AN OFFICER OF SIX NAVIES

The Life of Confederate Commander Hunter Davidson

John M. Coski
with Charles T. Jacobs

SB
Savas Beatie
California

First edition, first printing

Library of Congress Cataloging-in-Publication Data

Names: Coski, John M. author | Title: An Officer of Six Navies: The Life of Confederate Commander Hunter Davidson / by John M. Coski with Charles T. Jacobs
Description: El Dorado Hills, CA : Savas Beatie, 2026. | Includes bibliographical references and index. | Summary: "Hunter Davidson served in or with six different naval forces over his 45-year career. The range of his professional activities and the diverse cast of people whose paths he crossed make his a fascinating life story. Although his resume was rich and diverse and his accomplishments in the advancement of naval technology justify his indignant boasts to Jefferson Davis, Hunter Davidson does not merit the historical sobriquet of "forgotten naval hero." His career was hardly one of unbroken triumph and his character sometimes far from exemplary"-- Provided by publisher.
Identifiers: LCCN 2026009305 | ISBN 9781611217896 paperback | ISBN 9781954547797 ebook
Subjects: LCSH: Davidson, Hunter, 1826-1913 | Confederate States of America. Navy--Officers | Navies--Officers | United States--History--Civil War, 1861-1865--Naval operations | LCGFT: Biographies
Classification: LCC E467.1.D295 C67 2026
LC record available at https://lccn.loc.gov/2026009305

SB

Savas Beatie
989 Governor Drive, Suite 101
El Dorado Hills, CA 95762
916-941-6896 / sales@savasbeatie.com / www.savasbeatie.com

To Ruth Ann, with a lifetime of love.

TABLE OF CONTENTS

Abbreviations vii

Introduction ix

Acknowledgments xi

Prologue xv

Chapter One: Midshipman "Davie," U.S.N. (1841–1856) 1

Chapter Two: Lieutenant Davidson, U.S.N. (1856–1861) 41

Chapter Three: Lieutenant Davidson, V.S.N. and C.S.N. (1861–1862) 61

Chapter Four: The "Notorious Lieutenant Davidson" (1862–1864) 93

Chapter Five: Commander Davidson, C.S.N. (1864–1865) 139

Chapter Six: "Hard Up Confed" (1865–1868) 151

Chapter Seven: Captain Davidson, Maryland State Oyster Police Force (1868–1872) 175

Chapter Eight: *El ingeniero* Hunter Davidson (1873–1884) 195

Chapter Nine: "A Good Rebel" (1884–1913) 219

Bibliography 251

Index 262

About the Authors 270

LIST OF MAPS

U.S. Navy Service, 1842–1861 7

Hampton Roads and James River, 1862–1864 94

Confederate Navy Service, 1864–1865 141

Voyage of the *Henrietta*, February–July 1866 163

Hunter Davidson's Argentina and Paraguay, 1873–1913 196

Photos have been placed throughout the text for the convenience of the reader.

ABBREVIATIONS

AG	*Alexandria Gazette*, Alexandria, Virginia
BDE	Baltimore *Daily Exchange*
BP	Brooke Papers
CBF	Confederate Papers Relating to Citizens or Businesses, RG 109, M346, NARA
CMLS	Confederate Memorial Literary Society
CSN area files	Confederate States Navy area files, area 7, RG 45, NARA
CSN subject files	Confederate State Navy subject files, RG 45, NARA
CV	*Confederate Veteran*
LC	Library of Congress Manuscripts Division
LC P&P	Civil War photographs, 1861-1865, Library of Congress, Prints and Photographs Division
LRSN	Letters Received by the Secretary of the Navy from Commissioned Officers below the rank of Commander and from Warrant Officers, 1802-1886
LRSN (Squadron)	Letters Received by the Secretary of the Navy from Commanding Officers of Squadrons ("Squadron Letters"), 1841-1846
LR USNA	Letters Received by the Superintendent of the U.S. Naval Academy
LS USNA	Letters Sent by the Superintendent of the U.S. Naval Academy
MFM	Matthew Fontaine Maury
MSA	Maryland State Archives
MSOP	Maryland State Oyster Police
NARA	National Archives and Records Administration, Washington, D.C.
NH&HC	Naval History and Heritage Command, Washington, D.C.
NYH	*New York Herald*

ABBREVIATIONS (continued)

NYDT	*New York Daily Tribune*
NYS	*The Sun* [New York]
NYT	*New York Times*
OR	*War of the Rebellion: Official Records of the Union and Confederate Armies*
ORN	*Official Records of the Union and Confederate Navies in the War of the Rebellion*
RDD	*Richmond Daily Dispatch*
RG	Record Group
RTD	*Richmond Times-Dispatch*
SHC, UNC	Southern Historical Collection, University of North Carolina Chapel Hill
SHSP	*Southern Historical Society Papers*
USN Area File	US, Area File of the Naval Records Collection, 1775-1910
USNA	United States Naval Academy
VMHC	Virginia Museum of History and Culture
W&L	Special Collections and Archives, James G. Leyburn Library, Washington and Lee University, Lexington, Virginia
WES	Washington, D.C., *Evening Star*

Introduction

In December 1881, Hunter Davidson, late commander in the Confederate States Navy, penned an indignant letter to Jefferson Davis, asking the former Confederate president to "do an act of justice." In his recently published *Rise and Fall of the Confederate Government*, Davis had trumpeted the Confederacy's remarkable innovations in submarine or torpedo (mine) warfare, attributing the innovations to his West Point contemporary and friend, Brig. Gen. Gabriel J. Rains, but failing to mention the work of the Confederate Navy's Submarine Battery Service, which Davidson commanded for two years. Davidson laid before Davis the facts about the Submarine Battery Service's accomplishments, quoting the testimony of Confederate Navy Secretary Stephen R. Mallory and reminding Davis that he also had written a similar letter. "If your memory still fails you," Davidson wrote, "there are four well-known officers living who can testify to the exactness of what I have here written." He then reiterated his request "that as an act of simple justice you will answer this letter and correct the mistakes referred to."

"If you were surprised at not finding in my book your name mentioned in connection with torpedoes," Davis replied in January 1882, "I was certainly not less so at your arraignment of me as having done you an injustice by the omission." Davis tried weakly to conciliate Davidson with admiring words, but he reiterated his belief that Rains's torpedo work was the more effective and more appropriate for the Confederacy. He did not try to mask his contempt for what he clearly believed Davidson's petty complaint that his name had not appeared in *Rise and Fall.*

If Davis thought that his scolding would be the end of the exchange, he obviously did not know Hunter Davidson. Widely criticized for his tenacity and unwillingness to let things go, the former Confederate president unwittingly had engaged a kindred soul. Davidson regarded Davis's reply as "an aggravated repetition of the injustice you have done me in your book" which was filled with "repeated historical mistakes." The former Confederate naval officer seethed with sarcasm as he observed that the former president's memory was "remarkably retentive" concerning Confederate torpedo warfare "if not to my credit," "but where the case concerns me . . . you persist in being wholly oblivious." Davidson advised Davis that "I will use whatever means I am possessed to give them all possible publicity." Indeed, he soon published his exchanges with Jefferson Davis in his local newspaper, the Buenos Aires *Herald*.[1]

Reprinted in 1894 in the more accessible *Southern Historical Society Papers* under the title "Davis versus Davidson," the spat raises some obvious questions. Who was Hunter Davidson and where did he find the audacity to confront and contradict Jefferson Davis so forthrightly and publicly? Did his arguments have merit? And, incidentally, what was he doing in Argentina?

Hunter Davidson served in or with six different naval forces over his 45-year career. The range of his professional activities and the diverse cast of people whose paths he crossed make his a fascinating life story.

As an officer in the U.S. Navy, he was for brief spells assigned to the nation's largest and most famous wooden warships, attended the fledgling U.S. Naval Academy, served in the Mexican War, in the Caribbean, along the Pacific coasts of South America, Mexico, California and Oregon, the U.S. Coast Survey, in the Africa Squadron suppressing the international slave trade, and on the Naval Academy faculty. While at Annapolis, he received two patents from the U.S. government. Then, as an officer in the Virginia State Navy and the Confederate States Navy, Davidson fought against the men who had been his commanders and comrades in blue as well as with men who had been brothers in blue before they were brothers in gray. As a Confederate officer he commanded a gun crew on the CSS *Virginia* in the battle of Hampton Roads, assisted Matthew Fontaine Maury in torpedo development and deployment, succeeded Maury in command of the Submarine Battery Service, won promotion for leading a daring torpedo boat attack against a Federal frigate, followed Maury abroad to acquire torpedo supplies, assisted in fitting out an ironclad commerce raider, and took a turn as a blockade runner. After the war he commanded an abortive gun-running expedition for the Chilean navy and commanded Maryland's so-called Oyster Navy before finding a remunerative position with the navy of Argentina.

1 "Davis and Davidson," *Southern Historical Society Papers* (1896), 24:284-91 (hereafter cited as *SHSP*); *Bueynos Ayres Herald*, July 14, 1882, copy courtesy of George M. Brooke, Jr.

Although his resume was rich and diverse and his accomplishments in the advancement of naval technology justify his indignant boasts to Jefferson Davis, Hunter Davidson does not merit the historical sobriquet of "forgotten naval hero." His career was hardly one of unbroken triumph and his character sometimes far from exemplary. Six of the ships on which he served were lost by fire, shipwreck, abandonment, or explosion–though he survived those disasters unscathed. So, too, the cause for which he sacrificed his chosen career proved to be a metaphorical shipwreck, compelling him to begin his life and career anew. In common with many other former Confederate officers, Davidson found his postwar livelihood in the employ of a foreign navy. Almost uniquely among his former Confederates, Davidson never came home. He spent the remaining 39 years of his life in South America, estranged from his family and from a country he perceived to be ruled by "Black Republicans" and the Black people for whom he held a life-long contempt.

Acknowledgments

A life and career like that of Hunter Davidson begs the obvious question of why he has remained so obscure. The answer in part is that no known collection of Hunter Davidson papers survives. Approximately 100 Davidson letters (only a handful of them personal) are scattered among other collections and documents relating to his U.S. and Confederate naval career and are in the National Archives. Although he was hardly a shrinking violet, Davidson never wrote an autobiography, and his decades-long self-exile in South America distanced him from the mainstream of late-19th century Civil War memory—despite his sporadic efforts to remind his former comrades of his wartime accomplishments.

Davidson captured the imagination of Charles T. Jacobs, who couldn't fathom why he and most students of the Civil War were unfamiliar with his story. A career CIA analyst and Civil War enthusiast, Jacobs had met and befriended Davidson's grandson and namesake. Both men were residents of Montgomery County, Maryland, where Jacobs helped establish a local Civil War roundtable. With the grandson's encouragement and assistance, Jacobs began researching Hunter Davidson as a retirement project. Over the course of 18 years of diligent labor, he amassed a wealth of primary and secondary source materials, corresponded with Davidson descendants and historians who had written about Davidson or the many activities in which he was involved, studied the art of historical writing, and published an article in the February 14, 1996, *Washington Times,* entitled "Hunter Davidson: Unsung Naval Commander."

Sadly, Charles Jacobs contracted cancer and died in 2008. When he learned he was dying, he asked me to take over his notes and see to the publication of a Davidson biography. Although we never met, we had corresponded a decade earlier about Davidson, who was an important supporting character in my 1996 study, *Capital Navy: The Men, Ships, and Operations of the James River Squadron*, and one of the officers featured in my oft-delivered program entitled "The Four Most Valuable Men in the Confederate Navy."

For most of the years since then, the notes sat neglected—though not forgotten. During those years, the digitization of newspapers and the National Archives' naval records has made available valuable resources that supplement Charles Jacobs's prodigious research (what joy Mr. Jacobs would have found in mining those sources for new material).

This book is the collaboration of two historians who never met each other. Charles Jacobs conducted most of the archival research, primarily at the National Archives, the U.S. Naval Academy's Nimitz Library, and the Library of Congress, which I supplemented with research in newspapers, newly available primary and secondary sources, the Maryland Oyster Police records, and easier access to libraries and archives in Argentina. Mr. Jacobs roughed out the book that he intended to write in an 80-page draft that carried Davidson through 1864. Happily, his organizational scheme—which the course of Davidson's life and the available source material suggests—reflects my own approach. The writing is entirely my work, relying on Mr. Jacobs's draft for guidance and advice. I cannot be sure that the book that Mr. Jacobs would have written would resemble the one I wrote, but the organization of his research files and his several draft outlines suggest that our perception of the major chapters in Davidson's life coincide closely. Letters between Mr. Jacobs and Davidson descendants assure me that Mr. Jacobs recognized and would have dealt forthrightly with Davidson's egotism and the other unsavory aspects of his personality and character that readers will encounter in this book.

Research conducted sporadically over the course of 35 years has benefited from the assistance and kindness of many people. Mr. Jacobs's files reveal his voluminous correspondence with Davidson's grandson, Hunter Davidson (1906-1997), collateral descendant Mary Sheridan "Mike" Anderson, and Hunter family descendant Mr. Mayo Stuntz. He benefited from the research assistance of Dr. George M. Brooke, Jr., who provided access to the letters of his grandfather, Cdr. John M, Brooke, Kevin Foster, Naval History Center (now the Naval History and Heritage Command), Dr. Wilbur E. Meneray at Tulane University Libraries, archivist Mrs. Beverly Lyall and assistant archivist Jane H. Price of the Nimitz Library, U.S. Naval Academy, AnnMarie Price, photo archivist at the Virginia Historical Society (now Virginia Museum of History and Culture), the staff of the National Archives, and Mark J. Davidson and Karen Schinnerer of the U.S. embassy in Asuncion, Paraguay; and helpful communications with historians

Edwin C. Bearss, Stephen R. Wise, and Benton McAdams, historian and collector Dr. Charles V. Peery, Col. Morris J. Herbert, U.S. Army (regarding John Wynne Davidson). Jose Curcio translated Spanish language sources about Davidson's decades in South America. Historian Gary Gallagher taught a course on historical writing that assisted Mr. Jacobs with writing an outline draft of his notes.

In the course of my own work on naval history and retracing some of Charles Jacobs's steps, I too, have benefited from the generosity of Professor George Brooke and the inimitable Charlie Peery (now both deceased), as well as the assistance of many archives and archivists: Dr. Jennifer A. Bryan at the Nimitz Library, U.S. Naval Academy, Lucas Clawson at the Hagley Museum and Library, Wilmington, Delaware, Mel Frizzell, at the Old Dominion University Library, Lisa McCown at the Washington and Lee University Special Collections, Darby Nisbet at the Maryland State Archives, Hailey at the Dorchester Library information desk, Andrés at the Archives Department of the Mariano Moreno National Library, Buenos Aires, Argentina, and David Grabarek at the Library of Virginia. My former colleague, Robert Hancock, became a *de facto* research assistant, looking up citations in the American Civil War Museum library. Antonia Gowan, an English descendant of Hunter Davidson through his daughter, Leila Gowan, answered a long-distance appeal with family photographs and information.

Vital to my research have been the digitized newspapers available on the Library of Congress' "Chronicling America" website and on genealogical websites, and the published letters of Lt. Roswell Lamson edited for publication by James and Patricia McPherson. Thanks to Mike Gorman for providing access to additional digital newspapers.

I owe special thanks to Dr. Peter Luebke for research assistance and a critical reading of the manuscript as well as for a decades-long fellowship that has been the most gratifying of my career, and to Dr. David Werlich for assistance and advice about South American sources and historical context. Carrie Janney and Cynthia Nicoletti provided useful advice and sources in response to my several queries. Doug Crenshaw of the Richmond Civil War Round Table lit the fuse that reignited my commitment to this project and Terry Johnston, Dwight Hughes, and Chris Mackowski provided opportunities to publish the first fruits of my work. John Grady shared his valuable research on Matthew Fontaine Maury as well as camaraderie. My Richmond Civil War Roundtable beer buddies, Bert Dunkerly, Bernie Fisher, Richard Grosse, Rob Monroe, and Bill Welsch offered support and encouragement along with healthy doses of humor and snark.

A last-minute query about a photograph led me to Greg Bartles, retired historian of the Maryland Department of Natural Resources, and an authority on Davidson's command of the Maryland Oyster Police. He, in turn, introduced me to John M. McKee, of Illinois, who, unbeknownst to me, has been researching the life and career of Hunter Davidson. Mr. McKee's research skills are awe-inspiring. He generously shared his materials and insights with me, supplementing my work and Mr. Jacobs's and saving this book from numerous errors and oversights. I am grateful to both men for their generosity.

Cartographer and historian Edward Alexander translated my sterile lists of places into a series of masterful maps that track Hunter Davidson's travels perfectly.

I am grateful also for the work of indexer Derrick Lindow and to Sarah Keeney and Veronica Kane of Savas Beatie for translating words and images into a real book. As he did 30 years ago when we worked together on *Capital Navy*, publisher Theodore P. Savas has again transformed dreams into a reality—this time the dreams of two men—and continues to surprise me with the range of his interests and expertise.

To my co-author, Charles T. Jacobs, I owe enormous gratitude for his voluminous research and for his trust, which I hope has proven well placed.

To my wife, Ruth Ann, I owe pretty much everything. She has been the Center of my Universe for my entire adult life. Off and on for the last decade she has shared me with Hunter Davidson, often with the quip, "What's the old reprobate up to now?" I *think* she was referring to Hunter Davidson.

John M. Coski
Richmond, Virginia

Prologue

Hunter + Davidson (1826–1841)

Georgetown, located in the District of Columbia across the Potomac River from Virginia, was an appropriate birthplace for a man destined to serve in the navies of the United States, the Commonwealth of Virginia, the Confederate States of America, and the Maryland Oyster Navy and whose forebears served in the United States Army during the Revolution and early Republic.

Through both of his parents, Hunter Davidson traced his lineage to Virginia, the "Old Dominion." His father, William Benjamin (sometimes given as Baker) Davidson was born in Norfolk, Virginia (or, according to his tombstone, Botetourt County, Virginia) in 1796, the son of a Norfolk merchant. Hunter's mother, Elizabeth Chapman Hunter, was born in 1800, presumably at her family's home in Fairfax County, Virginia, across the Potomac from Washington, D.C. She was the daughter of Revolutionary War veteran John Chapman Hunter, of Scottish ancestry.[1] William Davidson attended the United States Military Academy at West Point, graduating in December 1815. Commissioned as a lieutenant, he was promoted to captain in July 1838.[2] He married Elizabeth on July 5, 1821.

1 Information on the Hunters and "Contemplation" from several articles by "The Rambler" published in *The Sunday Star* [Washington, D.C.], July 20, 1919, Aug. 10, 1919, and Mar. 7, 1920; and Historic American Building Survey by Nan Netherton, 1970, and related correspondence, copies from the Fairfax County Public Library. The house burned in the 1970s.

2 *The Madisonian* [Washington, D.C.], July 21, 1838. The Army Adjutant General's office sent William Davidson his formal commission in December 1838, but he did not receive it and sign the accompanying oath of allegiance until he was home in Fairfax County in August 1839. National Archives and Records Administration (henceforth NARA), Record Group [RG] 94, Records of the

Born on September 20, 1826, Hunter was the second of four sons. His brothers were John Wynne (born 1823), Roger Jones (born 1834), and Charles (possibly Charles Carroll, born possibly 1839).

The Davidsons were an Army family, following William from post to post as his orders dictated. Fortunately for the family, his postings–until his last–were along the settled Atlantic seaboard. Serving primarily in the artillery, William was assigned to Fort Monroe at the mouth of Hampton Roads, Virginia, in 1828, 1831, 1833, and 1838. The family reportedly spent much of their lives at their maternal estate, "Contemplation," in Fairfax County in what is now the sprawling northern Virginia suburbs of Washington, D.C. Hunter later reminisced about his boyhood at "Contemplation" and about his "Angel Mother" who "instilled into me all of the virtues I ever possessed. Its memories embrace the truest, purest moments of this uneasy life of mine." The only clue about the boys' early formal education comes from a 1909 letter Hunter wrote to an officer in the U.S. Artillery stationed at Fort Monroe. "In 1838 my father commanded where you are now," he wrote, "and my brother and myself were partly educated there."[3]

The Davidsons were not only an Army family, but a family of the Virginia slaveholding elite. In common with other military officers (including, for example, Robert E. Lee), William Davidson seems not to have owned slaves himself during his service. He was, however, raised in a slaveholding family. The 1810 census showed Davidson's father owning eight enslaved people. In 1820—the year before Elizabeth Hunter married William Davidson—census records show her father, John Chapman Hunter, owning 21 slaves. Elizabeth Hunter Davidson's second husband owned more than 50 slaves in 1840.[4]

It is not clear whether career naval officer Hunter Davidson ever owned any enslaved people, but he grew up in a slaveholding world and throughout his life evinced a deep-seated animosity toward dark-skinned people.

The Davidson family fortunes changed dramatically when William was assigned to Florida during the Second Seminole War in March 1839. Davidson was commander of Company K of the 3rd United States Artillery and commanded the post of Fort Lauderdale. He survived an ambush on the nearby New River in April 1840, but later that year contracted diarrhea during an expedition to

Adjutant General's Office, Letters Received, Virginia 1839. A family tree on Ancestry.com lists his birthplace as Tazewell, Virginia.

3 Davidson to Reginald Leach, Mar. 9, 1900, copy in Charles T. Jacobs research papers; [Hunter Davidson], "Correspondence" [letter to Major T. W. Winston, USMC]. *Journal of the United States Artillery*, (1909), 32: 94. *Journal of the United States Artillery*, volume 32 (1909), 94.

4 1810, 1820, and 1840 U.S. Census, accessed via Ancestry.com.

the Everglades. He died on Christmas day 1840 and is buried in St. Augustine National Cemetery.[5]

The death of their father had immediate implications for the Davidson family. Elizabeth Davidson continued, presumably, to live at "Contemplation" and benefit from her extensive family network. Her Revolutionary War veteran father died in February 1849. Perhaps not coincidentally, nine months later, on November 8, 1849, she married William Henry Pope, a distant cousin who had emigrated from Fairfax to become a wealthy farmer in Wilkes County, Georgia. She died a year later of diarrhea (the same malady that had killed her first husband) in Marengo County, Alabama, at the age of 50.

The memory of the years that followed his father's death exacerbated Hunter's post-Civil War animosity toward the government that he, his father, and his eldest brother once served. "The ungrateful Gov't never gave mother a pension nor assisted father's family in any way altho' father died on the field of battle [sic] when he had been fighting for his country," Hunter wrote to a nephew in 1900. "And thus it [is] because [of] that poverty of the family prevented the education of my younger brothers Roger & Charles & they had a hard time of it." Roger landed on his feet, working variously as a railroad clerk, baggage master, and conductor in Cincinnati and, primarily, St. Louis. Hunter's older brother, John Wynne, reportedly had secured an appointment to West Point before their father's death. He entered the Academy on July 1, 1841, graduated with the class of 1845, and became, like his father, a career Army officer, rising to the rank of captain by 1861.[6]

William Davidson's death compelled 14-year-old Hunter into an early career choice. He found it through the influence of his mother's younger brother, Thomas Triplett Hunter, who also had been raised at "Contemplation." A passed midshipman in the U.S. Navy, Thomas Hunter wrote to Navy Secretary James K. Paulding on January 30, 1841, applying for a midshipman's warrant on behalf of his nephew. Paulding replied that he could make no promises because of "the number of applicants pressing on the department at this time is so great." The appointment did come through, however, and on October 30, 1841, sitting at a desk in "Contemplation" before another cousin, Fairfax County justice of the peace Frederick A. Hunter, Hunter Davidson signed his oath. He solemnly swore

5 *Richmond Enquirer*, Mar. 16, 1839; *Alexandria Gazette* [VA], May 13, 1840; *The Pilot and Transcript* [Baltimore], Jan. 13, 1841; burial information accessed on www.Findagrave.com

6 Davidson to Reginald Leach; 1860, 1870, and 1880 U.S. Censuses, Ancestry.com. Homer K. Davidson, *Black Jack Davidson: A Cavalry Commander on the Western Frontier: the life of General John W. Davidson* (Glendale, CA, 1974), 22 and passim.

> to bear true allegiance to the United States of America, and to serve them honestly and faithfully against all their enemies or opposers, whomsoever, and to observe and obey the orders of the President of the United States of America, and the orders of the Officers appointed over me; and in all things to conform myself to the rules and regulations which now, are, or, hereafter, may be directed, and to the articles of war, which may be enacted by Congress, for the better government of the Navy of the United States and that I will support the Constitution of the United States.[7]

For the next 19-1/2 years, Hunter Davidson fulfilled that oath as an officer in the United States Navy.

7 NARA, RG 45 Letters sent by Secretary of Navy. Frederick A. Hunter also signed William B. Davidson's oath for promotion to U.S. Army captain at Fairfax C.H. on August 13, 1839.

Chapter One

Midshipman "Davie," U.S.N. (1841–1856)

Hunter Davidson's first orders as an officer in the United States Navy, dated February 8, 1842, assigned him to the U.S. Receiving Ship *Pennsylvania* stationed at Norfolk, Virginia.[1] Davidson entered the U.S. Navy in an eventful year that saw the commissioning of the Navy's first steam warships, the successful conclusion of the famed United States Exploring Expedition, and the execution of Midn. Philip Spencer (the "wild and uncontrollable" son of the U.S. secretary of war) and another officer and seaman charged with mutiny aboard the training brig, USS *Somers*. Those events and the ongoing evolution of naval technology augured important changes in the service during Davidson's naval career.

Midshipman Davidson's Navy

In an age before the telegraph and the trans-Atlantic cable, the world's navies represented the most regular and reliable means of communication between governments. Naval vessels were *de facto* instruments of diplomacy and intelligence gathering. The United States Exploring Expedition (1838-42) commanded by Lt. Charles Wilkes reinforced the navy's role in "showing the flag" around the world and, thus, the importance of training officers as gentlemen and diplomats. More immediately, the Wilkes Expedition, which explored broad swaths of the Pacific Ocean and Antarctica and gathered valuable data and specimens for the new

1 A. P. Upshur to Acting Midshipman Hunter Davidson, Feb. 8, 1842, Miscellaneous Records of the Navy Department, 1776-1930, RG 45, NARA.

Smithsonian Institution, transformed the navy into one of the nation's primary scientific organizations. The Wilkes expedition was the first of 17 expeditions undertaken before the Civil War.[2]

Beyond the exploring expeditions, the navy expanded its commitment to naval science. In 1844 the navy broadened the mission of its Depot of Charts and Instruments and relocated it to the U.S. Naval Observatory in northwest Washington, D.C. Supervising the Naval Observatory was Lt. Matthew Fontaine Maury. Lamed in a carriage accident, Maury proved his value to the service with his appointment in 1842 as Naval Hydrographer (developing, collecting, and distributing navigational charts and studies of oceanic currents). "The Pathfinder of the Seas," as Maury became known in the 1850s, transformed the Naval Observatory into an internationally significant center of oceanographic and hydrographic research. Davidson never served with Maury at the Naval Observatory, but he did earn a reputation in hydrography and became Maury's protégé in the Confederate Navy.

The decades in which Hunter Davidson served in the U.S. Navy were the last in the fabled "Age of Sail." The U.S. Navy already had introduced its first steam-powered floating battery, *Fulton*, in 1815 and a second experimental paddle wheel steam warship, also named *Fulton,* in 1837. Just over a month before Davidson reported for duty in February 1842, the U.S. Navy commissioned its first seagoing steam warship, the steam frigate *Mississippi*. She and her sister ship, *Missouri* (commissioned in March 1842) each carried a small battery of four heavy guns. Paddle wheel steamers obviously were vulnerable to enemy fire. Swedish naval engineer John Ericsson addressed this problem with the invention of a screw propeller, which Capt. Robert Stockton showcased in the USS *Princeton* in 1844. Best remembered for the explosion of Stockton's experimental 12-inch gun, the "Peace-maker" that wounded its inventor, killed the secretary of state and secretary of the navy, and nearly killed President John Tyler, the *Princeton's* February 28 sea trial on the Potomac River demonstrated the effectiveness of the screw propeller and portended the future of naval motive power.

Naval ordnance was also undergoing a revolution. In the early 1820s, French general Henri-Joseph Paixhans had designed guns that fired explosive shells. The effect of the guns was to rip ragged, irregular holes in wooden warships, making them virtually impossible to repair during battle. Paixhans's gun tilted the

2 David F. Long, *Gold Braids and Foreign Relations: Diplomatic Activities of U.S. Naval Officers 1798-1883* (Annapolis, MD, 1988); William P. Leeman, *The Long Road to Annapolis: The Founding of the Naval Academy and the Emerging American Republic.* (Chapel Hill, NC, 2010), 103-4, 157-8; Michael A. Verney, *A Great and Rising Nation: Naval Exploration and Global Empire in the Early U.S. Republic* (Chicago, 2022), 6 and passim.

advantage decisively in favor of ordnance over wooden ships. They were among the guns placed on the guns of the *Mississippi* class steam frigates.

Inevitably, the advent of Paixhans guns renewed the impetus to develop effective armor for warships. Two years after Davidson entered the service the U.S. Navy launched its first iron-hulled warship, the Great Lakes paddle wheel steamer, *Michigan*. Two years after that, naval constructor John Luke Porter drafted designs for an iron-clad floating battery, but the design sat on the shelf until 1861 when Porter resurrected it for the Confederate Navy.[3]

The advent of new technologies, as well as the increasingly important role of naval officers in American diplomatic affairs, intensified the periodic calls for reform in the education of American naval officers. The opening of the U.S. Military Academy at West Point in 1802 stirred some interest in naval education, but an analogous naval academy did not admit its first students until 1845. Meanwhile, the U.S. Navy trained its officers primarily on the job, but with a theoretical opportunity for formal education. A naval school opened at the Washington Navy Yard in 1807, and others followed in Boston and New York in 1825, but attendance was voluntary and poor. An 1813 act provided for schoolmasters on 74-gun ships of the line—of which there were none then in service. The Navy abolished the three naval schools in 1839 in favor of a single school at the Asylum in Philadelphia that sought to prepare midshipmen for their exams to become lieutenants. With the lessons of the *Somers* mutiny still fresh, Navy Secretary George Bancroft in 1845 succeeded where his predecessors had failed in convincing Congress to authorize and fund a naval school at Fort Severn in Annapolis, Maryland.[4]

Until then, U.S. Navy midshipmen learned their trade as most young officers always had: on the job, at sea. Hunter Davidson was among the first young American naval officers to receive their training both on the job and in the classroom.

Davidson was in good and plentiful company. The 173 young men warranted as acting midshipmen in 1841 constituted the largest cohort of newly minted officers in the antebellum and Civil War eras and represented nearly half of the acting midshipmen warranted during the 1840s. The navy admitted so many midshipmen in 1841 that it admitted only eight midshipmen in 1842, none in 1843, six in 1844, and 24 in 1845. Designated by their entrance date, not by the

3 For good summaries of these developments see Craig L. Symonds, *The U. S. Navy: A Concise History* (New York, 2015), 44-6; Robert W. Love, Jr., *History of the U.S. Navy, volume One, 1775-1941:* (Harrisburg, PA, 1992), chapters 10 and 11; Allan Westcott, ed., *American Sea Power Since 1775.* (Chicago, 1947), chapter 7; and Edward L. Beach, *The United States Navy: A 200-Year History,* paperback edition (Boston, 1986), chapters 8 and 9.

4 Charles Todorich, *The Spirited Years: A History of the Antebellum Naval Academy* (Annapolis, MD, 1984), 8-18; Leeman, *The Long Road to Annapolis*, 58-9, 70-95, 195-224.

varied years when they completed their formal education, the "Date of 1841" men were an accomplished group, producing 10 rear admirals, seven captains, seven commodores, eight commanders, and 11 lieutenant commanders in the U.S. Navy and numerous officers who were destined to make their marks in the Confederate States Navy. One of those men, John McIntosh Kell, known best to history as the executive officer of the Confederate commerce raider *Alabama,* wondered aloud in his memoir "if it be possible that any class of naval officers have ever formed so brotherly an attachment for each other as did the class of 1841."[5]

Reaching professional maturity just as the Civil War provided unprecedented opportunity for glory and promotion, the Date of 1841 resembled the celebrated West Point Class of 1846. The 1841 men similarly made their marks in the United States and Confederate navies. Never together in the same place at the same time, the 1841ers reported to ships and stations around the country. On those ships and at those stations they began their long apprenticeships, learning practical seamanship, navigation, gunnery, and, ideally, the code of gentlemanly conduct for officers.

The ship to which 15-year-old Hunter Davidson reported in February 1842, the U.S. Receiving Ship *Pennsylvania*, was the largest American sailing warship ever built. She carried 120 guns and was the only American three-deck ship of the line. She was more than 210 feet in length, almost 57 feet in beam, with a depth of more than 24 feet, and, ideally, a complement of more than a thousand officers and crew. She was, however, as feeble in fact as she was formidable on paper. Conceived the year after the War of 1812 ended, her keel was laid at Philadelphia Navy Yard in 1821, but tight budgets delayed her launching until 1837. Her first voyage—down the Chesapeake Bay to Norfolk, Virginia—made when she was still incomplete and not yet commissioned, proved to be her only voyage. She remained the rest of her life at Norfolk, where she received hundreds of boys and young men entering U.S. naval service. Some of them would be present for her ignominious death in 1861.

The enduring stereotype of American ship captains in the Age of Sail is that of the ruddy, weather-beaten Yankee from New England. Although the stereotype may have been true for the whaling fleet, clipper ships, and other merchant vessels, it was not accurate for the United States Navy. Three days before Hunter Davidson received his first orders, the *Boston Transcript* acknowledged a demographic trend:

5 Numbers from Mark C. Hunter, *A Society of Gentlemen: Midshipmen at the U.S. Naval Academy, 1845-1861* (Annapolis, MD, 2010), 27; John McIntosh Kell, *Recollections of a Naval Life* (Washington, D.C., 1900), 122.

The earliest identified photograph of Hunter Davidson taken when he was a midshipman, probably in the 1850s when he was in his mid-20s. (It was misidentified in the author's *Capital Navy* as being from the 1861 Naval Academy album.) *Charles V. Peery Collection*

If any State has cause to be proud of our navy, it would seem to be Virginia. The President of the United States, who is ex-officio commander in chief of the army and navy, is a Virginian; the Secretary of the Navy is a Virginian; the first clerk of the Navy Department is a Virginian; the President of the Navy Board is a Virginian; the commodore of the Mediterranean squadron is a Virginian; and the commander of the frigate Columbia, one of the Home squadron, (so called, we believe, from its staying at home,) is a Virginian. A noble list this, truly. Glory enough for one State."

The growing predominance of men from Virginia, Maryland, and the District of Columbia was evident among the men entering the new Naval School, including Davidson's Date of 1841. Forty-one percent (55 of 135) of the Date of 1841 men who graduated from the Naval School were born in or appointed from Virginia, Maryland, or D.C., half of them from Virginia.[6]

Sea Service

Two months after reporting to his first duty station, Davidson requested a transfer. "Being very desirous of seeing sea service, I respectfully request orders to the U.S. Frigate Constitution," he wrote to Navy Secretary Abel Upshur of Virginia, "knowing that sea service would be much more advantageous than the present employment."[7] The secretary approved the request, so Davidson transferred on May 1 from the largest warship in the U.S. Navy to the most famous American warship.

The USS *Constitution,* "Old Ironsides," as she became known after her victory over HMS *Guerrière* in 1812, was built at Charlestown, Massachusetts, in 1797. Commanded in 1842 by Capt. Foxhall Alexander Parker, Sr., *Constitution* was one of 10 warships in the U.S. Navy's newly established Home Squadron. Authorized in 1841, the Home Squadron assumed the duties of the old West Indian Squadron, patrolling the Atlantic coast from Newfoundland to the Amazon and the Gulf of

6 "VIRGINIA AND THE NAVY" quoted in *Army and Navy Chronicle,* Feb. 5, 1842, 45, from the *Boston Transcript.* The commanding officer to whom young Davidson reported, Captain Charles William Skinner, was in fact a native of Maine, but he was appointed to the service from Virginia. Leeman, *Long Road to Annapolis,* 53-4, noted this geographic trend and attributed it in part to the proximity of Maryland and Virginia to the nation's capital. Hunter, *A Society of Gentlemen,* 27-9, determined that the earlier dominance of Virginia, Maryland, and Washington, D.C., among naval officers had diminished by the end of the 1840s.

7 Davidson to Secretary Abel Upshur, Apr. 6, 1842, Letters Received by the Secretary of the Navy from Commissioned Officers below the rank of Commander and from Warrant Officers, 1802-1886 (hereafter cited as LRSN), vol. 282-283, RG 45, NARA.

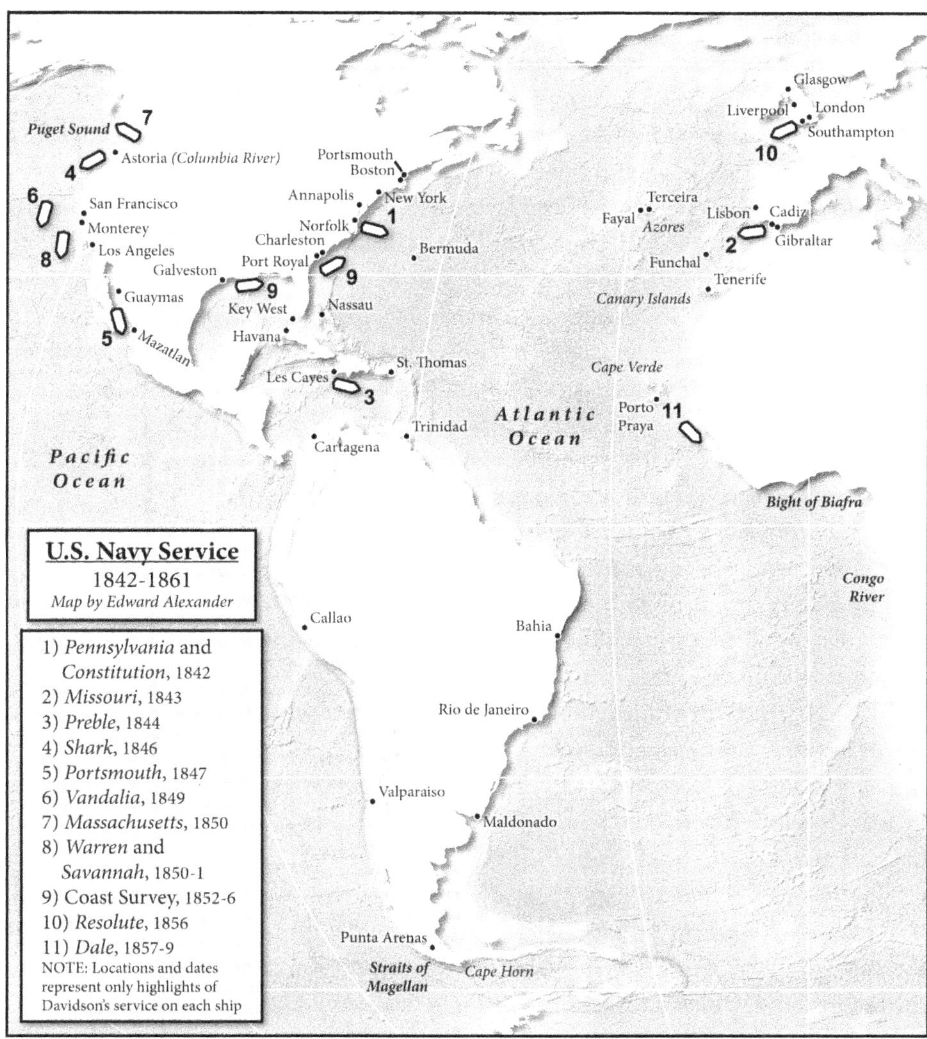

Mexico and Caribbean. It joined the Mediterranean Squadron (a legacy of the early 19th-century war against the Barbary Pirates), the Pacific, Brazil, and East Indian squadrons, established between 1821 and 1835, to protect America's expanding commercial, diplomatic, and missionary interests. The Navy created the Africa Squadron in 1842 to help combat the illicit Atlantic slave trade.[8] In his U.S. Navy career Davidson would spend time with the Home, Pacific, and African squadrons.

8 Annual Report of Secretary of the Navy, 1842, NH&HC, 535; Westcott, ed., *American Sea Power*, 91-95. Formally the Africa Squadron, it often appeared in period sources as African Squadron, and this book will use them interchangeably.

In November 1842, the *Constitution* prepared to leave Norfolk, reportedly for Vera Cruz, Mexico. She was to join a small armada of American ships intended to dissuade the Mexican government from trying to re-conquer Texas. The new steam frigate, *Missouri,* and the war sloop, *Falmouth,* showed the Stars and Stripes at Vera Cruz, but the *Constitution* never joined them. Instead of a mission to a hemispheric hot spot, Hunter Davidson's first sea duty apparently was a routine weeks-long cruise off the Virginia coast. The training cruise revealed severe leakage problems, and *Constitution* laid up at Norfolk waiting for repairs.[9]

Davidson, along with Captain Parker and *Constitution*'s other officers and crew, transferred in February 1843 to the frigate *Brandywine.* But Davidson soon parted from an officer whose son, William Harwar Parker, would become a close associate in both the United States and Confederate navies. In April Davidson received new orders for the new side wheel steamer frigate *Missouri.* In July 1843, the *Missouri* steamed up the Potomac River to rendezvous with America's newly appointed minister to China, Caleb Cushing, and transport him on the first leg of his journey to his post. Ominously, *Missouri* ran aground on oyster beds and had to retreat to Hampton Roads for repairs. Three weeks later, the *Missouri* picked up the minister and transported him via the Azores into the Mediterranean.[10] She put into port at Gibraltar to take on more coal.

At Gibraltar, as Minister Cushing dined ashore with the American consul, the *Missouri* caught fire while refueling. "[T]his costly ship—an ornament to the navy—was entirely destroyed," reported Navy Secretary Upshur. "All the accounts of this disaster concur in representing the officers and crew as having made the utmost exertion to extinguish the flames, and that their conduct during this perilous period, when an explosion of the magazine was momentarily expected, was marked by great coolness and intrepidity." Minister Cushing resumed his eastward journey, rendezvousing with Parker's *Brandywine* at Bombay, India, for the last leg. The *Missouri's* officers and men turned west. Hunter Davidson returned to the United States in October aboard the chartered vessel, *Rajah.* It was the first of many misadventures Davidson would experience in several different navies.[11]

As an officer aboard the ill-fated *Missouri* transporting Minister Cushing toward China, Hunter Davidson served the ambitious East Asian vision of his

9 "Naval," *New York Herald* (hereafter cited as *NYH*), Nov. 6, 1842; *New York Daily Tribune* (hereafter cited as *NYDT*), Nov. 25, 1842; *NYH,* Nov. 12, 1842; *NYH,* Dec. 6, 1842.

10 The *Army and Navy Chronicle* reported that Davidson's orders were dated Apr. 10, 1863. *Spectator* [NY], Apr. 19, 1843; Claude Moore Fuess, *The Life of Caleb Cushing* (New York, 1923), 1:421-424.

11 Annual Report of the Secretary of the Navy 1843, NH&HC, 482-3; "Official Report of the Loss of the United States Steam Frigate Missouri," printed in *NYH,* Oct. 7, 1843; Fuess, *Cushing,* 423-4.

fellow Virginian, President John Tyler. Davidson's next assignment served Tyler's similarly ambitious policies in the Caribbean and the Gulf of Mexico. On January 9, 1844, he reported in Boston for his next assignment aboard the USS *Preble.*[12]

In late January 1844, the U.S. war sloop *Preble* sailed from Boston on unspecified "special service." The second American warship named for Commo. Edward Preble (1761-1807), the officer who had commanded the expedition of the USS *Constitution* and six other ships against the Barbary Pirates, *Preble* was built in 1839 and carried 16 32-pound guns. As she sailed into the Atlantic in January 1844, she was under the command of Cdr. Thomas W. Freelon. Davidson was one of three midshipmen, as well as a passed midshipman and an acting midshipman. After 13 days at sea, *Preble* arrived February 6 at St. Thomas in the Danish West Indies—battered by a gale off Bermuda. Her mission then took her via Trinidad to Cartagena (now Colombia), then to Jamaica.[13]

A hint about the nature of *Preble's* mission came in a message that President Tyler sent to Congress, along with relevant documents, on May 15. The report listed U.S. ships, primarily belonging to the Home Squadron, under orders to the Gulf of Mexico, and including the unattached *Preble* "on a temporary cruise among the West India islands and to the ports in Central America, &c." The Mexican government was not reconciled to losing Texas, and the Tyler administration sought to deter any effort to re-conquer the breakaway republic. Tyler also noted reports of "domestic disturbances in the islands of Hayti and of Cuba, which will render the presence of a ship necessary to the protection of American interests."[14]

Even as Tyler delivered his report to Congress, Davidson and his fellow officers on the *Preble* were in the port of Aux Cayes (now Les Cay) on the southwest coast of Haiti, showing the American flag. Commander Freelon sent a cable reporting his arrival at Aux Cayes on May 5 and that the officers and crew were in good health. "This city is in possession of the negroes," he reported, "and the whole island is in a state of war, anarchy and confusion." Civil unrest between rival parties had led to threats against European and American ships and cargo in the harbor and appeals

12 See Edward P. Crapol, *John Tyler The Accidental President* (Chapel Hill, NC, 2006); Davidson to Hon. David Henshaw, Jan. 10, 1844, LRSN, vol. 304-305.

13 *NYH,* Jan. 24, 1844; *The Whig Standard* [Washington, D.C.], Jan. 29, 1844; *The North-Carolina Standard,* May 1, 1844; *NYH,* Mar. 18, 1844; *NYH,* Apr. 30, 1844.

14 *Alexandria Gazette* [VA] (hereafter cited as *AG*), May 20, 1844; *Iowa Territorial Gazette and Advertiser,* June 8, 1844.

for help. The commercial agent and British consul reportedly took refuge on the *Preble,* and the American ship furnished arms to the crew of a commercial vessel.[15]

"The presence of the sloop of war Preble is the only protection now afforded to the lives and property of Americans in the island of Hayti," reported the captain of one commercial vessel. The *Preble* "was outside the bar, and had her boats all armed, and ready to give any assistance that might be required," reported another captain. Freelon and his officers received formal thanks from the captain of a Boston-based ship "for the interest they took in regard to the property at risk, and the handsome treatment of himself."[16]

Preble's timely arrival in Aux Cayes was a classic example of the U.S. Navy's role in 19th-century American diplomacy. The eyes and ears of the United States government, naval vessels also carried the authority to protect life and property, especially when threatened by what western nations considered "uncivilized," typically dark-skinned, peoples. The periodic political instability on the island of Santo Domingo (Hispaniola) buttressed Americans' skepticism about the viability of the republic of former slaves that had thrown off French rule in the 1790s. Disorder on Santo Domingo threatened to invite European meddling in the Caribbean; it also fulfilled the prejudicial belief in the unfitness of dark-skinned people for independence. An anonymous U.S. naval officer recently arrived in Haiti from Jamaica, described a raging civil war "between the blacks and the browns," and that the vastly outnumbered browns "are flying from the different ports to Jamaica, for the preservation of their lives, leaving their own property, as well as that of foreigners consigned to them, (of which there is a great amount) to the mercy of the ferocious, half-civilized negroes."[17] It's unlikely that Midn. Hunter Davidson was the source of this account, but Davidson's subsequent actions and words suggested that he shared and possibly imbibed a deep-seated racial prejudice from the month he spent in Haiti in 1844.

The political situation in Haiti calmed down, at least temporarily, allowing *Preble* to depart about June 15. On July 1, after spending a short time in quarantine, she sailed up the Hudson, exchanging "the usual salutes" with the U.S. Receiving Ship *North Carolina.* It was to that 74-gun ship of the line that Davidson received his next orders. He asked that those orders be revoked "and that I remain attached

15 "Condition of Hayti," *NYH,* May 30, 1844; *The Whig Standard* [D.C.] June 21, 1844; *NYH,* May 19, 1844.

16 "FROM JAMAICA AND HAYTI, *NYH,* June 20, 1844; *NYDT,* May 30, 1844; *NYDT,* June 27, 1844.

17 *The Whig Standard* [Washington, D.C.] June 21, 1844.

to [*Preble*] being anxious to see my sea Service."[18] The young midshipman's second request for a change of orders was not as successful as his first, and he left *Preble* for *North Carolina.*

During this short, but eventful, cruise in the Caribbean, Davidson earned the commendation of his commanding officer. One of the few dozen existing documents relating to Davidson's early USN career is a letter dated August 8, 1844, from Thomas W. Freelon stating that Davidson's "conduct and deportment as an officer and Gentleman, have been uniformly praise-worthy and correct."[19]

California

In the waning days of the Tyler Administration in March 1845, the U.S. Congress annexed the Republic of Texas, which became the 28th American state in December 1845. With annexation the United States inherited a festering border dispute between Texas and Mexico. Without careful diplomacy the border dispute could erupt into war between the United States and its southern neighbor. Far from endeavoring to avoid war, the new president, Democrat James K. Polk of Tennessee, seemed intent on provoking war with Mexico and risking war with Great Britain over Oregon.

If war with Mexico did occur, it was an open secret that U.S. territorial ambitions extended well beyond Texas to include the Mexican provinces of New Mexico and California. What the U.S. Navy's role would be in such a war became manifest in October 1842 when Commo. Thomas ap Catesby Jones, acting on an unfounded rumor of war, landed troops at Monterey, California, and raised the U.S. flag over the provincial capital. Jones held the city for one day before learning of his mistake. The U.S. issued an apology, but Jones's *faux pas* betrayed American designs. Four years later, U.S. Navy warships returned to raise the Stars and Stripes over Mexican cities and towns along the length of the California coast, and Midn. Hunter Davidson was among the officers who helped consolidate American control of the territory.

After a few months on *North Carolina,* Davidson traveled to Portsmouth, New Hampshire, and reported for duty on the USS *Portsmouth* on November 11, the day after she was commissioned. The namesake of the navy yard where she was constructed, *Portsmouth* was one of six newly commissioned fast 20-gun

18 "Hayti," *AG*, July 2, 1844; "Late From Hayti," *NYH,* June 29, 1844; *NYH,* July 2, 1844; Davidson to Sec. John Y. Mason, July 26, 1844, LRSN, vol. 309-310.

19 Thomas W. Freelon affidavit dated Aug. 8, 1844, in Early Records (ZB) file of Hunter Davidson, NH&HC (hereafter cited as ZB files, NH&HC).

sloops-of-war. Davidson sailed with her south to Norfolk, Virginia, for her highly successful sea and speed trials. Under Cdr. John B. Montgomery (1794-1872), a New Jersey born War of 1812 veteran, *Portsmouth* received orders to join the Pacific Squadron.[20]

A sailing vessel measuring just over 151 feet in length and 37 feet wide, with a draft of 16-1/2 feet, *Portsmouth* lived up to her expectations for fast, smooth sailing, reaching Rio de Janeiro in 33 days. After a fast run down the east coast of South America, she made the difficult passage around Cape Horn into the Pacific, arriving at Valparaiso, Chile, in early April 1845.[21]

Although Midn. Hunter Davidson had been in the service for three years and had experienced sea duty, this months-long cruise was his real initiation as a sea officer. About 3 p.m. on Sunday, February 16, 1845, the 18-year-old officer sailed across the Equator for the first time. And although Davidson had set foot on the fabled Spanish Main the year before, this cruise introduced him to several ports on the continent of South America, where he would spend the last 40 years of his life. On May 20, 1845, Davidson was among a handful of officers invited to a sumptuous dinner with the American Chargé D'affairs in Chile.[22] Twenty years later Davidson would be back in Chile under contract of Chilean agents.

From mid-June to mid-July 1845, *Portsmouth* and other Pacific Squadron ships were stationed in and around the port city of Callao, Peru. In late July, *Portsmouth* sailed for Honolulu in what were known then as the Sandwich Islands. Eleven days after arriving in Honolulu, *Portsmouth* sailed on September 5 for Monterey, California, then to Mazatlán on the west coast of Mexico near the tip of Baja, or Lower, California to rejoin the rest of Commo. John Sloat's Pacific Squadron and await developments. Davidson was among several officers who fell ill during the return voyage.[23]

20 Davidson to Mason, Oct. 23, [1844] and Davidson to Mason, Nov. 11, 1844, LRSN. Vols. 313 and 314; Staunton *Spectator, and General Advertiser* [VA], Oct. 31, 1844; *AG and Virginia Advertiser*, Nov. 13, 1844; Joseph T. Downey, *Cruise of the Portsmouth, 1845-1847. A Sailor's View of the Naval Conquest of California*, Howard Lamar, ed. (New Haven, 1958), 2 n. 1; *American Republican and Baltimore Daily Clipper*, Dec. 6, 1844.

21 *Weekly National Intelligencer* [Washington, D.C.], Jan. 25, 1845, 2; *American Republic and Baltimore Daily Clipper*, Apr. 11, 1845, Apr. 22, 1845; July 12, 1845; and Aug. 2, 1845; Downey, *Cruise*, 33-4.

22 Charles R. Smith, ed., *The Journals of Marine Second Lieutenant Henry Bulls Watson 1845-1848* (Washington, D.C., 1990), 4, 18.

23 Downey, *Cruise*,75, 103-4; Watson Journals, 20-2, 28, 31, 45-6. Watson has Davidson "detached" from the ship before leaving for Honolulu, but among the sick on the way back from Honolulu; Downey's diary is silent on Davidson. "U.S. Navy in Mazatlán Roads," *The Yazoo City Whig* [MS], June 26, 1846.

Davidson was a young midshipman on the new sloop-of-war *Portsmouth*, at the start of the Mexican War in 1846. *NH&HC (86020-KN)*

On June 7, 1846, Sloat received credible reports from the Mexicans themselves that hostilities had broken out along the Rio Grande in Texas. This news triggered the implementation of orders that he carried from Secretary of the Navy John Y. Mason, dated June 24, 1845: If Mexico seemed "resolutely bent on hostilities, you will be mindful to protect the persons and interests of citizens of the United States near your station and should you ascertain beyond a doubt that the Mexican Government has declared war against us, you will at once employ the forces under your command to the best advantage." Sloat sailed immediately in his flagship, the frigate *Savannah,* to Monterey. Arriving on July 2, he demanded the city's surrender. When the Mexicans refused, Sloat landed troops to take possession of California's capital city on July 7, raising the Stars and Stripes as Jones had done four years earlier—this time permanently. Sloat's squadron of frigates and fast sloops then fanned out to blockade and occupy other California port cities. Sloat previously had ordered Cdr. John B. Montgomery to take the *Portsmouth* to Yerba Buena—the city that Americans know as San Francisco—and await further orders. Montgomery occupied San Francisco Bay and hoisted the American flag over the city on July 9.[24]

24 Annual Report of Secretary of the Navy, Dec. 5, 1846, published in *NYDT*, Dec. 14, 1846; Sloat to Bancroft, July 31, 1846, Letters Received by the Secretary of the Navy from Commanding Officers

Although Hunter Davidson eventually set foot in California, he was not with the *Portsmouth* when she sailed into San Francisco Bay and its men took possession of the city on July 9, and he did not participate in the conquest of the future Golden State.[25] He was instead serving aboard another U.S. warship, the schooner *Shark,* showing the flag in another of America's coveted Pacific coast prizes: Oregon.

Shipwrecked

Davidson's service record notes his transfer from *Portsmouth* to the *Shark* but is silent about the specific date. According to the contemporary journal of the *Portsmouth's* U.S. Marine commander, Lt. Henry Bulls Watson, Davidson was ordered to the store ship *Erie* on February 18, 1846. Watson may have been mistaken about Davidson's assignment, or Davidson's detail to the *Erie* (unrecorded in his service file) was short-lived. By the time the *Portsmouth* and *Shark* sailed from Mazatlán on April 2 to go their separate ways, Davidson was aboard the *Shark. Portsmouth* proceeded up the coast; the *Shark* headed west to Honolulu for thorough repairs and re-coppering before proceeding to Oregon on June 23, arriving on July 15.[26]

Built at the Washington Navy Yard and commissioned in 1821, *Shark* was a small vessel (86 feet in length, nearly 25 feet in beam, and displacing 10"4' of water) and carried a battery of 12 guns (later reduced to 10). In December 1839, she became the first American warship to sail through the Straits of Magellan from the Atlantic into the Pacific Ocean, where she spent the next six years patrolling the coast from Peru to Panama. Her up-and-coming young commander was Lt. Neil M. Howison, of Virginia. Among her other officers was the ship's master, James Dunwoody Bulloch, of Georgia.[27]

Shark's assignment in Oregon was "to obtain correct information of that country and to cheer our citizens in that region by the presence of the American

---

of Squadrons ("Squadron Letters"), 1841-1846 (hereafter cited as LRSN Squadron), M89, roll 32 (Pacific Squadron), vol. 33, RG 45, NARA.

25 *The Polynesian* [Honolulu], Aug. 8, 1846.

26 "Summary of the Movements of American and English Men-of-War," *California Historical Society Quarterly,* (July 1924), No. 2, 3:168 noted that both ships sailed from Mazatlán on Apr. 2, 1846; Howison's report, Feb. 1, 1847, published as House Miscellaneous Document 29, 30th Congress, 1st Session.

27 U.S. NH&HC website: https://www.history.navy.mil/content/history/museums/nmusn/explore/photography/ships-us/ships-usn-s/uss-shark-schooner-1821-46.html; Gregory Paynter Shine, "'A Gallant Little Schooner': The U.S. Schooner Shark and the Oregon Country, 1846," *Oregon Historical Quarterly* (Winter 2008), 536-565; *Register of the Commissioned and Warrant Officers of the Navy of the United States . . .* (Washington, D.C., 1847), 121 (hereafter cited as *U.S. Navy Register year*).

flag." Beyond reporting on the shipping channels, topography, and resources of the area, Lt. Howison reported on the people of Oregon—the settlers, the traders, and the officials of the English/Canadian Hudson's Bay Company — and directed his own officers "to seek all information respecting the country which their respective opportunities might afford."[28]

Unbeknownst to Howison, his mission took on a new complexion as his ship was undergoing repairs in Honolulu. On June 18, 1846, the U.S. Senate ratified a treaty, signed just days before, that finally settled the border between Oregon and British Columbia at the 49th parallel. An 1818 treaty provided for joint possession of the territory pending a formal agreement on the boundary. In the ensuing years, the British insisted on the Columbia River as the border. Americans insisted on sole ownership of the Columbia and American expansionists, egged on by incoming President Polk, adopted the war cry of "54° 40' or fight." With the ratification of the treaty, the rivers, inlets, and valleys that Howison, Davidson, and the other officers were exploring became American territory—the future states of Oregon and Washington. Or, as a *Shark* crew member recalled more than 60 years later, "At that time it was the cry, '54-40 or fight.' But they fought it out in Washington, D.C."[29]

The *Shark's* exploration of the Columbia River basin ended abruptly on the night of September 10, 1846, when she ran aground on an uncharted sand bar and was destroyed by the breakers. Howison took responsibility for misjudgment and a court of inquiry subsequently absolved him. The last hours of the *Shark* were harrowing. "We struck about 6 o'clock P.M.," recounted an anonymous officer a few months later, "and at 7 [Lieutenant Howison] summoned the crew upon deck, and in a brief and eloquent address represented the perils by which they were surrounded, and the extreme importance of silence, calmness, and the most absolute obedience to orders. It had a most happy effect, and every man went to his station with perfect confidence in our brave and collected commander." The violent breakers proved too strong for the lifeboats, so the men had to wait five

28 "Shark I (Schooner)," ship history on Naval History and Heritage Command website, URL: https://www.history.navy.mil/content/history/museums/nmusn/explore/photography/ships-us/ships-usn-s/uss-shark-schooner-1821-46.html published 9 September 2015; Howison report, 4 and passim.

29 George M. Himes, ed. "Letters by Burr Osborn, Survivor of the Howison Expedition to Oregon 1846: Reminiscences of Experiences Growing out of Wrecking of the United States Schooner Shark at Mouth of Columbia on Eastward Voyage of Expedition," *Oregon Historical Quarterly*, No. 4 (Dec. 1913) 14:361.

Watercolor of the U.S. schooner ***Shark*** by Charles Steedman (1790-1860). *NH&HC (NH 80398)*

hours for the flood tide. Howison charged Lt. Bulloch with supervising the boats and removing the crew.[30]

"About 11 o'clock p.m. she had 5 feet water in the hold; the flood tide set in; the other boats were got out and loaded with as many as they would safely carry," Howison reported. "Lieut. Schenck, Midshipman Davidson, and 21 men, remained with me on the wreck,—the flood-tide gradually crowding us into narrow limits, until the bow-sprint and the two quarter-deck houses were the only habitable spots on board, and these were frequently washed by the heavy swell. Each man was secured to the vessel by a cord passed around him—a precaution which may have saved some lives; for, towards daylight, the surf began again to set in heavily." The lifeboats returned and carried Howison, Schenck, Bulloch, Davidson, and the others to shore. "The wreck was completely untenable an hour after she was finally abandoned, and by 3 p.m. not a vestige of the poor Shark was

30 "Particulars of the Loss of the U.S.S. Schooner [*sic*] Shark." *NYH,* July 28, 1847; Walter E. Wilson and Gary L. McKay, *James D. Bulloch: Secret Agent and Mastermind of the Confederate Navy* (Jefferson, NC, 2012), 14.

visible." The captain's gig was destroyed as it departed from the *Shark,* taking with the ship's papers and an iron box with $4,000 in gold.[31]

Landing on a beach at the mouth of the Columbia without any loss of life, the crew and officers moved into vacant log huts at the old Astoria trading post. Within a week, remembered crewman Burr Osborn, "three-quarters of the crew were taken down with a fever and the rest of the crew we not much better." After the men recovered their health, they cut and hauled logs a mile downstream to build a double log house at a site they dubbed "Sharksville." There they spent October and part of November while Howison traveled to Vancouver to arrange for supplies and transportation.[32] He chartered the Hudson's Bay Company's schooner, *Cadboro,* but fierce gales delayed their departure for a month. The condition grew even more uncomfortable after they embarked onto the ship but were unable to take to sea. "The cabin was just 11 feet by 8. In that extensive apartment ten officers messed and slept, without fires, and the cold piercing, for seventy-five days," wrote the unnamed officer. "There we lay, wearied and freezing, in Baker's Bay, waiting for a fair wind to carry us to San Francisco, suffering with rheumatism, frost bites, and chilblains." In that cabin the men observed Christmas and New Year's Day before finally departing on January 18, 1847, and arriving nine days later in San Francisco.[33]

Mexico

Having finally escaped their ordeal in Oregon, Davidson and his comrades had to wait a few more months before rejoining their ship. As they waited, the Mexican-American War raged on without them. General Zachary Taylor's army, which had precipitated the war in April 1846, fought the battle of Buena Vista and secured American control of the Rio Grande Valley on February 22, 1847. General Winfield Scott's army landed at Vera Cruz and began its storied march to the "Halls of Montezuma."

The officers and crew who had remained on the sloop-of-war *Portsmouth* were as busy as the men detailed to the *Shark* had been idle. The U.S. forces that had compelled the surrender of Mexican forces all along the California and northern

31 Howison's report dated Sep. 15, 1846, printed in *The Daily Union* [Washington, D.C.] July 15, 1847; Shine, "Gallant Schooner," 554.

32 Osborn letters, 356-357.

33 "Particulars of the Loss"; Howison's "Report." Surgeon Marius Duvall, stationed on the frigate *Savannah* in San Francisco Bay, noted in his journal on February 14, 1847, that "the officers of the Shark are now living on board" and that "they gave a fearful account of the bar at the entrance of Columbia River[.]"

Mexican coasts were far too small to pacify the conquered territory. Ignoring their paroles, Mexican troops in September 1846 reoccupied key cities. In December, Pacific Squadron Commo. Robert F. Stockton converted his naval force into a land army. Along with 60 dragoons under Brig. Gen. Stephen W. Kearny, the jacks marched 150 miles from their base at San Diego to Los Angeles, where they defeated Mexican militia at La Mesa on January 8-9, 1847. The only American killed in the battle was a seaman from *Portsmouth.* Among Kearny's dragoon officers was Lt. John W. Davidson, Hunter's older brother. If Hunter had not been detached from *Portsmouth,* he would have fought a land battle in California shoulder to shoulder with his officer brother.[34]

On April 23, Cdr. Montgomery received orders to leave Lower California and proceed to Monterey—an order that he predicted correctly would allow the Mexicans to reassert their control in the area. *Portsmouth* reached Monterey on May 24. By June 11, when Montgomery received orders back to Lower (Baja) California and the Mexican coast, Midshipmen Hunter Davidson and George T. Simes had rejoined the ship. During the seven-week voyage down the California coast around Cape San Luca to Mazatlán on the Sonoran coast, Davidson got a taste of Mexican War sea duty. Davidson also enjoyed at least one day of shore leave. On the Fourth of July, Davidson joined Marine Lt. H. B. Watson's small party exploring on foot and on horseback the vicinity of San José del Cabo. Then it was back to San Francisco Bay by way of Monterey.[35]

As Scott's army was fighting its final battles outside Mexico City, Hunter Davidson finally got into the war. Mexican forces in Lower California and Sonora refused to be pacified, and the *Portsmouth* sailed back down the coast to re-impose American control yet again. Serving with the frigate *Congress* (a ship that Lt. Hunter Davidson, Confederate States Navy, would help destroy 15 years later) and under the ultimate command of her captain, Elie A. F. La Vallette, *Portsmouth* left Monterey on September 3 and arrived a month later at Guaymas, a port on the Sonoran coast of the Gulf of California. La Vallette and Montgomery spent several days preparing to bombard the small port city and gave the Mexican commander an ultimatum to capitulate. By the time *Congress* and *Portsmouth* began a full bombardment on the morning of October 20—the *Portsmouth's* first shots fired against an enemy during the war—Mexican troops had abandoned the city. Local

34 Watson Journal, 259-268; *Annual Report of the Secretary of the Navy 1847* in Exec. Doc. 1, 948; *Annual Report of the Secretary of the Navy February 16, 1849* in Senate Executive Doc. 31 (Washington, D.C., 1840), 37; *NYH,* May 28, 1847; Fred Rogers Blackburn, *Montgomery and the Portsmouth* (San Francisco, 1958) details the activities of *Portsmouth* and her officers and crew in 1846-1847.

35 Watson Journals, 331, 335, 341; Fred Blackburn Rogers, *Montgomery and the Portsmouth* (San Francisco, 1958), 99-101.

civil officials raised the white flag. American landing parties occupied the city, raised the Stars and Stripes, read a proclamation, then left. Mexican troops reentered the same night. Over the next several days, U.S. forces "occupied" Guaymas ("keeping guard over a few empty houses," as Marine Lt. Watson described the duty), while the Mexicans camped nearby and intimidated the local citizens. Davidson presumably played a junior officer's role in the October 20 bombardment, but it is not clear whether he was involved in the occupation of Guaymas.[36]

"It is truly laughable, to see us here pretending to be in possession of Guaymas," complained Marine Lt. Watson in his diary on October 27. Guard duty was no laughing matter to men who were at the end of their tether and their enlistments. The crew sent a letter to the squadron commander asking respectfully to be sent home. Captain Montgomery later endorsed their request, explaining to the squadron commander that the crew had been reduced to one-quarter of its full complement and that the enlistments of almost 100 men had expired already and the rest would expire before they returned home. On November 9, the sloop-of-war *Dale* relieved *Portsmouth* at Guaymas, but orders detained her in Lower California until there were enough ships and men to secure the area and to help turn back enemy attacks against an exposed garrison at San José. It was not until January 3, 1848 (by which time Winfield Scott's army had captured of Mexico City and peace negotiations began in earnest) that *Portsmouth* headed for home.[37]

Retracing her route along the Pacific Coast of South America and around Cape Horn, she endured strong gales, rough seas, and cold weather in the south Atlantic, which laid low many of the ship's officers with severe colds. Davidson was among those who avoided the sickness, and he won the confidence of at least one of his fellow officers. "Lieuts. Missroon, Revere, & Hunter, and Midshipman Simes sick," wrote Marine Watson in his journal on March 19, "Lieut. Bartlette & Midshipmen Grafton and Davidson, having both been seven [*sic*: six] years in service, are as familiar, and as capable of taking charge of the Deck now, as they ever will be, hence the fears of the Capt are not only unfounded as to the capacity of these officers, but is very annoying, & vexatious." On May 5, 1848, *Portsmouth* sailed into Boston harbor, almost 3-1/2 years after she had left Norfolk. Davidson

36 Watson Journals, 354-361 (quote 361); Rogers, *Montgomery and the Portsmouth*, 101-102. *The Daily Union* [Washington, D.C.], Nov. 16, 1847; "THE CAPTURE OF GUYAMAS [from *New Orleans Picayune* of the 22nd inst.] *The Democratic Pioneer* [Wyandot, OH], Jan. 14, 1848; Sunbury American and Shamokin Journal [Sunbury, PA], Feb. 5, 1848 [from Baltimore Republican and Argus from Monterey], Oct.10, 1847.

37 Watson Journals, 361-370 (quote 362); Rogers, *Montgomery and the Portsmouth*, 103-105; William B. Shubrick to J. B. Montgomery, Dec. 1, 1847, and Shubrick to Navy Secretary Mason, Dec. 1, 1847, U.S.N. Area File, (Area 9, East Pacific Ocean), RG 45, NARA.

was due for a period of leave, which he informed Navy Secretary John Y. Mason he would spend in Fairfax County, Virginia.[38]

Although Hunter Davidson had missed much of the action in the war on the Pacific coast, he was a veteran of the Mexican-American War. He had confronted his country's enemies and seen shots fired in anger. He had been on almost continuous sea duty for more than five years. Not only had he been at war, but he had also helped enforce order and protect American and European property from "uncivilized" peoples. He had been a willing agent of American imperialism in the Caribbean and in the Pacific. He had been on one ship that burned at its berth and on another that had run aground and was destroyed by the angry sea. It is easy to imagine that Davidson was not enthusiastic about his next assignment for which he reported on October 10: a year of classroom education at the Naval School.

The Naval School

The first class of students that entered the new Naval School at Annapolis in October 1845 comprised an unstable and often toxic blend of young men and boys in different stages of life and maturity and at wildly different levels of education and experience. Not until 1855 did a discrete, identifiable class of young men at the same stage of life and experience enter the Academy at the same time, follow the same course of study (eventually settling on the traditional four years), and graduate together. Before then, newly warranted 14–16-year-olds entered the school alongside selected young men who had been in the service for as long as six years and who resented being recalled from duty to attend school. The veterans, known colloquially as "oldsters" shaped the school's culture for its first decade. "In theory they were pupils," explained Naval Academy historian Charles Todorich. "In reality they 'regarded themselves . . . as officers on leave of absence from sea duty.'" Famed naval theorist and historian Alfred Thayer Mahan, who entered the Naval Academy in 1856 just after the last of the "oldsters" left, later imagined the circumstances and mindset of those men. They were, he wrote, "too young for ripeness," but had for five years "been bearing the not slight responsibility of the charge of seamen" and enjoying "the powers and privileges" of mature men. "How

38 Watson Journals, 380. The surviving log of the *Portsmouth* for Dec.1847-May 1848 reveals entries by Davidson only for six days in December 1847. Log of the *U.S.S. Portsmouth,* RG 24, NARA; *NYH,* Feb. 20, 1848; *NYH,* May 7, 1848; Davidson to Mason, June 13, 1848, LRSN, vol. 357-358.

could such be brought under the curb of the narrowly ordered life of the school, for the short eight months to which they knew their ordeal was restricted?"[39]

The result was predictable. "A spirit of insubordination prevailed among the Midshipmen during the whole of Captain [George] Upshur's Superintendence," wrote an early chronicler of the school, "and it was due partly to the defective organization of the School as originally established, and partly to the want of a strong will at the helm. There was a ceaseless struggle between the Superintendent and Professors on one hand, and the Midshipmen on the other, which generally resulted in favor of the latter."[40]

The Date of 1841 men were especially unruly. In Naval Academy lore, the huge cohort was long remembered as "the most spirited, rambunctious, regulation-flouting group of men to grace Severn's shores." If the entire 1841 group had been admitted all at once, wrote Naval Academy librarian and historian Thomas G. Ford, "'their combined power and relish for mischief would have rendered the maintenance of strict discipline simply impossible.'" Because of its unmanageable size, the Date of 1841 cohort was divided into two classes according to the men's warrant dates: those who received their warrants before June 30 entered the school in 1846, and those warranted after July 1 entered in 1847. An additional 40 men—some of whom were, like Davidson, far from Annapolis when the second 1841 cohort reported—entered the school in August 1848 to begin their year of formal education.[41]

No contemporary letters or diaries offer any details on Hunter Davidson's single year at the Naval School. We do not know whether he joined the Owls, Crickets, Apostles, or other social clubs. The absence of any recorded offenses for drunkenness or rowdy behavior suggests that he was not an active member of the clubs, known as they were primarily for drinking in Annapolis taverns. Nor did Davidson participate in any duels or incidents for which the Date of 1841 men were notorious.[42]

Official records of his year at the Naval School do suggest, however, that the 22-year-old Davidson was among those "oldsters" who chafed at the routine and discipline that he encountered at the school. At the end of Davidson's academic year in August, 1849 the school's famously lax superintendent, George P. Upshur

39 Todorich, *Spirited Years,* 37; Alfred Thayer Mahan, *From Sail to Steam: Recollections of Naval Life* (London and New York, 1907), 47.

40 Thomas G. Ford, "History of the U. S. Naval Academy" Nimitz Library, United States Naval Academy (hereafter cited as USNA), chapter 11, typescript page 15.

41 Ford quoted in Todorich, *Spirited Years,* 52; Parker, *Recollections,* 117.

42 Todorich, *Spirited Years,* 54-62.

(who supposedly told the midshipmen "I cannot govern you, young Gentlemen, so if you will only govern yourselves I should be delighted.") submitted a report to the president of the Board of Examiners on the "general deportment "of the midshipmen. Based on the school's official conduct roll as well as "personal observations" and "reports of the executive and other officers attached to the institution," Upshur's report graded the midshipmen as "Unexceptionable and Exemplary," "Excellent," or "Generally Good." Then, he added a list of 12 officers whom he was "pained to report" have "been frequently guilty of violating orders, rules and regulations and of irregularities at the School." Davidson's name was on that list.[43]

The School's Register of Delinquencies logs Davidson's list of offenses: one instance of "neglect of duty" (specifically, being absent from French recitation), two instances of tardiness at French recitation, two instances of breaking liberty, one instance of "loud whooping at the dinner table during the sitting of the Court of Inquiry in the adjacent building," and two instances of the much more serious offence of "unofficerlike conduct." Both of those incidents involved "indecorous," "disorderly," and "violent" conduct toward the school's African-American mess hall stewards. Those incidents constitute a pattern of behavior that extended beyond Davidson's year in Annapolis and warrant closer scrutiny.

On February 16, 1849, Davidson and three other midshipmen (two of whom did not graduate) were reported "for disorderly conduct at dinner, abusing and cursing mess boys." The register of delinquencies noted that they were "[s]uspended and quarantined." The punishment obviously had little effect on Davidson. On May 11, 1849, he was cited for "Disorderly and violent conduct in mess room during dinner. Cursing and striking several times one of the servants and afterwards pursuing him into the city with a carving knife in his hand and threatening to kill him." The record indicated he was "[a]rrested by civil authorities. Civil suit instituted against him."[44]

43 Todorich, *Spirited Years,* 48; Superintendent George R. Upshur to Commo. William B. Shubrick, President of the Board of Examiners, Naval School, Aug. 8, 1849, Volume 4, Letters sent by the Superintendent of the U.S. Naval Academy (hereafter cited as LS USNA), May 9, 1849 to July 27, 1853, RG 405, entry 1, NARA.

44 Register of Delinquencies, 1846-1850, USNA, RG 405, vol. 346, 6, 36, 37, 44, 45, 57, 73, and 74, NARA. The fate of the civil suit is unclear. A barely decipherable entry in the Anne Arundel County Court records shows Davidson appearing in court on July 2, 1849. A marginal notation ("Cepi") indicates he had been arrested and taken into custody, but other notes and names listed suggest that the case related to a debt, possibly the one discussed below. The docket contains no record of verdict or punishment. Anne Arundel County Court Docket 1849 October Term, Maryland State Archives (hereafter cited as MSA), Annapolis.

Superintendent Upshur ordered Davidson to write a detailed account of the incident, which he submitted the same day:

> I was sitting at the dinner table, and ordered the said servant to procure me a plate of soup, he replied "yes Sir" but was very tardy in obeying the order. I again said get me a plate of soup, you rascal, upon which he took the soup tureen from the table and went below in the kitchen. I then waited sometime until all the other officers had finished their soup, & partly through the rest of their dinner, when the soup tureen came into the room by another boy, but I was not helped, waiting still longer, the servant in question entered the dining room, with a plate of vegetables, but took no notice of myself whatever. I then arose from the table and struck him twice over the head with my fist, which he resisted by raising a dipper above my head in the act of striking me on the neck & shoulder with the dipper, which he had in his hand, and then immediately fled from the room into the yard. I pursued him for a short distance, but returned and sat down at the table, -- . Being still excited & aggravated by the negroe's [*sic*] conduct, I left the dining room and went in pursuit of the boy, whom I followed about three hundred [word missing in original] outside the Fort, and was just in the act of overtaking him, when I was arrested by a civil officer in the name of the law, & immediately desisted from proceeding further in the matter. The negro was taken in custody by the officer present, and I came directly in the fort & made my report to Mr. Lee, 1st Lieut.[45]

Davidson suffered no immediate punishment aside from being reported for "disorderly and violent conduct."

Davidson's attentiveness to his studies was similarly underwhelming. A final tabulation of attendance for the 42 members of his class list Davidson as one of five judged to be "Very Inattentive" (nine others were rated even lower as "Doubtful"). In most of the branches of study—Mathematics and Navigation, Mechanics, French, and Field and Battery Exercises—Davidson was absent more than one-third of the time; he missed 7 of 23 gunnery exercises. Only in Astronomy was Davidson's attendance record (82%) respectable. He was on the sick list 21 times for a cumulative 36 days—and those days on the sick list were not deemed "justified by the actual state of [his] health."[46]

45 Davidson to Upshur, May 11, 1849, copy in Phyllis Barbour Papers Virginia Museum of History and Culture (hereafter cited as VMHC).

46 Table of attendance upon the several branches and of general attention to studies, RG 405, NARA.

Despite his "very inattentive" record, Hunter Davidson succeeded academically. He passed his examinations in July 1849 with an aggregate score that ranked him 17th among the 40 midshipmen who passed. He ranked 12th in Mathematics and Navigation, 13th in Mechanics and Astronomy, 14th in French, and—ironically for an officer destined to command a gun section on America's first ironclad warship—24th in Gunnery and Steam.[47]

At his examination he confessed to having outstanding debts to a local citizen—a condition that, if unresolved, would prevent him from passing. Records suggest that his debt was to African-American barber Moses Lake, who was an employee of the school and maintained a shop in Annapolis. Davidson pledged to settle the debt by the time of his final examination in seamanship, and *thought* he had done so, and he was able to proceed to his examination in seamanship. A letter from Navy Secretary William A. Graham in December 1851 indicated that there had been a misunderstanding, involving a former classmate who ultimately failed his exams, and the debt was still outstanding.[48]

Three weeks after passing his academic exams, Davidson took his exam in seamanship. He already had five years and six months sea service. One segment of the seamanship exam was to present letters from his commanding officers and journals of his cruises. Davidson produced letters from Lt. Commanding Neil Howison of the *Shark* and Cdr. John B. Montgomery of the *Portsmouth* and a journal of 14-months service (probably February 1847-May 1848). "He lost, as he stated, the residue of his letters and Journal, in the occasion of the burning of the 'Missouri' and the wreck of the 'Shark.'" After sending him from the room to discuss his examination, the review board "decided that his letters and Journals, produced, were good; that he had passed his Examination in seamanship; and fixed the number to denote his standing therein."[49]

The "number to denote his standing"—the number that was of consuming interest to all military officers in a peacetime service—soon became a source of grievance for Passed Midn. Hunter Davidson. Navy Secretary William B. Preston's July 5, 1849, instructions to the members of the Members of the Board

47 Relative Standing in the Academic Branches combined, submitted for the Academic Board William Chauvenet President to Commander G. P Upshur Superintendent, U.S. Naval School Aug. 9. 1849, RG 405, Entry 202, NARA.

48 "Proceedings of the Board for the Examination of Midshipmen, convened at the United States Naval School Annapolis. July 26th, 1849," RG 405, NARA; Davidson to Secretary William A. Graham, Dec. 17, 1851, LRSN, vol. 398-399; Jim Cheevers, edited by Sharon Kennedy, "The United States Naval Academy, 1845-2020," unpublished paper: https://tinyurl.com/k5dv6ykr

49 Examination in Seamanship, Aug. 18, 1849 [From Nimitz Library, USNA]; *U.S. Navy Register 1849*, 80-81.

of Examiners explained that aggregate academic standings combined with the examination in seamanship would determine the "relative merit" of the candidates. "The list of merit thus obtained will be modified by the Board on the grounds of the officer-like qualities of the candidates, their moral and general character, the correctness of their journals and the character of the letters from the commanders with whom they have served." The Board must specify any such modifications in the list in their final report. Ballard then reminded the Board of unspecified "certain irregularities of a grave nature which have occurred at the school" that they may wish to consider.[50]

Preston did not mention or implicate Davidson in his instructions, and the Board did not mention any necessary modifications in its report. Nevertheless, Davidson did not, after all, escape the consequences of his record of unbecoming conduct at the naval school. As punishment for unspecified "pranks," Davidson was assigned a number below what he would have had based on merit alone, and below men who scored lower than he had on exams and even below men who failed their examinations initially. Davidson was not alone in suffering this ignominious demotion. His classmate and friend, Stephen Bleecker Luce of New York, a promising young officer whose academic record and conduct were otherwise exemplary, lost 77 positions, from 5th overall to 10th from the bottom—as a result of his participation in the March, 1849 "Guns, Bells, and Horns" affair (when midshipmen noisily protested their exclusion from a formal event). The Navy's 1850 "Active List" pegged Davidson as number 256 of the 268 passed midshipmen. Luce and the other three men punished for the "Guns, Bells, and Horns" incident occupied places 257-260. Only three Date of 1841 men fell below them on the list. Frustrated and indignant over this heavy anchor that he would have to drag along throughout his career, Davidson remained bitter in subsequent years and grasped at every opportunity to have the handicap removed. {See pages 33-35.}[51]

On September 29, 1849, Hunter Davidson received his warrant as passed midshipman to date from August 10, 1847. One month shy of his 23rd birthday, Davidson was about the age of a modern college graduate. Unlike the typical modern college graduate, Davidson was not facing the challenge of finding a job or deciding upon a career. He was nearly eight years into his career as a naval officer

50 "Proceedings of the Board for the Examination of Midshipmen," 5-6.

51 Rear Admiral Albert Gleaves, ed., *Life and Letters of Rear Admiral Stephen B. Luce U.S. Navy* (New York, 1925) 37-39; Todorich, *Spirited Years*, 67; *U.S. Navy Register 1850*, 74; Davidson to DuPont, Jan. 11, 1853 (W9-6597), Samuel Francis DuPont Papers, Hagley Library, Wilmington, DE (hereafter cited as DuPont Papers).

and fully prepared for the next phase of that career. Standing roughly 5 feet 9 inches (of average height for his time), Davidson was a slim and healthy man in the flower of youth. Photographs of him taken in the 1850s show a handsome man with piercing eyes and intense gaze sporting fashionable facial hair.[52] It is tempting for the biographer and the reader to see in his face the strength, confidence, and self-righteousness that he exhibited throughout his life. His record so far revealed him to be a competent, courageous, and dutiful officer, intelligent and capable when he applied himself, but sometimes "inattentive" to his studies, prone to a bad temper, and contemptuous toward servants and dark-skinned people whom he apparently considered his inferiors. Subsequent service reinforced all those qualities.

Back to the Pacific

From the Naval School Davidson received orders back to the Pacific Squadron. He served the next two years aboard three different vessels and was associated with a fourth. Those two years were tumultuous ones for the Pacific Squadron, punctuated by several mutinies and a wave of desertions, as sailors and officers alike yielded to the temptation of the California gold fields. They were also tumultuous years for Hunter Davidson.

Davidson received orders in August 1849 to the 20-gun sloop-of-war, *Vandalia,* and was aboard her for at least part of 1850. Built 1828 in Philadelphia, *Vandalia* had recently undergone a major overhaul and lengthening at the Gosport Navy Yard in Portsmouth, Virginia, across the Elizabeth River from Norfolk. *Vandalia* sailed from Norfolk for the Pacific in early September and was to pick up a stranded American merchant sailor in the Straits of Magellan.[53]

Among the young officers assigned to *Vandalia* was Davidson's classmate, Passed Midn. Stephen Bleecker Luce. The product of old New England stock, Luce was born in New York in March 1827. As a child he moved with his family to Washington, D.C. and was appointed a midshipman in the U.S. Navy in October 1841—10 days before Davidson. Assigned to the Mediterranean, Brazil, and Pacific Squadrons, Luce visited Japan, circumnavigated the globe, and served on the coast of California during the Mexican War. Unless they knew each other as boys in Washington, he and Davidson did not cross paths until they landed

52 NARA RG 24. Estimate of Davidson's height is based on 5-8-1/2 height listed on his late-life consular papers. The authors did not find any contemporary physical descriptions of Davidson or an official descriptive list that would reveal details about his complexion and eye and hair color.

53 *Times-Picayune* [New Orleans] of Sep. 11, 1849, lists Davidson as a PASSENGER on Vandalia bound for Pacific Squadron, but the *U.S. Navy Register 1850*, 122, lists him among the officers.

together at the Naval School in August 1848. Luce later recorded fond memories of his cruise aboard *Vandalia.* Among the midshipmen in the ship's steerage mess, Luce recalled, were his friends, Alexander Habersham, John B. Stewart, and Hunter Davidson—"'Habs,' 'Jack,' 'Davie,' and 'Tibby'—'cheeryble brothers.' A party of youngsters kept in strict discipline by their elders, worthy representatives of the innocent bravery of the Navy, ready instantly to enter upon grave situations if called upon and disappointed when the call did not come." Luce kept a journal of his service on *Vandalia,* but unfortunately for the Davidson biographer seeking details about his activities, Luce only began his journal long after Davidson had transferred from that ship for other duty.[54]

According to his service record, Davidson was assigned to the frigate *Savannah* for much of 1850-51, but Navy Department records indicate that he never spent any appreciable time on that ship. Instead, he was detailed to the steamer *Massachusetts* for duty at a place that he probably preferred to avoid: the coast of Oregon. A steamship that the U.S. Army had purchased as a troop transport during the Mexican-American War, *Massachusetts* was transferred to the Navy in 1849. Under the command of Lt. Samuel R. Knox, she was on what Navy Secretary William Ballard Preston described as "special service connected with the War Department." She was put at the disposal of a joint commission of army and navy officers appointed to select positions for lighthouses and fortifications along the coast of newly acquired Oregon. While *Vandalia* left San Francisco for service along the Pacific coast of South America in late May 1850, *Massachusetts* carried out her exploration duties in the vicinity of Puget Sound in what became the state of Washington. She reached Astoria on June 30, 1850, to begin exploring the Columbia River.[55]

Davidson's previous experience exploring the Columbia River vicinity no doubt made him a valuable addition to this "special service." But when *Massachusetts* returned from the Oregon coast to San Francisco, Samuel Knox had reason to regret the assignment of Passed Midn. Hunter Davidson to his ship. On August 31, 1850, Davidson wrote a letter to Secretary Preston "to report to you Commanders L. M. Goldsboro and G. J. Van Brunt (as Naval officers of the Joint Commission for Oregon & California) for neglect of duty, in not taking official notice of the drunkenness & unofficerlike conduct of Lieut. Saml. R. Knox, while

54 Lewis Randolph Hamersly, compiler, *The Records of Living Officers of the U.S. Navy and Marine Corps,* Fourth edition (Philadelphia, 1890), 47; Luce *Life and Letters.* Probably coincidentally, the passed midshipmen ordered to *Vandalia* also included Jefferson Maury, another of the men demoted for the "Guns, Bells, and Horns" incident. *U.S. Navy Register 1850,* 122.

55 Annual Report of the Secretary of the Navy, Dec. 1, 1849, in *The Daily Union* [Washington, D.C.], Dec. 28. 1849; *NYH,* July 9, 1850; *NYDT,* Sep. 7, 1850.

commanding this ship under the directions of this 'First Commission.'" Davidson explained that he considered it his "duty" to make this report because the conduct "and consequent disaffection in the ship" had "a tendency to injure the reputation of the Navy, and reflect discredit upon any scientific duties for which she might be commissioned. . . ." Knox himself dutifully forwarded the complaint to Pacific Squadron commander Charles S. McCauley who forwarded it to Preston.[56]

Six days after firing his official shot across his commander's bow, Davidson wrote another official letter directly to squadron commander McCauley concerning disciplinary charge lodged against him before *Massachusetts* returned to San Francisco. Because the complaint — abuse of a servant — was a familiar and recurring one, it is worth quoting Davidson's letter in full:

> U.S. Ship "Massachusetts"
> Saucilito [*sic*] Sept. 5th 1850
>
> Sir,
>
> Not having been permitted to defend myself in the conduct for which I am under suspension, I respectfully request to lay before you the circumstances of the case, and the sense of duty by which I was actuated, that you may think proper to reconsider the reasons for your decision.
>
> I had been informed by the acting master of the ship (at that time) that the servant in question was discharged; and under that impression when he came alongside, I ordered the Qtr. Master not to permit him to come on board; accordingly he was repeatedly told by the Qtr. Mr. not to come over the side, which however he obstinately insisted on doing. I then went to the Gangway myself and ordered the servant, twice, to leave the ship, and not making any demonstration to obey me, I pushed him to the Gangway ladder and he fell over the side.
>
> I was Executive Officer of the ship at the time Sir, and considered it my right and duty, to prevent a person from coming on board, whom I thought did not belong to the ship, and who had previously caused so much trouble in the ship, and I was so exceedingly vexed when the man showed so much contempt for orders from an officer, together, with his insolent manner (often exhibited on former occasions) and temerity in forcing himself on board, that I could not refrain from putting him out of the ship myself.—

56 Davidson to Preston, Aug. 31, 1850, LRSN (Squadron).

> Moreover, Sir, there being no marines, master at arms, or other person to enforce my orders on board, I had either to give way to the man or act as I did.
>
> The fact of this boy not being shipped Sir, has protected him from being punished on former occasions, when he violated the rules and regulations of the Service, by fighting and other misconduct, when the circumstance had to pass unnoticed by the captain altogether, with both parties. These acts of misconduct have been reported to Bvt. Col. Smith, and no more notice taken of them than advice or perhaps threats, the result of which has been to increase the disorderly and insolent conduct of the servant.
>
> As Executive Officer of the ship at the time sir, in the discharge of my duty and prerogatives, I again respectfully submit this case to your consideration, that I may be protected from the insolence and disrespect of these servants who are not amenable to any laws for their conduct.[57]

Commodore McCauley forwarded Davidson's letters to the secretary and noted the seriousness of Davidson's charges against his fellow officers. But he also explained that he did not let the charges prevent *Massachusetts* from resuming her important survey duties. The ship had been in port several weeks, McCauley noted, giving Davidson adequate time to lodge his complaint. It was, the commodore reasoned with understandable suspicion, "only when he gets in trouble himself that this complaint is made, showing clearly to my mind, that he was influenced more by personal motives, in preferring these charges, than from sense of duty to the service, a manifest sort of recrimination making his commanders alleged misrule, the basis to justify his own misconduct." Instead of convening any kind of disciplinary hearing, McCauley let *Massachusetts* sail on September 7 and addressed the personnel issue by removing "Mr. D." to the sloop-of-war *Warren* and assigning another passed midshipman to *Massachusetts*.[58]

The 137-foot, 20-gun *Warren* had been part of the Pacific Squadron since 1843, but, by the time Davidson joined her officer corps, she was not exactly a choice assignment. In his December 1850 annual report Navy Secretary William A. Graham noted that *Warren* had become "unseaworthy" and was serving as a store ship. Davidson's service on *Warren* was episodic and brief. Newspapers listed

57 LRSN (Squadron).

58 McCauley to Preston, Sep. 13, 1850, LRSN (Squadron). There is no evidence that Knox faced any discipline for drunkenness or unofficerlike conduct.

him as an officer aboard the frigate *Savannah* in February 1851 and again on *Warren* in April 1851.[59]

Davidson was able to get a final detachment from *Warren* (which remained in the Pacific) and return home aboard the *Savannah* (possibly with the status as passenger) in October 1851. Upon his arrival in Norfolk, Davidson received a three-month leave of absence, which he planned to spend in Washington, D.C. To his consternation, Davidson almost immediately received new orders back to Norfolk and the receiving ship *Pennsylvania.*[60]

Davidson's challenge to his unwelcome new orders was the result not of professional, but of personal, concerns. "In consequence of late and important changes in my domestic affairs, I most respectfully request to be detached from the U.S. RE[C] Ship Pennsylvania and granted the remainder of my 'leave of absence' received after returning in the U.S. Frigate Savannah.," he explained to Navy Secretary William A. Graham on November 11, 1851. "I am at present on a two weeks leave from Capt. Silas H. Stringham whose permission I have obtained to be detached, & my present residence is Annapolis Md."[61]

It is conceivable that the change in his "domestic affairs" related to the death of his "Angel" mother in March 1850, when he was far away from home in the Pacific. But it is more likely—given where he told the secretary he would be residing during his leave—that it had something to do with Mary Steele Ray of Annapolis. Five years Davidson's junior, the 20-year-old Mary Ray was the daughter of the late U.S. Navy surgeon, sometime Maryland officeholder, and slaveholding tobacco planter Hyde Ray (ca. 1787-1835) and Catharine Sarah Maria Steele Ray (1801–1891). She descended from two prominent Maryland families, the Steeles and the Bowies. Davidson apparently met her during his year at the Naval School. In 1850 she lived with her widowed mother and two sisters in Annapolis.[62] Subsequent

59 Annual Report of the Secretary of the Navy, Nov. 30, 1850, in *NYDT*, Dec. 5, 1850; *The Republic* [Washington, D.C.], Feb. 21, 1851; *Daily Union* [Washington, D.C.], Apr. 23, 1851.

60 *Washington National Intelligencer*, Oct. 11, 1851; *The Republic* [D.C.]. Davidson to William A. Graham, Oct. 16, 1851, and Davidson to Graham, Nov. 3, 1851, LRSN, vol. 396-397 and 398-399.

61 Davidson to Graham, Nov. 11, 1851, LRSN, vol. 398-399.

62 Walter Worthington Bowie, *The Bowies and their Kindred: A Genealogical and Biographical History* (Cottonport, LA, 1971), 104; John Thomas Gurney, III, ed., *Cemetery Inscriptions of Anne Arundel County, Maryland* (privately printed, n.d.), vol. I, 163; Eugene Fauntleroy Cordell, M.D., *The Medical Annals of Maryland, 1799-1899* (Baltimore, 1903), 544, gives Hyde Ray's first name as Jesse. In Oct. 1809, while assigned to *U.S.S. Essex,* Dr. Ray killed another officer in a duel. See "Fatal Duel," in *Federal Republican & Commercial Gazette* [Baltimore], Nov. 1, 1809, and reprinted in dozens of other newspapers). Upon Hyde Ray's death, his widow and brother-in-law sold his 836 1/2-acre farm on the Severn River near Annapolis, along with a stone house, multiple tobacco buildings, an unspecified number of slaves, cattle and other farm animals, and personal property. *The Baltimore Gazette and*

events suggest that Davidson used his three-month leave of absence in Annapolis to advantage.

Coast Survey

Upon the expiration of his leave, Davidson received orders attaching him to the U.S. Coast Survey. Established in 1816, the Coast Survey conducted hydrographic surveys and produced nautical charts. Bounced between the departments of the Treasury and the Navy between 1818 and 1836, the Coast Survey finally achieved stability and significance in 1843 within the Treasury Department under Superintendent Alexander Dallas Bache (1806-1867). A West Point graduate and physicist, Bache made the Coast Survey a center of American scientific research. In addition to its own staff of scientists, engineers, surveyors, cartographers, and artists, the Survey employed talented army and navy officers detailed to it. As of July 1, 1852, 13 army officers and 81 naval officers were detailed to the Coast Survey, distributed among 11 geographical sections and the central office in Washington, D.C.[63] The assignment suggests that, despite his demonstrated hair-trigger sensitivity to perceived challenges to his authority or integrity, Davidson also had established a reputation as an intelligent officer of promise. The four years that he spent with the Coast Survey augmented his scientific and technical education as well as his growing network of mentors and friends and gave him an intimate familiarity with the coastal waters of the southeast United States.

On January 17, 1852, Davidson reported to the Coast Survey steamer Légare in Baltimore and to his new commander, Lt. Commanding John Rodgers. Son and namesake of War of 1812 naval hero, Commo. John Rodgers, the younger Rodgers was born in Maryland in 1812, entered the navy in 1828, and had seen action in the Mediterranean Squadron as well as the Seminole Wars. As with other officers with whom Davidson served in the U.S. Navy, Rodgers was destined to encounter his new passed midshipman a decade later—as an enemy officer.

The Légare, a 160-foot screw steamer built in 1843 left Baltimore on February 16 and arrived a week later at Key West, Florida. The focus of her work during the four-month survey season was in and around Key Biscayne Bay. Rodgers divided specific survey tasks between two teams of junior officers, Davidson assisting

Daily Advertiser, Dec. 4, 1835. Giving no reference citation, a family tree on Ancestry.com indicates that Mary and Hunter became engaged in 1849.

63 https://nauticalcharts.noaa.gov/about/history-of-coast-survey.html; *Report of the Superintendent of the Coast Survey, showing the progress of the Survey during the year 1852* (Washington, D.C., 1853), 76-77.

Lieutenant (later Captain) John Rodgers, Davidson's commander in the Coast Survey in 1853, and wartime opponent on the James River in 1862. Photograph by E. Anthony. *NH&HC (NH 46934)*

Acting Master's Mate Julian Myers with inshore survey work. According to a report in the Baltimore *Sun,* Rodgers's survey team worked "with rapidity and vigor." After finishing their duties recording observations on currents, Légare and her officers and crew headed back to Baltimore on July 3. Upon his return, Davidson remained with the Coast Survey, assigned to the office in Washington, D.C.[64]

In between his return to Baltimore and reporting to the Coast Survey Office, Davidson attended to an important piece of personal business. On Tuesday, July 20, 1852, he married Mary Steele Ray in Annapolis, reportedly over the objections of her mother, who knew too well the life of a navy wife. Mary Ray was an obviously important, but elusive figure in Davidson's life. A surviving miniature purportedly of her shows her to have been an attractive young woman. As a teenager, she apparently attended the Patapsco Female Institute in Ellicott City, Maryland. The man who performed the marriage ceremony, Rev. Dr. Hector Humphreys, was president of the venerable St. John's College in Annapolis (which Hyde Ray had attended).[65] Marrying Mary Ray provided the 25-year-old Davidson with a new family and fixed Maryland's capital city as his new home, but it would not be accurate to conclude that it settled Hunter Davidson. He was still an ambitious career naval officer and a man of strong opinions and sensitivities.

Within two weeks of his marriage, Davidson officially reported to Rodgers at the Coast Survey office in Washington. At the end of the year, he joined the Coast Survey vessel, *Morris,* for the next season of survey work.[66]

As he was preparing to leave on the *Morris* from New York for survey work in Galveston Bay, Texas, Davidson learned "that the President contemplated restoring to those Passd Midn who were passed in 1849 . . . & were put down in their date for alleged improper Conduct, the numbers which they passed according to their merit." The 1853 Active List showed Davidson at number 169 among 197 passed midshipmen (Luce and the other "Guns, Bells, and Horns" men just behind).[67]

On January 11, 1853, he wrote to Cdr. Samuel F. Dupont, an officer who had served on the examination board that passed Davidson, and appealed to his sense of justice:

64 *Report of the Superintendent of the Coast Survey, 1852,* 42; Baltimore *Sun* quoted in New Orleans *Times-Picayune,* Mar. 15, 1862; Boston *Weekly Messenger,* July 14, 1852; Barbour Papers.

65 *The Republic* [Washington, D.C.], July 26, 1852; *The Cecil Whig* [MD], Dec. 31, 1842. Communication from John M. McKee, Aug. 21, 2025. Family tree on Ancestry.com.

66 NARA RG 24.

67 *U.S. Navy Register 1853,*72-73.

Permit me sir, to say a few words in my own behalf upon this subject. Although I shall not at this late period pretend to offer any excuses or extenuating circumstances for my conduct at the Naval School yet I would simply ask any one, who was influential in assigning me the number which I at present hold in my date, if I have not already been severely punished, to be made to serve three years constantly under those whom I passed far above, & whom I constantly taught, & not only this sir, but under those who at one time failed altogether to pass their examinations, & were afterwards put above me in the date to which they were not entitled, (by the customs of the service) from having once failed to pass in it.

If my present number is to be permanent what punishment can be so severe, so mortifying? & for my <u>lifetime</u>! Since I was not broken from the Service the sentence of a Court Martial however severe would have had an end, and my rank according to my merit restored me, but in this instance I am sentenced merely from suspicion, - I was not concerned in the difficulty of the 'Gun, Bell, & Horns' (about which the Hon. Court of investigation sat) as I testified before it, but several difficulties occured [*sic*] at the School, which led Capt Upshur to the belief that my influence was felt in every other which did occur; those things though wrong in the extreme were boyish freaks, which the man now regrets with his whole soul, but is made to suffer for & be mortified for to the latest day of his life.

Since I have no friend, either in or out of the Navy who has any influence at the Dept & beside sir, I deemed it proper to address you, as a member of the Court & Board alluded to, entertaining a faint hope, that you would employ some leisure moment in presenting this matter to the Hon Secretary of the Navy, that he might think proper to recommend the restoration of my number as I passed according to merit.[68]

Whatever hopes Davidson had for restoration soon dissipated. Subsequent correspondence with DuPont and with Navy Secretary James C. Dobbin made it clear that the administration of President Franklin Pierce would not restore the original numbers based solely on merit. Stephen Luce similarly appealed his demotion and managed to get a hearing from the U.S. Senate Committee on Naval Affairs. The committee agreed that Luce's punishment was excessive and unfair and recommended restoration of his original rank order. Despite that

68 Davidson to DuPont, Jan. 11, 1853, DuPont Papers.

recommendation, the Navy did not act. Luce finally won restoration of his rank in 1862 when Adm. Samuel DuPont wrote in favor of it, citing Luce's performance at the battle of Port Royal, South Carolina, under his own command. Luce reaped the rewards of loyalty to the old flag that Davidson's disloyalty denied him.[69]

"I have abandoned the idea, at this late period, of ever succeeding in having justice done me, by an administration, which it appears to me is governed more by political influence in any case than by any merit which the case may possess," Davidson concluded bitterly to DuPont. He added with some petulance that "If I should remain in the Navy, the good opinion of my brother officers is all I have to compensate me for the injustice which has been done me." Davidson did, of course, remain in the navy and won promotion to lieutenant in September 1855. Relative to his classmates, however, Davidson was still near the bottom of the list (number 251 out of 311 lieutenants on the 1857 list) which Davidson projected earlier would "make a difference of about four years in my promotion" as more officers competed for fewer senior positions. Officers who entered the service years after Davidson were just behind them on the list, including two future Confederate comrades Robert Randolph Carter (Date of 1842) at number 257, Beverly Kennon (Date of 1846) at number 267, and John Taylor Wood (Date of 1847) at number 274.[70]

Obsession about relative rank and promotion is, of course, endemic to military officers in every branch of service throughout history. Davidson was not unusual in that or in nurturing wounded pride and ego. Rank and promotion also carried tangible consequences for financial security and well-being. This became especially important to Davidson after his marriage in July 1852 and after he and Mary became parents in 1853 with the birth of a son they named for her father: Hyde Ray Davidson. On September 25, 1854, as Davidson' third season with the Coast Survey wrapped up, Mary gave birth to their second child, daughter Leila. The standard active service salary for a U.S. Navy midshipman in the 1840s-50s was $350 per year, $750 for a passed midshipman, and $1,500 for lieutenants. Records show that Davidson's total pay (salary plus travel and rations allowance) for his years after leaving the Naval School ranged from $951.13 in 1850 to $546.27 in 1852 (the year of his marriage and first in the Coast Survey) to $1,435.01 in

69 *Journal of the Proceedings of the Senate of the United States in Executive Session,* 37th Congress, 2nd session commencing Dec. 2, 1861, 153 (Mar. 6, 1862); Luce, *Life and Letters*, 37-38.

70 Davidson to DuPont, Mar. 5, 1854, DuPont Papers; Davidson to Secretary J. C. Dobbin, Feb. 2, 1854; Davidson to DuPont, Jan. 11, 1853, DuPont Papers; *U.S. Navy Register 1857,* 38-39.

1853 and a base pay of $750 in 1854.[71] Although his salary was respectable, it was neither consistent nor secure and was half the lieutenant's salary he believed his unjust demotion had delayed him. Throughout his career in four different navies, Davidson evidenced anxiety over his ability to provide for his family.

Even as he tried to expunge the consequences of his youthful conduct, Davidson found himself in yet another tiff with a commanding officer. He spent the 1853 survey season in Galveston Bay, Texas, on the schooner *Morris* under Cdr. Henry S. Stellwagon and under future Confederate blockade running captain, Lt. John Wilkinson (with whom he had served eight years earlier on the *Portsmouth*). Following several stormy months in Texas, during which a hurricane damaged the *Morris* and delayed their work, the crew closed out their work in late August and left for New York. Davidson received orders to the schooner *Gallatin* at Woods Hole, Massachusetts. In late August he reported to Lt. Commanding Maxwell Woodhull at Portland, Maine. Within two weeks of arriving there, Davidson wrote to Coast Survey Superintendent Bache requesting transfer owing to "the extremely [illegible] and abrupt treatment of Lieutenant Commanding Woodhull." Davidson soon withdrew his letter, and had it removed from his file, but not before Woodhull endorsed his transfer.[72] In November 1853 he was reassigned to the surveying party of Lt. John Newland Maffitt.

The son and namesake of an Irish-born Methodist preacher, the man who won renown as commander of the Confederate blockade runner *Florida* in the American Civil War was born at sea in 1819, on his way to America. He spent his first years in Connecticut, but his family moved to Fayetteville, North Carolina, when he was five. John entered the U.S. Navy as a midshipman at age 13 in 1832. By the time Davidson came under his command, Maffitt had spent most of 12 years assigned to the Coast Survey and was one of the country's most experienced and accomplished survey officers. In 1854 he was an assistant with the Coast Survey, commanding a section surveying the waters from Virginia to Georgia. Stephen Luce, who joined Maffitt's survey party later that year, recalled a half century later in a letter to Maffitt's widow that his experience with her late husband was "one of the most agreeable of my career. . . . My recollection of that period is that we had lots of hard work and no end of fun; for Maffitt had the rare art of getting all the work possible out of one with the least amount of friction. He was always in a good humor, nor

71 *Pay of officers of the Navy and Marine Corps, &c. . . . January 11, 1851*, 19; *February 1, 1853*, 21; *February 3, 1854*, 25; *February 2, 1855*, 20; *U.S. Navy Register 1854*, 5.

72 *Report of the Superintendent of the Coast Survey, showing the progress of the Survey during the year 1853* (Washington, D.C., 1854), 74-75; Letters of Sep. 23 and 29, 1853, Coastal Survey file, RG 24, NARA.

Known best as a successful Confederate commerce raider, Lt. John Newland Maffitt, USN, was Davidson's commander in the Coast Survey, 1854-56. *NH&HC (NH 48094)*

do I remember ever having seen him lose his temper even under the most trying circumstances."[73]

Davidson spent the next three years working under Maffitt's command, surveying the coasts of the Carolinas. The association proved a happy one for Davidson but threatened to get off on the wrong foot. In February 1854, Davidson forwarded through Maffitt and Bache a communication to the navy secretary complaining about—or possibly on behalf of—the crew of a vessel at Norfolk. Maffitt evidently concurred with Davidson's judgment and thought highly of Davidson's work. Later that summer Maffitt recommended Davidson's appointment to acting master of the Coast Survey Tender *Bouncer* to replace a transferred officer.[74] Among Davidson's comrades in 1854 was fellow Virginian and Date of 1841 classmate John Pembroke Jones.

Davidson, Jones, Luce, Maffitt, and all the officers working hard to survey the Atlantic coast received a bitter lesson in humility in September 1854. A severe hurricane slammed the Atlantic coast of Georgia and South Carolina, potentially altering shipping channels that Maffitt and his parties had surveyed in previous years. In the 1855 season Davidson went back to work in the waters around Charleston, South Carolina. He worked occasionally with his friend and classmate, Stephen Luce, who later described how he "and his old shipmate," Davidson (according to Luce's biographer)

73 Luce to Mrs. Maffitt, Sep. 29, 1906, in Emma Martin Maffitt, *The Life and Services of John Newland Maffitt* (New York, 1906), 122.

74 Maffitt to Bache, Feb. 11, 1854 and July 27, 1854, RG 23, NARA; RG 23, NARA; Maffitt, *Life and Services*, 120; *The Report of the Superintendent of the Coast Survey showing the Progress of the Survey during the Year 1855* (Washington, D.C, 1855), 65.

slaved day after day in open boats, angling, sounding and running in coast lines until at times they swore that they would rather be court martialed than serve any longer under such a driver. And then when tired and hungry and worn out they returned to the ship, often at sunset, fully determined to have it out with the 'old man,' they would find the Captain at the gangway to greet them with a cheerful, 'Well you have had a hard day's work today. As soon as you get washed up come up into the cabin and dine with me. My steward has found some ducks and terrapin on shore and we'll have a good dinner.' And then they would forget all their troubles and mutinous thoughts, and dine abundantly and copiously, enjoying the captain's best Madeira."[75]

The spring of 1855 found Davidson working again in South Carolina waters on the Coast Steamer *Crawford.* While measuring a base line at Port Royal, Davidson injured himself severely in the foot with a hatchet. "Mr. Davidson suffered so much for medical attention and ran such a risk without it," Maffitt explained to Bache on May 22, "that I deemed it my duty to allow him to go home where he can under his severe misfortune be properly cared for." Davidson was still out of service a month later.[76]

By the end of 1855, Davidson was back on the job, and it was Maffitt who was ill and absent. Superintendent Bache appointed Davidson acting master in charge of the *Crawford*—then at the Brooklyn Navy Yard—in Maffitt's absence. Instead of returning home after the survey season ended, Davidson remained in New York through October overseeing extensive repairs to *Crawford,* with orders to take the repaired ship back to Charleston to discharge its crew. In November he commanded the Survey schooner *Gallatin* on her voyage from New York to Charleston, where he met the now-repaired *Crawford.*[77]

Davidson returned to South Carolina and to command of the schooner *Gallatin* in the spring of 1856. His crew picked up where another crew left off the year before, two miles northeast of the mouth of North Edisto River, continuing southward to the bar and harbor of the South Edisto River. His work won the praise of Maffitt and Superintendent Bache.[78]

75 *Life and Letters* of Luce, 61-2.

76 Davidson to Bache, June 6, 1855; Maffitt to Bache, May 22, 1855 and June 21, 1855, RG 23, NARA.

77 Document dated Oct. 8, 1855, and Maffitt to Bache, Oct. 31, 1855, RG 23, NARA; *Charleston Courier* [SC], Nov. 21, 1855.

78 Maffitt, *Life and Services*, 125-6; Bache to Maffitt, July 7, 1856, roll 121, 239, RG 23, NARA; note that, according to RG 24, Hunter Davidson on May 21, 1856, was detached temporarily from

He was in Boston on the survey steamer *Bibb* in early October when he received his long-awaited promotion to lieutenant. The Navy announced his promotion in late September 1855, but the U.S. Senate did not approve the list until a year later. Davidson's promotion was dated September 15, 1855, placing him 51st among the 125 men (most from the Date of 1841) promoted to lieutenant in September 1855. Coast Survey comrades and classmates (both of whom joined the service 10 days before Davidson), J. Pembroke Jones and Stephen Luce, were 57 places ahead and two behind Davidson, respectively.[79]

After five years detailed to the Coast Survey and working in the tidal waters of America's eastern seaboard, Davidson's next assignment was a brief, but prestigious, mission across the Atlantic Ocean. A week after his detachment from the Coast Survey, Davidson received orders for Her Majesty's Ship *Resolute* and a rendezvous with Her Britannic Majesty, the Queen of the Kingdom of Great Britain. From his home in Cambridge, on Maryland's Eastern Shore, Davidson accepted the orders with enthusiasm and promised to report at the "[e]arliest available opportunity."[80]

Mafffitt's party and assigned to that of Commander Henry S. Stellwagon, with whom he served on the Morris in 1853.

79 Davidson to Dobbin, Oct. 10, 1856, LRSN, vol. 457-459; *U.S. Navy Register 1861*, 30-35.

80 Davidson to Dobbin, Nov. 5, 1856, NARA LRSN, Volume 457-459.

Chapter Two

Lieutenant Davidson, U.S.N. (1856–1861)

The story of the *Resolute* is a rich, but often forgotten, chapter in the history of the Anglo-American "special relationship." The *Resolute*, a 115-foot bark-rigged ship, was one of a succession of "rescue vessels" that the British Navy sent to the Arctic Ocean to search for the ill-fated 1845 Franklin expedition probing for the elusive Northwest Passage. *Resolute* and her companion, *Intrepid*, became stuck in the ice in 1854 and their officers and crews traveled hundreds of miles over ice to safety. More than a year later, an American whaling vessel discovered the *Resolute* floating freely, essentially undamaged, nearly 1,200 miles from where she had stuck. The whaling ship captain claimed her by right of salvage and placed a small prize crew aboard her. After a harrowing two-month cruise, the crew sailed her safely to New London, Connecticut. Recognizing her symbolic value, the U.S. Congress purchased her and appropriated $40,000 to repair and return her to the British as a gesture of friendship.[1]

Given his oft-demonstrated prickliness, Hunter Davidson was a curious choice for an assignment that was not only an honor, but diplomatic in its nature. Joining Davidson were two other freshly minted lieutenants, Clark Wells of Pennsylvania and Davidson's classmate, Edward E. Stone of Georgia. Their captain, Cdr. Henry J. Hartstene of South Carolina, was a more obvious choice for his assignment. A member of Charles Wilkes's legendary 1839-1842 Exploring Expedition,

1 For background and details, see Alfred Dunning, "The Return of the Resolute," *American Heritage* (Aug.1959), 10:14-17; and Fessenden Otis, "Presentation of the Arctic Ship *Resolute* by the United States to the Queen of England," *Magazine of American History*, (Aug. 1887), 18: 97-120.

Hartstene had given his name to an island in the Puget Sound, and, as commander of the bark, *Release,* he had found and rescued an American vessel, the *Arctic,* that had, like *Resolute,* been searching for the Franklin expedition.[2]

Departing New York on November 13, the notoriously slow sailing *Resolute* arrived at Spithead on December 12. Sailing to the dock at Portsmouth, *Resolute* hoisted the Union Jack. Hartstene traveled by train to London for official business with the Admiralty, while Davidson and the other officers were feted in Portsmouth. On December 16, the ship docked at Isle of Wight, where Queen Victoria and Prince Consort Albert traveled by carriage from Osborne House to inspect the recovered vessel. Commander Hartstene delivered a speech restoring the ship to Britain "not only as evidence of a friendly feeling to your sovereignty, but as a token of love, admiration and respect to Your Majesty personally." The queen invited Hartstene to dine and stay at Osborne House, and the other officers to tour its grounds. All the American officers traveled to London, where, on December 21, Vice-Adm. Sir George Seymour hosted a formal dinner at the Admiralty House. Davidson, Hartstene, and the other officers and American crew members traveled back across the Atlantic as passengers on the U.S. mail steamer *Washington,* arriving in New York on January 20, 1857.[3]

One symbolic gesture deserves another. In 1880, Queen Victoria ordered that timbers from the *Resolute,* recently broken up, be made into a handsome oak desk that she presented to President Rutherford Hayes "as a memorial of the courtesy and loving kindness which dictated the offer of the gift of the 'Resolute.'" The *Resolute* desk was a massive presence in the White House Oval Office through the Kennedy Administration (and was the desk under which John Kennedy, Jr., made his "house"); President Jimmy Carter restored it to its place.[4]

Service on *Resolute* was an honor for a young naval lieutenant, but as so often happens in any age, duty came at the expense of family. In early December 1856, as *Resolute* sailed toward England, Mary and Hunter Davidson's first-born child, Hyde Ray Davidson, died at the age of three years and seven months. Shortly after

2 Biography of Hartstene from Administrative/Biographical History for Henry J. Hartstene Collection, Scott Polar Research Institute Archives, University of Cambridge, accessed on https://tinyurl.com/mppnbe4p

3 *The Times* [London], Dec. 7, 1856; Hartstene's speech quoted in Dunning, 16; *The Times* [London], Dec. 22, 1856; *NYH,* Jan. 21, 1857; Dec.11, 1857.

4 Terrence Cole, "The Strange Saga of the President's Desk," *American Heritage* (Oct./Nov. 1981), 32:62-64.

Davidson was among the American officers who returned the Arctic exploring vessel HMS *Resolute* to Queen Victoria at Southampton England in December 1856. Davidson appears in this print (based on William Simpson's painting) standing on the deck to the left of the royal party. *NH&HC (NH-108332)*

Davidson arrived in New York on the *Washington,* the grieving Mary gave birth to second son, Percy, on January 12, 1857.[5]

Family concerns did not, however, preclude Davidson from seeking a new assignment to advance his career. Exploiting his five seasons with the Coast Survey and perhaps hoping to burnish his own credentials as a naval surveyor and scientist, Davidson threw his hat in the ring for a newly announced initiative. On March 29, 1857 he wrote to Navy Secretary Isaac Toucey requesting (and quoting from the recently published Congressional legislation) to "be attached to the Party detailed by the Navy Department 'for the purpose of making explorations and verification of the surveys already made, of a ship Canal near the Isthmus of Darien, to connect the waters of the Pacific & Atlantic by the Atrato & Truando rivers.'" His request crossed in the mail with new orders to travel to Norfolk and report on April 10th to the 16-gun sloop-of-war USS *Dale,* which Davidson dutifully obeyed.[6]

5 Burial information for Hyde Ray Davidson, accessed via Ancestry.com; birth date for Percy Davidson from www.Findagrave.com and from christening document accessed via Ancestry.com. Another source lists Jan. 25 as Percy's birthday.

6 Davidson to Toucey, Mar. 29, 1857, LRSN, vol. 460-462; see, for example, [Richmond] *Daily Dispatch* (hereafter cited as *RDD*), Mar. 17, 1857, and *AG,* Mar. 16, 1857; Davidson to Toucey, Mar. 31, 1857 and Apr. 10, 1857, LRSN, vol. 460-462 and vol. 463; *U.S. Navy Register 1858,* 113.

Africa Squadron

A sister ship to the *Preble,* on which he served his first extended cruise in 1844, the *Dale* was built at the Philadelphia Navy Yard and commissioned in 1839. She operated on the Pacific Coast of California and Mexico during the Mexican-American War (relieving *Portsmouth* at Guaymas in 1847) before transferring to the African Squadron in 1850. Reputedly the fastest of the five sloops-of-war authorized in 1837, *Dale* joined a squadron charged with suppressing the resurgent Atlantic slave trade.

Although the U.S. had abolished the slave trade in 1808 (after keeping it open for the entire 20-year grace period authorized in the Constitution), it had declined to enter into any international agreements to enforce it until 1841-1842. The 1842 Treaty of Washington with Great Britain obligated the United States to a joint cruising responsibility and necessitated the creation of the African Squadron. The U.S. still—until 1862, after the southern states had left the Union—did not allow its ships the "right of search" of vessels other than those flying under the U.S. flag. This restriction rankled British officials and undermined the effectiveness of the enforcement. After years of decline, the Atlantic slave trade increased leaps and bounds in the 1850s. Most of the vessels were American built and many reportedly operating out of New York and New Orleans (France was also rumored to be behind the resurgence). The British questioned the American commitment to suppressing the slave trade, not only because the U.S. denied the right of search, but because most of the ships assigned to the African Squadron were larger and more cumbersome sailing ships, not fast sailing ships or, better yet, fast steamers. During his two years as an officer on the *Dale,* Hunter Davidson experienced the difficulties and frustrations that plagued the African Squadron.[7]

One reason for the U.S. Navy's tepid approach to the slave trade interdiction duty was the real danger of "Africa fever" to the health of officers and men. In November 1844, four months after Davidson left the *Preble,* that ship had transferred to the Africa Squadron and spent two weeks anchored close to the African shore. More than half the men soon fell ill with fever. Ultimately, 90 of the crew of 144 fell ill with fever and 19 died. Perhaps not coincidentally, a few weeks after his assignment to the Africa Squadron in April 1857, Davidson asked and received permission "to allot Sixty Dollars per month of my salary, for support of my family." Still assigned

7 See W. E. Burghardt DuBois, *The Suppression of the African Slave Trade to the United States of America, 1638-1870* (New York, 1954), especially 143-148, 169-180; and Donald L. Canney, *Africa Squadron: The U.S. Navy and the Slave Trade, 1842-1861* (Washington, D.C., 2006), especially chapters 1-3 and 181-182.

to the *Dale* two years later—and expecting a salary increase to $1,500 per year—Davidson asked for an increase in his allotment to his family.[8]

The *Dale* left Norfolk on May 6, 1857, on her third and final cruise with the African Squadron. Her new commander was William McBlair (1807-1863) a 33-year U.S.N. veteran from Baltimore. Davidson was to be 3rd lieutenant, sharing the officers' wardroom with 1st Lt. and Executive Officer Joel S. Kennard of Alabama, 2nd Lt. Theodoric Lee Walker of Maryland (a fellow Date of '41 man), 4th Lt. Andrew Boyd Cummings of Pennsylvania, and Master (later Lt.) Thomas Pelot. Not unusually, five of the six senior officers on a ship whose mission was to suppress the slave trade hailed from slaveholding states and four of them later resigned from the U.S. Navy to join the Confederacy.[9]

The *Dale* arrived in the Azores in early June and at the end of the month sailed from Porto Praya, the primary base located on Cape Verde Island, for the coast of Africa. She arrived on the south coast of the Bight of Biafra in early September to patrol around the mouth of the Congo River. Over the next two years, McBlair exhibited great energy and ingenuity in the pursuit of his duties. In contrast to other commanders, McBlair and the *Dale* spent considerable time close to shore, south of the Bight of Biafra, and patrolling the river, and seemed determined to demonstrate that the U.S. Navy took its mission seriously. "It could easily be argued," wrote historian Douglas Canney, "that McBlair was one of the most motivated ship commanders on the station."[10]

Not yet a year since he had helped return the *Resolute* to Britain and met the Queen of England, Hunter Davidson found himself entangled in the diplomatic friction that characterized the Anglo-American relationship on the African coast. England dedicated more ships, men, and resources than any other nation to interdicting the slave trade, and British cruisers captured far more suspected slavers than did their American counterparts. A curious number of those ships were "captured without flag or papers." In October 1857, the British captured a suspected slaver (typically without human cargo on board), the U.S.-flagged commercial vessel *Bremen,* declared her papers "worthless," threw them overboard, and took her as a prize "without flag or papers." Commander McBlair sent Davidson and Thomas Pelot to the British senior officer, Commo. Charles Wise, to learn more about the circumstances of the capture. The two lieutenants' reports

8 Canney, *Africa Squadron,* 31-35, 66; Davidson to Toucey, Apr. 21, 1857, and June 20, 1859, LRSN, vol. 463 and 477.

9 *AG*, Mar. 11, 1863; *Evening Star* [Washington, D.C.] (hereafter cited as *WES*), May 7, 1857; *U.S. Navy Register 1857,* 113.

10 *RDD*, July 1, 1857; *The Washington Union*, July 23, 1857; Canney, *Africa Squadron,* 189-93.

of the interview were subsequently excerpted in newspapers and reproduced in official reports about the slave trade.

Davidson explained that McBlair wished to determine "whether he (Wise) used language or other means to intimidate the Captain of the Bremen and to influence him in hauling down the colors against his wish." Wise denied the implication. "Finally," Davidson wrote, "I asked Commo. Wise that in the event of his meeting with an American slaver under American colors and bearing genuine papers (which of course she would have obtained when she cleared for other purposes than slaving), if he would use means to induce the Captain to throw his colors and papers overboard. He replied, 'Well I might stretch a point and tell the Captain, the 'Dale' was just near us here." Wise's reply vindicated American suspicions "regarding the method which H. M. officers on this Coast, adopt to seize American slavers, as the latter would never choose the other alternative of being taken to an American man-of-war, sent to the United States and tried for their lives." (At the request of the secretary of the navy, Davidson later briefed Secretary of State Lewis Cass about the incident.)[11]

Captain Thomas H. Conover (1794-1864), the New Jersey-born commodore of the U.S. African Squadron, shared Davidson's interpretation of Wise's explanation and forwarded his report to Washington. In response to an article in *The Edinburgh Review* indicting Americans, specifically southerners, for their role in the resurgent slave trade, the *Richmond Enquirer* cited the *Bremen* incident, quoting Davidson and Pelot, and charged the British Navy with an elaborate scheme to profit by taking the prize money from ships, capturing their human cargo, and selling captured Africans to labor-hungry planters in their Caribbean possessions.[12]

National loyalty rather than sectional loyalty explained the actions and reactions of Davidson, McBlair, and *Dale's* other southern-born officers. Their suspicions of "Perfidious Albion" were not a façade to defend slavery or the slave trade, but a long tradition. Despite the symbolic return of the *Resolute* and the 20th-century "special relationship" between the United States and Britain, enmity between the two countries was more the rule than the exception. Britannia "ruled the waves" and, as a wag observed during World War I, often "waived the rules,"

11 Davidson to McBlair, Oct. 12, 1857, LRSN (Squadron); also in *African slave trade. . . December 6, 1860,* 532. A manuscript copy of the letter is available in the Gilder Lehrman Collection (www.gilderlehrman.org/collection/glc0583202).; *NYT,* Jan. 24, 1860.

12 *NYH,* Jan. 11, 1858; *Richmond Enquirer,* Dec. 14, 1858. Conover's squadron flagship was the sloop-of-war (formerly frigate) *Cumberland,* which Davidson would help destroy during the battle of Hampton Roads in March 1862.

and American naval officers had resented the British high-handedness since the Quasi-War of 1798.[13]

A month after the *Bremen* incident, it was *Dale* herself that captured a suspected slaver. Operating at the mouth of the Congo River, McBlair received a credible report of a slave ship upriver. He dispatched a launch under the command of his executive officer, 1st Lt. T. Lee Walker, up the Congo. Walker's party surprised the ship, *William G. Lewis,* at her moorings, found irregularities in her papers and the usual evidence of her true purpose, such as suspiciously large water casks in her hold, and took her as a prize. Walker escorted her down to the coast, where other officers, including Davidson, boarded and inspected her, endorsing Walker's conclusions. McBlair put 2nd Lt. Joel S. Kennard in command of a small prize crew and sent her across the Atlantic to a prize court in Norfolk. Although *Lewis* almost certainly was a slaver, prosecutors were—typically—unable to win their case in prize court.[14]

A few months later, *Dale's* concern shifted from her mission to the welfare of her own crew. An anonymous officer reported in April that most of the officers and men were suffering with "Africa fever." Lieutenant Walker, who had led the party that captured the *William G. Lewis,* died, and all but one of the lieutenants (apparently including Davidson) were suffering from the fever. "The captain was obliged to perform the duties of the Captain, 1st Lieutenant, and *watch* officer," wrote the unnamed officer. "When you see the commander of a man-of-war *keeping watch,* you may be sure the ship is in distress." The *Dale* left the African coast to recuperate in the Canary Islands. By July, McBlair was able to send home reports that the officers and crew were well and that only two men had died of the fever.[15]

When the *Dale* and other vessels of the squadron anchored at Porto Praya in early July 1858, Davidson found himself embroiled in another dispute with a brother officer. Unlike his previous disputes, this one resulted in a five-day court martial. Davidson was the chief accuser and star witness for the prosecution. Although the incident seems trivial in retrospect, the charge against Passed Assistant Surgeon Washington Sherman was serious: "Disobedience of the lawful orders of his superior officer and treating with contempt his superior while the

13 See, for example, Edward P. Crapol, *America for Americans: Economic Nationalism and Anglophobia in the Late Nineteenth Century* (New York, 1973). The loss of prize money no doubt also explained their reaction.

14 *RDD,* Dec. 24, 1857; *The National Era* [Washington, D.C.], Dec. 31, 1857; Joe Mosier, "United States v. The Bark William G. Lewis: The Navy Brings a Slave Ship to Norfolk," *The Daybook* [Hampton Roads Naval Museum] (2005), 10:7-9, 13-14.

15 *AG,* June 9, 1858; *The Daily Exchange* [Baltimore] (henceforth cited as *BDE*), Aug. 2, 1858.

execution of his office." Presided over by Capt. McBlair, the court convened on the USS *Vincennes* on July 5.[16]

The situation began on July 1, when Davidson, serving as executive officer, communicated McBlair's order to make out a written request for a medical survey of men that Sherman thought necessary to survey. According to Davidson, Sherman disobeyed the order, not even bothering to respond. The following morning at the wardroom breakfast table, the captain's orderly reiterated the order to Sherman, who acknowledged that Davidson had communicated the order the day before. Davidson went to the captain (intercepting Sherman and preventing him from seeing the captain first) and "earnestly hoped he would take official notice of the neglect on the part of Dr. Sherman." Davidson then sent for Sherman and reiterated the order, to which Sherman allegedly replied, "Well but I wish you to understand that I do not acknowledge your authority to [. . .]" To this pregnant incomplete sentence, Davidson ordered Sherman from the quarter deck three or four times and Sherman refused until Davidson summoned the sergeant and a Marine guard. Sherman obeyed but said that "I only go below to avoid personal violence."

Sherman was the "accused," but the trial revolved largely around questions concerning Davidson's authority and his behavior. Had Davidson made it clear that he acted under the captain's authority? Davidson explained that "The executive officer is always considered as acting under the authority of the Captain, and therefore when I give an order as Executive officer, I consider that the person to whom it is given should obey it as promptly as if it was given by the Captain." Asked why he had to prevent Sherman from getting first to the captain's cabin, Davis replied "Because he had defied my authority upon the Quarter deck, and I could not let it pass unnoticed for a moment." Exactly what authority Sherman implied that Davidson did not have was immaterial after he stated flatly that he did not recognize his authority.

The accused and his counsel posed to six witnesses leading questions contrasting Davidson's manner, language, and tone (characterized in the questions as "excited," "imperious," "loud," "offensive," "boisterous," and "calculated to exasperate the accused") with the accused's "remarkable calmness and forbearance under the circumstances." The witnesses agreed that Davidson was "excited" and "loud" and his manner "calculated to exasperate" Sherman and anyone else in his situation. Asked by the court how he knew that Davidson was excited when he left the breakfast table on July 2, Purser J. S. Cunningham answered, "Anyone who knows him can see it distinctly in his face." The court asked Davidson's fellow lieutenant,

16 Records of the Judge Advocate General (Navy), RG 125 (M273), NARA, Vol. 80, case no. 2363. The following paragraphs are from the 55-page trial transcript.

A. B. Cummings, whether Davidson's "general manner of carrying on duty" were "positive without being offensive." Yes, he replied, but his voice could be loud when giving orders, depending on the order and whether he was on deck.

After hearing the testimony and receiving a written statement of defense from Dr. Sherman, the court found Sherman guilty on the charge and both specifications and sentenced him to be reprimanded by the commander-in-chief, the reprimand to be read on the quarter deck of each ship in the squadron. A commentary added to the sentence indicated just how much the trial was as much about Davidson's behavior as Sherman's disobedience:

> [T]he Court add further, that in voting this very lenient sentence for an offence so grave as that of 'Disobedience of the lawful orders of his superior officer, and treating with contempt his superior being in the execution of his office' the Court have considered the very excited and irritating manner of Lieutenant Davidson, towards the accused, which may possible have tended to confuse the accused and provoke him to committing himself to a greater extent than he otherwise might have done.

The incident highlighted aspects of Davidson's character and personality evident in other episodes throughout his naval career: his sensitivity to having his authority challenged; his acute sensitivity to disrespect; his self-righteousness; his sense of duty; and his unwillingness to back down from confrontation. This incident revealed that his comrades—at least those in the wardroom of the USS *Dale*—perceived him as short-tempered and combative. Clearly, it was not only "insolent" African Americans whose perceived disrespect awakened Davidson's ire. As his earlier charges against Lt. Samuel Knox indicated, Davidson was more than willing to call his brother officers to account.

The *Dale* spent the next few months patrolling the southern coast of the Bight of Biafra and the Gulf of Guinea, without further drama. She arrived at the Portsmouth, New Hampshire, shipyard in late May 1859. The 20-year-old *Dale* was taken out of commission (though she was put back into commission during the Civil War and again after the war) and McBlair echoed Commo. Conover's complaints about the inadequacy of the squadron to its task. The Navy Department listened, and reconstituted the composition of the squadron, committing more ships and men to the suppression of the slave trade, most importantly including four steamers cruising around the principal destination of Cuba.[17]

17 *BDE*, Feb. 24, 1859; *AG*, Feb. 25, 1859; *RDD*, May 24, 1859; *The National Era* [Washington, D.C.], July 21, 1859; Mosier, "Bark William Lewis," 14; Canney, *Africa Squadron*, 201-205.

True to form, Davidson wrapped up the cruise of the *Dale* by raising a formal complaint about the "disrespectful and insubordinate" conduct of an unnamed brother officer. Upon reaching Portsmouth, McBlair left the ship with his baggage and moved on shore to await orders. A few days later, while Davidson was in temporary command of the ship, a junior officer followed McBlair's example and refused to obey Davidson when he refused him permission to do so. To Davidson's consternation, McBlair sided with the junior officer and allowed him to come ashore.

Rather than accepting that as a definitive answer, Davidson wrote to Navy Secretary Isaac Toucey. The question, Davidson, argued is whether it is proper for officers of a U.S. warship upon its arrival home to leave their ship before receiving formal instructions regarding ship and crew. "A moments reflection will show the inj[ury] that must result to the Service by permitting such a course of conduct," he explained. The obvious double standard undermined morale and indiscipline and posed an immediate danger to the service if the ship were called unexpectedly back into service. "I very respectfully request that the Hon Secretary will inform me whether I am right or wrong in my view of this case." Rather disingenuously, he concluded that "I have submitted it more from a desire to have the question decided for the future guidance of naval off[ice]rs and to promote the discipline & efficiency of the Navy, than that my conduct should be sustained, for individuals are but too liable to errors of judgment."

Davidson no doubt was smugly pleased when the officers to whom Toucey referred his query opined that "We are of opinion, that it is improper for officers to pack up & remove their baggage & effects on shore from a ship of war returned from a cruise before orders shall have been received to discharge the crew, or allow them to go on shore unless the officer shall be detached from the vessel."[18]

Assistant Instructor of Seamanship, Naval Tactics, and Practical Gunnery

After a two-year absence from his growing family, Davidson sought an assignment that would allow him to spend what would prove the remainder of his U.S. Navy career living in his adopted home city. On June 29, 1859, he wrote from his home in Annapolis to Navy Secretary Toucey, requesting "orders to the 'Executive Dept,' of the U.S. Naval Academy." Toucey honored his request, and, on September 20, Davidson reported to Capt. George S. Blake, superintendent

18 Davidson to Toucey, June 14, 1859, with endorsement by Smith and Ingraham, June 16, 1859, LRSN, vol. 489.

Portrait of Davidson from the Naval Academy 1861 class album. *Special Collections & Archives Department, Nimitz Library, USNA*

of the Naval Academy. Davidson, presumably with Mary and their children, Leila and Percy, lived on post (the "Yard" in Naval Academy parlance) initially in the Old Pinckney House, which Superintendent Blake described as "very much dilapidated." After a year in that "most uncomfortable house," Davidson was able to arrange an exchange whereby he was able to occupy the more spacious quarters occupied by Lt. George W. Balch. The move to Annapolis apparently succeeded in providing the desired domestic contentment. Almost 40 years later Davidson reminisced to his classmate and fellow faculty member, Stephen Luce, about how their children, "my Percy and your Carrie, little wee things between 3 & 4 years were lot one day in the naval school & made us all so uneasy until found by the Watchman away down by the side of the hillock near the water sound asleep in each other's arms!"[19]

Davidson's appointment as assistant instructor of seamanship, naval tactics, and practical gunnery reflected the evolution of the Academy and its academic program. The reforms of 1850-51, the year after Davidson passed his examinations—extended the years of study from one to four and established several departments: naval tactics and practical seamanship; mathematics; natural and experimental philosophy; gunnery and infantry tactics; ethics and English; modern languages. The longer term of study required more instructors, most of whom were, like Davidson, detailed from the officer ranks to supplement the regular faculty. Subsequent reforms made during Davidson's two-year tenure at the Academy further refined the course of study, instituted the tradition of a "summer cruise, and created an Academic Board intended to dilute the power of the core academic faculty.[20] When he took up his post as assistant instructor, Lt. Hunter Davidson was nearly 33 years-old and an 18-year U.S. Navy veteran with an impressive resume.

The faculty that Davidson joined in October 1859 included several men from the Date of 1841, suggesting that the famously unruly class had earned respectability at Annapolis. His fellow 41ers included Virginians William K. Mayo, Robert W. Scott, and John Upshur, and Kentucky-born William P. Buckner. Like Davidson, Scott and Upshur were assistant instructors of seamanship, naval tactics, and practical gunnery, but attached to the practice ship *Plymouth;* Mayo

19 Davidson to Toucey, June 29, 1859 and Davidson to Toucey, Sep. 20, 1859, LRSN, vol. 489 and vol. 492-493; *WES*, Sep. 14; Ford, "History," chapter 15, typescript pages 32, 36; Davidson to Blake, Nov. 26, 1860, LR USNA, entry 25; Blake to Captain George A. Magruder, Nov. 27, 1860, LS USNA, Entry 1; Davidson to Luce, Apr. 19, 1897, Stephen Bleecker Luce Papers (hereafter cited as Luce Papers), Library of Congress Manuscripts Division (hereafter cited as LC).

20 Todorich, *Spirited Years,* 68, 78-78, 180, 186; *U.S. Navy Register 1860,* 98; *U.S. Navy Register 1861,* 90.

Davidson's best friend at the Naval School and during his USN service was Stephen Bleecker Luce of New York, who rose to the rank of admiral and established the Naval War College. *Special Collections & Archives Department, Nimitz Library, USNA*

was assistant professor of ethics and English studies; and Buckner assistant professor of astronomy, navigation.[21]

In his second year at the Academy, two familiar faces joined Davidson on the faculty. William H. "Billy" Parker, son of Davidson's first ship commander, Capt. Foxhall A. Parker, and the top of the class of 1847-48 class, became assistant professor of mathematics in 1853 and returned to the faculty as instructor of seamanship and naval tactics and practical gunnery. More gratifying for Davidson was a reunion with his 1848-49 Annapolis classmate and Coast Survey comrade, Stephen B. Luce, whose punishment for the "Guns, Bells, and Horns" prank continued to handicap his rank standing, but not his growing reputation. Joining them was Lt. John Taylor Wood, grandson of President Zachary Taylor and nephew by marriage of Senator Jefferson Davis of Mississippi. Although he did not join the service until 1847, Wood was already a lieutenant and only 20 positions below Davidson on the list.[22]

In addition to sharing their practical expertise, the naval officers *cum* instructors found themselves sharing in the humdrum administrative tasks of a military school bureaucracy. During his two years at the Academy, Davidson, along with lieutenants Simpson and Buckner, received orders to "make a useful examination of the seamless overcoat" and recommend on its potential use for

21 *Official Register of the Officers and Acting Midshipmen of the United States Naval Academy* (Washington, D.C., 1859), [3]. Upshur had changed his surname from Nottingham to his mother's maiden name to align him with the ubiquitous Virginia naval family.

22 *U.S. Navy Register1861*, 32; *Official Register of the Officers and Acting Midshipmen of the United States Naval Academy* (Washington, D.C., 1860), [3].

acting midshipmen, and to examine the regulations relating to the duties of the storekeeper's department.[23]

The five classes of midshipmen whom Davidson knew during his two years on the faculty predictably included dozens of young men who confronted each other as enemies a few years later. Several of them—notably Hardin B. Littlepage, Robert Chester Foute, Walter Raleigh Butt, William W. Read, and Charles W. Read—would serve with their former instructor in Hampton Roads or on the James River. Roswell H. Lamson would draw the assignment of thwarting his instructor's wartime torpedo work. Another, William B. Cushing, would lead the Civil War's most celebrated torpedo attack and eclipse Davidson's own fame. The midshipmen of 1859-61 also included two young men—William T. Sampson and Winfield Scott Schley—destined to become national heroes for destroying the Spanish fleet at Santiago, Cuba, in 1898 and the most famous naval historian and theoretician of the era, Alfred Thayer Mahan.

It is difficult to determine how much contact Davidson had with any of the midshipmen whose paths he would cross in the Civil War. But he certainly became more intimate with the 12 faculty and 117 midshipmen who participated in the 1860 summer cruise. Beginning in 1851, the summer cruise quickly became an important ritual in the Naval Academy's practical education curriculum. The first cruises crossed the Atlantic on the sloop *Preble,* which Davidson knew well from his time aboard her in 1844. By 1860, the Academy's practice ship was the sloop *Plymouth,* sister ship to the *Portsmouth,* on which Davidson had sailed in 1844-1848. Commanding the practice vessel was the commandant of midshipman and the chief instructor of seamanship, naval tactics, and practical gunnery, Cdr. Thomas T. Craven.[24]

The midshipmen, primarily from the first and third classes, reported to *Plymouth* on June 9, 1860. They sailed the ship down the bay to Norfolk, then stood to sea on June 27. The cruise took them to ports where Davidson had spent time while serving in the African Squadron and would visit again in 1865-66—the island of Fayal in the Azores, Cadiz, Spain, and Funchal in the Madeiras and Tenerife in the Canaries—before making a swift passage back to Norfolk in early September. The practice vessel spent the remainder of September in the Chesapeake drilling the midshipmen on the guns and the spars and rigging and giving the first-class men

23 Orders dated 20 Sep. 1859, 15 Oct. 1860, 29 Sep. 1859, and 14 Dec. 1859, RG 405, entry 1000, NARA.

24 Todorich, *Spirited Years,* chapter 7; Hunter, *A Society of Gentlemen,* chapter 6.

practical experience as "officers of the deck" before returning the midshipmen to Annapolis in time for the new academic year.[25]

"A very intelligent officer in the naval service"

The most notable role that Davidson played during his two years at the Academy was not educator, but inventor. An unpublished history of the Academy's first decades explained that "While the students were thus actively engaged in the struggle for Academic honors and in general self-improvement, some members of the staff employed their leisure hours in supplying deficiencies in the text-books, in preparing new ones, and in the improvement of nautical apparatus." Of particular note, "Lieutenant Davidson introduced his ingenious boat-detaching apparatus, which, in a trial of efficiency with the apparatus of Blunt, Bishop, Brooke, Kynaston, and Tucker, bore away the palm of superiority, and for the use of which Congress awarded him the sum of $10,000."[26]

The story of Davidson's invention began during his cruise on the *Dale*. As the ship prepared for her return from Cape Verde to the United States, Davidson wrote to Navy Secretary Toucey informing him that he had invented what he described as "an Apparatus for Lowering, Detaching, & Attaching Boats alongside of vessels, whether in rapid motion, or still in the water." Commander McBlair and Commo. Conover had appointed a "board of officers" from the African Squadron flagship *Cumberland* to test the apparatus and "stated in writing that they are 'perfect.'" Davidson requested that Toucey appoint a board of officers so that, upon the *Dale's* return, they could test the apparatus "and report to the Navy Dept their opinion thereof in order that if considered useful to the Navy, it may be adopted."[27] This was the beginning of Davidson's relentless and successful campaign on behalf of an invention that profited him financially and in reputation.

Davidson applied for a patent for his device, and, on November 15, 1859, the U.S. Patent Office granted him patent number 26,094 for an "Improved Apparatus for Working Ships' Boats." "By means of this new apparatus it is contended," explained a widely published newspaper article about the patent, "a ship's boat, with its crew, can be lowered at sea by one man, with perfect safety, and without

25 "THE RETURN OF THE PLYMOUTH," *NYH*, Sep. 5, 1860.

26 Ford, "History," chapter 15, typescript pages 8-9 [MSS page 6]. A board of Naval Academy instructors that tested Davidson's invention noted that "[a]s to comparative merits, we know of no other apparatus now in use in the Navy with which to compare it." Thomas T. Craven, et al., to Superintendent Blake, Dec. 19, 1859, LR USNA, Entry 25, NARA.

27 Davidson to Toucey, Apr. 10, 1859, NARA LRSN, vol. 487.

the slightest danger of swamping, however stormy the weather or dark the night." With this public announcement came high praise, possibly inspired by Davidson: "The cost of construction is trifling, we understand, not exceeding fifty dollars. Lieut. D.'s friends predict that, ere long, no vessel will venture to sea without this apparatus on board," noted the article. "Lieutenant Hunter Davidson is a very intelligent officer in the naval service, and his invention is believed by many to be destined to secure his mechanical genius a world-wide reputation," added the *Charleston Courier.*[28]

The invention promised genuine benefits for ships and seamen around the globe. It also promised pecuniary benefits for its inventor. The Navy Department agreed to conduct its own tests of the apparatus on *Plymouth.* In advance of those trials, Davidson sought endorsements from influential brother officers. Samuel F. DuPont, who had been unable to assist Davidson with his grievance over rank, gratified Davidson with an unqualified positive reply to his query about the importance of the invention. "I have to say," DuPont wrote to Davidson on March 7, 1860, "that any apparatus which will accelerate even by <u>one</u> minute the lowering a quarter of waist boat, or increase the <u>safety</u> of the operation in a seaway,-over the present mode, particularly if it can be done by one man, is worthy of immediate consideration—and adoption—for human life is involved in the process, and many of us may look back & remember how a minute or two sooner in getting off a boat would have rescued a drowning man who had fallen overboard."[29]

The *Plymouth* trials in April 1860 in the waters off Annapolis went well. The apparatus passed three examinations and was referred to two boards of officers appointed by the secretary of the navy and another by the Naval Committee of the House of Representatives. *The Scientific American* featured Davidson's invention on the cover of its May 19, 1860, issue, describing it and the experiments in detail.[30]

Testing of the apparatus continued during the Summer Cruise on *Plymouth.* Commander Thomas T. Craven's official report of the tests described the successful operation of the apparatus and concluded with high praise for its inventor: "For the ease and safety, and very great expedition with which these operations have been performed, we are greatly indebted to the admirable boat-lowering, detaching, and attaching invented by Lieutenant Hunter Davidson." *The Pacific Commercial Advertiser* of Honolulu exceeded the many other newspapers reporting on the tests,

28 *Report of the Commissioner of Patents for the Year 1858: Arts and Manufactures in Two Volumes* (Washington, D.C., 1860), vol. I, 682 vol. II, 632 *The Charleston Daily Courier,* Nov. 22, 1859.

29 DuPont to Davidson, Mar. 7, 1860, DuPont Papers.

30 "Improved Boat-Lowering, Detaching, Attaching and Griping Apparatus," *The Scientific American,* (May 19, 1860), 321-322.

DAVIDSON'S BOAT-LOWERING APPARATUS.

"Davidson's Boat-Lowering Apparatus" from *Scientific American*, May 19, 1860.
Scientific American, digitized by Cornell University

gushing that "the dangers of the sea seem to be entirely overcome in this simple apparatus, invented by an American Lieutenant." Naval Academy superintendent Blake's annual report to Navy Secretary Toucey also noted the successful trial and opined that "there can be no doubt of the value of that invention."[31]

The "value of the invention" was very much on Davidson's mind. After overseeing a successful test on the *Plymouth* in April 1860, the House Committee on Naval Affairs (specifically Rep. J. Morrison, a Maryland Democrat) in June 1860 reported a bill "to enable the Secretary of the Navy to purchase Davidson's boat apparatus." The bill took a circuitous path through Congress, reappearing in the Senate in February 1861 as an amendment to a deficiency bill. Senator John Renshaw Thomson, a pro-slavery Democrat from New Jersey (whose brother-in-law and predecessor in that seat was former Navy Commo. Robert F. Stockton) introduced an amendment "[f]or the purchase of the right to use in the Navy, if in the opinion of the Secretary of the Navy, it shall be deemed expedient, Davidson's boat-lowering, attaching, and detaching apparatus, a sum not exceeding $15,000." In support of the expenditure Morrison quoted the endorsements by Craven, Blake, and *Plymouth's* executive officer, Lt. Edward Simpson. William Pitt Fessenden, Republican senator from Maine, concurred in the value of the apparatus, but opined "that $15,000 is a large sum for us to pay for this." At his suggestion, the Senate agreed to the purchase for $10,000. The generous payment to Davidson was part of an appropriations bill signed by President James Buchanan in the last days of his administration. "This wonderful apparatus, by which a boat can be lowered with perfect safety at sea, under any and all circumstances," exclaimed a widely printed newspaper article, "will now be offered to passenger steamers, and will, no doubt, soon come into general use, by which thousands of lives will be saved."[32]

31 Craven's report quoted in *Congressional Globe,* 36th Congress, 2nd Session, Feb. 11, 1861, (vol. 30), 843. According to a newspaper summary of Commander Craven's official report of the summer cruise, the "only point of special interest is his notice of David[son]'s boat-lowering and detaching apparatus." *BDE,* Oct.17, 1860; "Lt. Hunter Davidson's Boat Apparatus," *The Pacific Commercial Advertiser [Honolulu],* Dec. 6, 1860; *Message from the President of the United States. . . to Congress. . . December 4, 1860,* 29.

32 H.R. 855, 36th Congress, 1st session accessed via Congress.gov; *Congressional Globe,* 36th Congress, 2nd Session, Feb. 11, 1861, (vol. 30), 843 "Dangers of the Sea Overcome" *BDE,* Mar. 23, 1861; also, [New Orleans] *Daily True Delta,* Mar. 30, 1861; *Philadelphia Press,* Mar. 22, 1861; *Boston Evening Transcript,* Mar. 20, 1861. After the war, a correspondent calling himself "NAVY" wrote to the *Army and Navy Journal* regarding a current discussion about the lack of boat-lifting apparatus on U.S. Navy vessels. "At the commencement of the Rebellion Congress bought the patent right of a disengaging apparatus from Lieutenant Hunter Davidson, U.S.N., who remained in the service just long enough to finger the appropriation before going over to the Rebels, but this right thus bought

Meanwhile, Davidson made an improvement on the hook component of his apparatus. He applied for a second patent, and, on April 9, 1861, the U.S. Patent Office granted patent number 32,036 for an "Improved Hook For Attaching and Detaching Boats from their davits."[33]

Davidson's patents, his service on the Coast Survey, and his appointment to the Naval Academy faculty earned him a place among a growing fraternity of naval officers celebrated for their contributions to naval technology and science. Unlike his Date of 1841 classmate, Lt. John Mercer Brooke, who also had a pair of patents to his credit, Davidson did not have on his resume an apprenticeship with Matthew Fontaine Maury at the U.S. Naval Observatory. But, like Brooke, Davidson's career combined a generous amount of sea service (14-1/2 years out of 19-1/2 total years) with scientific and intellectual service. Davidson, Brooke, and many of their Date of 1841 brethren had successfully shed the unruly reputation of their youth and were poised to be leaders among a new generation of senior naval officers.

Less than a month after both Davidson and Brooke received their second patents from the U.S. Patent Office and Congress appropriated money to pay them for their inventions, both men—and 13 of their classmates—abandoned their promising U.S. Navy careers. Virginia had seceded from the Union, and they cast their lot with their ancestral state. A new chapter of their careers began.

---

and paid for has never been exercised." "BOAT-DISENGAGING APPARATUS FOR THE NAVY," *Army and Navy Journal* (Dec. 8, 1866), 4:250.

33 *Report of the Commissioner of Patents for the Year 1861: Arts and Manufactures* (Washington, D.C., 1863), vol. I, 287 and vol. II, 144.

Chapter Three

Lieutenant Davidson, V.S.N. and C.S.N. (1861–1862)

In 1901, Mary Bradford Crowninshield, wife of Rr. Adm. Arent Schuyler Crowninshield, wrote a story for the Washington, D.C., *Evening Star* dramatizing the dilemma confronting U.S. Naval Academy faculty in the spring of 1861. The story centered on a Lt. William "Billy" Buckner who, after much *angst*, submitted his resignation from the Navy on April 19, 1861. Crowninshield related the reaction to his rumored resignation among the midshipmen:

> "'Resigned? Old Buck?" "Well, I really thought he would stick.'
>
> 'I thought he had more sense,' said another.
>
> 'You must remember that he is a Kentuckian,' urged the first speaker, 'and that his state has seceded. Then, too, Hunter Davidson and Wood and Billy Parker have gone, you know; all friends of his, and southern men.'
>
> 'Well, perhaps that's natural. I don't know how I should look at it if I were a southerner.'"

The character "Billy Buckner," modeled on the real Kentucky-born U.S.N.A. assistant professor, Lt. William Preston Buckner, had second thoughts when his state failed to secede after all. Unlike another "Old Buck" (Capt. Franklin Buchanan of Maryland, the first superintendent of the Naval School), "Billy Buckner" acted quickly and decisively, and made a mad dash from Annapolis to Washington to intercept or withdraw his resignation. He met with Navy Secretary Gideon

Welles and pledged his loyalty to the old flag. Welles allowed him to withdraw his resignation without penalty, and, true to his word, Billy Buckner became a loyal member of "Gideon's Band."[1]

During the Secession Winter of 1860-61, the Naval Academy epitomized the loyalty dilemma facing U.S. Navy officers and, indeed, the entire U.S. military establishment. As South Carolina, then Mississippi, Florida, Alabama, Georgia, Louisiana, and Texas seceded from the Union between December 20 and February 1, many naval and army officers born in or associated closely with those states submitted their resignations (others from those states equivocated or bided their time). The senior acting midshipmen at the Academy in early January petitioned Superintendent George Blake asking that he and others be allowed to receive their certificates or the equivalents, "as may be deemed most proper, when it shall be incumbent upon us to resign and return to our homes." Blake forwarded it without comment to Navy Secretary Isaac Toucey, which the midshipmen interpreted as tacit consent to their request.[2]

Seventy-one naval officers, including 31 acting midshipmen, had resigned their commissions or warrants between December 1, 1860, and the end of February 1861. In March, during which no other southern state seceded, 37 more officers resigned, of whom 31 were passed midshipmen. Thomas Ford, who was then assistant librarian at the Academy and collecting material for a history of the school's first decades, noted how "a feeling of despondency and distrust pervaded the entire personnel of the institution. Officers, Professors, and students observed each other silently as if uncertain what course each would pursue, and so unconscious were all of the bloody drama about to be enacted that the seceders were treated, not as traitors but rather as erring brethren. It was not believed that they would actually go to the extremity of taking up arms against the mild and beneficent government which was educating them for its service, and hence their withdrawal from the Academy and from the service was commented upon only in language of sincere regret."[3]

Fort Sumter destroyed any illusions about peaceful secession and cast subsequent resignations in a sinister new light. The Navy Department printed and distributed loyalty oaths for officers to sign, pushing fence-sitters off their fences.

1 "Gideon's Band" in *WES*, Mar. 30, 1901; also, *Savannah Morning News*, Mar. 31, 1901. The real William P. Buckner went on the retired list in Sep.1862 and died in 1869. Admiral Crowninshield had been a first-year midshipman in 1861.

2 Ford, "History," chapter 16, typescript page 5.

3 William S. Dudley, *Going South: U.S. Navy Officer Resignations and Dismissals on the Eve of the Civil War* (Washington, DC, 1981), 16-17; Ford, "History," chapter 16, typescript pages 5-6 (MSS pages 3-4).

Officers who resigned after Sumter were no longer "erring brethren," but enemies who soon would be fighting against the men, the service, and the nation they left behind. Even before Sumter, several naval officers who had been allowed to resign had participated in hostile acts against Federal property in the seceded states—conduct that a Congressional investigation decried as "nothing less than treason."[4]

The new administration of President Abraham Lincoln and Navy Secretary Gideon Welles continued to accept almost all resignations in March and early April, but Sumter put the Navy and the Naval Academy upon a war footing. After the deadly confrontation between the 6th Massachusetts Infantry and a pro-Southern mob in the streets of Baltimore on April 19, Superintendent Blake mobilized the demonstrably loyal faculty—including Davidson's friend Stephen Luce—and midshipmen to prepare the school for possible attack (nestled as it was in the heart of pro-southern Maryland) and for temporary relocation to Newport, Rhode Island. The Commandant of Midshipmen at Annapolis "quietly read the 'Articles of War' to the whole body of students," Ford recalled, "leaving each to shape his own course without the slightest attempt at persuasion or coercion."[5] The 38 acting midshipmen who submitted their resignations in April were allowed to resign without dismissal.

It was a different story for the more senior officers who submitted their resignations after Sumter, including the trio of Naval Academy faculty members: Hunter Davidson, John Taylor Wood, and William H. Parker. After Sumter, Secretary Welles responded to most requests for resignation with dismissal, often accompanied by "striking" the officer's name from the rolls or by "order of the President," which made dismissal final and irrevocable. Of the 114 officers who resigned in April 1861, 62% of those above the rank of passed midshipmen (including Davidson, Wood, and Parker) were dismissed.[6] The difference between resignation and dismissal may seem trivial in retrospect after a divisive and bloody civil war, but it was a critical difference to career naval officers in the spring of 1861 and in subsequent decades. Men who cast their lots with their states and with the Confederacy realized how utterly they had forfeited their careers and struggled to find new livelihoods.

The Annapolis *Gazette* denounced the "horde of secessionists" at the Naval Academy, and the U.S. Senate passed a resolution inquiring of the school's superintendent whether any of the faculty or instructors "have allowed or countenanced in the young men under their charge, any manifestation or exhibition

4 Dudley, *Going South,* 13, 5-6.

5 Ford, "History," chapter 16, typescript page 6.

6 Dudley, *Going South,*4, 12-13.

(Left) William Harwar Parker was the academic star of the USN date of 1841 and Davidson's colleague on the Naval Academy faculty, 1859-1861. His father, Foxhall Parker, had been Davidson's first USN commander. *NH&HC (NH-66657)* (Right) John Taylor Wood, Davidson's colleague on the U.S. Naval Academy faculty and in the wardroom of the CSS *Virginia*. *Special Collections & Archives Department, Nimitz Library, USNA*

of feelings or sentiments hostile to the Government of the United States, and whether any of the officers of said Academy have manifested any sentiments of like character.'" Superintendent Blake solicited replies from 22 officers and professors and confirmed that the only secessionists had already left the Academy.[7]

Testifying to their military professionalism, Davidson, Wood, and Parker reportedly did not use their influence to sow seeds of discontent among the midshipmen. "Of the officers, who had openly announced their intention of joining the Southern cause, and of the Acting Midshipmen who had already sent in their resignations and were awaiting the acceptance thereof, it must be said that, until they were discharged from their obligations, all displayed true naval and manly spirit by a scrupulous and honorable discharge of their duties," wrote Thomas Ford. Robley D. Evans, a recently arrived 15-year-old acting midshipman from Floyd County, Virginia, echoed Ford. "Many of us came from the South, and as the States one after another either seceded or threatened to do so, we had to make up our minds what we were going to do," Evans wrote in his 1901 memoir when he was Rr. Adm. Evans and a Spanish-American War hero. "Conferences

7 Quoted in *Newport Mercury* [RI], July 26, 1862.

were frequent and serious, but never in one of them was there a disloyal word uttered. Every man followed the example set by the Southern men among the officers. So long as we were inside the Academy limits, or until our resignations were accepted, we were officers of the Navy and would behave as such." The officer "probably more responsible for this position than any other man" was, he wrote, "Lieutenant Hunter Davidson, afterward the torpedo expert of the Confederacy."[8]

"Stricken from the rolls of the Navy"

Davidson's scrupulous dedication to his duty as a U.S. Naval officer did not prevent him from abandoning the U.S. Navy upon learning of Virginia's secession on April 17. The new loyalty oath requirement no doubt made his decision even easier. On April 23, 1861, Davidson addressed to President Abraham Lincoln a simple letter forwarded through USNA Superintendent Blake: "I respectfully request your acceptance of my resignation, as Lieutenant in the Navy of the United States." In response, Davidson received from Secretary Gideon Welles the unwelcome reply dated May 5 [*sic*: 15] acknowledging his tendered resignation but informing him that "By order of the President, your name has been stricken from the rolls of the Navy from that date." Rather than wallow in self-pity, Davidson wrote a blistering response to President Lincoln via Secretary Welles and pugnaciously published it in the *Richmond Enquirer:*

> Sir: I have just received a communication from your Secretary of the Navy, stating that you had directed that my name should be stricken from the rolls of that service.
>
> "Herewith you will find that communication returned.
>
> "Be pleased to accept my thanks for the courteous manner in which you have acted touching my resignation. I am sure that the tens of millions of *freemen,* whose principles and cause I have espoused, will appreciate the motives which induced such a mild, just, and dignified exercise of your highest prerogative.
>
> "In future years, when one shall turn over the pages of impartial history, with what pride they will point their children to the example of a Washington, a Jackson, and last, not least, an Abe Lincoln!! Yours, &c, &c.

8 Ford, "History," chapter 16, page 10; Robley D. Evans, *A Sailor's Log: Recollections from Forty Years of Naval Life* (New York, 1901), 39-40. Although born in Virginia, Evans was admitted to the academy from the Utah Territory.

Hunter Davidson

Lieutenant, Va. Navy

Forwarded through Gideon Welles, Esq.,

Secretary of the late U.S. Navy[9]

This swaggering letter was the closest thing Hunter Davidson gave to an explanation of why he decided to resign his commission and forfeit his career—and violate the oath he had taken when he enlisted in the service almost 20 years earlier. His underscored use of "*freemen*" and his ironic and sarcastic references to Lincoln imply that Davidson believed the new Republican administration illegitimate, thus freeing him from his sworn obligation "to bear true allegiance to the United States of America, and to serve them honestly and faithfully against all their enemies or opposers, whomsoever. . . and that I will support the Constitution of the United States." The handful of officers who included explanations in their resignation letters appealed to a "higher law" interpretation of the Constitution to justify their actions. The absence of letters or documents makes it impossible to know absolutely Davidson's motives for resignation—whether he acted out of constitutional principle, defense of slavery and white supremacy, personal ambition, or a combination of factors.[10]

Of the 16 officers serving on the Naval Academy faculty in 1861, eight were northerners, and eight had associations with slaveholding states, seven of them with states that seceded from the Union. The only three who "went South" were Davidson who was born in the District of Columbia and appointed from Virginia (and who declared himself a citizen of Virginia); William Henry Parker, who was born in New York, but was appointed to the service from and was a citizen of Virginia (Parker's brother, Lt. Foxhall Parker, who had the same profile, chose to remain with the U.S. Navy in which their father had been a captain); and John Taylor Wood, who was born in Minnesota Territory, where his U.S. Army surgeon father was then stationed, but was appointed from Virginia and a citizen of Louisiana. Birth or residence in Virginia was not enough to prompt Lt. John H. Upshur or Lt. Robert W. Scott to resign, and Lt. George W. Balch and Lt. William Preston Buckner did not let their Tennessee or Kentucky birth or (in Buckner's case) residence in Arkansas determine their loyalties. Lieutenant Charles

9 Davidson to Lincoln, Apr. 23, 1861, RG 45, entry 76, NARA; Welles to Davidson, May 15, 1861, RG 24 Bureau of Navy Personnel, Appointments, Orders and Resignations, Entry 158, NARA; "Interesting Correspondence," *Richmond Enquirer*, May 31, 1861.

10 Dudley, *Going South*, 22.

W. Flusser, a Maryland born and Kentucky-bred officer then on leave from his Academy appointment famously resisted the blandishments of Capt. George Hollins of Maryland and later died under the Stars and Stripes.[11]

Loyalty to the service and the nation was stronger in the U.S. Navy than it was in the U.S. Army. A higher percentage of U.S. Navy officers and graduates of the naval school remained loyal to the service than did U.S. Army officers and U.S. Military Academy graduates. Still, the absolute number of men who "went South" in 1860-1861 (373 out of 1,554 officers in the service as of December 1860) was impressive.[12] Among the resigned or dismissed officers were captains Duncan Ingraham, Josiah Tattnall, French Forrest, Franklin Buchanan, Samuel Barron, and George Hollins, and commanders Ebenezer Farrand, Raphael Semmes, George Minor, John R. Tucker, and Sidney Smith Lee. Davidson's cousin and patron, Commander Thomas T. Hunter, resigned, was dismissed, and joined the Confederate navy.

Sixty per cent of the Date of 1841 men who were born in or appointed from slaveholding states and who were still in the service in 1861 "went South."[13] Several of the officers with whom Davidson had served during his U.S. Navy career left: lieutenants John Newland Maffitt, John Wilkinson, and John Pembroke Jones of the Coast Survey, Cdr. Henry J. Hartstene of the *Resolute,* and Cdr. William McBlair and lieutenants Joel S. Kennard and Thomas Pelot of the *Dale.* More importantly, the resigned and dismissed included men with whom Davidson was to serve closely in the Confederate Navy, most notably lieutenants Matthew Fontaine Maury, Catesby ap Roger Jones, and Date of 1841 classmates John Mercer Brooke and Robert Dabney Minor. Those and other men comprised the nucleus of the officer corps of the Confederate States Navy.

Before they became Confederate officers, those men—including Hunter Davidson—spent a few weeks or months as officers in the short-lived state navies. On February 21, 1861, the Provisional Congress of the Confederate States of America passed a law creating a Navy Department. President Jefferson Davis appointed Stephen Russell Mallory, a former U.S. senator from Florida and chairman of the Senate Naval Affairs Committee, to be Confederate secretary of the navy. Mallory's

11 *U.S. Navy Register* 1861; Todorich, *Spirited Years,* 191; Arthur Thurston, *Tallahassee Skipper: The Biography of John Taylor Wood, Merrimac Gunner, Soldier-at-Sea, Guardian of the Confederate Treasury, Adopted Nova Scotian* (Yarmouth, Nova Scotia, 1981), 58-59, 64-65.

12 Dudley, *Going South,* 13, 18-19.

13 Calculated from "Register of Alumni of the United States Naval Academy 1846 to 1957," 120-122. A high percentage of young men who entered the service were "non-graduates" or died, resigned, or were discharged from service before 1881.

department soon incorporated the navies—the ships and officers—that the lower South states had organized after they seceded from the Union. By the time Virginia seceded on April 17, 1861, the Confederate Navy Department was well-established. But Virginia and the other states that seceded after the war began—unlike the lower South states—made their secession contingent upon popular referenda. Virginia voters would decide on May 23 whether their state would leave the Union. Meanwhile, the Virginia Convention appointed an Advisory Council to oversee the creation of the state's military defenses and establishment. The members of the committee were Francis H. Smith, superintendent of the Virginia Military Institute; Col. Robert E. Lee, late of the U.S. Army; and Lt. Matthew Fontaine Maury, late of the U.S. Naval Observatory.

The Advisory Council appointed three naval officers to a joint commission of army and navy officers and asked them "to name all efficient and worthy Virginians and Residents of Virginia in the Army and Navy of the United States; for the purpose of inviting them into the service of Virginia." The three officers named to the commission suggested the wealth of experience available. Captain Samuel Barron represented the fourth generation of a Virginia-born naval dynasty. Warranted as a midshipman in 1812 at age *two* in tribute to his esteemed father, Samuel reported for duty at age six and was at sea by age 10. Sidney Smith Lee, older brother of Robert E. Lee, entered the U.S. Navy in 1819, commanded a ship on Cdr. Matthew C. Perry's historic voyage to Japan in 1853, and was, like Barron, promoted to captain before the war. Commander Robert Baker Pegram became a naval celebrity in 1855 when he commanded an expedition that rescued British ships from Chinese pirates.[14]

On May 2, 1861, the Advisory Council approved the joint commission's officer nominations, including Lt. Hunter Davidson. Davidson and the other officers entered a newly organized Virginia Navy Department modeled on the U.S. Navy Department, replete with the traditional administrative offices and bureaus: Orders and Detail (personnel), Provisions and Clothing, Ordnance and Hydrography, Medicine and Surgery, Yards and Docks, and Construction. As chief of the Office of Orders and Detail, Samuel Barron became the *de facto* head of the Virginia Navy Department and communicated with the Advisory Council and with Virginia Governor John Letcher. The ranking officer in the Virginia Navy was Capt. French Forrest, who had reached the rank of captain in the U.S. Navy in 1844 and had briefly commanded the Washington Navy Yard. With his seniority

14 John M. Coski, "'A Navy Department, Hitherto Unknown to Our State Organization," in *Virginia at War 1861*, William C. Davis and James I. Robertson, Jr, eds. (Frankfort, KY, 2005), 68-9.

and his experience, Forrest assumed command of Virginia's—and the South's—primary naval asset: the Norfolk Navy Yard.[15]

Davidson wrote his May 23 open letter to Abraham Lincoln from the "Ordnance Department, Norfolk (Va.) Navy Yard," which offers a clue about his brief service in the Virginia Navy. It is not clear whether he reported to Flag Officer Forrest in command of the Yard or to Cdr. George Minor, head of the Office of Ordnance and Hydrography. The assignment did indicate however, the direction of Davidson's contribution in the Virginia and the Confederate navies.

The same day that Davidson wrote his letter to Lincoln, Virginia voters went to the polls to ratify or reject the April 17 convention vote to secede from the Union. Although many counties west of the Allegheny Mountains (counties that later became the new state of West Virginia) rejected secession, the overall result was a foregone conclusion. By a vote of 129,950 to 20,373, Virginians approved the secession ordinance.[16] Ratification brought a predictable response from Federal troops who had refrained from any aggressive action in hopes that Virginians would remain in the Union. Troops marched across the Potomac and seized Alexandria and Arlington (Robert E. Lee's home) and from their base at Fort Monroe into the town of Hampton, which its defenders burned instead of allowing Federal troops—or enslaved African Americans—to occupy it. War had come to the Old Dominion.

In early June, in accordance with a secret arrangement made in April with Confederate Vice President Alexander Stephens, Virginia turned over its military assets to the Confederate States of America. As of June 10, 1861, Lt. Hunter Davidson, Virginia State Navy, became 1st Lt. Hunter Davidson, Confederate States Navy.[17]

For the first year of his career in the Virginia State Navy then the Confederate States Navy, Davidson was stationed in and around Norfolk, Virginia, which was as important to the Confederate Navy as it had been to the U.S. Navy. Formed by the confluence of the James, Nansemond, and three branches of the Elizabeth River, Hampton Roads was a large estuary that forms one of the world's largest natural harbors. The Roads flowed into the southern end of the Chesapeake Bay.

15 James I. Robertson, Jr., ed., *Proceedings of the Advisory Council of the State of Virginia, April 21 – June 19, 1861* (Richmond, 1977), 40; Coski, "A Navy Department," 69.

16 James I. Robertson, Jr., "The Virginia Convention of 1861," in Davis and Robertson, eds., *Virginia at War 1861*, 19.

17 *Register of Officers of the Confederate States Navy 1861-1865* (Washington, DC, 1931), 46. The *Register of the Officers of the Confederate Navy, 1862*, 4, indicates that Davidson accepted his commission on June 15, 1861.

The United States Army never relinquished Fort Monroe which guarded Old Point Comfort at the north side of the mouth of Hampton Roads and, as a result, the U.S. Navy was able to control Hampton Roads and the mouths of the three rivers that formed it. Virginia and Confederate forces controlled the south shore of Hampton Roads, including the cities of Norfolk and Portsmouth and the Elizabeth River that flowed between them. On the Portsmouth side of the river lay the Gosport Navy Yard (also, confusingly, called the Norfolk Navy Yard) which was the most important U.S. Navy installation in the South. Virginia state forces occupied the yard and the cities after Federal forces evacuated them in April 1861. Despite hurried attempts to destroy the naval resources before the evacuation, Virginia troops were able to salvage several of the U.S. naval vessels stationed there and more than 1,100 heavy guns.

It was not only an impressive officer corps and the resources of Norfolk and Portsmouth that the Virginia Navy bequeathed to the Confederate Navy, but a creditable assemblage of ships. Ten U.S. warships were at the Gosport Navy Yard in Portsmouth when Virginia seceded. Through a combination of indecision and incompetence, the commanders in Norfolk failed to get any of those ships out of the harbor when U.S. Navy authorities realized they could not defend Norfolk against Virginia's forces. On the night of April 20-21, 1861, U.S. authorities gave the order to evacuate and destroy the navy yard and its valuable stone dry dock and any remaining ships. Several of the U.S. Navy's largest warships, including the 120-gun *Pennsylvania*—the receiving ship to which Acting Midshipman Hunter Davidson had reported in 1842—went up in a blaze of ignominy. Another ship burned was the USS *Merrimack,* one of the impressive new steam frigates introduced in the mid-1850s. Six of the ships were beyond salvage. The oldest American vessel still in service, the receiving ship, *United States* (rechristened, predictably, *Confederate States*), survived untouched as an otherwise useless receiving ship, and Virginia authorities judged three of the vessels worthy of salvage and refitting. One of those, of course, was *Merrimack.*

In addition to *bona fide* warships, Virginia waters also yielded a handful of potential warships. The Virginia Navy Department leased several small steamers for use around the Norfolk Harbor and paid $6,000 to a Norfolk salvage firm for the Philadelphia-built tugboat, *Teaser.* Virginia forces also seized and retained two side wheel steamships, *Jamestown* and *Yorktown,* belonging to a New York-to-Virginia shipping company that were in Virginia waters when the Virginia Convention voted to secede. Although state authorities had doubts about the value of the *Jamestown,* Samuel Barron declared *Yorktown* "a valuable auxiliary to the defenses of James river." Built in 1859, she was 250 feet long and 34 feet wide at beam. Davidson's Date of 1841 classmate, Lt. James Henry Rochelle, who served as her executive officer during the war, later described *Yorktown* as "a side wheel steamer of beautiful model. . . . She was considered a fast boat, and deserved the reputation." Barron assigned Cdr. John Randolph Tucker to command the ship and supervise her fitting out "with as heavy a battery as she will bear." Under the direct supervision of master ship carpenter Joseph Pierce working at Richmond, not Norfolk, the Virginia Navy spent more than $11,000 converting the passenger vessel *Yorktown* into the formidable 10-gun warship *Patrick Henry,* with a paddle wheel protected by a layer of iron plate over her boilers.[18] When the state turned over her military resources to the Confederate Navy, *Patrick Henry* was the strongest vessel in the new James River Squadron. She remained the squadron's flag ship through the battle of Hampton Roads.

Pay and clothing records suggest that Hunter Davidson was assigned, at least nominally, to *Patrick Henry* in Hampton Roads from August into December 1861. At Davidson's request, in late August 1861, the Confederate Navy began allotting Davidson $150 per month to support his family, who had settled in Portsmouth. Except for three days leave in mid-August he collected pay for "Sea Duty" from August 1 through December 7, 1861. On that day, Davidson was stationed on the James River off Mulberry Island (the site of modern-day Fort Eustis) near the Confederate Army of the Peninsula's defense line.[19]

A month earlier, in early July, a *New York Herald* correspondent stationed aboard the U.S. frigate, *Roanoke,* in Hampton Roads spotted Davidson "flying around to and fro" in what he described as "a little rebel propeller"—presumably one of the small steamers used for ordnance work. Davidson's vessel escorted another flying an English ensign that carried a British consul from Norfolk to visit U.S. Commodore Silas Stringham aboard the flagship *Minnesota.* "It is very unpleasant to our sailor boys to watch the movements of this impertinent little craft and not be able to pop away at her," the correspondent observed. Apparently, it was not just the craft, but its commander specifically, that raised the sailors' ire:

> Lieutenant Davidson, who commands this rebel vessel-of-war, is the gentleman that Congress a few years ago voted $10,000 to for a great improvement in lowering boats in a way he discovered, and for which he, it is said, paid $5,000

18 Coski, "A Navy Department," 73, 75; James H. Rochelle, "The Confederate Steamship 'Patrick Henry,'" *SHSP* (1886), 14:127-28.

19 Bound volume of clothing and money issued to officers on *Patrick Henry,* 1861-1862, RG 45, NARA; Hunter Davidson pay account [Form No. 30] with C.S. Steamer "Patrick Henry, ZB file, NH&HC; also *Official Records of the Union and Confederate Navies in the War of the Rebellion,* 29 volumes (Washington, DC, 1894-1921), series II, volume 1, 299 (hereafter cited as *ORN,* series:volume, page.

> to get the bill lobbied through the two houses. He, with consummate assurance, continues to wear the same uniform in the service of the rebel government that he used to wear for Uncle Sam. He was yesterday dressed in the same coat that some of our officers recollected as the last they saw him muster in in [sic] the service of the United States government. If any of our fleet can get an opportunity to honorably punish him and his piratical craft they will blow it out of the water.[20]

It was not the last time that Davidson's "sauciness" provoked his former comrades.

In early September, Confederate Secretary of War Leroy P. Walker forwarded a request for Davidson's detail to Gen. Benjamin Huger, commander of Confederate army troops around Norfolk, as a naval aide-de-camp. Huger sought Davidson because of his "experience in the civil survey and his other qualities," suggesting that Davidson's duties were surveying waterways and adjoining land. Not for the last time in his career, Davidson's service with the Coast Survey made him an especially valuable officer. According to notations in the correspondence file, there is no evidence that Davidson in fact joined Huger's staff, and he continued to draw pay for "Sea Duty."[21]

The higher pay was especially welcome as the Davidson family continued to grow. On New Year's Day, 1862, Mary gave birth to a third son, Hunter, in Portsmouth, where the family was living.

"A great, unwieldy patched-up scarecrow"

Three weeks earlier, on December 8, 1861, Hunter Davidson received new orders—to report for duty aboard the vessel known formerly as the USS *Merrimack* and soon to be rechristened CSS *Virginia*.[22] The career of the CSS *Virginia* and the March 7-8, 1862, Battle of Hampton Roads represent one of the most famous chapters in Civil War naval history. Occurring as the battle did in a natural amphitheater under the gaze of thousands of soldiers, sailors, and civilians, there is no shortage of eyewitness accounts (most recorded after the war). Although he commanded a gun section on *Virginia* and was very active on

20 *NYH*, July 9, 1861. Davidson was not alone among Confederate officers in continuing to wear U.S. Navy blue. See James Morris Morgan, *Recollections of a Rebel Reefer* (Boston, 1917), 52-3.

21 Walker to [Mallory?], Sep. 7, 1861, Letters Sent by Confederate Secretary of War, Aug.-Nov. 1861, RG 109, Chapter 9, Vol. 2, NARA. According to a biographical timeline in the Davidson Family Tree on Ancestry.com, Davidson was reassigned to the North Carolina Squadron on September 30, 1861.

22 Date is from John V. Quarstein, *The CSS Virginia: Sink Before Surrender* (Charleston, SC, 2012), 285.

both days of the battle, Hunter Davidson makes only a cursory appearance in the accounts of eyewitnesses and historians. If Davidson submitted an official report of the battle, it has not survived or been found. At the request of Catesby Jones, Davidson in late October 1862 wrote a brief account of the battle and endorsing Jones's controversial decision to break off the engagement with *Monitor* on March 9. Davidson's letter to Jones has been the only source for Davidson's perspective on the fight to appear in the many histories of Hampton Roads.

Happily, Davidson did write a much longer account of the battle published in the May 9, 1897, New York *Sun* and reprinted (with significant portions omitted) in the *Daily Oregonian* three weeks later. Apparently not reprinted or even quoted or cited since, this article represents an undiscovered account of the battle of Hampton Roads and an important source for a biography of Davidson. Although he wrote it more than 35 years after the battle, Davidson noted casually that the article benefited from a "private journal" that he then still had in his possession.[23] With all the necessary caveats and qualifications about a post-war source written by a participant intent on fixing his place in history, the *Sun* article allows us to restore Hunter Davidson to the story of the *Virginia* and the Battle of Hampton Roads. What did Davidson write about his role in the battle of Hampton Roads and how does it compare with the other accounts of the battle?

The Battle of Hampton Roads—the historic first duel between two ironclad vessels—was the culmination of a naval arms race that was more dramatic and unlikely than the overwrought script of a Hollywood film. The concept of ironclad vessels was not new. American naval architects had designed and constructed armored floating batteries in the 1840s, and the Crimean War of 1853-55 had demonstrated the value of those weapons. On the eve of the American Civil War, France commissioned the first modern, self-propelled ironclad vessel, *La Gloire*, and Britain countered with HMS *Warrior*.

Fully aware of these developments, Confederate Navy Secretary Stephen R. Mallory determined to build an ironclad warship that could, if successful, compensate for the U.S. Navy's naval superiority. Rather than start from scratch, the Confederacy resolved to build an ironclad on the hull of the U.S. steam frigate *Merrimack* salvaged from the Norfolk harbor. At a meeting in Richmond in late June, 1861, Mallory received similar design proposals from two men: veteran Portsmouth, Virginia, naval constructor John Luke Porter, who had submitted a design for an ironclad vessel to the U.S. Navy in the 1840s and soon became the Confederacy's first and only chief constructor, and Lt. John Mercer Brooke,

23 There is reason to doubt the veracity of this claim as Davidson later wrote that he lost all is papers in the explosion of a vessel in 1877. See pages 210, 240-41.

Davidson's Date of 1841 classmate who had already established himself as the designer of naval ordnance and who would serve most of the war as chief of the Confederacy's Bureau of Ordnance and Hydrography. Brooke's important modification of Porter's casemate design was to submerge both ends of the raft-like hull below the waterline. Within months of the battle and for the rest of their lives Porter and Brooke crossed sabers over credit and blame for the strengths and weaknesses of the resulting experimental vessel.[24]

The Confederacy's ironclad project was underway in June 1861 and soon became common public knowledge. The U.S. Navy appointed an Ironclad Board to choose a design for its own experimental warship. In October 1861, the Board contracted three different designs, including one submitted by Swedish engineer John Ericsson. Despite his ship's revolutionary design and technical complexity, Ericsson contracted to deliver it to the U.S. Navy in less than 100 days. A naval arms race was on. Proximity to the scene of action gave the Confederacy the advantage, and it enjoyed a devastating naval supremacy for all of 12 hours.

Two days after receiving orders to report to the unfinished ironclad, Davidson learned from Capt. French Forrest, flag officer of the Confederacy's James River Squadron and commandant of the Norfolk Navy Yard, what his role would be in preparing *Virginia* for action: "As an order has been issued by the War Department directing Generals Huger and Magruder to discharge all seamen that may be wanted for the naval service, you will report to General Huger for permission to make the selection of such seamen as, upon examination, you may deem qualified for such service."[25]

If Davidson were involved in the final months of her conversion from *Merrimack* to *Virginia,* he did not write about it. But, like her other officers, Davidson did not hesitate to point out the many flaws that made the famous vessel incapable of doing those things that U.S. political and military authorities so feared. In his *Sun* article, Davidson described *Virginia* as "mainly covered with scrap iron" no thicker than four inches over wood with a shield sloped at about 36 degrees.[26] The sloped shield formed "a covering for the fighting deck, and the men at the guns had to work stooping." No other account emphasized the relationship between *Virginia*'s signature sloped casemate and the exhausting work that her gun crews endured on both days of the battle. Echoing her other officers and crew, Davidson underscored

24 See George M. Brooke, Jr., ed., *Ironclads and Big Guns of the Confederacy: The Journal and Letters of John M. Brooke* (Columbia, SC, 2002), 95 and John M. Brooke, "The Virginia, or Merrimac: Her Real Projector," *SHSP*, (1901), 9: 3-34.

25 *ORN,* I:6, 750.

26 Tredegar Iron Works rolled the scrap iron into two-inch thick plates, then bolted it on in two layers.

Conversion of the U.S. frigate *Merrimack* into the CS ironclad ram *Virginia* in the drydock at Gosport Navy Yard. Illustration after J. O. Davidson. *NH&HC (NH-314)*

the vulnerability of *Virginia*'s knuckle—the angle where the armored casemate joined the unarmored wooden sides. Brooke's design called for the knuckle to be submerged, but Porter's miscalculation of the ship's displacement left it riding at or above the waterline. A single shot from enemy guns could cripple the ship. "The Merrimac" (the technically incorrect name for his ship, but one that he and other officers continued to use), he wrote, "was a great, unwieldy patched-up scarecrow, without buoyancy or ability to maneuver, but she was the best the means of the South enabled it to do."

Without ceremony, the Confederate navy commissioned the CSS *Virginia* on February 17, 1862. A week later, Secretary Mallory appointed Capt. Franklin Buchanan to command her. Buchanan, a 36-year U.S. Navy veteran who had been the founding superintendent of the U.S. Naval Academy, was a reluctant secessionist. When his native state of Maryland seemed on the brink of secession, he submitted his resignation from the Navy. When Maryland failed to secede, Buchanan tried to withdraw his resignation. Predictably, the U.S. Navy instead dismissed him from the service. After further indecision, he eventually made his way across the Potomac and offered his services to the Confederacy. Mallory appointed Buchanan to the Confederacy's premier command despite his vacillation because of his well-known aggressiveness.[27]

27 Hunter Davidson, "MERRIMAC AND MONITOR. The Story of the Great Naval Duel Told in a New Way. . ." *The Sun* [NY] (hereafter cited as *NYS*), May 9, 1897. Much of the following and account and all the quotations not cited otherwise are from this article. For background on Buchanan, see especially Craig L. Symonds, *Confederate Admiral: The Life and Wars of Franklin Buchanan* (Annapolis, MD, 1999).

If Davidson had known his new commander, it was only a passing acquaintance. Buchanan resigned from the Naval School to serve in the Mexican War before Davidson entered the school, and the men never served together. Davidson encountered familiar faces in the wardroom housed within *Virginia*'s casemate. Not only was John Taylor Wood, his late Naval Academy faculty colleague there, but six of the ship's midshipmen had been among their students at the U.S. Naval Academy: Walter Raleigh Butt and Hardin Littlepage of Virginia, William J. Craig of Kentucky, Henry H. Marmaduke of Missouri, and Robert Chester Foute and James C. Long of Tennessee. The executive officer was Virginian Lt. Catesby ap Roger Jones, and Buchanan's flag lieutenant was another Virginian, Robert Dabney Minor, Date of 1841, who would become one of Davidson's closest naval acquaintances. Davidson's other fellow lieutenants, Charles C. Simms and John R. Eggleston, were also Virginians who had entered the U.S. Navy a few years before and after Davidson, respectively.

Workmen labored feverishly to finish the countless details of her conversion. Although she had her full complement of officers, she still lacked a sufficient crew, including men to work her 10 guns. (On March 6, Capt. Thomas Kevill's Virginia artillery company, volunteered to join *Virginia*'s crew and worked one of her 9-inch guns.[28]) Her sea trial was set for Saturday, March 8. Just as the conversion of *Merrimack* into the ironclad *Virginia* was an open secret, so, too, was the progress of John Ericsson's ironclad battery. The *Monitor* had been launched and commissioned and was steaming down the east coast toward Hampton Roads. *Virginia*'s sea trial might be her only opportunity to engage the wooden blockading squadron before *Monitor* arrived to defend it. The U.S. Navy assigned to Hampton Roads a large force of wooden warships carrying more than 200 guns and had additional batteries at Newport News point, Fort Monroe, and the Rip Raps (later Fort Wool).

Virginia "sallied forth from Norfolk against the Federal forces assembled there," Davidson wrote in his 1897 *Sun* account. "'All hands' had been up through the previous night, preparing the vessel to move, but without time for exercise at the guns, as everything had been rushed on board, working day and night for weeks previous in the desire to get the vessel out. In fact, most of the fighting crew were green hands, put on board at the last moment." *Virginia* left Norfolk, steamed down the Elizabeth River, and entered Hampton Roads at 1:30 p.m. It took the lumbering ship another hour to cross the Roads and reach her prey.

"Arriving in Hampton Roads the Merrimac directed her course for the wooden frigates Cumberland and Congress, anchored off Newport News," Davidson

28 Quarstein, *CSS Virginia,* 464.

continued. "The Congress was the nearest, but she was close in shore and tending down stream. The Cumberland was anchored well out and lying across stream at the time, thus presenting a far more favorable object for ramming, which Admiral Buchanan . . . availed himself." *Cumberland,* which had been razed from a two-deck frigate to a one-deck sloop, boasted two especially powerful guns that Buchanan believed to be the greatest threat to *Virginia*'s armor, which is why he chose to engage her first. Rather than offer details of his own work supervising two gun crews on March 8, Davidson's *Sun* article dwelled on the ramming of *Cumberland.*

"When one vessel rams another, it does not happen once in a thousand times that the vessel ramming goes in and backs out on the same line, or a parallel line," Davidson explained. More often than not, "the rammer is sure to turn or twist before her ram is fairly free again," which is what occurred when *Virginia* rammed *Cumberland.*

> The massive iron beak was wrenched from her old wooden bows, and her butt ends, opened and from that moment she leaked freely, and required to be pumped, in order to keep the water below her fires. The beak did not part from its bolts, however, without a struggle, but on entering the side of the Cumberland stuck fast. The Cumberland rolled once toward and apparently upon the bows on the Merrimac, which immediately became depressed, until the sill of the bow port was level with the water. Somebody in my forward division exclaimed: 'We are going down with the Cumberland!' There was a moment of awful suspense. There was but one small hatch over this part of the vessel, and the ladder was unshipped for action: there was no escape for the many. Suddenly, with a bound back, the Merrimac freed herself. The iron beak had been wrenched off, and we caught our breath again.

As did others of Davidson's brother officers, he expressed admiration for the "glory of the struggle" of the doomed *Cumberland.*

Freed, but leaking badly, *Virginia* made a laborious wide turn and headed toward the 52-gun *Congress.* She closed to about 200 yards—as close as she could get without grounding—and poured in a murderous fire that turned *Congress* into a slaughterhouse. *Congress* surrendered, but small arms fire from Federal infantry on shore frustrated several attempts to board and accept her surrender. A furious Captain Buchanan ordered *Congress* destroyed with incendiary shot, notwithstanding that his own brother was purser aboard the ship. Franklin Buchanan was wounded in the leg when he rashly climbed to the casemate roof to return the small arms fire. Command then devolved upon the executive officer, Lt. Catesby Jones.

Catesby ap Roger Jones commanded CSS *Virginia* during her epochal battle with *Monitor* at Hampton Roads. Portrait photograph ca. 1863-64. *NH&HC (NH-48723)*

Because his *Sun* article and his brief report in defense of Catesby Jones both focused on *Virginia*'s fight with the *Monitor*, Davidson wrote virtually nothing about his own role in the first day's action. He commanded the bow (forward) gun section consisting of two 6.4-inch Brooke rifles (one port and one starboard) firing ordnance roughly twice as heavy as the 32-pound shot fired from 6.4-inch smoothbore guns. Midshipman Marmaduke commanded gun #2 under Davidson's supervision, and Davidson personally worked gun #3. Assisting Davidson and Marmaduke were U.S. Navy veterans Boatswain Charles Hasker and Gunner Charles B. Oliver.[29] *Virginia* was the attacking ship with her bow to the enemy for most of the battle, so Davidson's section was extremely busy throughout the fight. It not only fired on enemy vessels but also received enemy fire.

Among the ship's details left unfinished on March 8 were the gunport shutters. Although *Virginia*'s iron-plated casemate proved impermeable to enemy guns, her gunports remained open and vulnerable throughout the battle. During the close combat with *Cumberland*, the doomed Federal ship fired shots that struck the exposed muzzles of two of *Virginia*'s guns, including one of Davidson's Brooke rifles. Midshipman Marmaduke, who had been one of Davidson's students at the U.S. Naval Academy, was wounded, but remained with his gun. The same shot killed Louis Waldeck, a South Carolina infantry soldier who had transferred to the *Virginia* crew in January. In his official report of the battle, Franklin Buchanan described and praised Davidson's work: "Lieutenant Davidson fought his gun with great precision. The muzzle of one of them was soon shot away. He continued, however, to fire it, though the wood work around the port became ignited at

29 Quarstein, *CSS Virginia*, 144.

each discharge. His buoyant and cheerful bearing and voice were contagious and inspiring."[30]

After ramming and sinking *Cumberland* and firing *Congress, Virginia* turned her attention to the large frigates that lay in the Roads near Fort Monroe blocking the entrance into Chesapeake Bay. *Virginia* opened on the 47-gun steam frigate *Minnesota,* a sister ship of *Merrimack* and the most formidable ship in the Federal squadron at Hampton Roads. Her commander was Capt. Gershon J. Van Brunt, a veteran officer with whom Hunter Davidson had a history. It was he and Louis M. Goldsborough—who was Van Brunt's commander and flag officer of the North Atlantic Blockading Squadron—whom Davidson had accused "neglect of duty" for their failure to discipline Lt. Samuel Knox for drunkenness & unofficerlike conduct in 1850. If Davidson thirsted for revenge, the battle of Hampton Roads afforded him the opportunity to slake that thirst. Witnessing what *Virginia* could do to a wooden warship and how little a wooden warship could do against *Virginia,* Van Brunt ran his ship into shoal waters. Davidson's guns were among those that pummeled *Minnesota* from just over a mile before the receding tide and approaching dusk compelled *Virginia* to break off the fight.

Davidson declined to call the action of March 8 a "battle" because the wooden warships lying at anchor were too overmatched to do battle, but, nevertheless, the work had taken its toll. "The officers and crew of the Merrimac were exhausted with twenty-four hours' continuous labor, much of it in stooping positions under the inclined shield," Davidson wrote. He claimed that Catesby Jones had "wanted to anchor somewhere near the ground, so as promptly to continue the destruction the following day," but that the pilots advised going back to the mouth of the Elizabeth River at Sewell's Point. They feared that any rough water could swamp the low-lying and leaking ironclad. "The Merrimac was in a ticklish condition under any circumstances, and especially so if leaking," Davidson reiterated several times in his *Sun* article. "Had she, at any time, gone into such a sea as to cause her to roll or pitch in the least, she would not have lived half an hour. . . ."

Davidson's account of the battle not only emphasized the vulnerability of the ship that seemed anything but vulnerable to the U.S. Navy and President Abraham Lincoln's panicked cabinet, but also was calculated to defend the actions and decisions of Catesby Jones, a man whom Davidson praised as "one of the most perfect gentlemen and ablest officers I have ever had the honor to know." Jones (1821-1877) was a native Virginian and, like Davidson, the son of a U.S. Army officer and a mother from an old Virginia family. His uncle was Commodore

30 Quarstein, *CSS Virginia,* 126, 424; *ORN,* I:9, 11; John R. Eggleston "Captain Eggleston's Narrative of the Battle of the *Merrimac,*" *SHSP* (1916), 49: 171.

Thomas ap Catesby Jones, the officer who had seized Mexico's California capital in 1842, four years before war began. Catesby Jones was five years older than Davidson, entered the U.S. Navy five years before Davidson, and received all his training on the job without attending the Naval School. While Davidson served on the Coast Survey in the 1850s, Jones became an ordnance specialist, working with Cdr. John Dahlgren at the Washington Navy Yard. If Davidson and Jones did not have more than a passing acquaintance from their decades in the U.S. Navy, they had an opportunity to know each other when both served in the Virginia State Navy and Confederate Navy at Hampton Roads.[31]

Their close association began when Davidson reported to the *Merrimack* in early December 1861. A month earlier Jones joined the ship as executive officer. Although the enormous project of converting *Merrimack* into *Virginia* fell under the command of the commandant of the navy yard, Capt. French Forrest, Jones oversaw the work. He had been an officer aboard *Merrimack* during her maiden cruise in 1856 and knew the ship better than any other Confederate officer. His comrades hoped that intimacy would translate into command, but they sensed correctly that the commander of the Confederacy's most important vessel would have to be a senior officer.

Returning to Sewell's Point, Jones gave his ship a quick inspection and sent a brief report of her condition to Confederate authorities. He noted that the ship's "prow was twisted," but, according to most accounts, did not realize that it actually had broken off and rested at the bottom of Hampton Roads inside the wreck of *Cumberland.* Jones wrote later that a pilot, looking at the burning hulk of *Congress* that lit up the night sky, noticed a "strange looking craft" pull up alongside the grounded *Minnesota* around 11:00 p.m., and identified it to Jones as John Ericsson's *Monitor.* Historians are skeptical of that claim and believe that Jones ended the day still believing that the next day's work would be finishing off *Minnesota* and the other wooden warships, *St. Lawrence* and *Roanoke.*[32]

In his postwar accounts, Hunter Davidson did not claim any insights as to what his friend and commander knew and when he knew it. He focused instead on the condition of the men and their ship after the first day's battle. "[E]very one slept in his clothes, I might even say 'at quarters,' for the probability of a boarding attack during the night had been discussed," he wrote, "and there was little rest on

31 W. S. Mabry, compiler, *Brief Sketch of the Career of Captain Catesby Ap R. Jones* (Selma, AL, 1912), 3-8.

32 *ORN,* I:7, 42; Catesby Ap R. Jones, "Services of the 'Virginia' (Merrimac)," *SHSP,* (Jan. 1883 [written 1874]), 11:70-1; Davis, *Duel,* 117. Jones did mention the loss of the prow in his report of the March 9 engagement. *ORN,* I:7, 47.

the hard deck, although all were so weary." Davidson then warmed to his subject: "It was in this condition of the Merrimac, with the ram bow disabled, the vessel leaking, the officers and crew well worn, and everything out of order in engine room and battery after such a day's work as that past, and with an experimental vessel, that the sun, on the 9th of March, 1862, shone upon the most important combat of single ships in history." Davidson gave no indication that he or anyone else on *Virginia* knew that *Monitor* had arrived. His silence on the subject could be further evidence debunking the story of the pilot's sighting, or it could be Davidson's attempt to insert himself more prominently into the drama of March 9.

"I was the first to observe the Monitor"

"It was my morning watch, as Lieutenant in charge. The weather was nearly calm, and a hazy atmosphere prevented objects from being distinctly seen during the first hours,' Davidson began his account of the day.

> I was the first to observe the Monitor anchored off near Newport News. It loomed up to an enormous size, under the influence of a partial mirage, so often seen in the Chesapeake and the adjoining waters. At first I could not imagine what it was, so totally different was the general outline from anything I had ever seen or heard of. In a few moments, however, I recalled the information we had not long before received from New York in reference to the Monitor. I immediately sent below to let Jones know that it had arrived and was anchored in sight.

In his account of the battle, Lt. John Randolph Eggleston, who commanded another of *Virginia*'s gun sections, used the editorial "we" in describing the crew's first sighting of *Monitor*.[33]

Davidson's description of Jones's reaction to this intelligence was perhaps disingenuously ambiguous. What was news to Davidson, Eggleston, and others might not have been news to Jones, although it does seem strange that he would keep such a pertinent piece of information from his officers. Jones was "a very quiet, reserved man" and Davidson remarked that "his face showed that he understood the situation." When Davidson asked the obvious question, "'What are you going to do?'" Jones replied "'Fight her, of course.'" Davidson had hoped they would focus on destroying the wooden warships and ignore the Federal ironclad, but he conceded that Jones's approach was "best for us in the end." According to Davidson, Jones then commented on his ship's "one great weakness"—her knuckle—which

33 Eggleston "Eggleston's Narrative," 174.

the previous day's expenditure of coal, ammunition, and stores had raised above the waterline. Probably not coincidentally, Jones noted those very things in his 1874 (published posthumously in 1883) account of the battle.[34]

In setting up his narrative of the first duel of ironclads, Davidson noted that *Monitor* was not without her own "difficulties and defects," but he always returned to *Virginia*'s defects and *Monitor*'s advantages, including her larger guns, greater maneuverability, her rotating turret, and sophisticated machinery, which the "agricultural pastoral" South could not hope to emulate. *Virginia*'s chief advantage was "the presence of a far greater number of regular naval officers on board."

"As soon as possible we were under way, and the contest began at close range," Davidson continued. He did not describe the nearly three hours of close ship-to-ship combat in the familiar terms of the two ironclads firing at each other at point-blank range without discernible effect. He emphasized instead that the "only serviceable weapons" *Virginia* had in the fight were a pair of 7-inch Brooke rifles mounted on pivot carriages, one mounted on the bow and the other aft. Because the ship's exposed steering apparatus was mounted aft, "we did not expose that end." Perhaps not coincidentally, Davidson himself commanded and personally worked the 7-inch bow rifle on March 9. Lieutenant Charles C. Simms, who had commanded the gun on March 8, succeeded Jones as executive officer, leaving Davidson in charge of three guns.

After more than an hour of inconclusive combat with *Monitor*, Jones, in his own words, "determined to run into her if possible." In his narrative, Davidson parsed his words carefully to explain this decision. Davidson drew a distinction between "running down" *Monitor* and "ramming" her. Jones did not try to ram "because we knew the bow was injured, but to run over it if possible. . . . The Merrimac did not maneuver to ram the Monitor, for that was at once seen to be useless."[35] Whatever term best describes it, the effort of a lumbering vessel to run down a more maneuverable foe resulted in a harmless glancing blow.

Like Jones, Davidson and the other officers searched for any literal or metaphorical chink in *Monitor*'s armor. Davidson noted that there seemed to be "something wrong" with *Monitor*'s port shutters because they remained open when the ship was not firing. In fact, the ship's executive officer, Lt. Samuel Dana Greene, decided to leave them open because closing the heavy pendulum covers consumed

34 Jones, *SHSP,* 67, 72. In contrast, Jones did not mention his ship's vulnerable knuckle in his after-action reports. Mabry, *Brief Sketch*, 17-27, notes that Jones submitted the article to *SHSP* in October 1874.

35 Jones, *SHSP,* 71. In his Oct. 25, 1862, letter to Jones (published in *ORN*, I:7, 60-61), Davidson emphasized Jones' "determination to sink & ram" *Monitor.*

too much time and manpower. Davidson determined to exploit the weakness and "made the men of my division fire into them as rapidly as possible with small arms while the chance offered." That, too, had no effect.

Davidson offered a uniquely personal account of how *Virginia*'s officers finally found a way to cripple their nemesis. "Jones sat in a small hatchway at the after part of my division, and we were in communication every few minutes during the action," Davidson wrote in his *Sun* article. "After an hour or so of ineffectual firing and maneuvering on both sides, I asked Jones: 'What is it trying to do?' He replied, with emphasis, that the same question had repeatedly occurred to him. 'Can't you try and hit the pilot tower?' he asked. At the same time, he ordered Lieutenant C. C. Simms, the executive officer, to go aft and direct the other division to do the same." Davidson admitted that he did not note "the intervals of time" during this period but asserted that the facts "are fresh in memory, and my account entered just afterward in the private journal I kept, is still with me."

Virginia's guns aimed for the pilot house, and *Monitor*'s movements suddenly "appeared wild," and she steered off toward Hampton into shoal waters where *Virginia* could not reach her. *Virginia*'s officers learned later that a shot striking the pilot house blinded *Monitor*'s commander, Lt. John L. Worden. That shot effectively ended the duel between the two ironclads. In Davidson's estimation, *Monitor*'s failure to return to engage *Virginia* meant that she "was as much defeated as an army that abandons the field of battle and leaves it in possession of the enemy."

According to Davidson, Jones then remarked: "'Well, we have disposed of her, let us see what we can do with the Minnesota.'" Not only is Davidson's the only account providing such vivid dialogue for the scene, but Jones's own accounts emphasized that *Virginia* had kept up an exchange with *Minnesota* whenever possible and was thus engaged when *Monitor* headed for shoal waters. Regardless of the sequence, *Monitor*'s withdrawal gave *Virginia* the opportunity to continue her destructive work from March 8. Unfortunately for the Confederates, *Virginia* ran aground on the same shoal where *Minnesota* lay helpless, with the frigate's impressive broadside facing the ironclad's bow. Davidson reckoned that *Virginia* was grounded for "nearly an hour," but most other accounts, including Catesby Jones's initial report, estimate the time as 15 minutes. "During this time I pointed and fired every shot of the bow 7-inch rifle with my own hands," Davidson boasted.[36] "The single gun we could bring to bear while aground hammered away at the Minnesota, doing considerable damage," he continued. His gun struck

36 Jones, *SHSP*, 72; Davidson's Oct. 25, 1862, letter to Catesby Jones (*ORN*, I:7, 60-1) estimated the time at three-quarters of an hour. He estimated that he fired "about eleven shells . . . six of which, not exploding prematurely as the rest did, appeared to take effect . . ."

and blew up what Davidson described as "a bay or river steamer" (the armed tug *Dragon*) that lay aside *Minnesota.* Davidson expressed surprise that the smaller ship had remained there, "taking things on board over the side." In his estimation, that steamer prevented *Minnesota* from using her full broadside against *Virginia.* Proving the folly of that inexplicable tactical error was the commendable work of a Federal gunboat at *Minnesota*'s stern which came close to firing shots into *Virginia*'s exposed bow ports. "Suppose the Minnesota's broadside, as well handled, had been added to that!" Davidson's insight did not prevent him from directing the shot that destroyed the *Dragon* and thus removed the obstacle in front of *Minnesota*'s broadside.

Other accounts corroborate the deadly effectiveness of Davidson's gunnery. Lieutenant Eggleston recounted how he was firing his guns "at ricochet," skipping them against *Minnesota.* "But Davidson, with his rifled guns, just forward of me was actually 'plumping' the target by direct fire, as we learned later by the enemy's official report." In his official report, Van Brunt described how *Virginia* "returned my fire with her rifled bow gun with a shell, which passed through the chief engineer's stateroom, through the engineer's mess room, amidships, and burst in the boatswain's room, tearing four rooms all into one in its passage, exploding two charges of powder, which set the ship on fire, but it was promptly extinguished."[37]

Thanks to the efforts of *Virginia*'s capable engineers, she soon freed herself from the shoal and could assume a more favorable position toward *Minnesota.* The ship that was to be the focus of *Virginia*'s attention on March 9 appeared now at her mercy. In his *Sun* article, Davidson creatively quoted Van Brunt as testimony to how close his ship was to destruction. "Seeing that the Monitor had retired from the action and could no longer render me any assistance, that my decks were covered with dead and dying, and my vessel unable to resist the enemy, I had gone on deck to make arrangements to abandon the vessel, when, to my surprise, I saw the rebel monster steaming toward Norfolk.'" Van Brunt told a different story in his official report. Although admitting that his ship was "badly crippled, and my officers and men were worn out with fatigue," he nevertheless "determined never to give up the ship to the rebels. . . ." Instead, he "ordered every preparation to be made to destroy the ship after all hope was gone to save her." It was then that Van Brunt noticed the *Virginia* steaming away toward Craney Island.[38] Davidson misquoted Van Brunt (who died a year later), but his account of *Minnesota*'s desperate condition was essentially correct.

37 Eggleston, "Eggleston's Narrative,"175; *ORN*, I:7, 11-12

38 *ORN*, I:7, 12.

Indeed, at noon, Catesby Jones ordered his ship to break off the battle and steam back to Norfolk. That decision was a pleasant surprise to Van Brunt and the U.S. Navy, and equally baffling and disappointing to Confederates. It shaped Davidson's account of the battle of Hampton Roads, as it compelled him to defend his friend and to explain how he could claim victory for *Virginia* even though she, too, left the field of battle, failing to accomplish her mission. Later that summer, when a Confederate officer who was not on *Virginia* made "ill-natured remarks in regard to the *Virginia*'s not taking on the *Minnesota*," Jones wrote to Davidson asking him to write an open letter defending the decision.

Jones offered Davidson what amounted to "talking points": that *Virginia* was leaking from her effort to "run into the *Monitor*"; that *Virginia* had "received a shot" from *Monitor* that "came near disabling the machinery"; that "*Minnesota* appeared so badly damaged that we did not believe that she could ever move again"; and that the pilots (who had already run her aground once) "refused to place us any nearer to [*Minnesota*]" and warned Jones that "if we did not go up to Norfolk then, that we could not do so until the next day." Based on that intelligence, Jones consulted with his executive officer, Lt. Simms, who expressed the "decided opinion . . . that the action should cease." Jones asked Simms to get Davidson's opinion, and Simms "informed me that you agreed with him." Expanding significantly on Jones's account of how he solicited feedback from Simms and Davidson, Lt. Eggleston's postwar account described Jones walking down the gun deck, holding a kind of progressive "informal council of war" (replete with full dialogue). All but Lt. John Taylor Wood concurred with Jones, Simms, and Davidson.[39]

"I am satisfied myself that you did all that any other officer could or would have done," Davidson replied in a September 12 letter that Jones found inadequate for his purposes. "It was unfortunate that you could not have had some idea of how near old Van Brunt was to leaving the ship."[40]

Neither in his more detailed October 25, 1862, reply to Jones or his 1897 article did Davidson recount anything like an "informal council of war," but he concurred fully with Jones's judgment and decision. To Jones's request for corroboration of his own account, Davidson dutifully responded that the impossibility of getting nearer to *Minnesota,*

> together with the fact that our officers & men were completely broken down by two days & nights continuous work with the heaviest rifled ordnance in the

39 Eggleston, "Eggleston's Narrative,"175-76.

40 Davidson to Jones, Sep. 12, 1862, *ORN,* I:7, 59.

> world, & that the ship was believed to be seriously injured by ramming & sinking the Cumberland, & remain so in attempting to reach the 'Minnesota', she would probably open forward where her horn had split the stem, & ~~cause us to~~ become an easy prey to the enemy, & in consideration also that the Monitor was drawn off and sought safety in shoal water, & that the Minnesota was ~~so badly riddled~~ crippled beyond the hope of safety, induced you, by the advice of the Lieutenants, whom you consulted, to return to Norfolk.

For good measure Davidson added: "I still think, as I then thought, that it was the proper course for you to pursue, & that you had made the best fight of the two days engagement." In his *Sun* article Davidson described how *Virginia*'s "worn out" crew "were rejoiced" when they perceived that they had the Federal fleet at their mercy, "but the old patchwork had nearly run her race. The grounding had spread her butt ends, as well as twisted her knuckle, and she was leaking rapidly. The carpenter and the chief engineer came up to report, and it was found necessary to return to Norfolk immediately."[41]

To those armchair admirals who insisted that *Virginia* could and should have run after the Federal fleet, Davidson offered a reality check. Had she not broken off the action, *Virginia* certainly would have destroyed *Minnesota.* But the other vessels could have escaped. *Virginia,* "in her leaking condition, with fires not cleaned for two days, steaming off and on, and the old rickety engine out of order, finally, with the officers and crew exhausted, would never have attempted to follow. If she had done so the most serious consequences to her might have resulted." Embroidering upon the pilots' assessment of the situation, Davidson concluded that "Had Jones been rash enough to follow the fleet, and escaped damage from it, the act would doubtless have necessitated his anchoring in the Bay of Roads for the night, and had the Merrimac been caught in rough weather in either place she would have foundered."

Beaten up as *Virginia* was, things could have been far worse had the Federal ships fought the battle more wisely. Echoing Jones, Eggleston, Wood, and other officers who wrote of the battle, Davidson underscored how vulnerable *Virginia* was to concentrated fire from *Monitor*'s large guns. According to Davidson, his friend and commander was "figuratively speaking, was trembling in his boots, fearing that Worden would concentrate his fire on some one spot on the water line, and steam rapidly around the Merrimac until returning to fire at the same point." Fortunately for the Confederate vessel, "the fire of the Monitor was wild in the

41 Davidson to Jones, Oct. 25, 1862, Confederate States Navy Area files, RG 45, NARA. The strikethroughs do not appear in the version published in *ORN,* I, 7:61.

extreme, for only once in the two hours did her shot have any effect. The armor was indented, the backing broken and splintered just near and above the starboard broadside gunport, but no person or material was put out of action. Had those two 11-inch shot only been fired at the water line (the Monitor being close to use at the time), I am pretty sure they would have started the knuckle, and the additional leak caused thereby would have been too much for us."

Emphasizing the vulnerability and condition of your own vessel after a two-day battle seems like a dubious basis for claiming victory in the battle of Hampton Roads. Davidson's claim was based on a certain sleight of hand and very narrow criteria for what distinguished victory and defeat in the battle of March 9. Most historians define *Virginia*'s objective for that day to have been the continued destruction of the Federal blockading squadron. *Monitor*'s objective was to prevent *Virginia* from accomplishing that. By those criteria, *Monitor* clearly won the day. Jones and Davidson argued that *Virginia* left *Minnesota* for dead, and that even her captain agreed with the desperateness of her situation when *Virginia* broke off combat and gave her a reprieve. *Minnesota* did not die, and Davidson himself would have to employ a new kind of weapon in a second failed attempt to kill her two years later.[42]

Be that as it may, destroying *Minnesota* and the other wood warships was not really *Virginia*'s objective on March 9, if we accept Hunter Davidson's explanation. In his October 1862 letter to Jones, Davidson laid the foundation for this argument. Even though *Monitor* fought consistently in a manner obviously intended to "relieve" *Minnesota* by "drawing us off," the southern officers decided the real battle would be with *Monitor* (a belief Davidson adopted only after Jones overruled his desire to go after *Minnesota*). "You expressed your determination to sink & ram her & to keep vigorously at her until the contest was decided," Davidson wrote to Jones, "and you left the impression upon my mind that the engagement could only end in the overthrow of either the enemy or ourselves." But, of course, the battle ended without the "overthrow of either" vessel. That inconvenient fact did not make the first duel of the ironclads a draw. For Davidson, the most salient fact was that *Monitor* left the field first, and did not return, leaving *Minnesota* at *Virginia*'s mercy. When *Virginia* failed to finish off *Minnesota* because she had run aground once and could not remain in Hampton Roads at the risk of rough seas, Davidson contorted that into further evidence of his ship's victory: "And now, while lying aground for nearly an hour, immovable, and deliberately trying to destroy the

42 See, for example, John V. Quarstein and Joseph Gutierrez, "Who Won the Battle of Hampton Roads?: A Historians' Debate," in *The Battle of Hampton Roads: New Perspectives on the USS Monitor and the CSS Virginia*, Harold Holzer and Tim Mulligan, eds. (New York, 2006), 141-54.

Minnesota, where was the Monitor?" he wrote in 1897. "Nowhere did she come, not a shot did he fire, and this I state as if standing in the 'witness box.'"

Even if *Virginia* failed to destroy *Minnesota,* the important thing is that she won her duel with *Monitor.* In his 1897 *Sun* account, he recalled a chance meeting in Annapolis two or three years after the war with Lt. Samuel Dana Greene, who had assumed command of *Monitor* when Worden was blinded. Introduced by a mutual navy friend, Greene asked Davidson why *Virginia* broke off and returned to Norfolk. I replied, 'Because when we got afloat we found she was leaking so badly we had to do so.'" Greene asked Davidson whether *Monitor* injured *Virginia.* "'None materially: the serious injuries to the vessel were all done by the Cumberland," I replied, to which, after a little hesitation, he remarked disconnectedly, and as I thought at the time, with some emotion: 'Well, I brought the Monitor back as soon as I could.' I asked, 'Do I understand you to say that the Monitor actually engaged the Merrimac again, after she had once retired?' He hesitated, and said: "Well, I did the best I could.'" *Monitor* did no material damage to *Virginia* (though she could have if her officers had exploited *Virginia*'s weaknesses). She left the field of battle and did not return. In Davidson's reckoning, this amounted to victory for *Virginia.*[43]

As *Virginia* turned back toward the Elizabeth River, Lt. John Taylor Wood, Davidson's former Naval Academy colleague who commanded the ship's aft 7-inch pivot rifle, came to Davidson and said, "'Dave, let's gives [sic] the Monitor a parting shot.' 'All right,' I answered, and our divisions each fired two shots low, so as to richochet [*sic*], for the Monitor was a long way off; and we thought one at least struck her, but the distance was too great to be certain. To those last shots the Monitor did not reply, and thus ended the day's contest."

There was no hint of controversy or disappointment when *Virginia* and her officers and crew received a heroes' welcome in Norfolk. The men went ashore, where citizens celebrated their victory. The Confederate Congress passed a resolution of thanks to the officers and crew of *Virginia* and the several ships of the James River Squadron for their "brilliant victory" at Hampton Roads.[44]

43 Greene had reason to be sensitive about his actions. *Monitor*'s inventor, John Ericsson, conceded that his vessel had quit the field, blaming the "miserable executive officer" (Greene) who "ran away with his impregnable vessel" instead of fighting on to victory as he could and should have done. Ericsson to Gustavus A. Fox, 24 Nov. 1874, typescript copy enclosed in letter from Gustavus A. Fox to Catesby ap Roger Jones, Dec. 2, 1876, Hardin Littlepage Collection, Confederate Memorial Literary Society (hereafter cited as CMLS) Collection under the management of the Virginia Historical Society, summarized in Mabry Tyson, "Believe Only Half of What You Read About the Battle of Hampton Roads," in Holzer and Mulligan, eds., *Battle of Hampton Roads*, 106-108.

44 Davis, *Duel*, 138-139; *ORN*, II:3, 131.

There was, however, no hiding how beaten up the victorious Confederate ironclad was from the two-day battle, and she spent the next month in dry dock undergoing what Davidson described as "extensive repairs." *Virginia* was never as formidable as Northerners feared. Her "great bulk," Davidson wrote in 1897, "magnified her powers proportionately, when in fact it constituted her greatest weakness." She was unseaworthy. "Imagine her being caught in rough weather at night or with her engine out of order—in Hampton Roads, or Chesapeake Bay!" Davidson was among those who feared that Cornelius Vanderbilt's self-named massive steamship fitted with a ram had the potential to sink *Virginia.*

When *Virginia* came out of dry dock in early April, she had a new commander, Capt. Josiah Tattnall, of Georgia. Not surprisingly, the Navy Department passed over Catesby Jones again for a senior officer. It was not to be a happy command for Tattnall. On April 11, *Virginia* "sallied forth" again in search of prey and with hopes of renewing her duel with *Monitor.* Still charged with protecting the wooden blockading fleet and with preventing *Virginia* from getting out of Hampton Roads and interfering with U.S. Gen. George B. McClellan's campaign against Richmond via the York River, *Monitor* was under orders to avoid combat.

If *Monitor* had accepted the challenge, Davidson was confident the Confederates could defeat *Monitor*–which he believed to be the stronger vessel—because they had a plan in place of Davidson's own devising. *Virginia* would be "accompanied by four fast tugboats, each one having a complete organization for boarding the Monitor," he explained. "We expected she would sink three, but by that time it was believed the fourth would have been enabled to give her the *coup de grace.* . . . I had charge of our tug, and we had determined to risk everything to capture the Monitor. . . . The experience and reflection of later years have confirmed my belief that we would have captured the Monitor had we met her."

Not everyone shared Davidson's confidence in the plan. Midshipman Robert Chester Foute, who had been a student at the Naval Academy when Davidson was on the faculty and who commanded one of *Virginia*'s guns at Hampton Roads, described the plan in an 1891 article. He declared it "entirely practicable, provided we should not all be blown out of the water before it could be carried out." In Foute's telling, each of the four tugs carried a few men from four different divisions, each carrying different tools: grappling-irons and lines, wedges and mallets, tarpaulins, and chloroform. "Well, the idea was for all four of these vessels to pounce down on the 'Monitor' at the same time;' Foute explained. "on a given signal, and from different directions, all hands were to rush on board, wedge the turret so as to prevent its revolving, then scale its sides, deluge the interior with chloroform by breaking the bottles on the upper deck, then cover the turret and pilot-house with tarpaulins, and wait for the crew to surrender." Regardless of

Foute's (*ex post facto*) misgivings, the plan evolved far enough for Davidson to take possession of a fast dispatch boat, *J. B. White,* and to sally out to challenge *Monitor.* The quarry refused to take the bait, however, so, Foute concluded, "we saved our chloroform and—our necks."[45]

There is no doubt that Davidson was the author of the plan. A few months later, Davidson's private memorandum book fell into the hands of the U.S. Navy. *Monitor*'s paymaster, William F. Keeler, read the book and recounted Davidson's plan in a letter to his wife. "It was minute in all its details," Keeler wrote, corroborating much of what Davidson and Foute later recalled. "The names of men were given, just what article each one was to carry, to what part of the *Monitor* he was to go &c., it even gave the men who were to carry the matches & sand paper to rub them on."[46]

A month after this aborted rematch with *Monitor,* the CSS *Virginia* was no more. She became the first of many Confederate ironclads destroyed by her own crew. As Gen. George McClellan's massive Federal army compelled the Confederate army to evacuate the defensive line across *Virginia*'s lower peninsula from Yorktown to the James River, Federal forces occupied Norfolk, cutting off *Virginia* from her base. A conference between naval and army officers on May 9 decided that *Virginia* should continue to help protect Norfolk, so the sudden decision to evacuate the city caught Capt. Josiah Tattnall by surprise. *Virginia*'s officers decided to lighten the ship as much as possible to steam upriver far enough to aid in the defense of Richmond. The pilots scuttled those plans when they warned Tattnall that *Virginia* could not ascend even the lower reaches of the James River without reducing her draft by several feet. Even lightening her draft—which raised her exposed knuckle and hull above the waterline—was not adequate. Tattnall decided that he had no choice but to destroy the ship. He later explained that "although not formally consulted, the course was approved by every commissioned officer in the ship." In the early hours of May 11, 1862, *Virginia*'s crew took her to Craney Island and blew her up. The officers and men of *Virginia* marched 22 miles to Suffolk, where they entrained for Richmond.

A court of inquiry later concluded that the destruction of *Virginia* was premature and convened a court martial against Tattnall for his decision. Davidson, Jones, Wood, Eggleston, and three other of *Virginia*'s former officers on June 26

45 R. C. Foute, "Echoes from Hampton Roads," *SHSP* (1891), 19: 247-48; Dinwiddie Brazier Phillips, "The Career of the Iron-Clad Virginia, (formerly the Merrimac) Confederate States Navy, March-May 1862," in R. A. Brock, ed., *Miscellaneous Papers, 1672-1865, now first printed from the manuscript in the collections of the Virginia Historical Society* (Richmond, 1887), 224-225.

46 Robert W. Daly, ed., William Frederick Keeler, *Aboard the U.S.S. Monitor 1862: The Letters of Acting Paymaster William Frederick Keeler, U.S. Navy, to his wife Anna* (Annapolis, MD, 1964), 184.

complained to Secretary Mallory that the court's conclusion "does great wrong to the officers of that vessel," and they asked "for some assurance of record to the effect that the court could not rightfully have cast any imputation upon our official character, and did not, in the judgement of the Department, intend such imputations." Mallory gave the officers the assurances they sought, and a court martial cleared Tattnall of the three charges brought against him.[47]

The evacuation of Norfolk and the destruction of *Virginia* left Richmond essentially defenseless against the advance of Federal naval forces. In April, the U.S. Navy ran the lower Mississippi fortifications, defeated the Confederate fleet below New Orleans, and compelled the surrender of the Confederacy's largest city before land troops arrived. Confederate officials and Richmond citizens feared that the same fate could befall the capital city.

The only effective defensive point between the Confederate capital city and the James River Flotilla of the U.S. Navy's North Atlantic Blockading Squadron was a recently constructed earthen fort sitting atop the high south bank of the river at Drewry's Bluff. Commanded by Davidson's 1852-53 Coast Survey commander, Capt. John Rodgers, the Federal flotilla—which included *Monitor* and another of the experimental ironclad vessels that the U.S. Navy commissioned, *Galena*—arrived at Drewry's Bluff on May 15. To obstruct the channel below the bluff, the navy sank the CSS *Jamestown,* which had won praise for her role in the battle of Hampton Roads. Crews dragged five guns from *Jamestown* and *Patrick Henry* onto the bluff to augment the battery. "[T]he Navy for the time being has been destroyed," John Taylor Wood wrote to his wife on May 24, "& we must seek other ways of rendering ourselves useful."[48] Accordingly, officers and sailors from the *Virginia* and from vessels of the James River Squadron joined a few artillery batteries and infantry regiments to defend Drewry's Bluff. Wood commanded a contingent of sailors stationed on the north bank of the river as sharpshooters.

The battle proved a lopsided victory for the *ersatz* Confederate defenders. *Monitor* could not elevate her guns enough to fire at the Confederate fortifications on the bluff and the lightly armored *Galena* proved vulnerable to plunging fire from the bluff. Initial accounts of the battle credited the Confederate navy, especially the officers and crew of the late *Virginia* with saving Richmond from the Federal flotilla. An Alabama infantryman who participated in the battle told his family that, while soldiers from a heavy artillery unit fled, the crew from the *Virginia* "stood their posts like men." The *Richmond Examiner* noted that it was fortunate

47 *ORN,* I:7, 336-37, 789-90.

48 Wood to Lola, May 24, 1862, John Taylor Wood Papers, Southern Historical Collection, University of North Carolina Chapel Hill (hereafter cited as Wood Papers).

that the guns were manned by the *Virginia*'s crew "and not Yahoos ignorant of command." Even artillery officers justifiably irked at the exaggerated credit given to the navy at the expense of the army, noted that the presence of *Virginia*'s crew boosted Confederate morale.[49] Was Hunter Davidson among the officers who helped repel the Federal flotilla at Drewry's Bluff? Davidson himself never wrote about the battle in his narratives about the career of the *Virginia* or mention any role he may have played in it. However, Lt. James Henry Rochelle, executive officer of *Patrick Henry*, included him in a list of officers who participated in the battle. John Thomas Scharf, a Confederate midshipman from Maryland who later wrote the first history of the Confederate States Navy, similarly included Davidson on a list of officers who manned a naval battery consisting of heavy guns dragged up the bluff from *Jamestown* and *Patrick Henry*.[50] Indirect evidence of his presence at Drewry's Bluff comes from orders dated May 19, 1862, *detaching* him from the James River Batteries for a new assignment.

Participating in the battle that purportedly saved Richmond in 1862 did not loom large in Davidson's account of his service. In contrast, the new assignment he received four days after the battle consumed his interest for the remainder of the war, dominated his narrative of his war career, and became the foundation of his place in history—which he defended zealously for the rest of his life.

49 For details of battle, see Ed Bearss, *River of Lost Opportunities: The Civil War on the James River 1861-1862* (Lynchburg, VA, 1995), 52-77, and John M. Coski, *Capital Navy: The Men, Ships, and Operations of the James River Squadron* (Campbell, CA, 1996), 41-52.

50 Rochelle, *Life of Rear Admiral John Randolph Tucker*. . . (New York, 1903), 42; J. Thomas Scharf, *History of the Confederate States Navy* (New York, 1887), 711.

Chapter Four

The "Notorious Lieutenant Davidson" (1862–1864)

The work that became Hunter Davidson's claim to fame began modestly with orders from the Confederate Office of Orders and Detail on May 19, 1862, four days after the battle of Drewry's Bluff: "You are hereby detached from the Batteries on Jas River, and will report to Command Robb, at Rocketts, for the Command of the Steamer, 'Teazer.'" Davidson reported to Rocketts—the port of Richmond—the same day.[1]

The *Teaser* was a shallow-draft, 80-foot tugboat that the Virginia State Navy purchased from a Norfolk salvage company in 1861 and armed with two guns. She became part of the Confederate James River Squadron and participated in the battle of Hampton Roads. When Davidson took command of *Teaser* in May 1862, the Confederate Navy had repurposed her to assist with creating a torpedo (submarine mine) defensive barrier in the James River. The officer to whom Davidson reported ultimately was not Cdr. Robert G. Robb, commandant of the Rocketts Navy Yard, but Cdr. Matthew Fontaine Maury, chief the Navy's Bureau of Coast, Harbor, and River Defense.[2] Maury had been experimenting with torpedo defenses for a year, and Davidson was to become his assistant, his protégé, his successor, and his occasional detractor.

1 ZB file, "Teaser," NH&HC.

2 The formal name of the bureau is from Herbert M. Schiller, *Confederate Torpedoes: Two Illustrated 19th Century Works with New Appendices and Photographs* (Jefferson, NC, 2011), 5; and W. Davis Waters and Joseph I. Brown, *Gabriel Rains and the Confederate Torpedo Bureau* (El Dorado Hills, CA, 2017), 40.

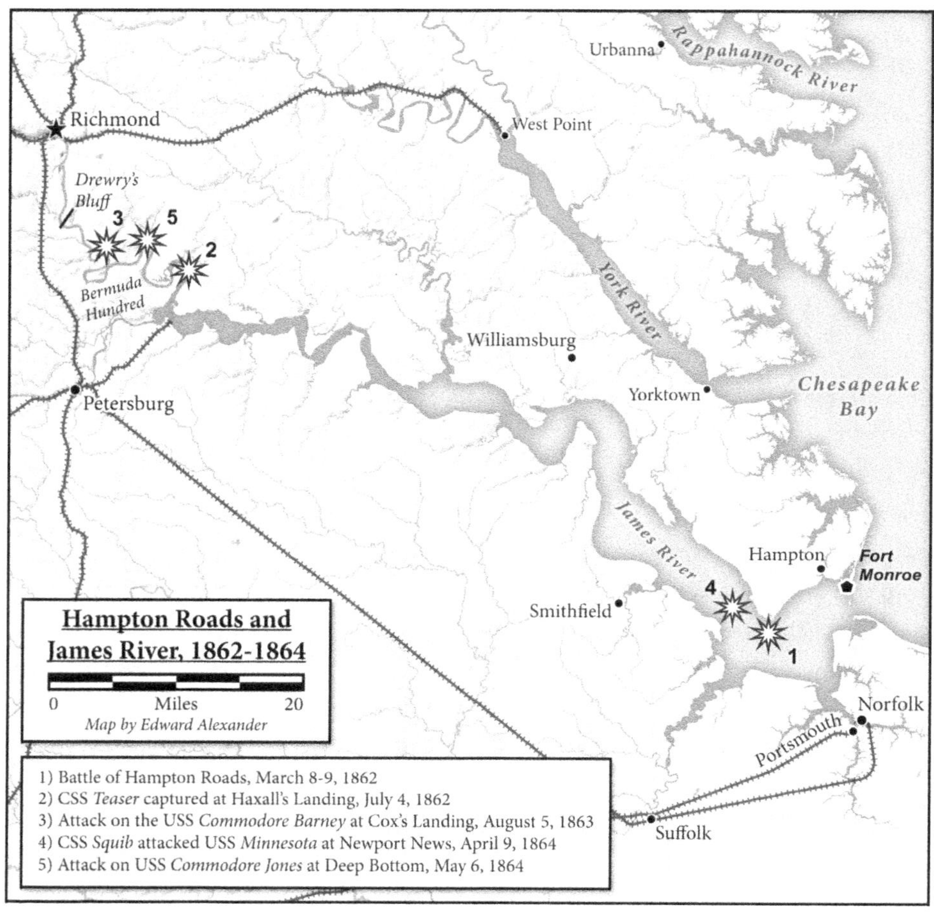

Belying the modest title he held in the Confederate States Navy, Matthew Fontaine Maury was one of the most celebrated American naval officers in the decade before the Civil War, a *bona fide* international celebrity renowned and rewarded for his work in charting the world's oceans and ocean currents. He was the "Pathfinder of the Seas." A descendant of several distinguished Virginia families, Maury had entered the Navy at age 19, but an 1839 carriage accident left him lame and unfit for sea duty. He had already authored a navigation textbook, and the U.S. Navy saw value in his work in naval science, giving him in 1842 command of the new Naval Depot of Charts and Instruments, later christened the U.S. Naval Observatory and Hydrographical Office. The navy assigned to Maury a succession of promising young officers who had demonstrated an interest in naval science, among them Davidson's Date of 1841 classmates John Mercer Brooke and Robert Dabney Minor. Despite occasional claims that Davidson had been

Commander Matthew Fontaine Maury established what became the Submarine Battery Service and was Davidson's mentor. *NH&HC (NH-58900)*

one of Maury's protégés, it had been the Coast Survey, not the Naval Observatory, to which Davidson had been assigned in the 1850s. Davidson certainly knew of Maury's scientific work, his maverick reputation, and the Southern nationalist sentiments that they shared, and the two officers may have met before May 1862, but there is no documentary evidence that they had ever worked together.[3]

Like Davidson, Maury did not hesitate to resign from the U.S. Navy after Virginia seceded from the Union. And, like Davidson, Maury was dismissed from the service and had his name stricken from the rolls. The U.S. government further alienated the "Pathfinder of the Seas" by insinuating that he had worked to undermine the U.S. Navy while he still served it. Befitting his prominence, Maury joined R. E. Lee and Virginia Military Institute superintendent Francis H. Smith on the Advisory Council to oversee the state's military preparations. When the Virginia State Navy folded into the Confederate States Navy in June 1861, Commander Maury found himself reporting to an old nemesis. Secretary of the Navy Stephen R. Mallory had been a U.S. senator from Florida and chairman of the U.S. Senate's Naval Affairs Committee. In that capacity Mallory had supported the work of the Retiring Board—nicknamed the "Plucking Board"—that had worked unsuccessfully to force Maury into early retirement in 1856.

In the year before his strained relationship with Mallory and his incurable penchant for speaking his mind resulted in exile to Europe, Maury employed his scientific mind and his reputation to help bolster the naval defenses of his native state. Just as the possession of a successful ironclad vessel could neutralize the numerically superior U.S. Navy, so, too, could the perfection of submarine mines

3 The best biographies of Maury are Frances Leigh Williams, *Matthew Fontaine Maury, Pathfinder of the Seas* (New Brunswick, NJ, 1963) and John Grady, *Matthew Fontaine Maury Father of Oceanography: A Biography, 1806-1874* (Jefferson, NC, 2015).

defend Virginia's rivers and harbors with minimal expense of scant funds and resources. Immediately upon leaving the U.S. Navy, Maury began experimenting with what his generation knew as torpedoes.

The concept of using submarine explosives against enemy warships was not new. Most famously in American history, David Bushnell of Connecticut tried using powder-filled barrels floated against British ships in the Delaware River and even developed a man-powered submarine, the *Turtle,* to attach time bombs to enemy vessels. Robert Fulton, inventor of the steamship, contemplated developing an electrical torpedo, and the famed firearms inventor Samuel Colt demonstrated a prototype electrical torpedo in 1844; although impressed by his invention, the U.S. government inexplicably declined to offer him a contract. British military technicians used electrically detonated torpedoes in demolition work, but it was the Russians who employed torpedoes in their defense of Sebastopol harbor during the Crimean War. The primary challenges were to develop fuses (often spelled fuzes in 19th-century sources) that would work under water and, ideally, a means of exploding torpedoes against specific enemy targets without endangering friendly ships. The obvious answer in the mid-19th century was electricity.[4]

On April 22, 1861, Maury sent to New York City for insulated wire to use in his experiments. Working with Prof. Socrates Maupin, Maury established a laboratory at the University of Virginia that worked in conjunction with the Virginia State Navy's Ordnance Department. Famously conducting his experiments in a washtub in his cousin's Richmond home, Maury developed fuses that would work underwater. In August 1861 at Rocketts, he staged an impressive demonstration of the *potential* power of submarine mines before an audience that included Virginia Governor John Letcher and several Virginia congressmen. The demonstration and Maury's lobbying secured a generous "Appropriation for Submarine Batteries" from the Confederate Congress that funded the Navy's torpedo work for several years. Assisted by his son, Richard, and by Lt. Robert Dabney Minor (who had been assigned to the U.S. Naval Observatory at the time of Virginia's secession), Maury continued his experiments and tried several times between July and October 1861 to detonate torpedoes against Federal ships in Hampton Roads. The Congressional appropriation for submarine batteries also paid for the work of Acting Master William G. Cheeney on a submarine boat that fell under Maury's authority.[5]

4 Timothy S. Wolters, "Electric Torpedoes in the Confederacy: Reconciling Conflicting Histories," *The Journal of Military History* (July 2008): 72:769-70; Edwyn Gray, *Nineteenth-Century Torpedoes and their Inventors* (Annapolis, MD, 2004), 4, credits Italian Frederico Gianibelli with inventing a proto-torpedo ca. 1585.

5 Williams, *Matthew Fontaine Maury*, 376-381; Grady, *Matthew Fontaine Maury*, 205-207; Maury to Franklin Minor, Aug. 11, 1861, Matthew Fontaine Maury Papers, LC (hereafter cited as MFM

By the time Davidson became his new assistant, Maury had shifted his focus from offensive to defensive torpedoes. President Jefferson Davis's March 25, 1862, special message to the Confederate House of Representatives underscored how important torpedoes had become in the defense of Southern waterways, specifically the James River. Prompting the message were alarmed reports that—pending the completion of the Drewry's Bluff earthworks—the Confederate capital city of Richmond was defenseless against the *Monitor* or other Federal ships. Davis assured Congress that obstructions and torpedo barriers were underway. "For want of insulated wire we are deprived of that class of submarine batteries exploded at will by electricity, which promises the best results," Davis explained. Experiments made since early in the war demonstrated that torpedoes exploded by impact were less effective because the enemy could render them harmless. Much to Maury's and Davidson's chagrin, Davis subsequently recanted or forgot his preference for electrical torpedoes.[6]

In a June 19, 1862, report to Secretary Mallory, Maury detailed the status of his torpedo work. "The James River is mined with 15 tanks below the iron battery at Chapin's [Chaffin's] Bluff," Maury began. "They are to be exploded by means of electricity. Four of the tanks contain 160 pounds of powder; the 11 others hold 70 pounds each. All are made of boiler plate." Arranged in rows, or ranges, the tanks were contained in water-tight casks anchored between three and eight feet below the surface. Maury described in detail the wiring and the galvanic batteries that enabled the ranges to be detonated at once. In addition to those 15 torpedoes were four other, much larger, torpedoes arranged in two pairs, which contained a collective 6,000 pounds of powder. Spring flooding had carried away the wires to operate one pair. "Lieutenant Davidson, who, with the *Teaser* and her crew, has assisted me with a most hearty good will, has dragged for the tanks without success." Despite this snafu, Maury was confident in the future of the torpedo work. "There are a quantity of admirably insulated wire, a number of shells for anchors or torpedoes, and a sufficient quantity of chains for the wires remaining." His operation also benefited from the service of talented assistants and

Papers); Gideon Welles to Robert Dabney Minor, Mar. 29, 1861, Minor Family Papers, VMHC (hereafter cited as Minor Papers); Betty Herndon Maury Diary, June 27, 1861, LC, 27; Mark K. Ragan, *Union and Confederate Submarine Warfare in the Civil War* (Mason City, IA, 1999), 12-18; sundry documents in Confederate States Navy Subject files (BM), RG 45, NARA (hereafter cited as CSN Subject files), Coski, *Capital Navy*, 116-121.

6 Williams, *Pathfinder*, 393, citing Maury's 1866 lecture in France, wrote that Davidson had begun working with Maury in April 1862, but Davidson's May 19, 1862, orders suggest that Maury was mistaken about the date. *The War of the Rebellion: A Compilation of the Official Records of the Union and Confederate Armies*, 128 vols (Washington, D.C., 1880-1901), series IV, volume 1, 1021. (hereafter cited as *OR*, series (if not series I), volume/part, page number.

the University of Virginia research facility. "My duties in connection with these batteries being thus closed," Maury concluded his report, "I have the honor to await your further orders."[7]

Having made himself a thorn in Secretary Mallory's side with public criticism and self-promotion, Maury's further orders were tantamount to an exile from the Confederacy. Congress rescinded his initial orders to Cuba, but Maury received new orders to Europe, where he was to use his reputation and connections in the cause of purchasing vessels and weapons. He finally left the country in October The day after Maury submitted his report, Secretary Mallory issued orders to Hunter Davidson: "You will relieve Commander Maury in the charge of devising, placing, and superintending submarine batteries in the James River, and you will exercise your discretion as to the ways and means of placing obstacles of this and any other character to oppose the enemy's passage of the river"[8]

An Inauspicious Start: The Seven Days

As Davidson reported at Rocketts on May 19 to begin his work with Matthew Fontaine Maury, Maj. Gen. George B. McClellan's Army of the Potomac had completed its march up the Virginia Peninsula from Yorktown and Williamsburg to the outskirts of Richmond. Because *Virginia* had blocked the Union navy from the James River, McClellan had made the Pamunkey River, a tributary of the York River, his supply line. Rather than wait for McClellan to attack, Gen. Joseph E. Johnston, commander of the Confederate army at Richmond (soon designated the Army of Northern Virginia) seized the initiative and attacked along the Williamsburg Road at Seven Pines on May 31. The two-day battle of Seven Pines/Fair Oaks was a bloody stalemate, but it did alter the strategic picture when Johnston fell wounded. To replace him—temporarily—President Jefferson Davis appointed Robert E. Lee. Lee reorganized his army and formulated plans for a second preemptive strike against McClellan's numerically superior army.

The result, of course, was the so-called Seven Days Battles fought between June 25 and July 1, 1862. McClellan's right flank lay on the north bank of the swampy Chickahominy River, which unusually heavy spring and early summer rains had swollen into a major barrier. Lee concentrated his forces to strike against that exposed right flank and roll up McClellan's army from the north. With the largest force that he was to command during the war, Lee was confident that he could

7 M. F. Maury to Mallory, Richmond, June 19, 1862, *ORN*, I:7, 544-546.

8 Grady, *Father of Oceanography*, 207-224; *ORN*, I:7, 546. Maury continued to sign vouchers for submarine work as late as Aug. 18, 1862. See CSN Subject files.

not only drive McClellan's army away from Richmond but punish his foe severely. Delayed attacks and lack of coordination led to missed opportunities. The largest battle of the campaign, Gaines's Mill on June 27, persuaded McClellan to move his army away from Richmond. And, while McClellan panicked, the Federal army managed to execute an orderly retreat—or "change of base" as McClellan insisted on calling it. On July 1, McClellan's army bloodily repulsed one last Confederate attack at Malvern Hill, a few miles north of the James River. McClellan then completed his "change of base" to Harrison's Landing on the James, 25 miles southeast of Richmond.

Davidson later remembered that he and his elder brother, John W. Davidson, "fought against each other in the seven days battles around Richmond and I came within less than five minutes of catching him, but he dodged into the Chickahominy and Clitz was caught." John Davidson did indeed participate in the Seven Days battles, leading a brigade of the Army of the Potomac's IV Corps and receiving promotion to brevet brigadier general. If his younger brother's account of their close encounter is accurate, both Davidsons would have to have been present along the Chickahominy River on June 27, the day that Maj. Henry Boyd Clitz of the 12th United States Infantry was taken prisoner. According to his official report, John Davidson was ordered to cross to the north bank of the Chickahominy on the evening of the 27th, but the order was countermanded. Instead, his brigade fought a sharp battle at Golding's farm on the 28th, then marched on the 29th from Golding's to Savage Station and was engaged in the battle there before moving to the White Oak Swamp Bridge. General Davidson was incapacitated with sunstroke from 4:00 p.m. on the 29th until the morning of the 30th. The brigade reached the James River at Haxall's Landing, several miles west of Harrison's Landing, on the 30th.[9]

John Davidson was in the vicinity of the Chickahominy on June 27, but was Hunter Davidson there? If so, what was he doing? His ship was on the James River, and there is no record of any torpedo defenses on the Chickahominy. If not for Hunter's allusion to the capture of Clitz, it would seem more likely that the brothers' near miss occurred near Haxall's Landing on the James River on June 30 or July 1.

Surviving official reports and correspondence shed no light on what Davidson and the *Teaser* were doing during the Seven Days Battles. Davidson and his riverine headquarters come back into focus in the first days of July when *Teaser* assisted the Confederate army with a new kind of reconnaissance. Beginning on June 27, as the battle of Gaines' Mill raged, the Confederate army sent aloft a reconnaissance

9 Davidson, "Correspondence," *Journal of the United States Artillery*, 32:94; *OR*, 11/2, 480-482.

balloon filled with coal gas from the Richmond gas works located on the city's eastern edge near the port of Rocketts. Conducting the aerial reconnaissance was Maj. Edward Porter Alexander, a Georgia-born officer who soon would become the chief of the Army of Northern Virginia reserve artillery. Alexander observed Malvern Hill "from a point about two miles out on the Williamsburg Road." "Ascensions were made daily," Alexander wrote in his memoir, "and when the enemy reached Malvern Hill, the inflated balloon would be carried down the river and ascensions made from the deck of a boat." A month later Alexander told his father that he made no ascent on June 28, but that he transported the balloon down river on a steamer on June 29.[10]

Teaser was well suited to her role as proto "aircraft carrier." Her draft was light enough to navigate the river, and her deck was generous enough for the balloon, Made in Savannah, Georgia, from strips of silk sewn together, the balloon leaked freely and could not stay aloft long before going back to the gas works for a refill. River transportation was ideal for the chore, and that may have led to *Teaser*'s detail to the army.

On what proved to be an eventful Fourth of July, *Teaser* took Alexander downstream to survey the Army of the Potomac's position at Harrison's Landing. The river between the new Federal base and Richmond's outer defenses had become a kind of neutral zone, nominally controlled by Confederate forces, but susceptible to Federal probes and patrols. From Harrison's wharf on the morning of July 4, Davidson's old Coast Survey mentor, Cdr. John Rodgers, reported that the enemy was at Haxall's. "They sent up a balloon this morning, but it remained up only a few moments. The *Monitor* and *Maratanza* will make a reconnaissance this evening in that direction."[11] Those two vessels managed to make the promised reconnaissance hours earlier, and the effect of their promptness proved disastrous for Hunter Davidson.

The Confederate aircraft carrier started downstream around 2:00 a.m., and "an hour or so before day" Alexander ascended from her deck. "About 9 AM the wind rose so that we had to exhaust & fold up the Balloon, & on [Davidson's] proposal, I agreed to go with him down the river nearly to City Point where we

10 Gary Gallagher, ed., *Fighting for the Confederacy: The Personal Recollections of General Edward Porter Alexander* (Chapel Hill, NC, 1989), 116-117; Alexander to father, July 24, 1862, in Judith Anthis and Richard M. McMurry, "Rebels in the Sky: The Confederate Balloon Corps," *Blue and Gray Magazine* (Aug. 1991), 22. Some secondary works claim incorrectly that all of Alexander's ascensions were made from *Teaser's* deck. See, for example, John Gutman, "The use of ships to transport balloons during the Civil War was the first example of modern-day aircraft carriers" *America's Civil War* (June 1998), 82.

11 *ORN*, I:7, 542.

Deck of the CS gunboat *Teaser* after her capture, July 1862. Photograph by James F. Gibson. *LC P&P*

could land & I could communicate with Gen Lee & the Army sooner than by returning to Richmond," Davidson wrote. Seeing Federal scouting parties on shore near Malvern Hill, Alexander asked to go ashore and capture them. About that time, *Teaser* ran aground, and could not be floated until the afternoon tide came in. Alexander went ashore to communicate with the army. "About 2 P.M. I came back and having loaded the row boat with arms, was just about pushing off to return to the Teazer when around the bend scarcely 800 yards off came the Yankee gunboat Maratanza." Alexander was able to "skedaddle" and only witnessed from the shore what happened to the *Teaser.*[12]

A newly commissioned 200-foot sidewheel steamship, *Maratanza* carried 6 guns, including a 100-pound Parrott rifle. Upon seeing the stronger enemy ship

12 Anthis and McMurry, "Rebels in the Sky," 22; Alexander's memoir (Gallagher, ed., *Fighting,* 117), differs slightly in details.

and sensing his predicament, Davidson fired a shot in apparent hopes of crippling *Maratanza*. The shot missed. *Maratanza* returned fire, and her third shot, fired from her 100-pounder, exploded *Teaser's* boiler. According to Alexander, "Davidson kindled a fire against the Magazine door and lashed down the safety valve so as to try & explode her boiler, & he & his men jumped overboard & swam & waded to shore, while the *Maratanza* showered grape & canister after them & after us in the woods and indiscriminately." *Maratanza's* commander, Lt. (later Adm.) Thomas H. Stevens, reported hours later that the *Teaser's* crew "at once precipitately abandoned her" only after the shot penetrated her boiler. Whether the explosion and fire were the result of *Maratanza's* big gun or her crew's actions, the *Maratanza* captured *Teaser* intact, along with what Stevens described as "public and private papers, and effects, even the side arms of her officers," which he forwarded with his report. He itemized some of the materials they found, including "a Confederate balloon, a quantity of submarine telegraphic wire, and other appliances for submarine batteries." James River Flotilla commander, John Rodgers, claimed the anchor, chains, and other supplies for his own use, and sent six "shells with peculiar fuzes" to Capt. John Dahlgren at the Washington Navy Yard.[13] The loss of the insulated wire—a resource that had made possible Maury's electrical torpedo work and was difficult to obtain in the Confederacy—was particularly damaging to Davidson's work and, potentially, his reputation.

Maratanza had gone upriver to interrupt Confederate balloon reconnaissance. She accomplished that and much more. From Davidson's perspective, it must have been a bitter irony that he lost his headquarters vessel and supplies not conducting the hazardous work of torpedo warfare but moonlighting for the Confederate army.

The loss of *Teaser* and the supplies and papers on board her was embarrassing for Davidson, both personally and professionally. According to an anonymous private letter excerpted in *The New York Times*, the haul of items captured included "officers' uniforms, swords, belts, pistols, muskets, silver, china, bedding, clothes, letters and papers," including not only the details about Confederate submarine batteries and fortifications, but also "a commission from the Confederate States Navy, running to Lieut. HUNTER DAVIDSON, formerly of the United States Navy." Midshipman Clarence Cary, who lost his own journal on the *Teaser*, wrote that Davidson lost his sword and a prayer book that his mother had given to him. Nearly 50 years later, Davidson wrote "that he would be very grateful if the fellow, who on that occasion came into the possession of the prayer book of his mother, would return it even at this late date." "Yesterday Davidson went down the River in his steamer the Teazer to reconnoiter, having onboard Maj. Alexander with a

13 *ORN*, I:7, 543, 544; Gallagher, ed., *Fighting*, 117; Anthis and McMurry, "Rebels in the Sky," 24.

balloon unfortunately running aground, the enemy came up & took his vessel with the crew barely escaping to the shores," John Taylor Wood confided to his wife in a July 5 letter. "[H]e lost everything, $200 in money clothese [*sic*] &c, but what is far worse all his papers, which will inform the enemy of the submarine batteries, their position &c. Davidson for some time has been engaged on the duty of placing them in the River, ready to blow the Yankees up. Really our little Navy seems doomed. They got his wifes [*sic*] letters also & I should not be surprised if some of them were soon published."[14]

Mary Davidson's letters were not published, but Federal officers enjoyed reading them. A description of their content provides rare details about the Davidsons' marriage. Davidson's wife "addresses him as 'My Splendid Hunter,' & goes on to say that 'you thought I never was good for anything but to spend money, now I want to tell you that I am making up that lawn dress I bought in Richmond to prove that I can do something else when I set out," chortled Paymaster Keeler of the *Monitor* in a letter to his own wife. "She tells him that she has sent him a tin pail filled with fried chickens & butter, a delicacy she thinks he hasn't tasted in a long time but wants him to be sure to return the pail as she was obliged to borrow it & as no more are to be had there a fuss will be made of it if is not returned." Keeler also described Davidson's minutely detailed plan for capturing *Monitor* (see Chapter 3) and diagrams showing the locations of the submarine batteries that Matthew Fontaine Maury had placed in the river.[15]

Possibly with Davidson's acquiescence or inspiration, Richmond newspapers sought to minimize the severity of the loss. "The capture of the gunboat Teazer, mentioned by us Saturday morning, will not prove much of a gain to the Yankees," reported the Richmond *Daily Dispatch* on July 7. Riddled with errors, the account had the *"Teazer"* (a common misspelling) running ashore just before encountering the U.S. steamer *Mustang* [*sic*]. Unable to get his ship afloat, Davidson felt compelled to abandon ship. "The Teazer was fired, and all hands got into the boats and pulled for shore. A terrific fire was opened on the boats from the guns of the Mustang, but without effect, though the shot ploughed up the water in every direction around the escaping crew." Only then, reported the *Dispatch,* did powder aboard *Teaser* catch fire and explode. "Capt. Davidson had destroyed her log and signal books, and everything valuable on board, before leaving her." The article praised Davidson as "one of the best officers" in the pre-war U.S. Navy,

14 *NYT*, July 10, 1862; Cary, *War Journals* quoted in James Morris Morgan Papers, LC; Davidson, "Correspondence," *Journal of the United States Artillery*, 32:94; Wood to "My darling Wife" [Lola], Drewry's Bluff, July 5, 1862, Wood Papers.

15 Daly, ed., *Aboard the U.S.S. Monitor,* 182.

but, inexplicably, mangled his biography as a Confederate officer: "He was on the steamer Jamestown in the memorable Merrimac engagement, and was afterwards transferred to the Merrimac."[16]

Accounts soon appeared in northern newspapers that revealed the extent of the *Dispatch's* creative fiction. A Washington, D.C., paper on July 8 reported that "Documents of great value were found on board the Teazer. They consist of papers showing the rebel plan of operations, and other matters of the utmost importance." A private letter, presumably from an officer of the *Maratanza,* dated July 5, appeared in several papers beginning in mid-July: "The officers and crew, after firing their gun, jumped into a small boat, taking with them their flag, but our second shot frightened them so they jumped out again, leaving everything behind. We got the officers uniforms, swords, belts, pistols, muskets, silver, china, bedding, clothes, letters and papers; among the latter a full description of all the fortifications at Drury's Bluff and a diagram of all the fortifications. We also found a balloon made of silk dresses and a commission from the Confederate States Navy, running to Lieut. Hunter Davidson, formerly of the United States Navy." *The Memphis Union Appeal* described in detail "complete and elaborate drawings of the Monitor, and a contrivance to be used in capturing her." The *Appeal* also claimed that the papers detailed the progress on the "*Merrimac 2*"—the Confederate ironclad that would become the CSS *Richmond.* In its July 16, 1862, issue, *Harper's Weekly* published conjectural drawings of that vessel based on the captured documents.[17]

Even allowing for error and exaggeration, there is no doubt that Davidson left behind at least a few important documents. Lieutenant Stevens of *Maratanza* enclosed in his official report Matthew Fontaine Maury's June 19, 1862, report on his torpedo operations and Davidson's June 20 orders to succeed him. Maury himself noted in a July 6 letter to his kinsman and confidante Franklin Minor that "The Yanks have got the Teazer & the plans of all the mines that you made."[18]

Perhaps because Davidson lost *Teaser* when he was on detail to the army, his naval superiors did not punish him, and personal embarrassment was the only price he paid for the incident. Davidson requested a court of inquiry. Secretary Mallory responded that "The Department does not deem an enquiry as to the

16 *RDD*, July 7, 1862.

17 *Louisville Daily Democrat,* July 15, 1862; also appeared in *Sacramento Weekly Union,* Aug. 16, 1862, attributed to the NY *Times*; also in *New England Farmer* [Boston], July 19, 1862; *The Memphis Union Appeal,* July 23, 1862; *Harper's Weekly,* July 26, 1862, 1.

18 MFM to Franklin Minor, July 6, 1862, MFM Papers. The loss of the plans compelled the relocation of the torpedoes. Based on intelligence he had received, the commander of the U.S. Navy's James River Flotilla reported to Navy Secretary Gideon Welles in September 1862 that "The torpedoes placed in the river have been entirely changed since the capture of the *Teaser.*" *ORN,* I:8, 69.

loss of the *Teaser*, by a court, necessary, nor does it attach blame to yourself, your officers or crew in consequence thereof. Your conduct under the circumstances was judicious and creditable to the service."[19] With McClellan's army holed up at Harrison's Landing, unwilling or unable to begin operations from its hard-won new base, Davidson could return to his work defending the James River.

The Submarine Battery Service

Much to Davidson's consternation, inter-service rivalry complicated his plans. On June 18, 1862, two days before Davidson's own appointment to succeed Matthew Fontaine Maury, the Confederate Army Adjutant and Inspector General's Office assigned Brig. Gen. Gabriel Rains "to the charge of the submarine defenses of the James and Appomattox Rivers." The general commanding troops (R. E. Lee) and the Engineer, Ordnance, and Quartermaster bureaus were to assist him. The order did not mention Maury, Davidson, or the Confederate Navy.[20] Gabriel Rains and his torpedo work were a thorn in Davidson's side that mortified his flesh and festered in his soul during the war years and for the remainder of his life. Davidson's disdain for Rains and his torpedoes grew into an obsession after the war.

Born in New Bern, North Carolina, in 1803, Gabriel James Rains graduated 13th in the U.S. Military Academy class of 1827. Among his West Point contemporaries were Jefferson Davis, Joseph Johnston, Robert E. Lee, and Leonidas Polk. Subsequent service together on the frontier deepened his friendship with Davis. As early as 1840 when he was serving in the Seminole War (the same year that Davidson's father died in Florida serving in the same campaign), Rains experimented with sub-terra torpedoes—essentially landmines. His work was well known enough that his former U.S. Army brethren guessed correctly that Rains was the man responsible for sowing sub-terra torpedoes into the Confederate earthworks at Yorktown and Williamsburg that killed numerous Federal soldiers in May 1862. Those landmines caused outrage among the northern public and high command. Gen. McClellan denounced them as "murderous and barbarous."[21]

Rains's landmines caused no small amount of outrage among the Confederate high command. Confederate officers, notably Maj. Gen. James Longstreet, shared McClellan's opinion of them. Confederate Secretary of War George W. Randolph launched an investigation into the question of whether mines were "contrary to the

19 Quoted in J. Thomas Scharf, *The Confederate Navy*, 728. The date and source of Mallory's letter is not clear.

20 *OR*, 11/3, 608-609.

21 Schiller, *Confederate Torpedoes*, 3-4; Waters and Brown, *Gabriel Rains*, 19-33.

Brigadier General Gabriel Rains has received what Davidson regarded as undeserved credit for developing and deploying submarine torpedoes. Photograph by Mathew Brady. *LC P&P*

usages of war." His conclusion was admirably judicious: "It is admissible to plant shells in a parapet to repel an assault or in a road to check pursuit, because the object is to save the work in one case and the army in the other." In contrast, "It is not admissible to plant shells merely to destroy life and without other design than that of depriving your enemy of a few men, without materially injuring him." And, in a pronouncement affecting the work that Rains and Davidson were to share: "It is admissible to plant torpedoes in a river or harbor, because they drive off blockading or attacking fleets."[22]

Through the summer of 1862, Davidson and Rains worked—apparently with little or no coordination—mining and obstructing the James River. The torpedoes that Rains deployed were much simpler and much less costly to manufacture than those that Maury and Davidson placed and managed. They consisted of metal or wooden kegs packed with small quantities of powder, anchored to the river bottom on wooden crates, and exploded on contact with what Rains described proudly as his "sensitive fuse" that exploded when contacted with a minimum of pressure. Obviously sick of hearing Rains wax on about them, Davidson later wrote that Rains was "daft on sensitive fuses, and his experiments were generally disastrous."[23] After the war, Davidson and his acolytes dismissed Rains's torpedoes as worse than useless because they were indiscriminate, as liable to destroy friend as foe, as indeed they were.

Happily, for Davidson, the overlapping command of torpedo operations on the James ended in September, and he soon received the title, the authority, and

22 *OR,* 11/3, 510.

23 Davidson. "The Electrical Submarine Mine," *Confederate Veteran* (hereafter cited as *CV*), (Sep. 1908), 16:459.

the resources he needed to pursue his work. On September 9, the Secretary of War issued orders that "Brig. Gen. G. J. Rains will turn over his submarine defenses in James River to Lieut. Hunter Davidson, C. S. Navy." A month later, the president gave Davidson command of a new Navy Department organization, the Submarine Battery Service. Simultaneously, Gabriel Rains, who had been working in North Carolina, was ordered back to Richmond to take charge of a new Torpedo Bureau situated in the War Department. Both organizations—and a Secret Service Corps created at the same time—were to be secret, and Rains also assumed titular command of the army's Conscription Bureau, probably as a cover.[24] Virginia's rivers, however, belonged to Davidson and the navy.

Davidson later described the charge he received on October 25, 1862 as "confidential instructions from the Secretary of the Confederate navy to organize a torpedo department for defence and offence under his direct authority—to form a corps of officers and men, purchase material, supplies, &c., and proceed to make experiments so as to get into active service as soon as possible."[25] Reporting directly to Secretary Mallory, the command was perfectly suited to Davidson's proven prickly personality. Although communication and coordination with line officers was obviously important, Davidson was not answerable to the successive commanders of the Confederacy's James River Squadron that operated on the James River between Richmond and Drewry's and Chaffin's bluffs.

The technical nature of his work meant that Davidson coordinated closely with the Confederate navy's Office of Ordnance and Hydrography, in which his Date of 1841 classmate, John Mercer Brooke, served, and, from March 1863 to war's end, commanded. He was also dependent on the work of the Confederacy's largest industrial establishment, Richmond's Tredegar Iron Works, which continued to produce iron tanks for Davidson's work as it had for Maury and Cheeney. Not surprisingly (and certainly not uniquely), Davidson complained privately about both Tredegar (for its tardiness) and about Brooke, whose promotion to commander "has disgusted me & almost taken away all desire I ever had to do anything gallant & meritorious as a naval officer." "Brooke is a valuable officer & has done good service in his way," Davidson confided to Catesby Jones, "but no amount of such

24 Special Orders No. 211, A&IGO, *OR*, 18, 743; Milton F. Perry, *Infernal Machines: The Story of Confederate Submarine and Mine Warfare* (Baton Rouge, LA, 1965), 31; Schiller, *Confederate Torpedoes*,5; Waters and Brown, *Gabriel Rains*, 42. I can find no primary source corroborating the simultaneity of those three bureaus.

25 Hunter Davidson, "TORPEDOES IN OUR WAR . . ." *NYS*, Mar. 28, 1897.

service should promote a man."[26] Reflecting the common enmity between line and staff, Davidson's complaint was both uncharitable (Brooke had desperately wanted a line assignment on *Virginia*) and ironic, considering how dependent Davidson was on Brooke's department and, after the war, on Brooke's assistance and advice.

Davidson's instructions from Mallory might imply that he was to be in command of a centralized torpedo department within the Confederate Navy Department. If that were Mallory's intention, such a centralized command did not come close to fruition until late in the war and under another officer. During the 22 months that Davidson commanded the Submarine Battery Service, its almost exclusive focus was the James River, the marine gateway to the Confederate capital. It also planted three 150-pound tanks in the Rappahannock River below Port Royal in the fall of 1862. Those tanks had to be removed after the Army of the Potomac, now under command of Ambrose E. Burnside, crossed the Rappahannock to assault Lee's army at Fredericksburg in December 1862, and an African American disclosed the torpedoes' location. The Confederates apparently replaced those torpedoes, as Davidson's electrical specialist subsequently made at least two trips there later in 1863 and 1864 and a May 1864 Federal raid reportedly exploded three torpedoes and raised two.[27]

Far from being centralized under anyone's control, Confederate torpedo warfare was virtually a free-lance operation—developed and sponsored by geographically diverse navy and army officers and private entrepreneurs. During the war, the Confederate States Patent Office granted at least seven patents for inventions related to torpedoes. The first torpedo to sink an enemy warship in combat was the work of a couple of inventors encouraged by a navy lieutenant. On December 12, 1862, the USS *Cairo,* an armored gunboat, struck a contact torpedo in Mississippi's Yazoo River and sunk without loss of life.[28]

26 Davidson to Jones, Oct. 25, 1862, CSN Area files, RG 45, NARA. This paragraph was omitted in the version published in *ORN*, I:7, 61.

27 R. O. Crowley, "Making the 'Infernal Machines': A Memoir of the Confederate Torpedo Service, *Civil War Times Illustrated* (June 1973), 26 [reprint of "The Confederate Torpedo Service" from *Century Magazine,* (June 1898)]; vouchers dated Mar. 30, 1863 and May 4, 1864 in CSN Subject files, RG 45, NARA; Mallory to Davidson, Jan. 6, 1863, which Davidson delivered to Lee; Lee replied on Jan. 22, RG 109, Chapter 8, volume 8, NARA; Crowley receipts dated Mar. 24, 1863 for inspecting torpedoes on the Rappahannock and May 4, 1864 for "expedition to Rappahannock River," CSN Subject files; report of Alonzo Draper, May 15, 1864, in *OR,* 37/1, 71-72. Crowley's Mar. 24, 1863, inspection trip may explain John Taylor Wood's letter of the same date to Catesby Jones stating that "Davidson is about starting on an expedition to the Chesapeake." *ORN,* I:9, 863.

28 H. Jackson Knight, *Confederate Invention: The Story of the Confederate States Patent Office and Its Inventors* (Baton Rouge, LA, 2011); Perry, *Infernal Machines*, 32-34; Edwin C. Bearss, *Hardluck Ironclad: The Sinking and Salvage of the Cairo* (Baton Rouge, LA, 1966).

By the time Davidson received his welcome new orders from Mallory, he had acquired a new headquarters vessel, the CSS *Torpedo,* and a new assistant, R. O. Crowley. Both proved vital to the success of his new command.

Torpedo was a screw steamer of unknown origin, 70 feet in length, 16 feet in beam, and a depth between six and seven feet. Her battery consisted of only one or two guns, but they were 20-pounders (Parrott rifles, according to Crowley), heavier than those on the ill-fated *Teaser.* Surviving crew lists suggest she was in service as early as July 1862, so she was adapted for the use of the Submarine Battery Service, not built for the service.[29]

Roy O. Crowley—R. O. Crowley in all Civil War records—received orders on September 8, 1862, to report to Hunter Davidson. His pay was $1,800 as an electrician. He never enlisted in Confederate service, and his name does not show up on lists of men assigned to the *Torpedo* or to the Submarine Battery Service. His relationship with the navy apparently was contractual, and he was paid and reimbursed for expenses he incurred from the navy's appropriation for submarine batteries.[30]

Born in Virginia in October 1834, Crowley established his reputation as a telegraph operator and energetic entrepreneur. In late 1852, the 18-year-old Crowley was an operator for the Lynchburg and Abingdon Telegraph Co. He announced the opening of a new office in Richmond and was "prepared to transmit dispatches with great regularity and promptness." Throughout the 1850s, Crowley extended his telegraph business to other Virginia cities and towns and was elected chief operator in Petersburg. He established his own business, R. O. Crowley & Co., Contractors and Builders, based in Richmond. The beginning of the war found him "out of employment in consequence of the inactivity of trade and commerce in Richmond" and applying for a clerkship in the Confederate Treasury Department.[31]

According to their narratives of events, Crowley and Davidson embarked immediately on experiments that resulted in a new and significantly improved system of electrical torpedo defenses. In the process, they disparaged the accomplishments of Davidson's torpedo mentor, Matthew Fontaine Maury. "Expensive and laborious

29 U.S. Navy Department, Naval History Division, *Civil War Naval Chronology* (Washington, D.C., 1971), vol. VI, 317; *ORN,* II:1, 307.

30 Mallory to Crowley, Sep. 8, 1862, CSN Subject files; documents in Confederate Papers Relating to Citizens or Businesses, RG 109, M346, NARA (hereafter cited as CBF).

31 Crowley's birth and death dates from Hollywood Cemetery burial records (URL: https://tinyurl.com/32tc44vt); *RDD,* Dec. 22, 1852, and Nov. 22, 1856; *Richmond Whig,* Mar. 2, 1858; P. H. Aylett endorsement for Crowley in Crowley file, CBF.

experiments were made to determine the effect of gunpowder at different depths of water," Davidson explained in the New York *Sun* in 1897 (a month before the publication in the same newspaper of his Hampton Roads account). "The galvanic batteries were designed so as to be efficient, portable, and quickly brought into service, to accomplish which was the greatest practical difficulty met with, for, when I took charge, the means of explosion known to us then were entirely too crude and clumsy to be of practical use."[32]

A year after Davidson published his recollections of his submarine work, Crowley authored an article for *Century Magazine* that echoed Davidson's criticism of the system they inherited and described in more detail the work that he and Davidson conducted to refine and improve Confederate electrical torpedo defenses. "The experiments made under the supervision of Captain Maury consisted of placing a series of hollow spherical shells of iron, containing about fifty pounds of powder, and extending across the bottom of the river, and connecting them electrically by insulated copper wires leading to galvanic batteries on shore," wrote Crowley. "Experiments soon demonstrated, however, that fifty pounds of powder from ten to fifteen feet of water would scarcely do any harm; and very soon the whole plant was entirely disarranged, the wires broken, and the shells lost, by a heavy freshet in the river."[33]

Funded by the Navy's "Appropriation for Submarine Batteries," Davidson and Crowley purchased the supplies and labor they needed for their experiments and to administer a small bureaucracy. They purchased not only boiler tanks and other iron products from Tredegar Iron Works, but also fixtures from Arnold & Fiske and Ettenger & Edmond; carbolic acid from R. E. Dupuy, sulfuric acid from W. Peterson & Co. and from Dove & Co., and bichromatic potash from R. W. Powers; metal from Union Manufacturing Company; hardware and tools from John N. Van Lew (brother of the famous Unionist spy Elizabeth Van Lew), W. S. Donnan, and John Henry; and sundry supplies and services from inventor and torpedo entrepreneur Robert Creuzbaur, Robert Reims, and others. No bureaucracy is complete without paperwork, so their expenditures also included record books, paper, pencils, pens, ink, and charges for messages sent and received via the Southern Telegraph Company. Vouchers for their work suggested that the precise name of Davidson's department was a matter of small concern: occasionally Submarine Battery Service, it was also called the "Submarine Battery Party" and the "Submarine Battery & Telegraph Service," which was probably the most

32 Davidson, "TORPEDOES IN OUR WAR . . ." *NYS*, Mar. 28, 1897.

33 Crowley, "Making the 'Infernal Machines'," 24-35.

accurate name given the background and work of R. O. Crowley and the number of telegraph operators on the payroll.[34]

In the cabin of the "small but swift steam-tug called the *Torpedo*," Crowley wrote, he and Davidson "studied, planned, and experimented for months with various fuses, galvanic batteries, etc., and finally we determined on a system." First, they devised new sensitive fuses on which "depends entirely the certainty of the explosion." Tredegar manufactured torpedo tanks of half-inch boiler iron. A screw plug filled the hole through which the powder was poured and into that plug were placed two wires to connect with the electrical battery. Further experiments revealed defects that broke the connections and caused the tanks to send their explosive force downwards. "We experimented for a long time with tanks of various sizes, and at various depths of water, and finally decided that a tank containing two thousand pounds of cannon-powder was sure to destroy utterly a ship of any size at a depth of not more than thirty feet." According to Crowley, their operations suffered from shortages of powder, insulated copper wire, fine-gage platinum wire, and of battery material, especially acids, which they had to scrounge from druggists. Conspicuously failing to mention the loss of such wire on the *Teaser*, Davidson noted that "insulated wire had to be procured from the North or from Europe, at great trouble and expense, through the blockade."[35]

On October 25, 1862, the day that he assumed formal command of the Submarine Battery Service, Davidson offered something of a progress report in a letter to Catesby Jones. "I am getting on slowly here with the submarines," Davidson wrote with obvious pride. "I shall soon have about 12,000 pounds powder down at different stations on the river. My late experiments prove that powerful galvanic batteries can be relied on to act with unerring certainty at the distance of a half mile under water. This is the way we should obstruct all our rivers if sufficient powder can be got. I don't believe you can find a Yankee to risk a blowing up."[36]

Tests conducted on November 14 vindicated Davidson's confidence, and the results even exceeded expectations. Working with tanks filled with 75 and 200 pounds of powder that had been placed in the river five months before, Davidson and Crowley connected them using insulated wire to a new type of galvanic battery located more than a half mile away. "Over the 75-pound tank I moored a 10-ton sloop, and in two and one-half seconds after the closing the galvanic circuit by

34 Vouchers and receipts in CSN Subject files.

35 Crowley, "Making the 'Infernal Machines'," 26; Davidson, "TORPEDOES."

36 Davidson to Jones, Oct. 25, 1862, *ORN*, I:7, 61. This was the same letter that Jones had requested from him regarding the battle of Hampton Roads.

connecting the wires from the battery the tank exploded, completely destroying the boat and throwing a column of water 30 feet in diameter about 45 feet high," Davidson reported to Mallory." The explosion of the 200-pound tank was even more impressive. Davidson concluded that "any ordinary sized gunboat or other vessel would have been sunk or destroyed when within 30 feet of the center of the column." What Davidson dubbed "the Crowley-Boynton galvanic battery" was "a vast improvement" over the Wollaston batteries that Maury had used, "and enables us to operate at any point with little expense or trouble where two men can be stationed in safety." Those experiments laid the foundation for their torpedo defenses on the James.[37]

Crowley described one of the stations that the Submarine Battery Service established along the banks of the James. Two tanks containing 1,000 pounds of powder each were submerged in 12 feet of water and connected by wire to galvanic batteries on shore. The batteries were

> concealed in a small hut in a deep ravine. From that battery-house the wires were led to an elevated position near by, where the man in charge could keep a lookout for passing vessels. The position of the torpedoes in the water was indicated by two sticks, planted about ten feet apart on the bluff, and in a line with each other and the torpedoes; and the watchman's instructions were to explode them by contacting the wires as soon as the enemy's vessel should be on a line with the two pointers. All this being prepared, we awaited the approach of a Federal gunboat.[38]

The course of military events in Virginia gave the Service nearly two virtually uninterrupted years to perfect the James River defenses. McClellan's Army of the Potomac left its base at Harrison's Landing in mid-August 1862 after Robert E. Lee sent a corps of his Army of Northern Virginia to confront Maj. Gen. John Pope's newly organized Army of Virginia approaching Richmond from the northwest. Lee then sent his entire army against Pope and routed it at the battle of Second Manassas, then crossed the Potomac River into Maryland. Although Lee's invasion of Maryland ended in defeat at the battle of Antietam (Sharpsburg) on September 17, the campaign succeeded in shifting the front from the James to the Rapidan and Rappahannock rivers, where it remained—with the obvious exception of the Gettysburg Campaign—until May 1864.

37 *ORN*, I:8, 848-849.

38 Crowley, "Making the 'Infernal Machines'," 26.

The only known images of Davidson's Submarine Battery Service stations along the James River were taken after Union forces overran them. *LC P&P*

The Submarine Battery Service's theater of war was limited to a stretch of the James downriver from Richmond's outer land defenses anchored at Drewry's Bluff on the right (south) and Chaffin's Bluff on the left (north) banks to City Point, where the Appomattox River flows into the James. Between those points the river flows as often north to south as it does west to east and features a series of tight loops. The effect is that the distance from Chaffin's Bluff to City Point by river is more than twice the distance on a straight line. The 1855 map of the river created by a party of the U.S. Coastal Survey shows its width between 1/8 and 1/3 mile and its depth at low water from 13 to 42 feet. A bar at Trent's Reach was a mere 8-1/2 feet at low water.[39]

Inventing, testing, and perfecting the torpedoes, fuses, and batteries was clearly the most important work of the Submarine Battery Service, but Davidson's charge also involved creating an effective organization. As chief of the service and commander of the *Torpedo*—for which he wore the functional title of "captain"—Davidson was responsible for acquiring supplies, recruiting and overseeing personnel, establishing procedures, and other aspects of administration for two distinct, but interrelated, commands. "It was," Davidson wrote, "a complete

39 "Preliminary Chart of JAMES RIVER Virginia from Richmond to City Point," prepared under direction of A. D. Bache, Superintendent of the Survey of the Coast of the United States, 1855. https://archive.org/details/dr_preliminary-chart-of-james-river-virginia-from-richmond-to-city-point-inc-13079000.

organization in every essential part, having a body of officers and men carefully selected for their character and intelligence, with relative rank and duties assigned them." Several of the men were from the surrounding neighborhood, suggesting that proximity must have been another criterion. The men of the Submarine Battery Service lived at their torpedo stations, so Davidson established storehouses "at suitable places for torpedo supplies, and a store vessel was anchored in the James River, with provisions and clothing, in charge of the paymaster." No doubt under the supervision of R. O. Crowley, telegraph lines connected the stations with each other and with the office of Secretary Mallory in Richmond.[40]

The screw steamer *Torpedo* was Davidson's headquarters vessel, but it was also a commissioned warship in the Confederate States Navy. In addition to Lt. Commanding Davidson, she had on board other officers, including an acting master, an assistant engineer, a quartermaster, several gunners, multiple seamen and ordinary seamen, cooks, and ship stewards, and several specialists—firemen and coal heavers—who served aboard Civil War era steamships.[41] Surviving lists suggest that there was no overlap between men assigned to *Torpedo* and those enlisted in Davidson's Submarine Battery Service, but the events of May 1864 reveal that at least one officer on the *Torpedo* participated actively in the work of the Submarine Battery Service.

Because theirs was a new mode of warfare not widely recognized as within the commonly understood rules of civilized warfare, the men who enlisted in the service assumed the same kind of risks that partisan rangers did. Just as Col. John Singleton Mosby's men carried papers identifying them as members of a legitimate military unit, so, too, did the men of the Submarine Battery Service carry special enlistment articles. Enlistees agreed to do their service "loyally and faithfully," obey "all lawful orders" issued by their superiors, and "Under no circumstances now, or hereafter, to make known to any one, not employed in this service, anything regarding the methods used for arranging, or Exploding its submarine batteries, excepting only by permission of the Hon. Secy of the Navy or the Commd officer of said service."[42]

As armies were converging on Gettysburg, Pennsylvania, and Maj. Gen. Ulysses S. Grant was tightening his grip on the Confederate garrison of Vicksburg, Mississippi, Davidson's torpedo work came to a brief halt. A year after the *Teaser* was captured while on detail to the Confederate Army, Davidson's new headquarters

40 Davidson, "TORPEDOES."

41 Consolidated muster rolls of the C.S.S. *Torpedo,* 1862-1864, in *ORN,* II:1, p. 307.

42 *ORN,* I:10, 11; facsimile of articles reprinted in William J. Morgan, "Torpedoes in the James," *The Iron Worker* (Summer 1962), 26:9.

vessel spent the Fourth of July 1863 on a diplomatic assignment. Navy Secretary Stephen Mallory assigned Davidson and *Torpedo* to transport Confederate Vice President Alexander Stephens and Confederate Commissioner of Exchange Judge Robert Ould down the James to Hampton Roads. At Fort Monroe they hoped to obtain permission to proceed to Washington, D.C. and communicate directly with President Abraham Lincoln concerning the moribund prisoner exchange cartel. Davidson received the orders on July 2. "At noon on the 3rd she started down the James River, hoisting and bearing a flag of truce after passing City Point," Stephens reported to Davis on July 8. *Torpedo* arrived at Newport News about 1:00 p.m. on the 4th.[43]

Over the next two days, Stephens sought direct communication with Lincoln—to deliver personally a letter from the Confederate president to the United States president—while Federal authorities used bureaucratic channels and the chain of command to frustrate Stephens's scheme. Admiral Samuel Phillips Lee, commander of the U.S. Navy's North Atlantic Blockading Squadron, acknowledged Stephens's request, but denied permission to proceed any further. Finally, on July 6, the official response came from Secretary of War Edwin Stanton through the Federal agent for exchange of prisoners that Stephens's request was "inadmissible" because "customary agents and channels" were "adequate" for such negotiations. *Torpedo* turned around and arrived back in Richmond on July 8.[44]

"A Yankee to risk a blowing up"

A month after this predictably frustrating diplomatic interlude, Davidson found a Federal vessel willing to risk being blown up. The ship was *Commodore Barney*, a 143-foot sidewheel steamship built as a ferry boat and converted into a warship carrying five guns.[45] She was one of four warships and an army transport that made a spontaneous reconnaissance up the James River in early August at the request of Maj. Gen. John G. Foster. Anchoring at Jamestown Island on the night of August 5-6, the flotilla proceeded upriver at first light and was six miles

43 *OR*, II:6, 94.

44 *OR*, II:6, 79-80, 84, 94; Alexander H. Stephens, *A Constitutional View of the Late War Between the States . . .* (Philadelphia, 1868), vol. II, 566. A month later, Davidson submitted a voucher for $1,617.75 "for expenses incurred in taking his excellency Vice President Stephens and suite down the James River to Newport News on board the steamer Torpedo by order of the Secretary of the Navy." CSN Area files. Stephens's mission and Davidson's auxiliary role in it received enormous press coverage—by far the most ink ever devoted to Hunter Davidson.

45 *ORN*, II:1, 62-63.

beyond Dutch Gap when the ships (except the monitor *Sangamon* which low water compelled to anchor at Dutch Gap) confronted Davidson's torpedo defenses.[46]

On August 6, 1863, Davidson reported to Mallory that "the enemy's squadron, consisting of one monitor iron clad and two wooden gunboats, proceeded yesterday afternoon rapidly up this river, shelling both banks indiscriminately on their way, and attempted to pass our lower submarine battery, near Cox's wharf; but as the leading gunboat came over the position, one of our tanks was exploded near her with effect, ripping off heavy timbers, careening the boat so as to throw nearly everything overboard from her spar deck; and, from the quantity of gun-gear picked up, I think her pivot gun also, which, no doubt, enabled her to right herself, as she was seen to disappear for a moment or so in the commotion of the waters." Davidson read the available tea leaves to conclude that the torpedo attack succeeded at least in part: "shrieks and cries could be heard a long distance," suggesting great panic; none of the other ships passed her to come upstream, suggesting that the explosion arrested the fleet's progress; and witnesses heard hammering and repairing all night from downriver at Dutch Gap, suggesting the ship was badly injured.[47]

Davidson's report was necessarily vague and written in the passive voice because he was not present for the explosion. "I was almost always near by, but on that day I was in bed with bilious fever, and rode to the station *en déshabillé* [a state of undress], hoping to arrive in time," he recalled in his 1897 article. "The officer in charge of the torpedo station had the 'buck fever,' and fired the torpedo from sheer nervousness, and when I arrived at the station half naked, from a bed of illness, he could hardly speak."[48]

Davidson was not the only Submarine Battery Service who was absent for what should have been their golden opportunity to prove their value. "As was usually the case," Roy Crowley recalled drolly, the Federal fleet "came when we least expected, on a beautiful clear day, when our entire force except the man stationed as lookout was absent in Richmond, preparing other war material."

> We were apprised by telegraph of the rapid approach of the gunboat, and immediately hastened toward our first station; but we arrived too late. The man in charge had not seen the United States flag for a long period, and never having previously seen a gunboat so near, lost his presence of mind, and fired one of

46 *ORN*, I:9, 146-147.

47 *Richmond Enquirer*, Aug. 11, 1863, reprinted in *Charleston Mercury*, Aug. 14, 1863.

48 Davidson, "TORPEDOES."

The failure of the Submarine Battery Service to sink the U.S. gunboat *Commodore Barney* on August 5, 1863, proved embarrassing to Davidson. Engraving from *Harper's Weekly*, Aug. 29, 1863. *NH&HC (NH-51932)*

the 1000-pound powder tanks when the gunboat was at least twenty to thirty yards distant. A great explosion took place, throwing up a large column of water to a considerable height; and the gunboat by her momentum plunged into the great trough, and caught the downward rush of a wave on her forward deck. The guards were broken away, half a dozen men were thrown overboard, and other damage to the gunboat was caused. The steamer then turned about as quickly as she could, and prepared to retrace her route down the river, after picking up the men who had been washed overboard. There as a brilliant opportunity to accomplish her total destruction by firing the remaining torpedo as she passed back over it. But alas! the man had been so astounded at the first explosion that he had fled precipitately, without waiting to see what damage had been done, and the gunboat was thus enabled to return down the river in safety.[49]

49 Crowley, "Making the 'Infernal Machines'," 26-27.

The failure to sink the *Commodore Barney* also caused consternation in the Confederate army. Brigadier General Henry A. Wise, the former Virginia governor who commanded the troops along the left bank of the river where the torpedoes were located, complained to his department commander that apparently "no competent person was left in charge" of the submarine batteries while Davidson was sick on August 5-6. From one of his colonels, he learned that at about sundown on August 5, "young Aiken, a youth of about eighteen years of age, came up and reported that he had exploded one of the torpedoes," Wise wrote. "He was in a great excitement and trepidation, and could give no clear account of the effect. Doubtless, had a competent person been at the batteries, the explosion would have destroyed one or more of the enemy's boats." Wise intimated that this was a recurring problem that needed to be addressed. "Certain it is, that, heretofore, the submarine batteries and works have not at times been guarded at all. I beg that attention may be called to this, and that more certainty of effect may be relied on in future."[50]

Modest as it was, the damage that the torpedo inflicted on *Barney* was even less than Davidson and Crowley reported. "When just beyond Cox's, two torpedoes exploded under the starboard bow of the *Barney*, producing a lively concussion and washing the decks with the agitated water," reported the expedition's commander, Capt. Guert Gansevoort. "Some 20 men were either swept or jumped overboard, two of whom are missing and may have been drowned. The engine of the vessel was partially disabled by the cutting of steam pipe and the connection of steam whistle. The *Commodore Barney* was then taken in tow by the *Cohasset*, and they came to anchor at Dutch Gap about half past seven." On the following morning, the flotilla came under artillery and small arms fire from shore. Along with the *Sangamon*, *Barney* returned fire. During this and a subsequent exchange of gunfire more than 30 shots penetrated *Barney*, including one that struck her boilers below the waterline and "disabled" her. Her commander, Acting Volunteer Lt. Samuel Huse reported that the torpedo perforated the hull on the starboard side and carried away a steam whistle that let steam out of the boiler; the crew was able to repair the damage the same night. The damage incurred by the shore fire the following day was far more extensive (though it did not result in further loss of life). *Sangamon* towed *Barney* downriver to Newport News. She went into Baltimore for repairs but was back on blockade duty at Newport News by early November.[51]

50 *OR*, 29/1, 24-25. "Young Aiken" was probably the Submarine Battery Service operator listed on a May 1864 muster role as A. M. Aikin, whose duty was "On Tel Line" and whose salary ($30 per month) was the lowest in the Service. Submarine Battery Service payroll May 1864, CSN subject files.

51 *ORN*, I:9, 147-148, 226, 258.

In his official report, Gen. John Foster inflated the number of torpedoes that exploded against the *Barney* to three. The ship was only temporarily disabled, but Foster corroborated Davidson's claim that the explosion forced the expedition to return. In the best bureaucratic tradition, Foster characterized the reconnaissance as "perfectly successful, and valuable information was obtained."[52]

"The partial success of this attempt at exploding torpedoes by electricity immediately established the reputation of the Torpedo Division," Crowley wrote 35 years later, "and created great excitement all over the South, it being an undisputed fact that but for this explosion a Federal gunboat would have been moored at the wharf at Richmond that morning, and would have captured the city."[53]

His boss nurtured a very different recollection of what he considered a failure. Davidson mourned not the failure to destroy the *Barney* as she went upriver, but the failure to let her pass and destroy the Federal monitor (the USS *Sangamon*), then use a second torpedo to destroy *Barney* as she retreated downriver. "The failure to destroy the Barney made a most unfavorable impression at Richmond, and increased the howl of my opponents against the service I was engaged in, but I was always firmly supported by Mr. Mallory, who had the greatest confidence in the success of that means of warfare, and by our mutual friend Capt. John M. Brooke, who, later on, became Chief of Ordnance, and then the Torpedo Department feared no enemy in the rear."[54]

In the subsequent 10 months, the Submarine Battery Service worked to extend and improve the torpedo defenses "Immediate steps were now taken to establish other torpedo stations at several points lower down the river, using in every instance 2000-pound torpedoes," wrote R. O. Crowley. "At our lowest telegraph station, which was located on General [George] Pickett's Turkey Island Plantation, opposite Presquile Isle, we erected a lookout tower, about one hundred feet high, from which the Federal gunboats at City Point could be seen distinctly. At Presquile Isle we stationed a scout whose duty it was to signal the man in the tower when anything suspicious occurred. . . . The lowest torpedo station was at a place called Deep Bottom, about five miles above City Point by land, but more by water." Surviving appropriation records show expenses for clearing land for telegraph on Presquile Island and for clearing land and building a dwelling

52 *OR*, 29/1, 23.

53 Crowley, "Making the 'Infernal Machines'," 27-28.

54 Davidson, "TORPEDOES."

house for telegraph operators and assistants at Signal Hill on the north bank of the James.[55]

As the Battery Service extended and improved its defenses—even before the *Commodore Barney* episode—Davidson was extremely sensitive to the issue of security. He needed to shield his stations from the prying eyes of anyone who could betray their location to the enemy. As both Confederate and Union authorities understood, the most likely sources of such intelligence were African Americans. "As there were a good many free Negroes in the vicinity of Deep Bottom, we had to do our work with great secrecy, generally planting the torpedoes at night, in a position previously surveyed by day," Crowley remembered. "At Deep Bottom we located the galvanic battery on the right bank of the river, in a pit about four or five feet deep, the top covered over with twigs and brush, and in another pit, some distance off, a place was prepared for the lookout; this pit was also concealed by twigs and brush."[56]

The Service took more extreme measures to prevent local Blacks from observing their work. On July 11, 1863, Davidson authorized payment to Crowley for "transportation of civil officers in removing free negroes from Deep Bottom in James River, by order of the Hon. Secy. of the Navy, for submarine battery purposes."[57] In late December 1863, Davidson wrote to Brig. Gen. John H. Winder, commander of the Confederacy's Department of Henrico and *de facto* chief of Confederate prisons, about four African Americans being held at Davidson's insistence in Richmond's Castle Thunder prison. Davidson explained that these men had been found "lurking without permission about the grounds now occupied by the Naval forces for Secret Service" at Deep Bottom after they were told to get out. Davidson recounted how "after much difficulty with the civil authorities and consequent delay, to remove certain free Negroes residing in the immediate locality." Davidson was certain that one of the men, William Scott, "is disloyal." Two others, named Braxton and Stephen, "are in the employ of this Scott, and were caught on the 21st inst., lurking without permission about the grounds at 'Deep Bottom,' now occupied by the Naval Forces, for secret service, and from which grounds they had been duly warned." In late January 1864, Davidson placed classified advertisements in the Richmond newspapers offering $100 for the arrest and confinement in Castle Thunder for negro boy Lewis, "the

55 Crowley, "Making the 'Infernal Machines'," 28; Invoices dated Oct. 31, 1863 and Oct. 2, 1863, in Crowley file, CBF.

56 Crowley, "Making the 'Infernal Machines'," 28.

57 Invoice dated Aug. 10, 1863, Crowley file, CBF.

son of Ellen Tyler, who formerly lived near the corner of 18th and Marshall streets, Richmond, but who is now living in the employ of Mrs J C, Petersburg, Va."[58]

African Americans were not the only threats to security. In early November 1863, newspapers south and north reported the arrest and imprisonment of J. W. McBroom (given also as McBrown), supposedly a "SUB-MARINE BATTERY SUPERINTENDENT." "Suspicions say that he had run off with a view of getting to the enemy," reported the *Daily Richmond Enquirer.*[59]

As 1864 began, family concerns piled on top of security concerns for Hunter Davidson. In early January, newspapers reported that "Mrs. Davidson, wife of Lieut. Hunter Davidson, formerly of the U.S. Navy, was captured a few days ago while crossing the Potomac in a skiff and has been committed to the Old Capitol prison. She was going to visit friends in Annapolis, Md." Commander Foxhall A. Parker, brother of Davidson's Date of 1841 classmate and Naval Academy faculty colleague, William H. Parker, reported that Mary Davidson was among a small group captured on the night of December 27, 1863, trying to cross from Virginia's Northern Neck into Maryland. Federal provost marshal Capt. Henry B. Todd reported that the captured ladies "state that they left Richmond, Va. on December 22 on papers from and with the consent of the rebel authorities to visit friends North and procure supplies and funds with the intention of returning." Despite Mary Davidson's relation to a Confederate officer toward whom Federal authorities held a particular animus, Todd recommended "their speedy return beyond our lines."[60]

Accordingly, January 25, 1864, found Hunter Davidson at Signal Hill on the James casting his eyes downriver for something other than a Yankee ship to blow up. "I am waiting down here for the next Flag of Truce," he wrote Robert Dabney Minor, "expecting Mrs. D., who tried to run the Blockade to see her fast sinking old Mother and was captured by Fox Parker." He was pleased to report that, despite reports of his wife being held in Old Capitol, she was taken to the Washington Navy Yard and was "staying with some Naval Officers family & not treated as a prisoner, except in regard to certain ground limits."[61]

58 Davidson to Winder, Dec. 30, 1863, Department of Henrico Papers, VMHC; *RDD,* Jan. 22, 1864; also, *Richmond Whig,* Jan. 22, 1864; and *Richmond Examiner,* Jan. 23, 1864.

59 *The Daily Richmond Enquirer,* Nov. 2, 1863; *Providence Evening Press* [RI], Nov. 11, 1863. Surviving official documents are suspiciously silent on McBroom / McBrown and census records yield no likely suspects.

60 *National Intelligencer,* Jan. 6, 1864; also, *AG,* Jan. 5, 1864; *ORN,* I:5, 381-382 Statement of Henry B. Todd, Jan. 3, 1864, case file #3251, Turner Baker Case files, RG 94, NARA.

61 Davidson to Minor, Jan. 25, 1864, Minor Papers. Mary's 63-year-old mother, Catharine Steele Ray, was not sinking as fast as Davidson thought. She lived until 1891. According to Steele family

The war years had been difficult for Mary Ray Davidson and her family. On January 1, 1862, she gave birth to her third son, Hunter Davidson, Jr., in Portsmouth, Virginia. A month later, while her husband was helping to prepare the CSS *Virginia* for action, Mary was "quite ill" in Norfolk and her three children were sick with scarlet fever. Presumably upon the Confederate evacuation of Norfolk, Mary and the children relocated to Oxford, North Carolina, a small town not far south of the Virginia border. Davidson visited her there in September 1862. By late October, she had settled in the village of Chester, just south of Richmond.[62]

Mary Davidson apparently remained in the Richmond vicinity for the months after her return from Federal custody—long enough to conceive a fourth son, Charles Steele, born in December 1864 in Oxford, North Carolina. In May 1864, she was close enough to her husband to forward a message on his behalf. The sparse documentary record is silent on a dubious claim attributed to Davidson shortly after the war—that Mary, "with her own hands skillfully prepared the electrical cartridges that were employed" in sensitive fuses that Davidson himself "planned."[63]

"For gallant and meritorious conduct in command of the Torpedo boat, *Squib*"

As 1864 dawned, torpedoes had become commonplace in the defense of southern rivers and harbors, and, increasingly, as *offensive* weapons. U.S. navy officers learned to expect torpedo defenses virtually anywhere their vessels went and they adopted effective countermeasures. Nevertheless, by April 1864, Confederate torpedoes had sunk five and damaged nine ships or boats in the waters of Georgia, Mississippi, Louisiana, South Carolina, and Florida.[64]

Torpedoes were especially central to the Confederacy's defense of Charleston, South Carolina, which became the focus of a years-long land and sea offensive beginning in April 1863. Beyond creating a formidable barrier of Gabriel Rains's contact torpedoes, Confederate authorities experimented with vessels capable of taking torpedoes to the Federal ships operating outside the harbor. Captain

---

correspondence, Mary's mother was not so much sick as bored and wished to see her family and obtain personal supplies. Communication from John McKee, Aug. 21, 2025.

62 Catesby Jones to John Brooke, Feb. 5, 1862, in Brooke, Jr., ed., *Ironclads and Big Guns*, 64; Davidson to Catesby Jones, Sep. 12, 1862 and Oct. 25, 1862, CSN Area files.

63 Mary Davidson to John Mitchell, undated [May 1864], John K. Mitchell Papers, VMHC published in *ORN* I:10, 633; John Barnes to Alfred Thayer Mahan, May 5, 1883, CSN Subject files. Based on this testimony, Charles Jacobs speculated that Mary Davidson may have gone north in December 1863 for the purpose of obtaining supplies for her husband's torpedo work.

64 Perry, *Infernal Machines*, 199-200.

Francis D. Lee of Gen. P. G. T. Beauregard's staff designed a torpedo ram that used a long spar to explode a torpedo against an enemy vessel. Several attempts to test the ram against the U.S. Navy's largest ship, the ironclad *New Ironsides,* failed through no fault of Lee's design. It was another kind of torpedo boat—the semi-submersible "David"—that attacked *New Ironsides* on the night of October 5, 1863, inflicting far more damage than the U.S. Navy acknowledged.[65] Most famously, the Confederate man-powered submarine boat, *H. L. Hunley,* attacked and sunk the USS *Housatonic* off Charleston harbor on the night of February 17, 1864, sinking herself and killing her eight crew members in the aftermath of the attack.

Not surprisingly, Davidson was interested in deploying an offensive torpedo weapon under his command. Possibly inspired by the promise of Francis Lee's project, Davidson may have begun his own preparation for an offensive torpedo a month before the *Commodore Barney* incident. In June 1863, he apparently requested assignment to the Department of South Carolina and Georgia, commanded then by Gen. P. G. T. Beauregard. On July 11, 1863, he authorized $28 in expenses incurred by R. O. Crowley for "fitting out Boat-expedition to Chesapeake Bay by authority of the Hon. Secy of the Navy." In January 1864, Davidson authorized a payment for $245 for work on a torpedo boat named the *Squib.*[66]

Built, presumably in one of the Richmond naval yards, specifically for the Submarine Battery Service, *Squib* was customized for her mission to attack Federal warships in Hampton Roads. One of the seamen on that mission, Master's Mate John A. Curtis, credited the boat "to a Richmond electrician named Crawley who took the idea to the Navy Department." Curtis described her as "thirty-five feet long over all, four feet wide, and drew, with coal and crew on board, three and one-half feet of water, with about a foot and a half freeboard." She was built of wood, but with a "cockpit" that was "protected by an iron casing, which covered the boiler and engine to protect them from the effects of small arms." Crowley—who claimed no credit for her existence—described her as only about 20 feet long with a beam of about five feet, and drawing three feet of water. He corroborated Curtis's description of her armor. "She was fitted with a small double engine amidships, and there was sufficient space in her bow for three men, and aft for an engineer, who

65 Perry, *Infernal Machines,* Chapter VII; Gray, *Nineteenth-Century Torpedoes,* 106-113, credits Robert Fulton with inventing the spar torpedo in the War of 1812 era. Lee's name occasionally appears as "Frederick" is secondary literature and even in primary sources, but contemporary autographed documents verify his name as Francis.

66 Reference card no. 1-55-536-D, NARA; Crowley file, CBF, NARA; Perry, *Infernal Machines,* 125-126, claimed that Lee's work inspired Davidson. Voucher for $245 for "Squib," dated Jan. 15, 1864, CSN Subject files.

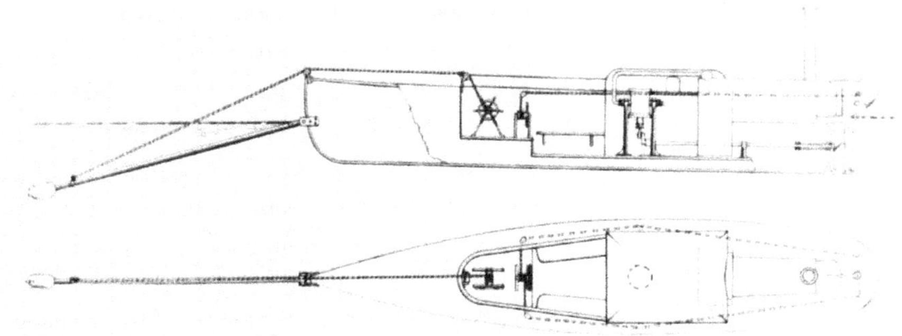

A line drawing of Davidson's custom-built torpedo boat, *Squib*. *NH&HC (NH- 108833)*

also acted as fireman. An iron shield was then fixed on her, completely covering the men from plunging rifle-shots."[67]

Squib's only armament was what Davidson described later as a "Lee-Spar-Torpedo" with 53 pounds of powder mounted on a 16 or 18 foot-long (sources vary) wooden spar. Crowley described the spar torpedo as "a formidable weapon, and one extremely dangerous to handle." He and Davidson conducted a test at Rocketts, attaching a spar carrying a copper cylinder with leaden fuses one to "a small steam launch" (possibly *Squib* herself) and "ramming" an old bulkhead at Rocketts. The first experiment failed. They tried it again with 25 pounds of powder, lowering the spar about two feet below the water level. "The effect of the explosion shattered the old wharf and threw up a column of water, completely drenching the occupants of the launch."[68]

The target of *Squib*'s torpedo was the Federal blockading squadron in Hampton Roads and, in particular, the flagship of the fleet operating there, the frigate USS *Minnesota.* She was, of course, the same vessel that the CSS *Virginia* had failed to finish off on March 9, 1862. Her commander was Lt. Cdr. John Henry Upshur, who had been one of Davidson's southern-born Naval Academy faculty colleagues who declined to resign in 1861 and son of George Upshur, the Naval School superintendent during Davidson's troubled year of schooling. According to Acting Master Curtis, the *Squib*'s mission was "to avenge the death of

67 "Built the First of Modern Boats," *The Times* [Richmond], May 29, 1900; *Richmond Times-Dispatch* (hereafter cited as *RTD*), Sep. 20, 1908; Crowley, "Making the 'Infernal Machines'," 33; the *Official Records* of the Navies offers no data for *Squib.* The *Civil War Navy Chronology* (vol. 6, 303) lists *Squib* as a steam torpedo boat 46 feet long and 6'3" at beam with a 3'9" displacement.

68 Davidson, "Electrical Torpedoes as a System of Defence.," *SHSP* (July 1876), 2:5; Knight, *Confederate Invention,* 281; Perry, *Infernal Machines,* 125; Crowley, "Making the 'Infernal Machines'," 33.

any sailor or soldier who had met death in battle[.]" Davidson himself commanded a small crew consisting of Curtis, Acting Master G. W. Smith, Acting Boatswain Thomas Gauley, First Assistant Engineer H. X Wright, First-class Fireman Charles Blanchard, and Pilot William A. Hines.[69]

"We left Richmond on April 6, 1864, conveyed down the James River by the Confederate States tug Juniluska' [*sic*] to Claremont," Curtis remembered. "Before day on the 7th we hid behind some low piles of an old wharf on the southern side of the river, just below Jamestown Island, a Federal gunboat then lying off Hog Island. At about 11 P. M. we got under way and proceeded down the James passing the gunboat, and before daylight on the 8th went into Pagan Creek and hid for the day." Stealth being *Squib*'s only other weapon, it was vital that her engine was quiet and her smoke invisible. Crowley wrote later that the more commonly available bituminous coal produced smoke and sparks. "Some one suggested that we might obtain anthracite coal by dredging at the wharves and in the docks at Richmond. This was accordingly done, and we obtained a supply of anthracite, for which an almost fabulous sum was paid."[70] The investment paid off handsomely.

At 1:45 a.m. on the morning of April 9, 1864, *Squib* approached the USS *Minnesota*. A quartermaster officer notified Acting Ensign James Birtwhistle of a boat adrift off the port beam. Birtwhistle hailed her, and the *Squib*—likely Davidson himself—replied "Roanoke." A tug, *Poppy*, had been assigned to act as guard, with her engines ready, but her engines were cold, and she was not able to run down the intruder as ordered. Birtwhistle ordered sentries to fire at the unseen boat and prepared a IX-inch rifle, but the iron shield deflected the small arms fire. "My torpedo struck the side of the Minnesota and exploded in just about one second after contact an excellent result for the fuse of the day," Davidson wrote of the incident in 1897. To avoid being sunk or damaged by the impact, Davidson had practiced "direct ramming at an angle, always stopping the engine before striking, and practicing the engineer to go full speed astern as soon as he felt the blow, without waiting for orders." The *Squib* backed off about 50 yards, then reversed, only to have her engine stall. "And there we remained—it seemed to me about forty years—under the fire of the Minnesota," Davidson wrote. "The engineer, Mr. Wright (one of the bravest and coolest men I ever knew), got the engine free again, having to feel for the different parts in the dark. The little steamer was peppered all over with bullets. Several passed through my clothes, but we got off without any

69 John A. Curtis, "The Old Minnesota. . ." *Virginian-Pilot* [Norfolk], Sep. 3, 1901; *ORN*, I:9, 604. and according to Charles Jacobs's research notes, an unnamed secret service agent.

70 John A. Curtis, "Cruise of the Squib, C.S.N.," *RTD*, Sep. 20, 1908; Crowley, "Making the 'Infernal Machines'," 33.

injury whatever. I then steered in the direction of Norfolk to throw pursuers off the scent, which proved successful." "There was hardly a square foot on the little boat not marked by a bullet," he elaborated 44 years later, "and my hat and clothes were perforated." The only damage incurred was his own broken left thumb, which happened when a close shot from *Minnesota* threw him against a metal shield.[71]

The tug, *Poppy,* which was to find and follow *Squib,* did not have her steam up and failed in her second assignment of the night. Upshur reported that the attacking torpedo launch may have gone up the Nansemond River. A small U.S. Navy expedition went up the James on April 13 and into the Pagan River to Smithfield, where they learned from black and white eyewitnesses that the torpedo launch had come up to that point the morning after the attack, then headed up the James to Richmond the next afternoon.[72]

From Turkey Island on April 11, Davidson sent a telegram with a preliminary account of his expedition. *Minnesota,* he reported, "has not sunk, and I have no means of telling the injury done."[73] Davidson was hopeful that he had inflicted considerable damage to *Minnesota.* He may have been encouraged by a preliminary intelligence report sent by Maj. James F. Milligan of the Confederate Signal Corps describing *Minnesota* as "much damaged" and having had nine guns dismounted, three ports blown into one, and her cabin torn to pieces. "She now lies off Old Point," Milligan wrote on April 13, "and they say she will never be fit for a war vessel again." Milligan's report was beyond exaggeration. On the night of the attack, Upshur assured U.S. Navy Secretary Gideon Welles that there was no indication of leakage. A thorough inspection revealed widespread damage to the ship's frame and planking and the disabling of three IX-inch gun carriages and two elevating screws. Far from being put out of action, the indomitable *Minnesota* never had to leave Hampton Roads.[74]

71 *ORN,* I:9, 93-594; Davidson, "TORPEDOES'"; Hunter Davidson, "Mines and Torpedoes During the Rebellion," *Magazine of History* (Nov. 1908), 8:259; Davidson, "Electrical Submarine Mine" *CV,* 1908.

72 *ORN,* I:9, 597, 625-626, 631. Curtis confirmed that *Squib* had hid in Pagan Creek. Curtis, "Old Minnesota" and "Cruise of the Squib." The commander of the *Poppy* earned a demotion for his failures.

73 *ORN,* I:9, 603.

74 *OR,* 51/2, 858; *ORN,* I:9, 593, 599-600. *Minnesota* remained at Fort Monroe, replaced as flagship by the *Malvern* which could more easily navigate the James. Good summaries of *Squib*'s attack on *Minnesota* appear in "Hunter Davidson and the '*Squib*'" by John Grady, posted 6/9/2014 on "The Civil War Monitor Commentary" (URL: https://tinyurl.com/tyttztdb) and Brian D. Kowell, "David vs. Goliath at Hampton Roads: The CSS *Squib* vs. the USS *Minnesota.*" *The Charger.* (Sep.-Oct. 2021). https://www.clevelandcivilwarroundtable.com/david-vs-goliath-at-hampton-roads-the-css-squib-vs-the-ussminnesota/ Kowell's article emphasizes the extensive damage inflicted on Minnesota.

From the perspective of the officers and men on *Minnesota,* the attack came frighteningly close to achieving its objective. Acting Ensign John W. Grattan, secretary to flag officer Samuel P. Lee, described his experience in a letter to his parents later that day:

> About 2.15 A.M. this morning, I was thrown out of my bunk by the concussion of an immense torpedo. . . . I immediately guessed what was the matter, as I could hear the ring of the torpedo striking the side of the ship, below the water line. The ship tottered and rolled like a small boat in the sea. The whole ship was lifted completely out of the water and came down with a tremendous jerk. . . . Every one thought the ship was sinking. . . . I looked out towards the port quarter and could see a small sigar [*sic.*] shaped steamer, about the size of the Captain's Gig, moving very rapidly towards the rebel shore. . . . I never saw such excitement and confusion before . . . The torpedo went off within 10 feet of the magazine bulkhead. The Gunner says it is a miracle that the ship [w]as not blown into a thousand atoms.

"It was subsequently ascertained," Grattan wrote in his diary, "that Hunter Davidson, formerly a lieutenant in our navy, had command of the torpedo boat and in addition had general supervision of all the torpedoes and obstructions in the James River."[75]

Despite failing to destroy her prey, the *Squib's* daring attack brought much praise to her commander. "The extent of the injury inflicted upon the ship has not yet been ascertained, but is believed to be serious," reported Secretary Mallory on April 30. "The cool daring, professional skill, and judgment exhibited by Lieutenant Davidson in this hazardous enterprise merit high commendation and confer honor upon a service of which he is a member." Taking their cue from Mallory's report, the Confederate Congress voted in June to promote Hunter Davidson to commander, retroactive to April 9, 1864. Mallory wrote to Davidson on June 16, 1864 that "the President has appointed [you] by and with the advice of the Senate a Commander in the Provisional Navy of the Confederate States for gallant and meritorious conduct in command of the Torpedo boat, *Squib,* in passing through the enemy's fleet off Newport News on the night of the 9th of April 1864 and attacking the Steam Frigate *Minnesota.*"[76]

75 Quoted in Robert J. Schneller, ed., *Under the Blue Pennant, or Notes of a Naval Officer* [John W. Grattan] *1863-1865* (New York, 1999), 82, 83, 218n.

76 *ORN,* I:9, 603; *Journal of Confederate Congress,* vol. 4, 212. By the same act, Congress also promoted H. X. Wright two grades to engineer, RG 45, NARA. In a newsy and gossipy letter about

Stephen R. Mallory, a former U.S. senator from Florida, served as a Confederate secretary of the navy throughout the war and encouraged Davidson's work on torpedo defenses. Portrait photograph, 1861-65. *NH&HC (NH-48061)*

For the rest of his life, Davidson was understandably proud of the *Squib*'s expedition. Unlike the *H. L. Hunley*, which was lost with all her crew after attacking the *Housatonic*, and, unlike U.S. Navy Lt. William B. Cushing's more famous torpedo boat attack against the Confederate ironclad ram *Albemarle* at Plymouth, North Carolina, in October 1864, Davidson brought his crew back alive on his boat and didn't have to swim to safety leaving the rest of his crew killed or captured. Despite his pride in this accomplishment, even Davidson had to concede the crucial differences: both the *Hunley* and Cushing's torpedo launch succeeded in sinking the ships they attacked.[77]

A month after the *Squib*'s attack on *Minnesota*, Federal officers got an unexpected opportunity to inspect the torpedo launch up close. Davidson had the "impudence" (sneered the *New York Herald*) to steam downriver in the *Squib* to the Federal James River flotilla under flag of truce requesting permission to meet a prisoner exchange vessel from Fort Monroe. While Davidson waited for a reply from Adm. Samuel P. Lee, officers examined *Squib* closely enough to make a drawing of her. They were all in admiration of her design and construction. Fleet Captain John S. Barnes described her to Adm. Lee as "of sharp model, moves

their mutual acquaintances in the navy, Robert Minor in Richmond wrote to Catesby Jones in Selma, AL, that "'Dave' made an attempt on the *Minnesota* not long since with his torpedo, but it failed, though it was not his fault." The letter, as published in the *Official Records*, is dated Mar. 23, 1864, more than two weeks before the *Squib* attack. Judging by the known dates of the many personnel actions referenced in the letter, it probably was written on Apr. 23. It is significant both for the perception that the *Squib*'s attack failed and for the use of Davidson's occasional nickname. *ORN*, I:9, 806.

77 Admiral David Dixon Porter credited Davidson with performing this "daring exploit, but surmised that Davidson "has, no doubt, since rejoiced that he did not succeed in sending many of his old friends and shipmates to the bottom." David Dixon Porter, *Naval History of the Civil War* (New York, 1886), 473.

rapidly under steam, and turns with great quickness. Her engine is covered with boiler iron, making a low, cupola-shaped, musket-proof house." Through Lt. Roswell H. Lamson Lee replied "that he would hold communication with no such infernal craft, and that if he appeared again he would seize him." Lamson, who had been a midshipman at the Naval Academy when Davidson was on the faculty, wrote that Davidson left in "a very bad humor that a Confederate naval officer, and a Confederate man-of-war should be so treated."[78]

Lee's indignant reaction should have been no surprise to Davidson. If his night-time torpedo attack on *Minnesota* were not enough to earn the enmity of his former U.S.N. comrades, a week before his appearance with a flag of truce he had committed another act that had made him "notorious."

"The first successful application of electrical torpedoes . . . in time of war"

The same Confederate Signal Corps intelligence sources that had declared *Minnesota* badly injured reported in mid-April a build-up of river transports at Hampton Roads, the arrival of Maj. Gen. Benjamin F. Butler, and a rumored expedition destined for the right (south) bank of the James River above the mouth of the Appomattox.[79] Those reports proved accurate. Butler, who had made himself "infamous" to Confederate southerners, primarily because of his administration of occupied New Orleans in 1862, was given command of a new force, the 30,000-man Army of the James. Moving up its namesake river on transports, the army was to disembark south of the river at Bermuda Hundred then march north to the lightly defended "back door" to Richmond. It was one of multiple prongs of the spring offensive planned by the new commander of U.S. armies, Lt. Gen. Ulysses S. Grant. Traveling with the Army of the Potomac—still under the titular command of Maj. Gen. George Meade, who had commanded the army at Gettysburg—Grant supervised the main strike: a swift move around the right flank of Lee's Army of Northern Virginia that would put the Federal army between Lee and Richmond.

78 *ORN*, I:9, 601; *NYH*, June 7, 1864. It seems irresponsible and inexplicable that Davidson chose to pay a call on the enemy in a specialized weapon of war instead of his headquarters vessel, *Torpedo* (as the *Herald* called his craft) or an unarmed steamer, but the description and drawing suggest that he did indeed come down river in *Squib*. James M. McPherson and Patricia R. McPherson, eds., *Lamson of the Gettysburg: The Civil War Letters of Lieutenant Roswell H. Lamson, U.S. Navy* (New York: 1997), 162. Davidson described Lamson as an officer "whom I knew and liked before the war . . ." *Magazine of History*, 258.

79 *OR*, 33, 1293 and 51/2, 859.

Butler's operation was apparently news to U.S. Navy Secretary Gideon Welles, who recorded in his diary on April 28 that Butler had requested ironclads and gunboats to accompany his transports. "Only four days to improvise a navy, and they are to proceed up a river whose channel is not buoyed out," Welles recorded. "The scheme is not practical, yet it has the sanction of General Grant."[80]

On May 5, 1864, Hunter Davidson sent a telegram to Mallory: "Four monitors, the *Atlanta,* 5 gunboats, 2 ironclads, 59 transports coming up the river; also 3 rafts have passed Fort Boykin." As the flotilla advanced, Davidson's men tracked their progress. Thomas H. Friend, in charge of the battery, telegraphed to "Mr. Smith" (probably Acting Master Peter W. Smith) that A. M. Bingley, a member of the Signal Corps working with the Submarine Battery Service, reports 3 gunboats in sight of Presqu'isle." "We can see no movements of the enemy this morning," Davidson wrote early on May 6, "but suppose from the sound of their drums they are marching up on the other side of the river."[81]

Even without the chastening experience of *Commodore Barney's* near miss in August 1863, the U.S. Navy was fully alive to the danger of Confederate torpedoes in 1864. After passing the confluence of the Appomattox and James River at City Point, U.S. warships shelled and demolished the Submarine Battery Service's watch tower and telegraph station at the Presquile Island station just upstream and prepared to negotiate the torpedo barrier. Protocol called for smaller vessels—essentially "mine-sweepers"—to advance ahead of the flotilla and drag for torpedoes and the connecting electrical wires. Alerted by local African Americans of torpedoes at Deep Bottom, Cdr. J. C. Beaumont of the USS *Mackinaw,* anchored and ordered two other vessels, *Commodore Morris* and *Commodore Jones,* not to advance any further. The commander of the *Commodore Jones* "disregarded the repeated orders she had been given," Beaumont explained to Adm. Lee, "ran over a torpedo, which exploded instantly and totally destroyed her." The stricken ship's commander, Volunteer Lt. Thomas F. Wade, wrote his report a week later from the U.S. Naval Hospital in Norfolk, and explained that he had been "dragging for torpedoes and covering the boats, which were also searching for them" when the torpedo exploded "causing her destruction instantly, absolutely blowing the vessel to splinters." Captain Barnes quoted an eyewitness who described the explosion lifting the *Jones* out of the water, "her wheels rapidly revolving in mid-air," after which a fountain of water shot through her. "She absolutely crumbled to pieces—dissolved as it were in mid-air, enveloped by the falling spray, mud, water, and

80 Gideon Welles and Edgar Thaddeus Welles, *Diary of Gideon Welles Secretary of the Navy Under Lincoln and Johnson with an introduction by John T. Morse,* Jr. (Boston, 1911), vol. 2, 19.

81 *ORN,* I:10, 11.

The destruction of the U.S. gunboat *Commodore Jones* was, Davidson boasted, "the first successful application of electrical torpedoes . . . in time of war." Engraving from *Harper's Weekly*, May 28, 1864. *NH&HC (NH-55305)*

smoke," Barnes wrote. "When the turbulence excited by the explosion subsided, not a vestige of the huge hull remained in sight, except small fragments of frame which came shooting to the surface."[82] As many as 69 U.S. seamen died.

R. O. Crowley's postwar account narrated the episode from the Confederate perspective. "A squadron of boats, heavily armed, went in advance of the fleet, dragging the river for wires and torpedoes. Their grapnels, however, passed over and over our wires, without producing any damage, our lookout, from his concealed station in the pit, noting all the movements of the men in the boats, and hearing every word of command." Not finding any torpedoes at the mouth of Four Mile Creek, the *Jones* sent landing parties ashore on the left bank at Deep Bottom—something that neither Beaumont nor Wade mentioned, but which Admiral Lee's clerk, John W. Grattan, included in his account. Crowley claimed that the *Jones* then steamed up to the wharf at Deep Bottom, found a torpedo station abandoned, then headed back downriver. Confederate submarine battery operators had declined to blow up the *Jones* because they had their eyes on a bigger, more symbolic, target: the *Atlanta,* a Confederate ironclad captured the previous summer near Savannah, Georgia, and now part of the U.S. flotilla. When it looked like the flotilla was turning back, the operator resolved to destroy the *Jones.* "As she retreated she passed immediately over one of the two torpedoes planted there," wrote Crowley. "All at once a terrific explosion shattered her into fragments, some

82 Crowley, "Making the 'Infernal Machines'," 28; *ORN,* I:10, 9, 15; Lieut.-Commander J. S. Barnes, U.S.N., *Submarine Warfare, Offensive and Defensive. Including a Discussion of the Offensive Torpedo System, Its Effects Upon Iron-Clad Ship Systems, and Influence Upon Future Naval Wars.* (New York, 1869), 99.

of the pieces going a hundred feet in the air. Men were thrown overboard and drowned, about forty being instantly killed. The whole Federal fleet then retreated some distance below."[83]

Davidson's own account, published in 1897, claimed that the destruction of the *Jones* benefitted from even more cunning and nuanced planning. "The fleet had on board a late servant of mine—a negro boy—who warned the officers that they were on dangerous ground," Davidson wrote.

> I was aware that the negro had deserted in the direction of the fleet, and for that reason had wires leading to the batteries on both sides of the river, believing that if the fleet cut the wires on the high left bank they would be content with that and proceed, not supposing that there was a battery with mines on the other side also, which was a swamp.
>
> My surmise was somewhat correct, for, had the battery station on the left bank been occupied, we should have been discovered, as at one time the Commodore Jones was high enough up stream to have seen into the station; she could have been destroyed minutes sooner, but we were waiting for an ironclad. The orders given on board were distinctly heard by us and it was in consequences of certain orders that the Commodore Jones was destroyed as she dropped back and over the mine.

According to Davidson's 1908 account of the incident, it was Acting Master Peter W. Smith—"one of the bravest men I ever met—who fired the torpedo.[84]

Although there was much disagreement over what *Commodore Jones* was doing when she destroyed, there was complete unanimity about her fate and its chilling effect. Quoting Hunter Davidson, the Richmond *Sentinel* reported the Jones "blown to atoms," and that, in Davidson's words, there was "'hardly a piece left as big as a row-boat.'" Lieutenant Roswell Lamson, U.S.N., described to his fiancée that the *Jones* "looks as though she *had been ground through a mill*—she was literally torn into *splinters.*"[85]

83 Crowley, "Making the 'Infernal Machines'," 28-29; Schneller, ed., *Under the Blue Pennant,* 98-99.

84 Davidson, "TORPEDOES"; Davidson, *Magazine of History,* 257. The "negro boy" may have been the runaway Lewis. In the later account, he attributed his security concerns not to a deserting "negro boy" but to a report from "our signal corps" that "some of the many negroes prowling about the region" might alert the enemy. Hunter Davidson, "The Electrical Submarine Mine — 1861-65.," *CV* (Sep. 1908), 16:457. Hunter Davidson, "Mine and Torpedo," *NYS,* Oct. 19, 1908.

85 *Sentinel* [Richmond], May 7, 1864; McPherson and McPherson, eds., *Lamson,* 162.

If there were no Federal landing parties ashore already before *Jones* met her fate, parties swarmed both shores after the explosion. The measures that the Submarine Battery Service had taken over the preceding years to conceal their stations and batteries bought some time but did not prevent the Federal landing parties from discovering the men responsible for the *Jones*'s destruction. Seeing three men running from the scene, Federals shot one and captured the other two. According to Dr. Carthon Archer, who was the attending physician for the Submarine Battery Service, a battery operator named "Brittain" feared capture and ran for a boat on shore. One of the survivors later told Archer that "if Brittain had not made the attempt to escape their hiding place would not have been discovered." Thomas H. Friend, a fellow battery operator identified the dead man as J. T. "Tom" Britton, the operator in charge of the battery. [86]

The two captured men, Acting Master Smith, and battery operator Jeffries (or Jarvis) Johnson, both of whom were residents of the area, initially refused to divulge the location of other torpedoes. Johnson feigned ignorance and claimed that he had been conscripted into service, but when Fleet Cdr. John Barnes placed him in the forward vessel dragging for torpedoes, "he signified his willingness to tell all he knew about them." The interrogation yielded information about the location and size of remaining torpedoes. Hunter Davidson later claimed that the man who was shot "was a carpenter of no torpedo importance"—a claim the muster rolls and the accounts of Archer and Friend contradict. Admiral David Dixon Porter (who succeeded Samuel P. Lee in command of the North Atlantic Blockading Squadron) later described the captured men as "'very communicative.'" "I am sure Admiral Lee thought they were, and that was just what I wanted," Davidson rejoined in 1897. "They were as good and true men as ever stepped in shoe leather, and had often been well drilled as to how much and what to say, in case of capture, for we were always much exposed. Had they been untrue the fleet could have captured me, and also destroyed the backbone of the James River torpedo defences, that same afternoon."[87]

86 Archer in *RTD,* Mar. 6, 1904, Magazine Section; Thomas H. Friend, "Torpedoes in the James," *RTD,* Mar. 9, 1904; "Monthly Pay Roll of Submarine Battery & Telegraph Service James River, Va. for the month of December 1863 / Hunter Davidson C.S. Navy, Lieut Comdg," CSN Subject files.

87 *ORN,* I:10, 10, 26-27; Davidson, "TORPEDOES"; Dr. Archer, *RTD,* Mar. 6, 1904, claimed that Smith and Johnson (the latter from Gloucester County) were "placed in irons on the deck of one of the gunboats." Upon learning of this, Davidson "demanded that they should be treated as prisoners of war" and threatened the same treatment for two Federal prisoners in his custody. "An exchange was effected and Smith and Johnson were released." Strangely, none of Davidson's accounts of the episode mentioned this bold and successful gambit, which casts doubt on its accuracy.

The man who the U.S. Navy and the northern press wanted captured was none other than Hunter Davidson, who briefly took on the *persona* of an elusive phantom. John W. Grattan recorded in his diary that, following the destruction of the *Jones,* "four men were seen running up the banks. One of them was recognized as being the notorious Lieut Davidson." Davidson was not among the men rounded up on shore. "We have had some skirmishing with the rebels along the banks which we had to clear before we could find the wires and lines by which the torpedoes are exploded," Roswell Lamson wrote his fiancé on May 17th. "I came near capturing Capt. Davidson at one of his torpedo stations." That incident may have been the basis of a report from a correspondent for the *New Bedford* [Massachusetts] *Evening Standard* that, thanks to their pickets, "Lieut. Hunter Davidson, of the Confederate States navy, has been captured, with his assistants" The correspondent paid Davidson a back-handed compliment when it identified him as "formerly an officer in the old navy, standing at the head of his date [*sic*], and the South did well in securing the services of so able an officer. Shortly before the breaking out of the rebellion he was paid by the government $10,000 for some valuable invention connected with the sciences of naval gunnery." The report of his capture was erroneous as the report of his class standing and the nature of his invention.[88] Little wonder Lee refused to meet with Davidson when he voluntarily showed himself under a flag of truce.

Although Davidson himself escaped Federal vengeance, the torpedo defenses his Submarine Battery Service had worked hard to construct did not. On May 12, Adm. Lee appointed Lt. Roswell H. Lamson to command a new Torpedo and Picket Division. Consisting initially of three ships and later expanded to nine ships, the division's charge was "to clear the river as far as possible to Richmond." According to Lee's clerk, John Grattan, Lee decided it was not "prudent to advance any further until the torpedoes were cleared out of the channel[.]"[89]

For the remainder of May, Lamson's division led the Federal fleet up the river, "clearing the river and banks[.]" "My orders were to clear the river of torpedoes, and open the way for the fleet," he boasted to his fiancée on May 24, "and I did it thoroughly up to the guns at Fort Chaffin, getting further up the river than anyone has been since the war commenced, except Commodore John Rodgers." In his May 23 report to Lee, Lamson noted that his operation included three vessels, 11

88 Schneller, ed., *Under the Blue Pennant,* 98; McPherson and McPherson, eds., *Lamson*, 164; *New Bedford Evening Standard* [MA], May 26, 1864.

89 McPherson and McPherson, eds., *Lamson,* 159-60, 178; Schneller, ed., *Under the Blue Pennant,* 97.

armed cutters, and 175 sailors, marines, and soldiers (from the 85th Pennsylvania Infantry) deployed along the riverbanks.[90]

With the assistance of an "old Negro" and often exchanging fire from Confederate soldiers on shore, Lamson's division located, raised, and disarmed dozens of torpedoes—the monster tanks that Davidson had placed as well as the smaller ones that Maury had placed and the "mechanical" torpedoes that Rains had placed. "It is quite wonderful the curious inventions they have devised for blowing up our vessels," Lamson mused with admiration as well as contempt. As did other Federal officers, Lamson judged Confederate torpedoes a more effective threat than the three ironclad rams and the other vessels of the James River Squadron. "The iron clads would be *nothing* to the infernal torpedos [*sic*] that fill the river, and of whose whereabouts we are entirely ignorant," he explained to his fiancée. "They explode some of them by pulling a trigger, and some by galvanic batteries." The galvanic torpedoes, he noted particularly "are constructed with great ingenuity and scientific skill, and when taken from the water were in as good a state of preservation when first put down, except one . . ." Acknowledging their danger, Lamson also acknowledged their value. He fashioned his own torpedoes for defense of the Federal vessels operating in the James, and even "refitted" captured Confederate torpedoes for his own use and "made a small bombproof ashore for the galvanic battery."[91]

On May 28, Lee ordered Lamson to put down obstructions in *front* of the fleet. Lamson judged his barrier to be "a good protection for the iron clads," but he also realized that "it tells the rebels we do not intend to advance at present." Indeed, the defeat of Butler's army at the second battle of Drewry's Bluff on May 16-17, in conjunction with the presence of strong Confederate batteries at Howlett's on the south side the James, had stalled the advance of the army and the navy toward Richmond. "I am sorry we cannot do more, but it would be useless for us to advance without the army," Lamson lamented on June 26, "so we can only hold the river, protect Butler's flank, and be ready to move when the time comes, which will probably not be very soon."[92] To use the popular metaphor of the day (still popular among historians), the "Beast" (Butler) had been "bottled." Shortly after, Lee disbanded Lamson's Torpedo and Picket Division, and the naval war on the James River settled into a nine-month-long period of primarily static warfare that mirrored the situation on land.

90 McPherson and McPherson, eds., *Lamson,* 164, 168; *ORN,* I:10, 92-3; *OR,*36/2, 49, 559, 745, 766.

91 McPherson and McPherson, eds., *Lamson,* 162-163, 173, 177; *ORN,* I:10, 92-93.

92 McPherson and McPherson, eds., *Lamson,* 169, 184.

Davidson and the Confederate navy were alive to the danger that Lamson's division posed. On May 15, Secretary Mallory shared a report from Davidson with Capt. John Kirkwood Mitchell, the new commander of the Confederate James River Squadron. The enemy, Mallory wrote "is slowly feeling his way to discover our submarine batteries, and that if permitted to pursue his present methodical investigation, those under Lieutenant Davidson's control will soon be discovered and captured." Davidson believed that one of Mitchell's warships would be sufficient to disrupt Federal minesweeping operations and tempt the enemy to send a warship or even an ironclad forward, where one of Davidson's torpedoes could destroy it. Mitchell could not comply with the request, however, because the Confederate army, which controlled the river obstructions at Chaffin's Bluff, had not yet opened a channel for Confederate warships. Secretary Mallory complained to Secretary of War James Seddon on May 19 that, as a result of the failure to clear the obstructions, the enemy had been "methodically sounding and dragging the river" and had "succeeded in gradually pushing back Lieutenant Davidson and his torpedo party to Chaffin's Bluff" and "captured the submarine batteries" to that point and "rendering the labors of our submarine-battery abortive." All but helpless as the Federals dismantled his work, Davidson was reduced to providing and receiving intelligence about the positions of Federal vessels as John Mitchell prepared his James River Squadron for a full-scale attack against the enemy that never came.[93]

After the war, Davidson and Crowley boasted that their destruction of *Commodore Jones* was responsible for slamming shut the "back door" to Richmond. Davidson acknowledged the importance of Butler's defeat at Drewry's Bluff, but he claimed that the support of Lee's fleet was key to the success of Butler's advance. "Certain it is that there was nothing to prevent Admiral Lee from doing so but the torpedo defences, and these, as already shown, compelled his retreat for the time." Davidson also argued that the temporary halt of Lee's fleet—a result of the shocking destruction of the *Jones*—accounted for Butler's defeat. "If Admiral Lee could have sent a few ironclads to within sight of the Bluffs, the gunners stationed on the river batteries would have been retained there. Without them at the rear, Gen. Butler could not have been repulsed, and Drury's Bluff, the key to Richmond, would have fallen that 16th of May, 1864."[94] The demonstrated difficulties that U.S. ironclads had navigating that part of the river or elevating their guns to the high bluff in May 1862 and August 1863 make Davidson's hypothetical narrative unconvincing.

93 *ORN*, I:10, 636, 645, 664-677.

94 Davidson, "TORPEDOES."

The destruction of the *Jones* "astonished the world," wrote Crowley with considerable hyperbole, "and its immediate result was the safety of Richmond from a second peril. General Butler, finding his army completely uncovered on the right wing, was unable to accomplish anything by land, and retired to Bermuda Hundred." Unconsciously echoing his adversary, Roswell Lamson, Crowley also noted accurately the dependence of naval forces on the progress of land forces. "Shortly [after the destruction of the *Jones*]," Crowley wrote, "the land forces again advanced, and compelled us to abandon all our torpedo stations below Dutch Gap."[95] Butler's advance beyond the eastern side of Dutch Gap occurred *before* the battle of Drewry's Bluff, so it was not the torpedo defenses that stopped Butler's advance.

The destruction of the *Jones* certainly made the Federal advance up the James slower and more timid. It was one of several tactical and strategic factors that prevented the success of Butler's campaign. Not the least of those other factors was the slow progress of Grant's Overland Campaign. The destruction of *Commodore Jones* figures more in the history of mine warfare than it did in the outcome of the spring 1864 campaign. It was, as Davidson never tired of asserting, the first use of electrically detonated torpedoes to destroy an enemy vessel.

The interdependence of submarine torpedoes and Confederate land defenses meant that the U.S. Navy was unlikely to challenge the torpedo barrier as long as the Confederates held Battery Dantzler (Howlett's) and outer defenses at Chaffin's Bluff. Lamson and his Torpedo and Picket Division had defanged the torpedo defenses downriver from Chaffin's, rendering Davidson's Submarine Battery Service almost superfluous.

As the opposing armies and the opposing navies settled into a prolonged fixed position warfare, Davidson's own presence along the James River had become extraneous. Already, in early June, the Confederate Army Adjutant General had assigned Gabriel Rains "to the Superintendency of all duties of torpedoes." All (army) officers and agents involved with torpedoes were to report to him. In place of the electrical torpedo barrier that Maury and Davidson had established was a mushrooming number of smaller torpedoes with sensitive fuses and torpedoes floated downstream against the Federal fleet. When Federal forces discovered a dozen torpedoes far downstream from Confederate lines in mid-July, a *New York Times* correspondent was quick to attribute them to "HUNTER DAVIDSON, arch fiend of the torpedo corps," but the floating torpedoes he described were certainly the work of Davidson's arch-rival Rains. By the end of August, Davidson had yielded command of the Submarine Battery Service to Lt. John Pembroke

95 Crowley, "Making the 'Infernal Machines,'" 29.

Jones of North Carolina, yet another Date of 1841 classmate. Davidson traveled to Wilmington, North Carolina, to meet with Maj. Gen. W. H. C. Whiting in Wilmington, North Carolina, about the use of torpedoes to defend the Confederacy's last remaining open port on the Atlantic Coast.[96]

"Nothing more of consequence took place on the James River" in 1864, wrote R. O. Crowley in 1898, "and we were transferred to Wilmington, North Carolina [in early 1865], to defend Forts Fisher and Caswell." Ostensibly, as Davidson later wrote, the Service's duties were "extended to include the whole South," but defending Wilmington and the Cape Fear became the sole focus of its efforts. With the Federal capture of Fort Fisher in January 1865 and Wilmington in February, Crowley and the other members of the Service returned to Richmond. The young telegraph operator turned electrician was in the Confederate capital in April 1865 when Union forces occupied the city. U.S. naval officers sought him out so that he could locate and help remove remaining torpedoes from the James so that President Abraham Lincoln could safely visit the conquered city on April 4, 1865.[97]

Although Davidson had surrendered operational control of the Submarine Battery Service and the James River torpedo defenses ceased to matter, the destruction of *Commodore Jones* had established once and for all the importance of torpedoes to Confederate defenses. "The submarine battery and torpedo force organized by the department under the command of Commander Hunter Davidson, has proved efficient, and an increase of the appropriation for this service is recommended," Navy Secretary Stephen Mallory reported to Congress in November 1864. "The importance of this weapon of defensive war is becoming daily more evident as experience develops means of surmounting difficulties heretofore regarded as insuperable." Mallory specifically cited the sinking of the *Commodore Jones,* which "materially retarded" and ultimately arrested the Federal ascent up the James to Richmond.[98]

Commander Hunter Davidson's next assignment was to find a way to improve and extend torpedo defenses for an ever-shrinking Confederacy.

96 *OR,* 36/3, 883; Perry, *Infernal Machines,* 165; *ORN,* I:10,737; *NYT,* July 20, 1864.

97 Crowley, "Making the 'Infernal Machines'," 30-31, 35; Davidson, "TORPEDOES"; *ORN,* I:11, 102.

98 *ORN,* II:2, 634-635. The published report is misdated Apr. 30, 1864. Because it describes not only the *Commodore Jones,* but the appointment of J. Pembroke Jones, it probably dates to August 30.

Chapter Five

Commander Davidson, C.S.N. (1864–1865)

"Commander Davidson has arrived, and I have had much conversation with him in reference to submarine defenses," Cdr. James D. Bulloch wrote to Navy Secretary Stephen Mallory from Liverpool, England, on September 29, 1864. "By his advice I shall send out a quantity of material, such as acids, zinc, copper, small chains, etc."[1] Davidson's presence in England obviously was an extension of his work for the Submarine Battery Service, but through it he entered into an entirely different realm of Confederate Naval operations.

Although no other nation formally recognized the Confederate States of America, the United Kingdom and, to a much lesser extent, France, were vital sources of material, ships, and men for the Confederate navy. So important was Europe to its operations that Secretary Stephen Mallory sent Capt. Samuel Barron to Paris in 1863 to be flag officer of Confederate Naval Forces in Europe. Barron's "Forces" consisted of dozens of officers whom the Navy Department assigned to command the ships that purchasing agents acquired from British shipyards to raid enemy commerce or to run the Federal naval blockade with desperately needed war supplies. For the nine months after his arrival in England, Hunter Davidson was immersed in the challenges of obtaining torpedo equipment and transporting it from England and Europe into one of the dwindling number of open Confederate ports.

The officer at the center of Confederate naval operations in the United Kingdom was an old acquaintance of Davidson's. James D. Bulloch and Davidson

1 *ORN,* II:2, 730.

James Dunwoody Bulloch was Davidson's shipmate on the ill-fated U.S. schooner *Shark* in 1846 and the officer who directed his activities for the Confederacy in England in 1864-65. *Scharf, History of the Confederate Navy*

had spent months together in 1846 on the schooner *Shark* and shipwrecked on the chilly and damp shores at the mouth of the Columbia River. Since that shipwrecked winter together, Davidson and Bulloch had gone their separate ways. In the early 1850s Bulloch served on a civilian mail steamer under contract to the U.S. Navy and resigned from the service in 1854 after the death of his first wife. He and his second wife settled in New York City, but his loyalties remained with his native Georgia. Bulloch offered his services to the Confederacy, and Secretary Mallory ordered him abroad in May 1861 to purchase vessels. Bulloch was the most effective of the several purchasing agents that the Navy Department sent abroad. Working with and through the firm of Fraser, Trenholm & Co. (based in Charleston, South Carolina, with offices in Liverpool), Bulloch and the other agents leveraged southern cotton as capital. He became conversant in the fine points of British neutrality laws—and how to evade them—and played a cat-and-mouse game with U.S. diplomats and consuls in Britain and British possessions in the Atlantic and Caribbean. Through his efforts, the Confederacy was able to crew, arm, and supply the commerce raiders *Florida, Alabama,* and *Shenandoah,* which, together, captured or sunk more than 134 northern commercial vessels.[2]

Beyond acquiring and outfitting commerce raiders, Bulloch was also the point man for shipping supplies between Great Britain and the Confederacy. He and Davidson evidently worked closely together in October 1864 to acquire supplies needed to deploy a system of electrical torpedoes to defend Wilmington, North Carolina, Galveston, Texas, and the few other remaining port cities. On October 20, Bulloch updated Mallory on the status of an order for torpedo wire that Mallory

2 Ibid., II:2, 83-7.

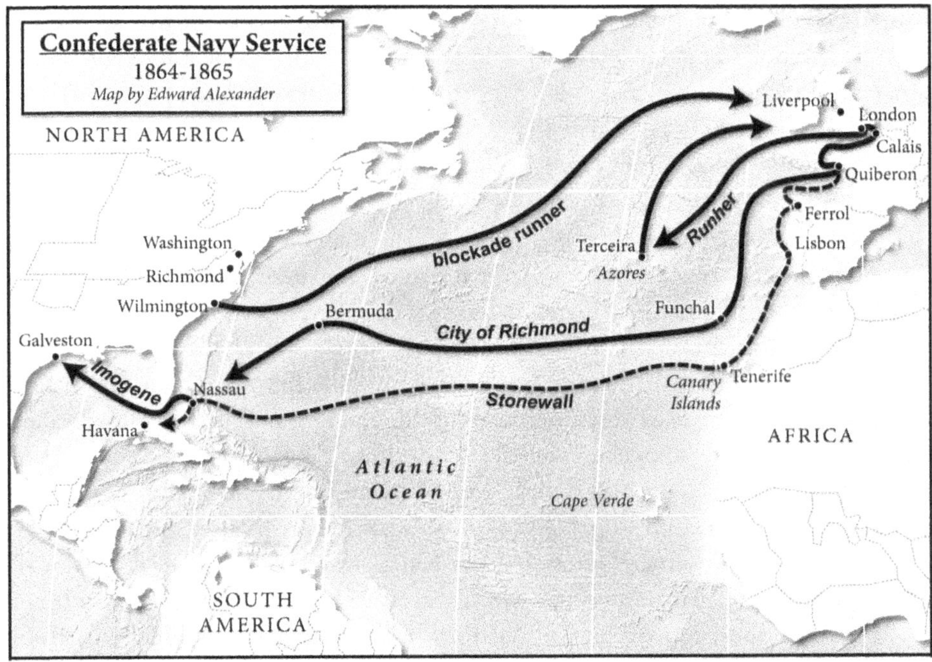

placed in April. "Having reason to believe from a conversation with Commander Davidson that this is not the wire which is required, I have suspended the balance of the order and have ordered 50 miles of such as his experience suggested to be prepared for the purpose required," Bulloch explained. Bulloch was shipping the wire along with other supplies (including three boxes from Matthew Fontaine Maury) on the blockade runner *Stag*[3]

A more substantial shipment of torpedo supplies followed several days later. On November 19, Bulloch sent Mallory invoices for goods recently "shipped on account of the Navy Department" by several specified ships. "The goods by *Runber* [*sic*: *Run Her*], *Whisper, Deer,* and *Crocodile* are almost exclusively for submarine defenses, and have been purchased at the suggestion of Commander Hunter Davidson, of which I have previously informed you," Bulloch wrote. On the steamer *Deer* were "several cases forwarded for Commander M. F. Maury; one of them marked [label] 4 contains an Ebonite machine, and with the invoice is enclosed a memorandum 'how to treat it.'"[4]

Davidson himself was aboard one of those vessels, though Bulloch did not state which. On October 24, Bulloch wrote Mallory that he was sending

3 Ibid., II:2, 735.

4 Ibid., II:2, 769. An Ebonite machine transformed vulcanite into insulated material.

"important dispatches" via Cdr. Hunter Davidson who "sails for a Confederate port via Bermuda in a day or two[.]" He also entrusted to Davidson details about other sensitive matters that he dared not trust "to ordinary conveyances." Those dispatches and details pertained to torpedo defenses and torpedo boats—much like Davidson's *Squib*—for which Bulloch, at Mallory's request, had contracted with British shipyards. "Commander Davidson will inform you of all he has said to me on the subject of submarine defenses. The material he has advised for that purpose shall be forwarded as quickly as it can be prepared." The intelligence also included details about the armament for two twin-screw steamers that a British yard was building for service at Wilmington.[5]

Neither Davidson, his cargo, nor the intelligence he carried made it into a Confederate port–at least not immediately. Surviving Confederate records shed little light on what happened, but U.S. consuls tracked Davidson's course. On October 28, the U.S. consul in London reported to Secretary of State William H. Seward about a suspicious ship, likely a blockade runner, named "Runher": 400-50 tons; paddle wheel steamer, fore and aft schooner rigged, draws 11 feet, capable of 19 knots, with her two funnels painted black. The ship was "[n]ot registered, not entered out, not on Lloyd's books, and they know nothing of her at the customs house." On November 4, the consul informed Seward that "Runher left 29th ult for Bermuda. Captain Courtney." On November 16, the U.S. consul at Fayal, Azores, forwarded information from an agent at Terceira, another island in Azores, "that on the 15th, the British steamer RUNNER, Davidson, master (of 700 tons) of and from London bound ostensibly to Bermuda, put in there for coal, she was a new iron steamer of great speed. She made the passage from London to Terceira in five days. The Bay of Angra is very narrow. The master probably presuming on the very superior qualities of the vessel ran close in and too late observed that there was not sufficient room to turn. She went onto the rocks where she down bilged and filled with water. 13,000 cases, said to be preserved meat, and some machinery have been saved." The consul added that he sent someone "to ascertain if possible the real contents of the cases saved from the "RUNNER."[6]

The wreck of *Run Her* and the waylaying of her cargo were a blow to the Confederate navy. Torpedo supplies were a high priority for Secretary Mallory. In early December, he wrote to Cdr. John Newland Maffitt (Davidson's former commander in the U.S. Coast Survey and more recently the captain of the Confederate commerce raider *Florida*) in Wilmington bound for Bermuda in the blockade runner *Owl:* "It

5 Ibid., II:2, 738, 740, 741.

6 Despatches from consul in London, Oct. 28 and Nov. 4, 1864, and from consul in Fayal, Azores, Nov. 16, 1864, Records of the Department of State, RG 59, NARA.

is desirable also that all articles for submarine purposes should reach us as early as practicable, and you will also take on board a portion of these articles."[7]

On December 24, Bulloch confirmed in a dispatch to Mallory that the *Run Her,* "by whom I made a considerable shipment of articles for submarine defenses, was wrecked in Angra Bay, Island of Terceira[.]" He added that "most of the goods were saved and have been reshipped from Angra in a small steamer called *Ruby*, under the control of Mr. Kavanaugh, agent for Mr. Merritt of Alabama." Bulloch said nothing about Davidson's involvement with the wreck of the *Run Her,* but an English crew member later identified a "Confederate Captain Davis who I know well having sailed with him in the "Run her" when she was wrecked at Terceira"[8]

Unless he made an extraordinarily speedy journey, Davidson did not accompany the trans-shipped cargo or complete his journey across the Atlantic. Instead, he found passage back to England. By New Year's Day, 1865, Davidson was back in London meeting with his submarine warfare mentor Matthew Fontaine Maury. "Davidson called. Had long talk with him about his torpedoes and James River," Maury wrote in his diary January 1. "Invited him to meet at Reeds so that I might show him how to use Mag. [probably the Magnetic Exploder] and Ebon[ite]."[9]

Three days later, on January 4, Maury recorded that he "spent the day with Davidson—showed him how to use Mag. & Ebonite. Explained to him my plan of torpedo boats and attaching torpedo by shooting bolt into the side of enemy." Maury recounted in detail Davidson's description of a test he made (time and place not specified). "He tells me he used Boynton's battery—20 cells—for exploding iron & zinc with copper connections" as well as a "porous cell" of nitric acid and sulfuric acid. Using 200 pounds of powder the test explosion knocked down spectators standing 150 yards away. Another test torpedo loaded with 50 pounds of powder and roughly a half ton of paving stones and scrap iron and lead created a destructive circle 200 yards in diameter. Davidson, Maury noted, planned to sail on Saturday the 7th.[10]

7 Emma Martin Maffitt, *The Life and Services of John Newland Maffitt* (New York, 1906), 346.

8 *ORN,* II:2, 784; deposition of William Hall, Dover, England in dispatch [#329] from Consul J. W. Morse, U.S. Consulate, London, to Seward, July 14, 1865, RG 59, NARA. The Ancestry.com Family Tree for Davidson suggests that Davidson carried the blockade runner *Deer* and her cargo safely into Wilmington and then returned to England. That is remotely possible, but stronger evidence places Davidson on *Runher.* His association with *Deer* seems to derive from Bulloch's November 19 letter to Mallory noting that Davidson suggested the purchase of her cargo.

9 Matthew Fontaine Maury Diary, 1864-65, entry of Jan. 1, 1865, LC (hereafter cited as MFM Diary).

10 MFM Diary, entry for Jan. 4, 1865, The tests described closely resemble those that Davidson and Crowley made on Nov. 14, 1862. {See pages 111-12.}

The days spent with Maury were significant. Despite Davidson's uncharitable tendency to diminish the effectiveness of Maury's torpedo work, the senior officer was continually studying and experimenting with modern technologies, especially those developed in England and Europe, and conferring with experts from other nations. Crowley and Davidson may have improved upon the Wollaston batteries that Maury had employed in the James in 1862, but Maury obtained and sent to Wilmington Wheatstones's Magnetic Exploder, then regarded as the most sophisticated electrical torpedo system available.[11] Maury's Ebonite machine was on the steamer *Deer* that ran the blockade in November and more supplies that Maury acquired likely were among subsequent shipments.

Davidson himself was to return to the Confederacy in command of the 230-foot side wheel steamer *City of Richmond*, a blockade runner owned and operated by William Graves Crenshaw. A wealthy merchant from Richmond, Crenshaw raised, outfitted, and commanded an artillery battery—the Orange Artillery—before throwing his patriotic energies and his wealth into blockade running. In February 1863, Secretary Mallory wrote to Bulloch to introduce Crenshaw, whom he described as "an enlightened merchant of large experience and views" who had gone to England "for the purpose of executing a plan for the regular transmission of Army, Navy, and other supplies to our country." Mallory urged Bulloch to avail himself of Crenshaw's services; within weeks Bulloch had dispatched with him a large quantity of uniforms and supplies for Confederate seamen.[12] In early 1865, Bulloch found another way of taking advantage of Crenshaw's largesse—and of his friendship with Hunter Davidson.

For several years, Bulloch and other agents had sought to acquire a seagoing ironclad warship. U.S. diplomacy had successfully intimidated the British and the French into preventing delivery of seagoing ironclads intended for the Confederacy. Denmark, suddenly at war with Prussia over the province of Schleswig-Holstein in 1864, claimed the French-built vessel. The war, however, was over before she could be delivered, and Denmark refused to take ownership. Bulloch seized the opportunity and purchased the ship from her Bordeaux builder. Destined to be known as the CSS *Stonewall*, she was an ironclad ram of nearly 172 feet length and 33 feet beam, drawing 14'4", and powerfully armed. Bulloch had his seagoing ironclad, but he found himself without a tender, or consort ship, to bring officers, arms, and supplies to the would-be warship. "Happily," Bulloch wrote in his memoir, "there was in London a handy unnamed steamer built for blockade-

11 Perry, *Infernal Machines*, 175.

12 Details of vessel from Stephen R. Wise, *Lifeline of the Confederacy: Blockade Running During the Civil War* (Columbia, SC, 1989), 294; *ORN*, II:2, 368, 375.

running, and the owners had employed Lieutenant [*sic*] Hunter Davidson, of the Confederate navy, to take charge of her for a proposed voyage to Bermuda, *en route* for Wilmington." That the vessel was "in charge of an officer whom I knew, and whose discretion I could trust, at once suggested her employment as the tender for our Danish ram." In a series of communications with Bulloch in the last weeks of December, 1864, Crenshaw agreed to let Bulloch use *City of Richmond* to fit out the *Stonewall* (known until her formal commissioning as *Olinde*), but emphasized that she should proceed with "as little delay as possible to Bermuda" so that she could fulfill her originally intended mission of delivering badly needed commissary stores and railroad materials to the Confederacy. Neither Bulloch, nor Crenshaw or Davidson was under any illusion that serving as tender for the *Olinde/Stonewall* would in fact delay the delivery of her cargo to the South. Davidson informed Crenshaw "that the plan and arrangements of the ship would have to be altered" to accomplish Bulloch's objective.[13]

On January 10, 1865, on the eve of *City of Richmond's* departure from London, Bulloch wrote Davidson a letter explaining the planned rendezvous with *Olinde* on the French coast. "We have conversed so frequently and fully on the subject that a formal official letter to you is unnecessary, more especially as I have no instructions to give, but simply wish to record for your future reference a few important points already discussed, and concerning which I think we are in perfect accord." Approaching the rendezvous point in Quiberon Bay from different countries, both ships were subject to detention by authorities as well as winter storms in the channel and the danger of seizure by the U.S. warship *Niagara* which was patrolling the English Channel in search of the ram or her consort. "I am well aware that you are actuated by the same desire for the success of this expedition as I or any other Southerner can be, and when you have sailed I shall await the result with hopeful confidence," Bulloch concluded. "God bless you, my dear Davidson, and grant you success."[14]

Bulloch's myriad preparations and his implicit trust in his old comrade paid off. The rendezvous went off with any number of hitches that Bulloch had anticipated. As instructed, Davidson had taken *City of Richmond* down the Thames before January 10 to Greenhithe. On January 11 at Gravesend, she took on human cargo from London and from Calais: approximately 100 officers and men who had been waiting for months to go on board another European built vessel—the *Rappahannock*—that was never delivered and others who had been on

13 James D. Bulloch, *The Secret Service of the Confederate States in Europe*, 2 vols (London, 1883); Bulloch, II:84, 85; dimensions from *Civil War Naval Chronology*, VI, 304.*ORN*, I:3, 725.

14 *ORN*, I:3, 726-27.

the commerce raider CSS *Florida,* which a Federal ship had seized illegally in the neutral port of Bahia, Brazil, in October. Those officers and men were destined now for the CSS *Stonewall.* According to the depositions of two English crew members, *City of Richmond* left behind two additional boat loads of men because the captain—probably the vessel's English captain, [William] Scott, thought he was being watched and could not wait. As it was, Davidson reported to Bulloch that "We are rather crowded, 125 on board all told, and the men must be somewhat uncomfortable, but we manage very well.'"[15]

Almost immediately, *City of Richmond* ran into rough weather in the Channel. "It was indeed most lucky that I determined to come down Channel on the French coast," Davidson wrote Bulloch from Cherbourg on the 13th, "for the steamer would have suffered on the English side from the heavy sea, besides which, I might have been forced into one of the harbours on that side. Your officers and men are all very manageable, and we get on very well. The chances are now that this part of the expedition is all right." After a few days in Cherbourg, Davidson took the ship to Quiberon Bay on the Atlantic coast of France near Belle Isle. Davidson wrote Bulloch "we obtained a snug harborage on the 20th, and laid quietly, permitting no communication with the shore," though the English crew members testified that a "small screw steamer" approached and "asked us where from, and what was our cargo." Captain Scott "answered Machinery from London," and the other ship "steamed away."[16]

On the morning of January 24, "the old *Stonewall* hove in view, to the rapturous delight of all in the secret," Davidson reported to Bulloch. The newly christened warship was in what Davidson described as "a horridly filthy condition and required more labor to clean her than to receive and get things in order afterwards." The men spent the next few days working in wet weather transferring supplies to *Stonewall.* The two ships left Quiberon Bay together on the 28th, headed for the Azores.[17]

Davidson adopted a colorful narrative voice when he told Bulloch what happened next. "But on the morning of the 29th old Neptune thought proper to pay his respects to the first ironclad expedition across his waters, and so he

15 Bulloch, *Secret Service,* 93; Warren F. Spencer, *The Confederate Navy in Europe* (Tuscaloosa, AL, 1983), 202; depositions of James Davis, Mar. 13, 1865, and William Hall, Mar. 14, 1865, RG 59, NARA; U.S. consul in London, to Charles Francis Adams, Jan. 10, 1865, Despatches from the U.S. Consul, London, Records of Foreign Service Posts of the Department of State RG 84, NARA.

16 Bulloch, *Secret Service,* 93; Davidson to Bulloch, Feb. 6, 1865, *ORN,* I:3, 732; deposition of Davis.

17 *ORN,* I:3, 732-33.

Davidson commanded the vessel that transported armaments and officers and crew to equip the French-built ironclad christened CSS *Stonewall*. *NH&HC (NH-43993)*

commenced. It blew a storm at times, with as heavy a sea as I have ever seen in any part of the world. The *Stonewall,* which we kept close to night and day, would often ship immense seas, they seeming at times to cover her from knightheads to taffrail; but yet she never seemed to be injuriously affected by them, and would keep her heading very steadily." Both vessels weathered the storm, but they became separated by about five miles on the morning of the 30th. They soon reestablished contact, and *Stonewall* indicated she needed coal and proposed to go into port at Ferrol, Spain. Given the choice of whether to accompany *Stonewall,* Davidson decided that it would arouse more suspicion if he did—and further delay his original delivery of cargo to Wilmington. With a final signal of "Adieu," Davidson watched the Confederacy's first seagoing ironclad head toward the Spanish coast.[18]

Stonewall arrived in Spain, but only after suffering damage in yet another gale that required repairs. U.S. diplomatic pressure on Spain delayed the work. Nearly

18 Ibid., 733-34.

two months after Davidson bid her "adieu," *Stonewall* left Spain and evaded the dragnet of U.S. warships but had to take on coal again at Lisbon and at Tenerife in the Canary Islands. By the time she reached Nassau, Bahamas, on May 6, nearly all major Confederate field armies had surrendered, and the war was essentially over. By the time she reached Havana, Cuba, five days later, Federal forces had captured President Jefferson Davis. Rather than challenge the Federal ships awaiting her outside Havana, Page sold his ship to the Spanish on May 19, but the Spanish soon sold it to the U.S. government. A few years later the former *Stonewall* became the first ironclad vessel in the Japanese navy.[19]

Things went more smoothly for Davidson and the *City of Richmond,* but the fulfillment of his orders similarly confronted the reality of a quickly collapsing Confederacy. The same gale that caused problems on *Stonewall* compelled Davidson to take his ship into port at Funchal on the island of Madeira. From there he would go to Bermuda, where he would deposit the several officers and the quantities of powder and mess stores for which there was insufficient room on *Stonewall.* Despite Davidson's praise for the officers and men as "very quiet and orderly," several men claimed later that Davidson detained them when they tried to leave the ship at Madeira—allegedly to report the *City of Richmond's* role in fitting out a "privateer"—to British authorities. Another sailor, who joined the crew at Nassau, reported tension between captain and crew and that the captain had made unfulfilled promises to the crew in Bermuda to persuade them to finish the journey. Davidson gave high praise to Capt. Scott, the *City of Richmond's* British commander of record, telling Bulloch that he "took great interest in the expedition and used every effort to advance it without promise of reward, until near the last I was so much pleased with his conduct I made some promise, and would really like to make him a present, but don't know how or what." That obtuse reference suggests that Scott did indeed have to smooth the waters with the largely foreign crew.[20]

City of Richmond reached Bermuda on March 5 and Nassau on March 18. American officials at Nassau knew that she had supplied the *Olinde* off the French coast. They had also received a report that "Captain Scott gave her into the hands of Captain Davidson not a British subject who had come out in her from London and was the agent of the owner Crenshaw." In Nassau, the much-delayed cargo was

19 Lee Kennett, "The Strange Career of the *Stonewall,*" *United Naval Institute Proceedings* (Feb. 1968), 80-4; Wise, *Lifeline*, 218-19.

20 Davidson to Bulloch, Feb. 6, 1865, *ORN,* I:3, 734; depositions of John Morgan, Davis, and Hall.

transferred to other ships, then William Crenshaw himself accompanied his ship back to London and paid off the crew.[21]

The weeks-long delay in *City of Richmond's* departure altered completely the nature of her mission. Between the time that she left London and arrived in Nassau, Wilmington had fallen. Federal forces captured Fort Fisher defending the mouth of the Cape Fear River, on January 15, 1865, effectively closing the port, and Wilmington itself on February 22. Galveston, Texas, was the last remaining Confederate port still open to blockade runners. It was to Galveston that Hunter Davidson headed with her cargo of telegraph wires, "submarine battery fixtures," and provisions in the new Scottish-built blockade runner *Imogene*.[22]

The largest city in Texas, Galveston was the port city for the rich cotton trade of east Texas. Located on an island, Galveston was not defended by any masonry or earthen fortifications. Artillery emplacements and warships kept Federal forces at bay until October 1862 when Federal gunboats compelled the city's surrender. U.S. control of Galveston did not last long. Confederate forces under Maj. Gen. John Bankhead Magruder, supported by several "cotton-clad" warships defeated the token Federal garrison and recaptured the city on New Year's Day, 1863.[23]

Davidson was well-acquainted with the waters around Galveston, having spent months there on the Coast Survey vessel *Morris* in 1853. When he returned there in April 1865, Galveston was a city on the brink of chaos. Desertions among the garrison led to several military executions. News of Robert E. Lee's surrender at Appomattox had convinced many Confederate soldiers that the war was essentially over and further undermined discipline among remaining forces. Even the appointment of a popular officer, Col. Ashbel Smith, to command the garrison could not stem the decline in morale. District commander Magruder had moved his headquarters from Galveston inland to Houston.[24]

Magruder's change of base complicated further Davidson's already forlorn hope of improving Galveston's defenses. By April 19, Davidson was in Galveston and charged with establishing submarine defenses in Galveston harbor. Special

21 Log of vessels in Bermuda and Nassau, 1861-1865, Confederate States of America records (Navy), roll 120, LC; C. A. Dana, Asst. Secretary of War, to Seward enclosing letter of May 18, 1865 from HQ Department of the East, NY, to Maj. Gen. John Dix including the testimony of Ernest W. Pratt and Robert Green, RG 59, NARA. The testimony said that Scott gave the ship to Davidson at Nassau on March 4 or 5, but that was when she arrived in Bermuda; deposition of Morgan.

22 Deposition of Morgan; *ORN*, I:3, 734. *Imogene* arrived in Galveston on April 16th. Andrew J. Forrest to son, June 13, 1865, Mariners Museum, Newport News, VA.

23 Edward T. Cotham, Jr. *Battle on the Bay: The Civil War Struggle for Galveston.* (Austin, 1998).

24 Cotham, *Battle on the Bay*, 176-78; Paul D. Casdorph, *Prince John Magruder: His Life and Campaigns* (New York, 1996), 291; *The Dallas Herald*, Mar. 23, 1865.

Orders issued from Houston assigned a chief of ordnance to him and transferred to his control the steam launch, "Little Rebel." Another special order issued on April 25 assigned Major E. Von Harten of the 1st Texas Heavy Artillery and Capt. Charles Benton, Chief Ordnance Officers, Defenses of Galveston, to report to Davidson "for instruction in the use of Sub-marine appliances, now deposited at the Ordnance Office at Galveston."[25]

By the time Davidson had trained those officers in the use of the submarine battery "appliances," he had a new concern: getting out of Galveston. He requested permission to leave the same way he had entered—on the blockade runner *Imogene*—but found himself entangled in red tape. He learned that "permits to proceed to sea beyond our waters can only be given when evidence is shown that the regulations of the Treasury Department have been strictly complied with." If the local agent would "yield the claim of the government on the tonnage of the steamer *Imogene* as established by the regulations of the Treasury Department under the exhibition of the requisite papers from the collector of customs, the necessary permits will be signed by Major General Magruder." Fortunately, Davidson was in Houston and probably able to appeal directly to Magruder.[26]

Evidence that Davidson left Galveston on May 3 on *Imogene* is circumstantial. A U.S. consul reported that the ship arrived in Cuba on May 12 with "Jeff Davis" on board. Before Federal cavalry captured the Confederate president in southern Georgia on May 10, Federal authorities feared that he would make it to the Gulf coast and escape the country on the *Stonewall* or another ship. It was not surprising that a consul would believe that every vessel coming out of Galveston as the one carrying America's Most Wanted Man—especially if that vessel had on board a Confederate officer named Davis or Davidson. Whether he left on *Imogene* or another ship or simply slipped across the Rio Grande to Mexico, Davidson was not in Galveston on June 2 when Gen. Kirby Smith boarded the Federal steamer *Fort Jackson* in Galveston harbor to consummate the surrender of the Confederacy's sprawling Trans-Mississippi Department.[27]

Nevertheless, the Civil War was over for Hunter Davidson. A new struggle—to make a living and to defend and exploit a reputation—had begun.

25 Special Orders no. 109, paragraphs 18 and 19, and no. 115, Apr. 25, 1865, vol. 103, page 140, Records Relating to Confederate Naval and Marine Personnel, RG 109 (M-260), NARA. *Little Rebel* was turned over to a U.S. quartermaster at Galveston in July 1865. *OR,* 48/2, 1121.

26 Letter to Hunter Davidson, Apr. 24, 1865, vol. 123, page 212, RG 109 (M-260), NARA.

27 *Imogene's* departure from Andrew Forrest letter; despatch from U.S. consul in Havana to State Department and Stribling letter, May 12, 1865, RG 59; Robert Dunkerly, *To the Bitter End: Appomattox, Bennett Place, and the Surrenders of the Confederacy* (El Dorado, CA, 2015), Chapter 13.

Chapter Six

"Hard Up Confed" (1865–1868)

Hunter Davidson was just short of his 39th birthday when the Civil War ended, and he was forced to begin life anew. He and Mary were the parents of four young children: Leila, almost 11 years old; Percy, almost eight; Hunter, three; and infant Charles. Having been dismissed and had his name stricken from the rolls of the United States Navy, Davidson could not return to the only career he had ever known—at least not in his own country.

Even his status as a full citizen of his native country was uncertain. President Andrew Johnson's May 29, 1865, amnesty proclamation granted "amnesty and pardon" and "restoration of all rights of property, except as to slaves" (and confiscated property then involved in legal proceedings) to persons who had participated in the rebellion. The proclamation, however, listed 14 categories of people exempted from the general proclamation. At least four of the categories applied to Davidson as a naval officer who had been educated by the U.S. Government at the Naval School, tendered his resignation from the U.S. Navy, served in the Confederate navy, had been absent from the U.S. while participating in the rebellion, and arguably a fifth—that he had "engaged in the destruction" of commerce on the high seas. Exempted persons could take the oath of allegiance and apply to the President for a special pardon. There is no evidence that Davidson ever took the oath or applied for a pardon under that proclamation. Johnson's September 1867 amnesty proclamation removed the exceptions that pertained to Davidson but still required an oath of allegiance. Eventually, Davidson recovered most of citizenship rights under Johnson's December 25, 1868, general amnesty proclamation, which declared a "full pardon and amnesty for the offence of treason" to all persons who

Portrait of Hunter Davidson in civilian dress probably taken soon after the end of the Civil War.
NH&HC (NH50688)

had participated in the rebellion, "with restoration of all rights, privileges, and immunities under the Constitution" except for property in slaves—and required no oath of allegiance.[1]

Independent of President Johnson's amnesty proclamation, Section 3 of the Fourteenth Amendment to the Constitution, ratified in July 1868, disqualified Davidson and other Confederates from holding any national or state office unless relieved of that disability by a two-thirds vote of both houses of Congress. Davidson was not among the thousands of former Confederates who sought and received Congressional clemency. Congress in 1872 passed its own Amnesty Act removing the disabilities defined in section 3 of the Fourteenth Amendment *except* for members of Congress on the eve of the war and "officers in the judicial, military, and naval service of the United States," and a few other categories of persons. Davidson lived long enough to see President William McKinley sign the Universal Amnesty Act of 1898, which repealed the disability imposed by section 3 of the Fourteenth Amendment—and required no oath.[2]

Davidson's adoptive state of Maryland was a particularly unfriendly place for former Confederates in the first year after the war. A new state constitution adopted in 1864 abolished slavery and effectively disenfranchised "rebels." An August 1865 act empowered election officials to refuse to register men who fell into a broad range of categories—many of which included Davidson. At the same time, the U.S. Army, wary of former Confederate soldiers from Maryland returning to their homes and disrupting their communities, required "rebels" to register with local provost marshals and to restrict their movements around the state. Maryland's triumphant loyalists rebuffed efforts of allegedly penitent Confederate sympathizers to lift the restrictions.[3] If he chose to return home, Davidson could not vote in state or federal elections or seek employment in any branch of public service.

The obvious alternative for Davidson and other men in his predicament was to go or remain abroad. John Taylor Wood, with whom Davidson had served on the U.S. Naval Academy faculty in 1861 and on the CSS *Virginia* in 1862, chose to remain in Canada, where his later war (secret service) duties had taken him. Wood opened a mercantile business in Halifax, Nova Scotia, with Cdr. John Wilkinson, with whom Davidson had served in the Coast Survey, and who had become the

1 Jonathan T. Dorris, *Pardon and Amnesty under Lincoln and Johnson: The Restoration of the Confederates to Their Rights and Privileges, 1861-1898* (Chapel Hill, NC, 1953), 111-12, 343-57.

2 Ibid., 375-376, 391.

3 J. Thomas Scharf, *History of Maryland from the Earliest Period to the Present Day*, 3 volumes (Baltimore, 1879), 659, 668-71, 673-79; Caroline E. Janney, *Ends of War: The Unfinished Fight of Lee's Army After Appomattox* (Chapel Hill, NC, 2021), 186-87, 231, 244.

Confederacy's most successful blockade running captain. Wilkinson eventually returned to the United States; Wood, grandson of an American president, did not. Matthew Fontaine Maury left England for an uncertain destination before resolving to go to Mexico, where the Hapsburg Emperor Maximilian appointed him director of the National Observatory and Imperial Commissioner of the Office of Immigration. Officers of the CSS *Shenandoah,* the Confederate commerce raider that succeeded in decimating the American whaling fleet in the Arctic two months after Appomattox, chose to remain in England for fear of being prosecuted for piracy. Several of the younger officers then sailed to Argentina to try their luck as sheep farmers. James Bulloch, with whom Davidson had been shipwrecked on the coast of Oregon in the winter of 1846-1847, and who more recently had purchased, equipped, and armed *Shenandoah, Alabama, Florida,* and *Stonewall* for the Confederate navy, remained in England the rest of his life. John Randolph Tucker, Davidson's commander on the *Patrick Henry* in 1861, accepted a commission in the navy of Peru and recruited other Confederates to join him.[4]

The "notorious Lieutenant Davidson"—the man responsible for blowing up a U.S. warship and killing as many as 69 men—had good reason to steer clear of the United States during the first months of Reconstruction. Davidson may have steered—directly or indirectly—across the border to Mexico, along with many hundreds of Confederate officers and soldiers from the Trans-Mississippi Department. The evidence for this brief sojourn is sketchy. On June 21, 1865, a Galveston paper reported that a "Mexican schooner Emma, Capt. Davidson, arrived at our wharf yesterday morning." She had come from Bagdad, a Mexican port town near the mouth of the Rio Grande (known also as the Port of Matamoras), with 37 passengers, most of them American refugees returning from Mexico. "Capt. Davidson informs us that all Texans at Bagdad are preparing to return home, via Galveston." Two additional vessels loaded with returning refugees were scheduled to leave for Galveston in mid-July.[5]

A cryptic reference in Matthew Fontaine Maury's diary suggests that, while he was shepherding American refugees *out of* Mexico, Davidson had given thought to how to entice them *into* Mexico. On July 28, 1865, Maury met with the Empress

4 Royce Gordon Shingleton, *John Taylor Wood: Sea Ghost of the Confederacy* (Athens, GA, 1979), 202-5; Thurston *Tallahassee Skipper*, chapters 42-45; Williams, *Pathfinder of the Seas,* chapter 21; Grady, *Father of Oceanography,* chapter 23; Andrew F. Rolle, *The Lost Cause: The Confederate Exodus to Mexico* (Norman, OK, 1964), chapter 14; John Thomson Mason Papers, CMLS Collection under the management of the Virginia Historical Society; Brianna Kirk and John M. Coski, "'What am I to do for a living?': Two Brothers in the Aftermath of War," *The American Civil War Museum Magazine* (summer 2017), 8-15.

5 "FROM MEXICO, VIA GALVESTON. . . . *Daily Picayune* [New Orleans], June 22, 1865, from the Galveston *Daily News,* June 21, 1865.

Carlota who gave him "Davidson's mem[orandum or memorial] on colonization . . . to examine & suggest action &c." He returned the document the following day with his own remarks.[6] Emperor Maximilian's November 1865 *Decrees for the Encouragement of Immigration and Colonization* are silent on any involvement Davidson may have had in formulating Maury's vision for a "New Virginia" in Mexico. It was just as well for Davidson that he did not become involved with Maximilian's doomed regime. By the first days of March 1866, Commissioner Maury left Mexico for England with a promise to return, but the recently announced withdrawal of the French troops that propped up Maximilian made that promise moot. Fifteen months later, Mexican rebels toppled and executed the emperor.

Davidson's foray into Mexican territory and Mexican politics is uncertain and based on skeletal evidence. It is possible that Davidson did, in fact, leave Galveston on a blockade runner (likely *Imogene*) and retraced his journey back to England via Havana and Nassau, arriving in London on May 27. In early August 1865, Davidson passed an examination to earn a Certificate of Competency as master from the United Kingdom Council of Trade. He spent some time that summer as master of the *Louisa Wallace* out of Glasgow, Scotland. He gave as his address the firm of Charles H. Reid [*sic*: Reed] & Co. (forge, chain, and anchor works), East India Avenue, Leadenhall St., east London (presumably the same company where Davidson met Maury in January 1865).[7]

Did Davidson ever return home to the re-united States in year after hostilities ended? The only documented sighting of Davidson in the U.S. in 1865 comes ironically from a U.S. Naval officer who had witnessed the tense flag-of-truce meeting between Davidson and Adm. Samuel P. Lee on the James River in June 1864 and who had drawn a sketch of the *Squib*. Sometime in the "winter of 1865," Lt. Cdr. John Sanford Barnes, an 1854 Naval Academy graduate who was then an instructor at the Naval Academy, interviewed Davidson for his 1869 book about torpedoes. Barnes recounted details of the interview in an 1883 letter to Adm. Alfred Thayer Mahan. "Davidson," Barnes wrote, "had at that time and has today probably more personal experience with the use of torpedoes than any man living." Barnes told Mahan that he considered Davidson more credible than other

6 MFM Diary, 1864-1865, images 256-257; David P. Werlich, *Admiral of the Amazon: John Randolph Tucker, His Confederate Colleagues, and Peru* (Charlottesville, 1990).

7 Davidson's Certificate of Competency as Master, Aug. 4, 1865, and Section (B) of Application for Renewal of certificate, Jan. 21, 1875, both accessed via Ancestry.com; information on Reed from https://www.gracesguide.co.uk/C._H._Reed_and_Co.

authorities he had interviewed.[8] If he had not realized it already, Davidson soon understood that his reputation as torpedo expert and sage was his best hope for a new career.

If Barnes were correct in his recollection of when that interview occurred, he saw Davidson just before his first crack at exploiting his reputation as a torpedo expert. The Shipping News section of the February 16, 1866, New York *World* carried the simple notice: "Cl[eare]d at London 30th ult, Henrietta, Davidson, San Francisco."[9]

Lieutenant Commander Hunter Davidson, Chilean Navy

Other newspapers revealed more about *Henrietta,* her captain, and her mission. "We learn from private sources likely to be thoroughly informed, that a formidable Chilean cruiser is now on her way from England to the Pacific coast, where we may reasonably expect to hear of her within a few weeks, making sad havoc with the Spanish fleet," reported the *San Francisco Bulletin* in late March 1866. Chile, along with Peru, Ecuador, and Bolivia—the so-called Quadruple Alliance—were at war with Spain, which had been trying to intimidate or reassert some degree of control over her former South American colonies. The *Henrietta* (sometimes given as *Henriette*), an English-built screw steamer, that left England in early February bound for Chile, was said to have on board "an abundant store of ammunition," including torpedo boats of the kind that Lt. William B. Cushing used to destroy the Confederate ram *Albemarle* (an incidental allusion that must have wounded Davidson's pride). "Ex-Lieut. Hunter Davidson of the United States Navy—subsequently in the rebel service—is on board the steamer and expected to command her," the report continued. "With the exception of a single English officer, lately in the South, and once in the British navy, *all* her officers are men who served in the late rebellion." The ship's supposed mission was to raise Spain's naval blockade of her former colony. According to the *Bulletin, Henrietta* would be rechristened *Cochrane* and sink every Spanish ship she could. "The officers of the *Cochrane* are not only brave but desperate men, who, having lost fame and country

8 Barnes to Mahan, May 5, 1883, in CSN Subject files; *U.S. Navy Register . . . to January 1, 1866*, 95. Barnes was an instructor of seamanship and assistant to the commandant—Stephen B. Luce. Barnes was in Annapolis through 1866, so the interview could have occurred after 1865.

9 *The World* [NY], Feb. 16, 1866.

by their own misguided conduct, are doubtless to accept any risks as the price of future success," the report concluded.[10]

Although Hunter Davidson's was the name most closely associated with the *Henrietta* in the American press, he uneasily shared command of the venture with another man. H. H. Doty was an archetypical 19th-century adventurer who could have sprung from the imagination of Mark Twain or George MacDonald Fraser. He seems to have been equal parts entrepreneur, inventor, and charlatan, altruistic citizen and merciless self-promoter.

Appearing in the historical record as "H. H. Doty," Henry Harrison Doty was born in Herkimer County, New York, in 1824, the second of 10 children of Lucretia and Henry Doty. "Being of an adventuresome disposition, he early left home, and, engaging in business, traveled throughout the country," wrote a late 19th-century Doty family genealogist with considerable understatement. Doty and his family moved to Wisconsin, and he first appears on the public record in 1846 in Milwaukee, where he denied being in debt to a local hotel. A year later he made headlines as a pioneering daguerreotype artist who had taken a photo of Venezuelan military hero José Antonio Páez, and for bearing back to Washington diplomatic messages about civil unrest in Caracas. In addition to owning a daguerreotype studio in Philadelphia, he was also the principal officer of an Arts Union Gallery, which won praise for encouraging the art of painting in the city, but was also prosecuted and fined for operating an illegal lottery. In the early 1850s, Doty promoted "Grand Concerts" of music from Albany to Buffalo to Cleveland, before deciding that California was the place he ought to be. In June 1854, he precipitously retired as a partner in Robb & Company's Ice Cream, Breakfast and Tea Saloon in San Francisco, to head further west—to Japan—where he was among the first Americans to exploit Commodore Matthew Perry's treaty that "opened" the country to western commerce.[11]

10 "A Formidable Chilean Cruiser Afloat—Sharp Work to be Expected," [San Francisco] *Evening Bulletin*, Mar. 30, 1866.

11 Ethan Allen Doty, *Doty-Doten Family in America: Descendants of Edward Doty, an Emigrant by the Mayflower, 1620* (Brooklyn, NY, 1897), 91; *Milwaukee Daily Sentinel*, Mar. 7, 1846. The entries in Ethan Allen Doty's book contain inaccuracies about H. H. Doty and his siblings. By a strange coincidence, Doty's younger sister, Frances Doty Guernsey, is author John Coski's great-great-grandmother. *Philadelphia Enquirer*, Oct. 22, 1847; *Charleston Courier* [SC], Mar. 3, 1848; "THE FINE ARTS AND LOTTERIES," *Sunday Dispatch* [Philadelphia], Feb. 3, 1850; "DOTY'S GALLERY," *Philadelphia Inquirer and National Gazette*, Feb. 14, 1850; *Philadelphia Inquirer and National Gazette*, Apr. 11, 1850; *Albany Journal* [NY]Feb. 10, 1852; *Rochester Daily American*, Feb. 16, 1852; *Buffalo Express* [NY], Mar. 1, 1852; *Morning Daily True Democrat* [Cleveland], Apr. 26, 1852; *California Farmer* [Sacramento], Apr. 6, 1854; *Daily Placer Times And Transcript* [SF, CA], June 1, 1854.

A witness to this most exotic of Doty's antebellum adventures was none other than the young U.S. naval Lt. John Mercer Brooke. An officer on the USS *Vincennes* of the North Pacific Surveying Expedition, Brooke arrived at the port city of Shimoda in 1855, and among the first sights greeting him was a group of three men in western dress, whom he correctly judged to be Russians and Americans. The Russian was a sailor from a vessel wrecked during a recent earthquake. The Americans were H. H. Doty and William C. Reed, merchants who (along with their wives) had come to Japan with their ship, *Caroline E. Foote,* loaded with provisions hoping to open a chandlery business in Japan and to remain there, as they believed Perry's treaty would allow. Instead, they were rebuffed by the Japanese. Brooke approvingly described Doty and Reed as "pioneers of American progress." Their complaint against the Japanese government became the first test of the landmark treaty. Although they received official and public sympathy and support, they spent three months in Japan trying in vain to establish their business.[12]

Doty was the first merchant to visit Japan a second time. After a brief stay in December 1855, he returned home bearing diplomatic papers for the Russian consul in San Francisco, a widely published eyewitness description of earthquake damage in "Jeddo" (Tokyo), and seeds and other "agricultural productions" that Doty lavished on the California State Agricultural Society. His hopes to become the John Jacob Astor of Japan frustrated, Doty found other ways to profit from his futile journey—and a second journey later that year. In San Francisco, he hawked a "GREAT JAPANESE REMEDY FOR SORE EYES"—a "Speedy and effectual cure of Sore and Inflamed Eyes" supposedly obtained from one of Japan's "Most Distinguished Oculists." Having been one of the first Americans in Japan, Doty became a self-proclaimed authority on that exotic country's "system of government, habits, customs, religion, commerce and commercial resources, and other matters," and offered public lectures on "Japan and the Japanese" in Trenton, Philadelphia, and Baltimore.[13]

12 George M. Brooke, Jr. *John Brooke: Naval Scientists and Educator.* (Charlottesville, VA, 1980), 113. "FROM JAPAN," *The Weekly Chronicle* [SF], Sep. 22, 1855; "Very Important from Japan," *Philadelphia Inquirer,* Oct.16, 1855; "TROUBLE WITH JAPAN," *New-York Daily Tribune,* Oct. 16, 1855; "ANOTHER DIPLOMATIC AFFAIR," *New York Semi-Weekly Tribune,* Nov. 2, 1855; Allan B. Cole, ed., *Yankee Surveyors in the Shogun's Seas: Records of the United States Surveying Expedition to the North Pacific Ocean, 1853-1856* (Princeton, NJ, 1947), 15-17, 103-11. Howard F. Van Zandt, *Pioneer American Merchants in Japan* (Tokyo, 1980), is a microhistory of the *Caroline E. Foote* and her crew, including Doty.

13 Van Zandt, *Pioneer American Merchants,* 337-9, 356; "JAPANESE VEGETABLE PRODUCTIONS," *Weekly Journal of Commerce* [NY], Oct. 18, 1855; "JAPANESE CURIOSITIES," *Sacramento Daily Union,* Feb. 19, 1856; "GREAT JAPANESE REMEDY / FOR SORE EYES," *Daily Evening Bulletin* [SF], Apr. 4, 1856; Sore Eyes and Rheumatism. . . . ASTONISHING CURES! . . . ." *The Nevada Journal* [Nevada City, California], July 4, 1856; "ACCOUNT OF EARTHQUAKE AT

Early in 1858, "H. H. Doty of Philadelphia" arrived in Norfolk, Virginia, to deliver his popular lecture. By late 1859, a Norfolk newspaper described him as "our enterprising townsman H. H. Doty, Esq." who had established the North Carolina Steam Transportation Company in Norfolk and was operating a profitable cotton trade through the newly opened Albemarle and Chesapeake Canal.[14]

Doty's activities and whereabouts during the Civil War are more elusive. An 1867 letter from Davidson to his 1841 USN classmate and Confederate Navy comrade Robert Dabney Minor suggests that Doty had been "false to both sections" during the war. Doty had apparently spent some time during the war in Richmond, where he befriended a young Confederate surgeon, William ("Willie") Whistler, younger brother of an ambitious young American artist. Doty spent part of the war years abroad, developing expertise—or, at least, a reputation—in torpedoes. In 1864, "Captain Henry Doty" and "Captain William Porter Downer" received a patent in England for "Improvements in Submarine Batteries" (reportedly a retractable spar torpedo). Fourteen years later, H. H. Doty of Washington, D.C., claimed to have been "the first and only inventor of a submarine outrigger torpedo" and that in 1865 he sent the plans from London to the U.S. secretary of the navy and did not receive a response—only to learn that the U.S. Navy employed the same technology on the ship, *Alarm.* Describing himself as a citizen of the United States who also held the rank as "captain of frigate" in the Chilean navy—then on leave without pay—and claiming to possess corroborating evidence from English and French authorities, Doty petitioned the U.S. Congress for recognition of and remuneration for his invention. The House Committee on Naval Affairs considered, but rejected, his claim. Despite his failure to earn credit and remuneration for that invention, Doty established credibility as a prolific inventor beginning in the Civil War years and received numerous patents in several countries.[15]

JEDDO," *Weekly National Intelligencer* [Washington, D.C.], Apr. 26, 1856; "THE EARTHQUAKE AT JEDDO," *New York Observer*, May 8, 1856; "JAPAN," *Sunday Dispatch* [Philadelphia], Nov. 15, 1857; "LECTURE ON JAPAN," *Daily True American* [Trenton, NJ], Dec. 1857; *The Sun* [Baltimore], Jan. 13, 1858.

14 *The Day Book* [Norfolk], Feb. 1, 1858; "MORE COTTON," *The Day Book* [Norfolk], Dec. 5, 1859; *Richmond Whig and Public Advertiser*, June 12, 1860; *The Sun* [Baltimore], Oct. 29, 1860.

15 Davidson to Robert D. Minor, May 26, 1867, Minor Papers; Daniel E. Sutherland, "James McNeill Whistler in Chile: Portrait of the Artist as Arms Dealer," *American Nineteenth Century History* (Mar. 2008): 9:65; British patent information on Doty family tree on Ancestry.com (the patent was voided two years later for failure to pay a required stamp duty); "H. H. Doty." House Report No. 626, House of Representatives, 45th Congress, 2d Session, 1878. "The Inventor of an Ugly Craft Asking for Credit for His Own Invention," T*he Farmer and Mechanic* [Raleigh], Feb. 21, 1878 [from the *Washington Telegram*]; *The Daily Critic* [Washington, D.C.], Mar. 8, 1878. Between

It was in London in January, 1866 that Doty signed a contract with Special Commissioner Ambrosio Rodriguez of the Chilean government to transport a ship to Valparaiso laden with three torpedo launches and various kinds of offensive torpedoes with orders to "destroy the Spanish ships found there, making use of whatever means at your disposal." The potential rewards were enormous: a bounty of 100,000 Chilean pesos (£20,000) for sinking the Spanish ironclad *Numancia* and half that amount for each of the frigates for a total of £60,000 that he would share with his partner, Hunter Davidson, and their crew. The contract made Doty a captain in the Chilean navy. Davidson received a commission as lieutenant commander and would command *Henrietta,* but with the understanding that he would take his "immediate orders" from Doty.[16] According to Doty's July, 1866 after-action report of the venture, Commissioner Rodriguez had "previously made" an agreement with Davidson, by which Rodriguez communicated to Davidson a document by which the Chilean government named Davidson "an Officer of the Navy of the Republic." Davidson evidently interpreted that agreement as making him responsible to the Chileans, not necessarily to Doty. Indeed, Davidson later dismissed Doty as "officially only as a contractor with a Chilian [*sic*] Agent in London in 1865 and afterwards as a shipped seaman on board of my Ship the "Henrietta" in which I took a Torpedo expedition to Chili [*sic*]."[17] The dual command led to a dueling command, fueled by an intense mutual animosity between Doty and Davidson.

It is not clear whether Davidson was in the right place at the right time to participate in this mission or whether he traveled to England to put himself in the right place. The short-lived War of the Quadruple Alliance provided a golden employment opportunity for Confederate-American naval officers. The South

186 and 1890, Doty received patents in Great Britain, France, Belgium, and the U.S. for lamps, signal lights, improvements in oil-burning apparatus, improvements railway rail-joints, and a process for disintegrating fibrous plants. His patents described him variously as "naval officer" and "engineer," residing either in Norfolk, Virginia, or London, England. Doty's patents are available as PDFs on Google Patents. Communication from John M. McKee to John Coski, July 13, 2025. John McKee's research also places Doty on the British blockade runner, *Victory,* carrying a cargo of cotton out of Wilmington, NC, and captured off Cuba in June 1863; Doty was detained in New York.

16 Contract terms quoted in Sutherland, "James McNeill Whistler," 65 and in Werlich, *Admiral of the Amazon,* 105.

17 *MEMORIA que el Ministro De Estado EN EL DEPARTAMENTO DE MARINA PRESENTA AL CONGRESO NACIONAL DE 1866* [translated as: *REPORT THAT THE MINISTER OF STATE IN THE DEPARTMENT OF THE NAVY PRESENTS TO THE NATIONAL CONGRESS OF 1866* (Santiago De Chile, 1866), 78 [Translated via Google Translate]; Davidson to Minor, May 26, 1867, Minor Papers.

American republics needed experts in modern naval technology and warfare, and the former Confederate officers needed gainful employment.

A month before Davidson and Doty signed on in London, another Chilean special commissioner in New York City recruited 26-year-old Edward Gaines Read. A Virginian and 1860 graduate of the U.S. Naval Academy, where he no doubt met Davidson, Read also served on the CSS *Patrick Henry* with Davidson in 1861 and was among the officers on the *City of Richmond* in 1865. He spent the years between serving in New Orleans, Jackson, Mississippi, and Mobile. Read assembled a four-man team of former Confederate junior officers (several of whom had been USNA midshipmen during Davidson's tenure as instructor) who left for Chile at the end of 1865. Before departing, they received some tutelage about torpedoes from Lt. William Glassell, the Confederate officer who had piloted the semi-submersible *David* in an attack against USS *New Ironsides* in 1863. Otherwise, the men had no practical experience with torpedoes. Nevertheless, they were the first of the Confederate mercenaries to arrive in Valparaiso—and the only ones to arrive before the war ended.[18]

American newspaper accounts claimed that the officers aboard *Henrietta* were almost exclusively former Confederates. Doty's report mentioned a Thomas S. Hunter, which was most likely Davidson's cousin, Thomas T. Hunter, and a "Lieutenant Lynch," who seems to have been Doty's chief ally on *Henrietta*. He may have been William F. Lynch, son of a prominent U.S. and C.S. captain who had served as an assistant engineer in the Confederate navy. The exceptional English-born officer to whom the San Francisco *Bulletin* alluded no doubt was Henry Bolton Edenborough, a young, Australian-born self-described soldier of fortune who later claimed to have served with Garibaldi in Italy, the Confederate navy, and as a torpedo expert for the Ottoman Empire before dying in poverty in New York City in 1890. Edenborough did in fact serve as master's mate on the CSS *Virginia II* and acting lieutenant in several late war raiding expeditions in the Chesapeake Bay, collecting his final pay in England in August 1865. Davidson's own correspondence confirm that he was an officer aboard *Henrietta*.[19]

18 *Register of Officers of the Confederate States Navy 1861-1865*, p.161; David P. Werlich, "The Allied Project to Liberate Cuba, 1866-67: Chile, Peru, and Colonel Barreda's Confederate Navy," Paper presented at the 2007 Naval History Symposium, Annapolis, MD, 4-6, 23-24. Read and his team unsuccessfully sought an opportunity to attack the Spanish vessels blockading Valparaiso with spar torpedoes.

19 Doty's July 24, 1866, report published as Appendix 11 in *REPORT . . . TO THE NATIONAL CONGRESS, 1866*, 76, 78-79; "UNDER SEVEN FLAGS. / Edenborough Bey's Experiences as a Soldier of Fortune . . .," *NYH*, Apr.15, 1888; OBITUARY, *NYH*, Jan. 10, 1890; *ORN*, I:12, 187; *Montgomery Advertiser* [AL], *July 5, 1903* (reprinted from *Baltimore American*, Oct. 1882); 1861 England Census accessed via Ancestry.com. The research of John McKee (email to John Coski, July

Henrietta traveled past the Madeira Islands when a storm injured her machinery and compelled her into port for repairs. Facilities in the Madeiras and Lisbon were inadequate, so *Henrietta* put in at Bordeaux, France. The New York *Herald's* Madrid correspondent on April 2, 1866, noted that there did not seem to be any armaments on board, but that the crew of 57 men seemed large for an alleged merchant vessel. "She will doubtless be heard from under another name, doing damage to Spanish commerce," the correspondent noted. The Spanish government was on high alert, but unable to stop the vessel.[20]

In Bordeaux, *Henrietta* "has excited no little curiosity and suspicion," according to the *Herald.* Repeating earlier reports about her supposed mission and crew, the correspondent reported that Davidson "claims to be her principal owner" and that he intends to run between San Francisco and Oregon. "Her papers are all regular, and the authorities here have not been able to get any hold of her." The correspondent offered an error-riddled reminder to readers that "Captain Davidson, who now claims to be an Englishman, is the man who got out the Stonewall when she took her little excursion to Denmark previous to being delivered into the hands of Captain Page."[21] By the time the repairs were finished, *Henrietta's* mission had become a moot point. The Alliance fought off the Spanish fleet at Callao, Peru, on May 2nd. When *Henrietta* arrived in Valparaiso on July 24, 1866, the Spanish had abandoned their half-hearted attempt to reclaim her former colonies.

Upon *Henrietta's* arrival, Doty gave to Chilean authorities a detailed report of the expedition, in which he blamed its failure on his partner in command, Hunter Davidson.[22] According to Doty, Davidson was uncooperative and obstructionist from the beginning of the mission. As the ship left the London docks, Doty tried to give Davidson his commission and instructions from the Chilean government. Davidson rebuffed him and claimed that because he was "sailing this ship with a British captain's certificate, he could not, in accordance with this, see them or recognize anyone on board in the character of Agent of the Government of Chile, while the ship sailed under the British colors." The ship sailed into the port of Cherbourg to drop off the channel pilot when a strong gale began on February 3 and blew for five days. Davidson took her out on February 8 only to encounter another fierce storm. Without Doty's knowledge or consent, Davidson took the

---

13, 2025) suggests that Edenborough's claims were substantially true. In 1880, Edenborough enlisted in the U.S. Navy and claimed to have been born in Virginia. "Return of the U.S. Naval Rendezvous at Boston for the week ending Saturday, October 30, 1880," accessed via Ancestry.com.

20 "SPAIN. / Our Madrid Correspondence," *NYH*, Apr. 22, 1866.

21 "Our Bordeaux Correspondence," *NYH*, Apr. 29, 1866.

22 The following paragraphs from are Doty's July 24, 1866, report, 76-80.

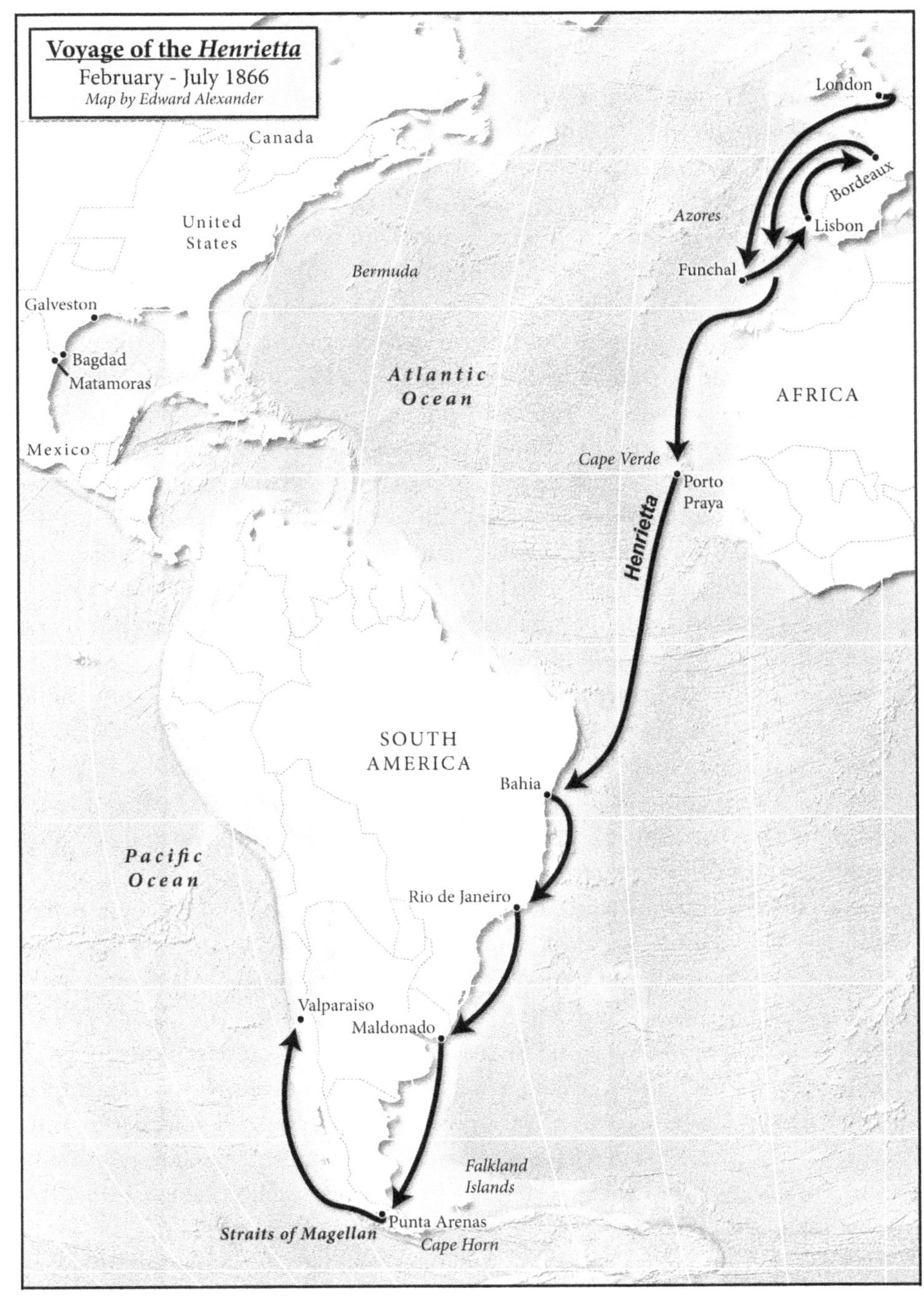
Voyage of the Henrietta
February - July 1866
Map by Edward Alexander
Canada
United States
Galveston
Bagdad
Matamoras
Mexico
Bermuda
Atlantic Ocean
Azores
London
Bordeaux
Lisbon
Funchal
AFRICA
Cape Verde
Porto Praya
Henrietta
SOUTH AMERICA
Bahia
Rio de Janeiro
Pacific Ocean
Valparaiso
Maldonado
Falkland Islands
Punta Arenas
Straits of Magellan
Cape Horn

ship to Funchal in the Madeiras to take on coal. "On the morning of the 18th," Doty wrote, "the Captain told me the astonishing news that the ship was taking on water and he told me that it was necessary for everyone to work on the pumps." Neither her own officers nor authorities in Funchal were able to discover or address the cause of the leak, so they unloaded the coal and headed to Lisbon for repairs.

Meanwhile, according to Doty, a man-made crisis compounded the problems that nature had wrought. For reasons that Doty obviously believed merited, *Henrietta's* crew grew restive, if not mutinous. The ship's inefficient accountant failed to distribute provisions and there was a "general lack of order on board." Doty blamed the situation on "the apparent ineptitude of the Commander to govern a crew made up of men hastily picked up at a London recruiting office." In response to the crew's "strongly expressed" unhappiness, "the Captain adopted and followed rigorous measures" that only exacerbated the discontent." Upon reaching Lisbon, it was advisable to dismiss part of the crew and await replacements from England. While awaiting the new crew, a Chilean special commissioner, Mr. J. D. Merino Benavente, arrived in Lisbon and authorized placing the ship in dry dock for inspection (though Doty observed that the leaking seems to have abated).

As the American newspapers had reported, *Henrietta* proceeded to Bordeaux, France, where she succeeded in getting the repairs. According to Doty, as *Henrietta* approached Bordeaux "in the midst of a strong wind and heavy sea" and failing to obtain a pilot to guide them into the harbor, the principled Capt. Davidson "relaxed his authority as a British Captain to the point of offering me, and giving me, the responsibility of leading the ship into the bay." *Henrietta* left Bordeaux on May 3rd three months after her departure from London—successfully evading Spanish warships determined to capture her.

From the Cape Verde islands, Davidson insisted on going into harbor at Bahia, Brazil, over Doty's protests "Then," Doty wrote, Davidson "once again reiterated his determination to act independently of the Government Agent and me." *Henrietta* made additional port calls for repairs at Porto Praya and Rio de Janeiro before proceeding to Maldonado, Uruguay, in mid-June to communicate with the Chilean consul, took on coal at Punta-Arenas in the Straits of Magellan, then sped north along the Chilean coast to Valparaiso. "In submitting this report to Your Excellency," Doty concluded, "I am deeply aware of my position and responsibility for some of the embarrassments we have experienced through the ship's immediate commanding officer."

If Davidson wrote his own narrative of the expedition, it was not published or did not survive. Uncharacteristically, he did not publicly refute Doty's thorough indictment of his performance and his character. The Chilean government published Doty's report months later (in Spanish) as part of a larger report of naval operations during the War. Davidson never mentioned the report among the grievances he aired about Doty in the following years. (Among other things, Doty reportedly borrowed $700 from Davidson and had failed to pay him back.) It is possible that Davidson never saw the report, but he did learn of its essential contents through another man connected with the expedition who had his own reasons to hate Doty.

James McNeill (a middle name he had only adopted recently) Whistler was a 31-year-old painter who spent the Civil War years abroad establishing his international reputation. Both he and his younger brother Willie were in London in late 1865 where they became willing participants in the Chilean scheme. The artist was not on *Henrietta,* but sailed ahead of the warship, escorting Doty's supposed wife and another woman, and was apparently tasked with gathering intelligence in Valparaiso. During their months-long voyage, Whistler allegedly had an affair with "Mrs. Doty," who in fact may have been Doty's mistress (Doty was married as many as four times in his life, possibly bigamously). News of the affair caught up with Whistler when he returned to London, where Doty also landed. Whistler's club was investigating the rumor and threatening the artist with expulsion.

Whistler wrote Davidson in January 1868 asking him to come to his rescue. "Knowing that you yourself have been annoyed by presumption on the part of this man, and have suffered from attempted fraud," Whistler wrote, "I think that you will willingly assist me with such knowledge in refuting the calumnies against me he has circulated, all of which would of necessity fall to the ground were the calibre of the person known." To further fan the flames, Whistler noted incidentally that Doty now claimed to have "command[ed] the important expedition, in which you were supposed to have taken a subordinate part."

Davidson obliged with a bitter denunciation of Doty as a man of low character ("a wretched criminal" and "snake-like abject coward") and wondered aloud "Why have you any difficulty in proving the character of such a wretched criminal—When Capt. Mr. Edenborough and others are near you who know all about him[?]" In contrast, Davidson flattered Whistler as "a gentleman," but his advice was not helpful. If Doty belonged to a club in London, Davidson asked rhetorically, "What kind of club can it be." Not long after, the Burlington Club found James Whistler unfit for membership.[23]

23 Whistler to Davidson, Jan. 19, 1868, and Davidson to Whistler, Feb. 7, 1868, Center for Whistler Studies, Glasgow University Library, Scotland; Daniel E. Sutherland, *Whistler: A Life for Art's Sake* (New Haven, 2014), 95-97, 106, 367, 369, 370, 424; Sutherland, "James McNeill Whistler in Chile," 65-68.

In the summer of 1866 in Valparaiso, when Whistler and Davidson forged a friendship based on their shared contempt for Doty, Whistler was happy to find new subjects for his paintings. Davidson, on the other hand, was unhappily unemployed. It is not clear whether he received any recompense for his failed mission (he and Doty certainly received no bounty for sinking Spanish ships). In any case, he found himself back at square one—a naval officer without a country, now in a foreign country.

When he arrived in Valparaiso, he found that several other former Confederate officers were there for much the same reason. To help repel the Spanish *reconquista,* the Peruvian government had gone in search of unemployed American naval officers and hired John Randolph Tucker, late captain, C.S.N., to be *contralmirante* of the Peruvian navy for a salary equivalent to that of a U.S. navy admiral. Tucker hastily assembled a staff of former Confederate officers and arrived at Callao on June 15, a month before Davidson arrived at Valparaiso, but nearly a month after the Peruvian foreign minister had ordered his agent to cancel the search for a foreign naval commander. Faced with the fact of Tucker's contract and presence, the Peruvian government retained him as *contralmirante.*[24]

Tucker and Davidson knew each other well from the Virginia State Navy and the Confederate Navy, especially when Tucker commanded *Patrick Henry* at Hampton Roads. Describing Davidson as "the most experienced and practical 'Torpedo' officer in the United States or Confederate Navies," Tucker recommended that Peru offer his old comrade a commission as flag captain and exploit his torpedo expertise. The Peruvians demurred but held out the possibility of commanding an ironclad they hoped to acquire in the U.S.[25] Davidson left Valparaiso in September 1866.

Despite the intense national newspaper coverage of the "privateer" *Henrietta* and Hunter Davidson's association with it, Mary Davidson apparently remained innocent of her husband's first post-war employment. A week after *Henrietta* finally anchored at Valparaiso, she wrote to John Brooke to introduce a cousin who was about to enter a school in Lexington, Virginia, where Brooke had settled. "As you probably feel an interest in my husband's welfare & whereabouts, I take occasion to mention here that he is doing well & was in good [h]ealth when last heard from," she informed Brooke. "He has a fine position in the Chilean Navy with a good salary & the prospect of making money. I shall probably join him with my

24 Werlich, *Admiral of the Amazon,* 88-93.

25 Ibid., 105-6.

Captain John Randolph Tucker followed his USN and CSN careers as *admiralte* of the Peruvian Navy and head of Peru's hydrographic exploration of the Amazon. *NH&HC (NH-42225)*

little flock about the 1st of October at Valparaiso."[26] It was probably only a short time later that Mary learned that her husband's Chilean prospects were not so promising after all and that she and flock of four children would remain in eastern Maryland for the time being.

"I am out of employment"

Judging from surviving correspondence, the months following Davidson's return from Valparaiso in late 1866 through 1867 may have been the most unhappy and desperate of his life. Not only was he unemployed and struggling to find a suitable position, but the political situation had turned dramatically against former Confederates. The fall 1866 elections gave Radical Republicans a majority in Congress, which overturned President Andrew Johnson's forgiving posture toward the former Confederate states, passed a series of Reconstruction Acts and the Fourteenth and Fifteenth Amendments to the Constitution.

Davidson made clear his disdain for Reconstruction and for Federal authority on several occasions. While he was in Valparaiso in the summer of 1866, he was an interested bystander during the so-called "War of Salutes," in which one U.S. navy officer accused *Contralmirante* John Tucker of disrespectful gestures, and another refused to salute the Peruvian admiral's flag. A year later Davidson wrote (an unsigned) open letter to the New York *World* defending Tucker's character and actions and casting aspersions on the character and motives of U.S. Adm. John Dahlgren. He accused Dahlgren of playing the "rebel" card and needlessly dragging his nation into a controversy with a foreign nation in violation of U.S. Navy regulations and for petty personal reasons: "vindictiveness" for his own failure to defeat Tucker's naval squadron and capture Charleston, South Carolina, in 1863.

26 Mary Davidson to Brooke, Aug. 1, 1866, John M. Brooke Papers, courtesy of George M. Brooke, Jr. (hereafter cited as BP).

Davidson struck back, noting "how easy it is, just now to heap reproach, through the government and the press upon 'rebels'!" Dahlgren defended his failure to salute Tucker's flag because he was a "criminal fugitive" and Peru had insulted the U.S. by hiring him. If that were true, why did the U.S. not extradite Tucker to the U.S.? "The United States government has never tried and probably never will try, any one engaged in the late revolution, for treason," Davidson argued, "nor has it ever even restricted the privileges of a person for treason. . . . how then can the press expect the United states government to find fault with Peru for employing an officer in whose conduct the government itself saw nothing punishable?" Davidson concluded by quoting approvingly the New-York *Herald's* advice to U.S. naval officers: "they must 'make obeisance to unpardoned rebels.'"[27]

Living in Annapolis, Maryland, Davidson was not affected directly by the Reconstruction Acts that Congress passed in 1867 to establish military rule over the seceded states and compel them to adopt new state constitutions. But he resented the acts and feared what they would mean for his native state and his own career. "Do drop me a line & tell me what is going on in your part of the Kingdom of Dixie," Davidson wrote to John Brooke on March 12, 1867. Davidson expressed "much interest" in Brooke and others in Lexington, where Brooke had taken a position on the faculty of the Virginia Military Institute. "Is Old Virginia going to sign & seal her <u>own</u> degradation?" Davidson mused to Brooke. "What does Genl Lee think of it—& how is he? God bless him!" He then confessed something of his own position: "My family are all well just now & <u>I am out of employment</u> but shall go into the merchant service soon."[28]

Davidson's correspondence with Brooke had everything to do with Davidson's employment prospects. Brooke, Robert Dabney Minor, and Catesby Jones had established what Brooke described as a "Civil Bureau of Supply." In addition to his two antebellum U.S. patents and his role in designing the CSS *Virginia,* Brooke was the inventor of the highly successful rifled gun that bore his name and had commanded the Confederacy's Bureau of Ordnance and Hydrography for the last two years of the war. Minor was a protégé of Matthew Fontaine Maury on the eve of the war and his first torpedo assistant and commanded the Naval Ordnance Works in Richmond for most of the war. Jones, the former executive officer of CSS *Virginia,* had spent the last two years of the war superintending the Confederacy's second most important naval ordnance works at Selma, Alabama. His prewar mentor in naval ordnance had been John Dahlgren. Their prospectus announced

27 "The Dahlgren-Tucker Affair." New York *World,* July 2, 1867. Davidson enclosed a clipping of the article in his July 4, 1867, letter to Robert Dabney Minor, Minor Papers.

28 Davidson to Brooke, Mar. 12, 1867, BP.

John Mercer Brooke (1826-1906), Davidson's Date of 1841 USN classmate, Confederate Navy comrade, and postwar correspondent. *NH&HC (NH-58902)*

that the officers would "offer their services as Agents to select, purchase and forward on Commission, all Products of American Manufacture or Invention, that may be required to promote the efficiency of Navies and Coast Defences: as WOODEN and IRON-CLAD VESSELS, TORPEDO BOATS and TORPEDOES, IRON LAND DEFENCES, ORDNANCE and ARMS of all descriptions." Brooke and Minor managed to retain or recover many of their wartime papers and received tacit assurance from the U.S. Navy that they could operate without violating U.S. laws. They also determined to avoid aiding what the partners deemed "wrong causes." Davidson obviously was angling to get in on whatever action the Civil Bureau of Supply might bring.[29]

Given Davidson's reputation as (quoting John Randolph Tucker) "the most experienced and practical 'Torpedo' officer in the United States or Confederate Navies" and that a request for torpedo drawings had been the occasion for launching the business, it would seem natural that Brooke, Minor, and Jones would invite Davidson to join them. That they did not begs obvious questions. Did the partners not think their old comrade brought enough expertise into the business to justify dividing potential proceeds by another share? Was there something about Davidson's character, personality, temperament, status, or unreconstructed attitude that made him seem too risky? (Brooke and Minor had applied for and received presidential pardons under the terms of Andrew Johnson's May 1865 proclamation; Jones apparently had not.) Indirect answers come from John Brooke's letters to Robert Minor. Discussing various ways to drum up business, Brooke informed Minor in September 1866 that he had drafted a paper on "the construction and use of torpedoes (except electric which everybody understands)."

29 Undated prospectus in Catesby ap Roger Jones file, Minor Papers; Brooke, Jr. *John Brooke*, 300-310.

According to his grandson and biographer, Brooke had been focusing his own intellectual energy on torpedoes since the war, which suggests that he believed that Davidson's expertise would add no real value to their work. A few months later Brooke mentioned Davidson's interest in their business. "I will do all that can be done for him," Brooke wrote. "Matters are not sufficiently advanced to effect a proper arrangement at this time, we must avoid confusion." Excluding Davidson seemed to be a business decision, not a personal one.[30] Whatever the reasons, the partners never invited Hunter Davidson to join them, and he spent the next several years maneuvering for a seat at the table and accepting occasional crumbs from it.

A month after his first letter, Davidson wrote Brooke again on April 25 and did not even attempt to feign optimism about his future. "I have sought for employment in New York since xmas but without success," he wrote. "I have many promises for the future—but you know what promises are. I want bread & butter & must do something for it & that quickly." Davidson had returned that morning from New York, where he learned from a Date of 1841 and Confederate comrade about other former Confederates working for the Pacific Mail Steamship Company. "McLane—Presdt of the P.M.S.S. Co is a splendid man—but he is as everyone else north M[ason] & D[ixon]'s line, afraid to touch Confeds," Davidson concluded. With that door of opportunity slamming shut, Davidson hoped that Brooke could open another door for him. "I see by the papers that you have been 'rewarded by the Prussian King for y[ou]r scientific attainments,' . . . I write now hoping for a little success in the same direction." He asked Brooke for an introduction to the Prussian minister in Washington. To the man whose promotion he had criticized behind his back five years earlier because the promotion was a result of his scientific and technological accomplishments, not active service, Davidson now fawned: "You are a man whose opinion I value & hence this epistle."[31]

John Brooke had not only a stable job and a stellar reputation for his intelligence and his character, but also many potentially lucrative contacts in Japan, Prussia, and Russia. Brooke had spent considerable time in Japan shortly after Commodore Matthew C. Perry "opened" the island nation to western trade in 1853. And while Davidson spent much of his U.S. Navy career on the eastern side of the Pacific and spent a winter shipwrecked on the Oregon coast, Brooke was on a ship that surveyed the Japanese coast and shipwrecked for six months on the Japanese coast. Brooke maintained contacts with the Japanese.[32]

30 Brooke to Minor, Sep. 19, 1866 and May 13, 1867, Minor Papers; Brooke, *John Brooke*, 321-23.

31 Davidson to Brooke, Apr. 25, 1867, marked confidential, BP.

32 Brooke, Jr. *John Brooke*, chapter IV.

"I have just seen in the Herald that the Japs are making inquiries about the use of Torpedoes & harbor defenses," Davidson wrote to Brooke on May 6, 1867. "Would not a line/word from you get me a position in those harbor defenses? . . . You could tell the Japs—in a letter of recommendation that I am the man who brought submarine defenses to practical use and success in this country." Obviously excited by this new prospect, Davidson wrote again three days later. "Just think!" he gushed. "Suppose you could get the contract to defend their harbors, we could purchase all the material here—freight a ship and with the exports in and about Richmond formerly of my party (including Crowley the best electrician in the country). We could all start off together & have a grand time & lay by a nice little nest egg."[33]

Davidson also communicated with Brooke's partner, "Bob" Minor, about the Bureau's business prospects and his desire to work for it. Following up his earlier queries with Brooke, Davidson noted incidentally that Brooke had failed to reply to his query "about the Japs and Torpedoes." He reported to Minor on his meeting with Prussian officials in Washington. "I think there is very little chance for me at the P[russian] Legation—The Old Baron [Friedrich von Gerolt, the Prussian minister to the United States, with whom Brooke had a close relationship] is very kind & polite, & I think, more anxious to oblige people than his Govt will be. He talked to me about Brooke's offer—but I think that all such things will find a [secure] 'pigeon hole' in some desk at Berlin for the present."[34]

Davidson also raised the alarm about the man who had become his *bête noir.* "I have just rec'd a letter from that fellow H. H. Doty virtually denying that he [owes] any money," Davidson wrote on May 26, 1867. True to form, the peripatetic Doty was in Riga, Latvia (then Russia), out of Davidson's reach. Davidson endorsed Minor's suggestion to work through some of Matthew Fontaine Maury's contacts in Russia to recoup the money. Doty not only owed Davidson money but posed a material threat to Minor's company. "Farther than this, & which concerns you, I think naturally, is the fact that the fellow is now in Russia imposing himself upon the Govt. Torpedoes which he claims to be the original inventor of. He has gone extensively into that business, & I suspect is now engaged in the defenses of some of their harbors. Of course his impositions will render the govt unwilling to touch any more American Ex-Confederates (as the fellow claims to be) & that govt at least would regard us all as adventurers,—imposing upon folks for a livelihood." Davidson proposed obtaining evidence that Doty had been "false to both sections"

33 Davidson to Brooke, May 6 and May 9, 1867, BP.

34 Davidson to Minor, May 26, 1867 and July 3, 1867, Minor Papers.

during the war and forwarding it, along with a statement from Maury, and his own report about Doty to Russian authorities "& thus head off this rascally fellow. I don't care so much about getting my $700 but the [cool] audacity of the fellow! That audacity which brought him south to spy makes me mad & I want to expose him."[35]

No longer content to beat around the bush, a frustrated Davidson confessed frankly to Bob Minor, who was everyone's friend and confidante: "I am up for any thing now & if you find any one that wishes to employ a hard up Confed why just say so."[36] The cocky young officer who had taunted Abraham Lincoln in 1861 had hit rock bottom.

Meanwhile, Davidson realized that if he hoped to find employment or land contracts with foreign governments, he needed endorsements from men whose names could open doors. In May 1867 he sent out several letters soliciting high-profile endorsements. Consistent with his wartime commendation, former Confederate Navy Secretary Stephen Mallory gratified him with effusive praise that he later quoted in pamphlets and articles: "I regarded your service as equivalent to that of a well appointed fleet or army." Robert E. Lee responded in characteristically careful language appropriate for an officer in another service who had little direct contact with Davidson. Lee stated matter-of-factly that Davidson had commanded the James River torpedo defenses and had served on the "Merrimac" and reputedly had a good reputation in the U.S. Navy. "He was distinguished for enterprise and gallantry, and his services were considered very important by the Secty of the Navy, Mr. Mallory." Davidson later chose to cite Lee's endorsement only indirectly.[37]

35 Davidson to Robert D. Minor, May 26, 1867, Minor Papers. Other sources are silent on Doty's supposed presence in Riga, Latvia. Davidson did not succeed in "exposing" Doty. Far from it. In 1875, "Mr. H. H. Doty, of London," offered to provide at his own expense "the necessary light . . . for the memorial monument proposed to be erected in the harbor of New York by the joint action of the people of France and the United States"—what became the Statue of Liberty. Three years later, Doty won a silver medal at the Paris Exhibition for his lighthouse lamp. See "THE CENTENNIAL," *North American and United States Gazette* [Philadelphia], Nov. 25, 1875; "AMERICAN PRIZES AT THE PARIS EXHIBITION . . .," *Staunton Spectator* [VA], Oct. 29, 1878; "AMERICA AT THE PARIS EXPOSITION," *WES*, Mar. 11, 1878. According to a history of the Doty family (Doty, *Doty-Doten Family*, 91, H. H. Doty married an English woman, Emma Crozier Bohn, in 1868, and died in England, ca. 1888. In fact, the 1891 English census found Henry H Doty, a "lighting engineer," living in Chelsea, London, with yet another (American-born) wife. Doty died in London on January 15, 1896. 1891 England Census and List of deaths registered in Jan., Feb., and Mar. 1896 in England-Wales Death Register, accessed via Ancestry.com.

36 Davidson to Minor, July 3, 1867, Minor Papers.

37 Quoted in "The First Successful Application of Electrical Torpedoes or Submarine Mines In Time of War and As a System of Defense," 2, 3; and "Electrical Torpedoes as a System of Defence," *SHSP* (July 1876), 2:3. Mallory's original letter not found. Lee to Davidson, June 10, 1867, Lee Letterbook, VMHC.

The endorsement that Davidson sought from former Confederate president, Jefferson Davis, was a classic case of over-reach that Davidson later had cause to regret. "If you can find a few moments leisure whilst recruiting your health from the long suffering and pain to which you have been subjected," Davidson wrote Davis less than three weeks after the latter's release from two years of imprisonment at Fort Monroe, "I desire to beg that you will honor me with a brief statement of your opinion of the value of my services in command of Submarine and Torpedo operations, as applied to the purposes of the War during the late Revolution." His object, he explained with considerable hyperbole, was "that not being able to find prosperous employment in this Country for the support of my family I am about to enter the Prussian Service for the defence of their Harbors with Torpedoes, Subm. Batteries &c., and the Prussian Minister looks very favorably upon it." Acknowledging that Davis would have little recall of those services, Davidson provided them in some detail. He concluded with the explanation that the "burning of Richmond caused the destruction of all of my official documents, papers &c., hence I am now dependent upon the expression of good opinion of those under whom I had the honor of serving."[38]

Davis's reply was, like Lee's, cautious, but very congenial. "Be assured that the high regard and respect in which I hold you makes it a real pleasure to me to serve you in any manner you may think it practicable for me to promote your welfare," wrote Davis. "Your correspondence with the Secretary and his endorsements as well as my own, would most specifically attest the favorable estimate placed upon your suggestions and services." After echoing the talking points that Davidson had provided, the former Confederate president concluded "Your services entitled you to the grateful remembrance of your compatriots, and will I hope secure for you a favorable reception in the foreign land in which you propose to seek a new home." Sensing perhaps Davis's reluctance to credit the value of his torpedo work, Davidson did not include Davis's endorsement in any of his self-promotional writings. He expressed "painful surprise" when Davis failed to recall this letter or even allude to Davidson's service in his 1881 memoir. Stung by Davidson's sharp reproach, the former president confirmed that he wrote his 1867 letter simply "to serve you and evince my esteem for you as an officer, and my regard for you as a man." His failure to endorse Davidson's claim of his own importance in the development of torpedoes was no oversight.[39]

38 Davidson to Davis, May 28, 1867, in Dunbar S. Rowland, ed., *Jefferson Davis Constitutionalist: His Letters, Papers, and Speeches*, 11 vols. (Jackson, MS, 1923), 7:107-9.

39 Davis to Davidson, July 3, 1867, Rowland, ed., *Jefferson Davis* Constitutionalist, 7:109-110; "Davis and Davidson," 286, 289.

By the second half of 1867, financial pressures as well as the deteriorating political situation had Davidson looking for safe harbor. He wrote to Bob Minor in late July to inquire about a place to rent in a village along the Orange & Alexandria Railroad within a four-hour train ride of Washington. "I must leave here soon for it is too expensive & I prefer the comparative seclusion of a country life for the present," he explained. "I have four children, the oldest thirteen—the youngest three years, & I hope never to have any more—This I mention because some houses or Hotels do not like to take babies - & you must tear this up as soon as you read it." He clarified that he "should be content with any kind of accommodation & only want to get away from Cities for the present." Two weeks later he updated Minor: "I wrote to Mrs. Lucas about board & she [answered] me very promptly & kindly—but they are all too expensive for me. I want to get my family somewhere for $100 per month—plain fare—in the country & am ready to put up with anything for awhile. I shall probably go to some little country town in Western Maryland among the mountains & hide away whilst the political storm is blowing over." He would even consider going abroad "for a fair salary." Declaring that he was "rather discouraged by the prospects in this country," Davidson concluded: "I am satisfied that my day—at least—is over in Yankeedom & would rather bear a stronger govt elsewhere than put up with the painful changes & uncertainties of this."[40]

40 Davidson to Minor, July 25 and Aug. 7, 1867, Minor Papers.

Chapter Seven

Captain Davidson, Maryland State Oyster Police Force (1868–1872)

Ultimately, it was not necessary for Davidson to leave the city for the country or seek employment abroad. Conservatives in Maryland clawed their way back into power at the end of 1866. With a narrow Democratic Conservative majority, the 1867 General Assembly restored the right to vote and hold office to men who swore allegiance to the United States and pledged to be loyal citizens in the future—without consideration of their past loyalty. Buoyed by the relaxed suffrage requirements, voters in April 1867 approved a new Constitutional Convention and ratified the resulting document in September. Stunned by this turn of events, Republicans boycotted the Constitutional Convention and the fall 1867 elections, resulting in a state legislature consisting entirely of Democrats.[1]

The new State Senate appointed Davidson as its journal clerk. On January 3, 1868, Davidson took an oath by which he swore or affirmed that he would "to the best of my ability, protect and defend the Union of the United States, and not allow the same to be broken up or dissolved, or the government thereof to be destroyed under any circumstances, if in my power to prevent it, and that I will at all times discountenance and oppose any political combinations having for their object such dissolution or destruction." The *Baltimore American*, a Republican

1 Scharf, *History of Maryland*, 684-703; Robert J. Brugger, *Maryland: A Middle Temperament, 1634-1980* (Baltimore, 1988), 306-7; Frank Atkinson Kent, *The Story of Maryland Politics* (Baltimore, 1911), 9-10.

The only known photograph of the four Davidson brothers, taken in Annapolis in January 1870. Left to right: Charles, John, Roger, and Hunter. The photograph represents not only a reunion of four brothers, but also a reconciliation between Bvt. Brig. Gen. Davidson, USA, and Cdr. Davidson, CSN, who are clasping hands across the table. *Black Jack Davidson*

organ, recounted Davidson's rebel pedigree and concluded drolly: "Such are the men that Maryland Democracy delights to reward."[2]

During the January 1868 legislative session, Davidson served not only as journal clerk of the Maryland Senate but occasionally sat in the chair as that body's acting secretary or secretary *pro tem.*[3] By February, when he replied to James McNeill Whistler's appeal for help, Davidson declared Annapolis his "headquarters" for the time being.

As he was settling into his new position, Hunter Davidson—recipient of two U.S. patents—indulged in a curious example of early product endorsement. He wrote an open letter to the Wilcox & Gibbs Sewing Machine Company (published in the *Jersey Journal* under the title "Mrs. Davidson's Conclusion—And What Brought her to It") relating how pleased Mary Davidson had been with their machine, but that she had to dispose of it when compelled to travel in 1864 (conveniently neglecting to mention her arrest trying to cross the Potomac). She acquired another brand that she found inferior to theirs, and "she now wishes to exchange it for one of yours. Please answer immediately, if you will exchange."[4] Things finally were looking up for the Davidson family.

Upon the conclusion of the legislative session at the end of March, Davidson slid into a new position in the Maryland state government that suited his background, training, and temperament. "Hunter Davidson, who deserted from the United States Navy at the commencement of the rebellion, went South, joined the Rebels and commanded a torpedo and other vessels in James river," announced the *Cecil Whig*, "has been appointed Commander-in-Chief of the 'Maryland Navy,' to enforce the Oyster law passed by the late Legislature."[5]

The position seemed so perfect for Davidson that it is tempting to believe that it was a sinecure created for him specifically. In reality, the creation of a state "Oyster Navy" was another step in the state's continuing effort to protect an increasingly valuable natural resource. After Delaware and New England oystermen had depleted their own state's oyster beds early in the 19th century, they expanded their range to Chesapeake Bay. In response, Maryland passed an act in 1830 prohibiting oystermen from other states from harvesting oysters in Maryland waters. An 1865 act required Maryland oystermen to obtain a license. By June 1867, the state code

2 Scharf, *History of Maryland*, 689-90; *Journal of The Proceedings of the Senate of Maryland January Session, 1868* (Annapolis, [1868]), 6. The appointment of Davidson and the other officers was made on motion of Democrat Eli J. Henkle, of Anne Arundel County *Baltimore American*, Jan. 4, 1868.

3 *Journal of the Proceedings of the Senate*, 15, 19, 23, 24, 46, 71, 119.

4 *Jersey Journal* [Jersey City], Jan. 11, 1868; also Jan. 14, 22, 1868.

5 *The Cecil Whig* [Elkton, MD], May 9, 1868.

included a 33-section article detailing the issuing of licenses, the how, where, and when of catching oysters, and the punishment of violators.[6]

The law approved on March 30, 1868, repealed the 1867 law and "re-enacted" the law with amendments (now totaling 52 sections) intended to enforce the laws. The new law established a State Oyster Police Force, budgeted $22,000 to purchase a steam vessel and two tenders, and funds to pay, arm, and equip a commander, chief mate, pilot, engineer, assistant engineer, three firemen and coal heavers, a steward, cook, and as many seamen as deemed necessary. The commander would be accountable to a commission of state officers and earn an annual salary of $2,500. The commander's duties were "to keep his vessel constantly cruising, when circumstances will permit, wherever opposition to the oyster law has arisen, or is likely to arise, within the boundaries of the State, and that every locality where a violation of the law exists, or is likely to arise, shall be visited as often as the duties of the force and the conditions of the vessel will permit," to make a monthly report to the commissioners, and keep a monthly journal.[7]

As news of the new oyster bill—introduced by the chairman of the House Committee on Oysters and Oyster Trade, William Henry Legg[8]—became public, prominent men wrote to Maryland officials recommending Davidson for the prospective new position of commander. The officers of the Board of Maryland Pilots endorsed him, citing particularly his "experience on the Chesapeake Bay and its tributaries" (thanks in part to the 1860 Naval Academy Summer Cruise) and his management of steamboats. Seventeen men from Dorchester County expressed themselves "extremely anxious that the command of this force should be given to the proper man" and "most earnestly recommend Capt. Hunter Davidson of Annapolis for that position." They described Davidson as "well known and very popular here" and opined "that his great intelligence, force of character, and nautical expertise point him out as preeminently qualified for the discreet and efficient discharge of its duties." Another group of men from the newly re-empowered planter class, led by the influential Edward Lloyd and his kinsman, Davidson's former CSS *Virginia* commander, Adm. Franklin Buchanan, applauded the bill and noted that a police force had been long needed. If the act passed, "we can with perfect confidence recommend Captain Hunter Davidson for the command.

6 Adm. Mark Belton, "Hunter Davidson: Fighting Naturalist" (Maryland Department of Natural Resources, Mar. 30, 2018). URL: https://tinyurl.com/yb6z9dyv; Lewis Mayer, *Supplement to the Maryland Code, containing the Acts of the General Assembly, passed at the sessions of 1861, 1861-62, 1864, 1865, 1866 and 1867...* (Baltimore, 1868), 171-184.

7 The full text of the law was printed in several newspapers, most legibly in the *Saint Mary's Beacon* [Leonard Town, MD], May 7, 1868.

8 "The Oyster Law," *Saint Mary's Beacon*, Mar. 12, 1868.

He is an intelligent gallant officer whose naval training admirably qualifies him to organize such a police force as is required." The men also described Davidson as "anxious for any honorable employment which will enable him to support his family," suggesting that the self-described "hard up Confed" had inspired this and possibly other letters of recommendation.[9]

Upon passage of the new act, every state senator and most of the delegates petitioned the newly created Board of Commissioners of the State Oyster Police force to "solicit the favorable consideration. . . on behalf of Capt Hunter Davidson for the position of Commanding officer of the 'Oyster Police Force' of the state, believing him eminently qualified for the position." On April 22, 1868, the Oyster Police commissioners (consisting of the state governor, treasurer, comptroller, Superintendent of Labor, and the Clerk of the Court of Appeals) voted unanimously for Davidson over five other candidates for the job.[10]

Davidson hit the ground running. Anticipating his election, he wrote to the state comptroller underscoring "the necessity of taking immediate action in regard to building or buying a Steamer to carry out the object of the Law." He advised further that, in the interest of efficiency, the board should delegate one of its members to coordinate with the commander of the police force. Davidson posted the required $20,000 bond and took the oath of office on April 27. He chartered the Baltimore steamer *Emma Dunn* for a month as a temporary headquarters vessel, fitted her out for service, and, on May 7, with the statutory complement of officers and seamen proceeded down the Bay to duty. By June 1, the Oyster Navy had contracted with the Baltimore firm of Shaw & Co. for a new purpose-built steamship to be delivered within three months. Davidson also sought and received permission to arm his vessel with a 12-pound Dahlgren gun that he ordered from Tredegar Iron Works—the Richmond firm that five years earlier had supplied his Confederate Submarine Battery Service.[11]

He began his duties by inspecting the oyster boats to insure that they were properly licensed. Within a few days, he arrested the captain of a boat caught

9 John H. Cooper, et al., to the Oyster Police Commission, undated; Francis Henry, et al., to Robert Fowler, Mar. 6, 1868; and Edward Lloyd, et al., to Senator Leonard Hammond, Mar. 19, 1868, in Records of the Maryland Oyster Police [S302], folder 7 (recommendations). Maryland State Archives (hereafter cited as MSOP Records).

10 James T. Earle, et al., to the Board of Commissioners, undated, folder 7, MSOP Records; Minute Book, 1868-1878, of the Commissioners of the State Oyster Police [S303], entry for 22 Apr.1868, MSA (hereafter cited as MSOP Minutes).

11 Davidson to William L. McPherson, Apr. 22, 1868, folder 7, MSOP Records; Davidson to Governor Swann and the Board of Commissioners, May7, 1868, folder 5, MSOP Records; and Davidson monthly report, June 1, 1868 (for May 1868), folder 2, MSOP; MSOP Minutes, entry for July 30, 1868.

dredging illegally and took him to court, which fined the captain. He and his men distributed 200 printed copies of the 1868 law, introducing oystermen to the new rules as well as to the proverbial new sheriff charged with enforcing them. After three weeks on the job Davidson filed his first monthly report to the Commission, which included a tabular report of vessels seized, their offenses, and the adjudication of those offenses "Before Justice," and other information and remarks.[12]

In his first narrative report Davidson offered some preliminary observations about the opportunities and challenges facing his new police force. He found that many oystermen were operating without state licenses and were under the impression that licenses obtained from the U.S. Customs House for coastwise trading were all they needed. He pointed out flaws in the legislation, such as provisions that made it difficult and inefficient for cooperative violators to pay their fines. And, contrary to the widespread belief that "dredgers" (boats using dredges to harvest oysters in massive quantities, thus depleting the oyster beds) were the imminent danger to the oysters and to the livelihoods of the tongmen or "tongers," Davidson believed that the new act handicapped the dredgers, "thus cramping the labor and [resources] of the State." He was pleased to report that his force "has been met everywhere with good will, and expressions of respect for the Law, not even a harsh word has yet occurred during the performance of my duties, and there has been sixteen cases, all of which have gone in favor of the State."[13]

Among Davidson's early accomplishments as commander of the Oyster Police was in a capacity for which he would not seem ideally suited: diplomat. "Some time ago there was a conflict of opinion relative to the oyster boundary between Virginia and Maryland," reported the Alexandria [Virginia] *Gazette* on December 30, 1868. Thanks to an agreement negotiated between Davidson and Virginia's chief inspector of oysters, "the matter has been amicably arranged." In his January, 1869 monthly report, Davidson claimed that the boundary seemed to be working well and that "the people in its vicinity have rendered a cheerful compliance with its provisions, and the officer having charge of the Virginia Oyster Revenue Force has promised to make every effort in his power, and to cooperate with me for the promotion of good feeling and a due observance of the laws of our respective states, on the border." The Oyster Police Board of Commissioners ratified the agreement,

12 "The Oyster Police Force. *The Sun* [Baltimore], May 9, 1868, "CAPTURE." *The Sun* [Baltimore], May 15, 1868; Davidson monthly report, June 1, 1868 (for May, 1868), folder 2, MSOP Records; tabular reports in folders 2, 8, and 9, MSOP Records.

13 Davidson monthly report June 1, 1868 (for May, 1868), folder 2, MSOP Records.

though at least one member of the Board later claimed that the agreement worked to Virginia's advantage and proposed its repeal.[14]

Davidson complained that the lack of a suitable vessel "circumscribed" his ability to perform his primary duties, but he hoped and expected to have that vessel in service by the beginning of the new oyster season in September. As September 1 approached, it became clear that the new vessel would not be finished, after all. The Commission leased an ice boat from the state River and Harbor Relief Board for Davidson's use until the amended completion date of November. Davidson, typically, grew impatient and indignant. Rather than representing a great triumph for Davidson, his headquarters steamer, which he named for his daughter Leila, proved to be an enormous ongoing embarrassment. "I have reason to believe," Davidson told the Board of Commissioners in October 1868 that the builders "are not acting in good faith" and have no intention of delivering the steamer on time. Davidson asked for permission to seize the boat material and have her built by another company at the expense of the original contractor. He repeated that request several times over the following months, as Shaw & Co. missed one promised delivery date after another. Davidson intimated to Commission member Colonel William J. Leonard that the contractors "state that I have detained them by not giving proper and necessary instructions, this of course I wholly deny, but it requires investigation."[15]

Finally, on March 30, 1869, the Board of Commissioners authorized Davidson to take immediate possession of *Leila* "and proceed to complete the equipment for service as rapidly as possible, and to superintend and hasten her completion by the contractors according to the contact specifications." Davidson did so and discovered that *Leila* was not only nine months behind her original delivery date, but also seriously defective. In an angry letter to the contractor, Davidson enumerated her defects—a list of 16 items that included only those "which are absolutely necessary for the present efficiency of the vessel," ranging from missing bureaus in the officers' quarters to an absence of putty around the deck seams, missing hand pumps on the decks, and insufficient pressure from the

14 "Oyster Boundary between Md. & VA," *AG*, Dec. 29, 1868; ***Baltimore American***, Dec. 29, 1868; Davidson report of Feb. 1, 1869 (for Jan. 1869), folder 8, MSOP Records; entry for Oct. 19, 1870, MSOP Minutes.

15 MSOP Minutes, entry for Sep. 19, 1868; Davidson to W. J. Leonard, Oct. 3, 1868 and Oct. 14, 1868, folder 5, MSOP Records; Davidson monthly reports of Jan. 1, 1869 (for Dec. 1868) and Feb. 1, 1869 (for Jan. 1869), folders 2 and 8, MSOP Records.

boilers. "There are still other articles not furnished, and requirements not fulfilled which are important specifications of the Contract."[16]

On April 3, Davidson transferred materials from the chartered steamer *Kent,* returned that vessel to her owners, and took the still incomplete *Leila* on an "experimental trip" down the bay to Cambridge, Maryland. The trip revealed just how seriously flawed she was. To Governor Oden Bowie (a distant kinsman of Mary Davidson) Davidson described a harrowing 68-mile journey that took 9-1/2 hours "and this was only accomplished by the use of sail when the steamer was before the wind." The steering gear failed even before leaving Baltimore and had to be replaced. As predicted, the unsealed decks leaked in several places, and the vessel proved "crank"—very unstable. As they came up the Choptank River toward Cambridge, the vessel "laid over on her side with one wheel nearly a foot out of the water" and "it was only by the energy & skill of Chief Engineer Benners Department, working with defective pumps and the low steam which the vessel careys [*sic*] that we were enabled to keep her free." Davidson concluded that if he had taken on the full complement of coal "or had the weather been much rougher, it would have become necessary to run the Steamer ashore to prevent her from sinking."[17]

Davidson reported that *Leila* "was not in any condition for service until the 21st April," and he complained bitterly to the contractor, the governor, and the commissioners that he was unable to perform any of his duties for nearly a month as he and his vessel lay in harbor waiting for delivery and making repairs. This had enormous fiscal implications, "as it occurred during the busiest part of the oyster season, when the fines & forfeitures would have been the greatest."[18]

Cognizant that *Leila's* problems reflected badly on his own management of the Oyster Police Force, Davidson conducted damage control, deflecting blame from himself. "My constant attention to the defects of this vessel is a painful duty," he wrote to the Commission as he reported hundreds of dollars in repair bills. Anticipating that the Maryland legislature would call for his monthly reports and his correspondence, Davidson "desire[d] to show that I have used every effort in my power to protect the interests of the State in this matter, and to prevent the Contractors from getting any more money than they contracted for[.]" He noted the tendency of contractors to act differently toward governments than toward

16 MSOP Minutes, entries for Mar. 31, 1869, and Apr. 8, 1869; Davidson to Messrs. Shaw & Co., Apr. 2, 1869, folder 12, MSOP Records.

17 Davidson to Gov. Bowie, Apr. 6, 1869, folder 12, MSOP Records.

18 Davidson report of May 1, 1869 (for Apr. 1869), folder 9, MSOP Records; Davidson to Messrs. Shaw & Co., Apr. 2, 1869, and Davidson to Gov. Bowie, Apr. 6, 1869, folder 12, MSOP Records.

private contractors and ventured the opinion "that in legislation M[aryland] has failed to observe a method for the protection of the Government in the matter of Contracts." To substantiate his portrayal that the contractors had no scruples about chiseling the state, Davidson quoted remarks he received in his meetings with them: "'Well, we did'nt [*sic*] know any better—we've done our best—and are in for it now, and the State is better able to lose the amount of our bill than we are.'"[19]

Leila's defects did not become an issue with the legislature, the Commission, or the public, but Davidson's performance of his duties and the very existence of the Oyster Police did.

Not surprisingly, a law that limited access to an increasingly profitable natural resource was not universally popular, and Davidson's Oyster Police confronted active resistance. Although not as violent as the aptly named "Oyster Wars" of the 1880s and 1890s, the first Oyster Police were engaged in an occasional shooting war. Much to the consternation of oystermen who had become accustomed to flouting the laws without fear of punishment, Davidson's force did not hesitate to fire warning shots against fleeing vessels. "That mighty Admiral and sworn guardian of bivalvular mollusks, Captain Hunter Davidson, of the Maryland Oyster Police, on Thursday last discovered three schooners taking oysters near the mouth of the Great Choptank River, in Dorchester waters," the *Delaware Tribune* reported sarcastically in January, 1870, "and upon approaching them they hoisted sail and attempted to escape, but a shot fired ahead of them brought them to. . . ." A story repeated often in modern histories of Maryland's Oyster Wars describes Davidson narrowly escaping an assassination attempt by a notorious pirate named Gus Rice in January 1871. The dramatic story did not appear in Davidson's reports or contemporary newspaper accounts. Gustavus Rice, a native of Virginia's Northern Neck, was indeed a brawler and a captain of a notoriously lawless oyster boat, but his encounters with the Oyster Police date from the late 1880s.[20]

19 Davidson monthly report, June 1, 1869 (for May, 1869), folder 8, MSOP Records.

20 See "The Oyster Pirates," *NYS*, Dec. 9, 1888; "Violation of the Oyster Laws," *Delaware Tribune* [Wilmington, DE], Jan. 20, 1870 or Jan. 18, 1870; also *Cecil Whig* [Elkton, MD], Jan. 30, 1869; John R. Wennersten, *The Oyster Wars of Chesapeake Bay* (Centreville, MD, [1981],) 42-3, 76-7; Brugger, *Maryland: A Middle Temperament*, 326; William S. Dudley, *Maritime Maryland: A* History (Baltimore, 2010), 112; "OYSTER WARS," *Saint Mary's Beacon* [Leonard Town, MD], Dec.20, 1888; 1850, 1860, and 1870 U.S. Censuses, accessed via Ancestry.com; Maryland Marriage certificates from Ancestry.com. Those sources also identify Hunter Davidson as a "Kent Island man," apparently conflating him with his son, Rev. Hunter Davidson, who lived on Kent Island, MD. The Oyster Police archives contain no narrative or tabular reports for 1871, thus making it impossible to conclude that no assassination attempt occurred that year.

Davidson and his police came under fierce criticism, primarily from Republican newspapers, for capricious and inconsistent enforcement of a law calculated to cripple the oyster industry and rob the public treasury. The *Baltimore American* characterized the new oyster law and its enforcement as "downright robbery of the honest gains of oystermen. . . . It comes, then, to *this:* That Captain Hunter Davidson, late of the Rebel navy, and Lieutenant John C. Henry, late of the Rebel army, and their whole squadron, are supported by the toil and sweat of our honest oysterman, while their 'expenses absorb all the receipts.' Instead of *protecting,* they 'absorb' the revenue, and create a nuisance that ought to be abated, if it can be done by any means short of an extra session—a remedy worse, if possible than the disease itself."[21]

On February 10, 1869, the *Baltimore Gazette* published a letter from a "Licensed Tongman" in response to an earlier letter from "Citizen" that praised Davidson's "ability and circumspection" in the performance of his duties. "A Licensed Tongman" scoffed at that characterization. He and his fellow tongmen considered Davidson's force "a nuisance," and charged Davidson with willfully allowing "marauders" to dredge for oysters on bars legally reserved for tongmen.[22]

The letter evoked from Davidson the kind of indignant response that he had exhibited often during his U.S. Navy career. Under the pen name, "ONWARD, Davidson published a long and blistering rejoinder in the February 16 Baltimore *Gazette* (later reprinted in other papers). Offering his arguments in the third-person voice, Davidson wrote that "The officer commanding the police force not only denies these charges but would treat them with silent contempt were it not for the character and influence of the able journal in which they appear." If the commander were guilty of the charges, the Commission would investigate and remove him, and Davidson urged "Licensed Tongman" to file a formal complaint to initiate an investigation. Davidson angrily refuted the charge that his force willfully permitted illegal dredging, but he acknowledged that the Oyster Law was "imperfect" and suffered from vagueness in defining geographic boundaries for various kinds of oystering. "The defects and insufficiency of the present Oyster law do not afford the Police Commander the means of reconciling the conflicting interests of the dredgers and the tongmen," he explained, "which is the one great difficulty after all." He offered statistics about seizures and revenue from fines to refute "Licensed Tongman's" charge that the police force was "a useless expenditure

21 *Baltimore American and Commercial Advertiser*, Feb. 9, 1869.

22 "Citizen," "Trouble Among the Oystermen," Baltimore *Gazette,* Jan. 28, 1869, and "A Licensed Tongman," "The Oyster Question." Baltimore *Gazette,* Feb. 10, 1869, exhibits no. 1 and no. 2 in folder 10, MSOP Records.

of public money." Davidson admitted that the police force was not a "great success," but it was "no longer an experiment" and in its "infancy." He closed by suggesting that "Licensed Tongman" acted from "some selfish ambition or sinister motive."[23]

Not surprisingly, "Licensed Tongman" fired back against "Captain 'Onward,' or rather Captain Backward," thus coyly signaling that he knew the identity of his protagonist. In his response, he not only accused Davidson of turning a blind eye to illegal dredging, but of conspiring with the dredgers. He appended an affidavit from oystermen certifying "that we have seen from twenty to sixty vessels dredging on Holland's Point Bar daily from the beginning of the season to this date, and knew they do it with Capt. Davidson's consent, as he has been present several times without preventing them or attempting to do so."[24]

Davidson as "ONWARD" responded with a letter that focused on the "Tongman's" month-long effort to find a paper to publish his latest letter—accomplished finally by signing another man's name on the original letter given to the *Gazette*. Davidson personally visited that man, who denied any knowledge of the letter. "You will therefore perceive that some infamous person, who dares not bring his charges against Captain Davidson, before the "Commissioners of the State Oyster Police Force," has deliberately forged the name of one person, in order to effect the ruin of another—for reasons best known to himself." "ONWARD" reiterated that Davidson welcomed an investigation of the charges, confident that it would "expose all these shameless attempts to discredit the State Oyster Police Force, in their true characters, and to the satisfaction of all concerned." He concluded by instructing the editor to "Please give my name to any one who may ask for it—but here, I prefer to sign, ONWARD."[25]

Davidson then took off not only his gloves, but also his mask. He corresponded directly with "Licensed Tongman," whose identity he had ferreted out as Frank Lewis (or Louis) Griffith of Anne Arundel County. Through his friends on the Oyster Police Commission Davidson may have learned that Griffith had written to Governor Bowie in March 1869 about Davidson's reported willful neglect of his duties and to apply for the job as Oyster Police commander after Davidson's inevitable removal. The son of a boat captain, Griffith was also one time captain of a state police boat. And, as he reminded the governor, Griffith also remained

23 Letter from "ONWARD," Baltimore *Gazette*, Feb. 16, 1869 reprinted in *State Capital Advertiser* [Annapolis, MD], exhibit no. 3 in folder 10, MSOP Records.

24 "Licensed Tongman," "The Oyster Police," *The Annapolis Gazette, and General Advertiser*, May 6, 1869, exhibit no. 4, folder 10, MSOP Records.

25 Letter from "ONWARD," *Maryland Republican* [Crisfield, MD], May 8, 1869, exhibit no. 5, folder 10, MSOP Records.

loyal to the Union during the war, whereas he knew Davidson to be "a[n] ex Reb." On May 26, Davidson wrote to Griffith a brief note asking him to confirm or deny the intelligence he had received that Griffith was the author of the "Licensed Tongman" letters. When Griffith failed to reply, Davidson reiterated his request on September 28.[26]

Griffith replied on October 1 with an indignant defense of his own honor, additional imprecations against Davidson's integrity, and abject fear of the Oyster Police captain (echoing the fear of "personal violence" that Dr. Washington Sherman of the USS *Dale* had expressed his 1859 court martial trial). He asked Davidson whether he possessed enough property "to make good to me all damages I may yet obtain" from Davidson's calumnies against him and denied "infamous reports" he had heard that Davidson claimed to have a letter from him offering to pay Davidson's salary if he would hire Griffith as his first officer. "I have been also informed that you have made personal threats against me—to use the language of another 'had often gone on shore looking for him, a 'walking armory & magazine'[.] I [hope] this is incorrect—for I think fighting never settled anything, & am opposed at any & all times to settling anything by [violent?] arm[s]. . ." Griffith then declared their correspondence closed.[27]

Griffith's rambling, occasionally semi-literate, and pusillanimous letter incited Davidson's scorn:

> It is quite evident from the tone of your letter that you are the hapless person who committed the forgery, in publishing the article & its accompanying certificate in the Annapolis Gazette of the 6th May last, headed "The Oyster Police" and signed "Licensed Tongman."
>
> I have never before had personally exposed to me a moral obliquity such as yours, and am therefore somewhat at a loss how to deal with you, unless I treat you as deranged. . . .
>
> Have you reflected that you have deliberately attacked the character of a man whom you have never seen, and know nothing of, and that acting from a one sided impulse, you have rushed blindly into an insane attempt to ruin his character that your attempt has gone so far you cannot retrace your steps, and that even at this point you have never heard one word on the other side? . . .

26 F. Lewis Griffith to Gov. Bowie, Mar. 17, 1869, folder 12, MSOP Records; Davidson to Griffith, May 26, 1869 and Sep. 28, 1869, exhibits no. 6 and 7, folder 10, MSOP Records.

27 F. L[ewis] Griffith to Davidson, Oct. 1, 1869, exhibit no. 8, folder 9, MSOP Records.

> Whilst I pity your derangement, I abhor your crime, I have nevertheless a duty to perform, in upholding the honor, & dignity of my state, and the attempt you have made; must be thoroughly investigated, that she may know her servants are good & true.
>
> The article and letters in this matter, will therefore be laid before the Hon. Comm[issione]r of the State O.P. Force, for their consideration & judgment, and no opportunity of avoiding the issue therein, as is betrayed in your letter, will be left you.
>
> In regard to my property—I will say that I hold amply sufficient to compensate you for any loss of character you could possibly sustain.[28]

Even as Davidson defended himself against charges of incompetence and corruption, he was digesting what he had learned from his first 15 months in command of the Oyster Police into a report for the Maryland General Assembly. Submitted in October 1869 and published in February 1870, Davidson's *Report upon the Oyster Resources of Maryland to the General Assembly* proved to be a landmark in marine resource conservation. In it, Davidson argued persuasively that effective enforcement of laws that protected oysters was in everyone's best interests and would assure that oysters would remain a source of wealth and revenue for Maryland well into the future. He underscored the harmful effects of unrestricted dredging upon oyster beds and the need to protect the welfare of the "tongers" against the dredgers. Davidson reiterated those concerns in his second bi-annual report in 1872: "These are the men whose labor requires the fostering care and protection of the State, because this labor has been directed in the proper channel, and the men acquire, after long years of toil, that knowledge of the Oyster in the different localities, and the circumstances best adapted to its nature and growth, of which the planter must avail himself in the future, when it is to be hoped the trade will be established upon a sure and permanent basis."[29]

In response to those who complained against the laws and the enforcement of them, Davidson mounted a vigorous counterattack. "The use of the dredge for upwards of fifty years, has been the means of keeping afloat a class of sailors,

28 Davidson to Griffith, Oct. 29, 1869, exhibit no. 9, folder 10, MSOP Records.

29 *Report upon the Oyster Resources of Maryland to the General Assembly by Hunter Davidson, Esqu., Com. State Oyster Police Force.* (Annapolis, MD, 1870); [Hunter Davidson], *Report on the Oyster Fisheries: Potomac River Shad and Herring Fisheries, and the Water-Fowl of Maryland to His Excellency the Governor and other Commissioners of the State O. P. Force, January 1872,* Maryland House of Delegates, Document E, Jan. 10, 1872, 13.

who, from the free and roving habits of their lives, removed from the restraints of society, and even the law, (until the Police Force was appointed,) have grown to think of themselves masters of the Oyster situation, and the advantages and working of their trade have been kept to themselves by a tacit agreement, in order that they might reap all the profits without interference." Far from spending too much of the people's money, as his critics charged, Davidson contended that his force suffered from lack of funds. "It is impossible," he argued, "to execute any practical method of regulating the taking and trade of Oysters, without a force *afloat;* private rights, the maintenance of the peace, and even the majesty of the law, are but names without it. The State is entitled to a revenue from her Oysters, and the people demand protection in the trade thereof. . . . The present force cannot be reduced and be efficient; on the contrary, it cannot now do more than half the duty required of it." He responded to those who charged him with corruption: "The journals and books of record, regularly kept, will show the amount of duty performed, and are always open to, and shown, any citizen interested." He then described in more detail the challenges his force faced:

> We have but one small, slow steamer, with which to visit twenty-five different Oyster localities scattered sometimes far apart, over tortuous routes, the extremes of which are one hundred miles from north to south, by seventy-five miles from east to west. I mention these facts *here*, because the people have been led to expect too much of this force, without considering the imperfections of the law under which it operates. It is expected to be in every locality at intervals of a few days, whereas about two months are required to make a complete tour of inspection, taking into account the time consumed by the average number of arrests and trials.
>
> Those who are in the habit of violating the law, keep the run of our movements by a regular system of reports from one to the other, and thus are often enabled to escape punishment for their offenses; but because all is not done that is desired, is no evidence that the force is not necessary; it rather shows that the force should be increased to a proportion that will cover the field of duty."

Assuming the tone of a booster, he predicted that Maryland's oyster beds "could be made to give profitable employment to twenty thousand laborers, in a very few years from this, under the administration of proper laws." He then proceeded to suggest specific modifications to the oyster laws, including an extension of his authority "to enforce the laws relating to the fisheries, as well as the Oyster trade, so that the duties of the force would be, the 'Inspection of Fisheries,' construed by law to include Oysters."[30]

The reception of Davidson's widely distributed report was largely favorable. "The Report contains much information in regard to the coveted bivalve, portions of which we publish, and which the majority of our readers will find new and interesting," editorialized the often-critical *Cecil Whig.* "From this report which appears to be entirely reliable, it is evident that the oysters need the protection of the state authority, or it will erelong be entirely cleaned out of the Maryland waters of the Chesapeake and its tributaries." A Wilmington, Delaware, paper quoted and endorsed Davidson's warnings against depleting the oyster beds.[31]

Having demonstrated mastery of the oystering industry, Davidson also was able to defeat the designs of his critics. As promised, he amassed his correspondence with F. L. Griffith, and clippings of Griffith's "Licensed Tongman" letters, and "ONWARD's" responses, presented them to the Commission, and requested a formal inquiry. At its April 20, 1870 meeting, the Commission (still firmly under Democratic control) read "sundry letters . . . complaining of neglect of official duty" by Davidson, conducted an investigation of the charges, heard a presentation by an attorney representing the complainants, then passed a resolution "that it is the opinion of the Board that the charges ad[vanced?] against Commander Davidson are not sustained by the evidence but Commander Davidson is honorably acquitted on each and every of said charges, and that his official action, so far as brought to the knowledge of the board , is hereby fully endorsed as that of a faithful and official P[olice] Officer." The Commissioners then unanimously re-elected Davidson for another two-year term as Commander of the Oyster Police Force.[32]

Davidson's reappointment promised the kind of stability that he and his family had not enjoyed since early 1861. The Davidsons lived in the city of Cambridge in Dorchester County, on Maryland's Eastern Shore, across Chesapeake Bay from Mary Ray Davidson's hometown of Annapolis. In addition to Leila (16 in 1870), the Davidsons had sons Percy (13), Hunter (9); and Charles Steele (5). Contrary to his 1867 assurance to Bob Minor that they would have no more children, they

30 *Report of the Oyster Resources*, 11, 13, 14, 17-18.

31 "The Oyster Trade and Oyster Navy of Maryland," *The Cecil Whig* [Elkton, MD], Feb. 12, 1870; "MARYLAND OYSTERS. / POSSIBILITY OF THEIR BECOMING AN ARTICLE OF EXPORT—DREDGING DESTRUCTIVE—PROTECTION DEMANDED" *Wilmington Daily Commercial* [DE], Mar. 11, 1870.

32 MSOP Minutes, entry for Apr. 20, 1870; "LOCAL MATTERS. Meeting of the State Oyster Commissioners," *The Sun* [Baltimore], Apr. 23, 1870; *Annapolis Gazette*, Apr. 28, 1870; *The Cecil Whig* [Elkton, MD], May 7, 1870.

had two more sons, whom they named for their father's Confederate comrades: Franklin Buchanan (born January 28, 1869) and Maury (born July 7, 1872).

Stability for his family, however, was not apparently all that Hunter Davidson sought. A few months after his vindication and reappointment for another term as commander of the Oyster Police, Davidson requested a leave of absence to travel to London. "Circumstances have transpired of much import to my future, and it is absolutely necessary that I should visit London for a few weeks to work up the matter," he intimated to James S. Franklin, his closest confidante on the Board. "I believe I have been a hard working faithful officer, and I have never asked for a days absence from duty," Davidson explained, promising to leave the Force in "good hands." He needed to act quickly, sailing from New York in eight days, and he appealed for secrecy: "My success depends upon my movements not being known except to the Comm[issione]rs."[33]

The "good hands" in which Davidson left the force were those of his first officer, Samuel Copper. Davidson—rather condescendingly ("I am aware that you have had no experience in the operations of the Force . . .")—wrote detailed instructions that provide a window onto his own approach to his duties as commander:

> Do not arrest parties unless the evidence is conclusive, & in every case ask the Justice to put on a fine which will not cause the parties to appeal, for when you get before Court there is no end to your troubles. Be careful in all you say and do with the oysterman to be impartial, don't make the least differance [*sic*] anywhere. Be careful in using the [Tredegar] Gun, not to fire at a vessel unless she has first fired at you. You can throw a shot across their bows to bring them to—but try not to hit them. Be firm with them all and don't talk to them any more than you are oblige [*sic*] to . . . As soon as you take charge commence to inform yourself about the duties and the law, so as to be posted by the commencement of the oyster season. Keep the vessel clean and be regular with the men in regard to their work meals &c. Keep an accurate statement in a book of all bills you pay."

Testifying to how desperately Davidson wished to get away, he left behind several unpaid bills and charged Copper with receiving the delivery of two new sloops for which the Board had contracted in May.[34]

33 Davidson to Franklin, Aug. 9, 1870, folder 16, MSOP Records.

34 Davidson to Copper, Aug. 11, 1870, folder 16, MSOP Records; MSOP Minutes, entries for May 13, 1870, and Sep. 7, 1870; undated report from Samuel Copper for Aug. and Sep. 1870, folder 13, MSOP Records.

Davidson's ultimate destination was not London, but Prussia, which was then at war with France. The trip revealed that Davidson had not surrendered his hopes of finding a more remunerative relationship with a foreign government or joining the Civil Bureau of Supply that Brooke, Minor, and Jones had created. It was, in fact, at least in part a mission on behalf of that business. Davidson was to show the Prussians drawings and specifications for an invention. Upon his return, Davidson confessed to Brooke that he failed to receive the drawing the latter had mailed to him. "I am quite sure that something could have been realized on it. But it's all over now—and we can only regret it." Davidson was not impressed with the Prussian naval establishment and believed that they "have been shamefully humbugged, in Torpedo affairs, by the English in general, and some yankee imposters who have been hanging around European govts ever since our lost Revolution trying to palm off—and in fact succeeding in palming off the most miserable combinations called inventions—that completely disgusted me when I was there." Combining flattery and reproach, Davidson concluded: "If you had been earlier in the field & gone at once to Prussia, you would now be worth $100,000 easy. But before we got anything there the poor devils were as sure as possible on the subject and believed that every one was trying to filch money out of them." Even when Davidson was in Europe, the North German Confederation was in the process of overwhelming the French, and the Germans showed no interest in what the former Confederates were peddling. But Davidson was hopeful for other opportunities. "Write me sometimes—and if anything turns up in our line let me know," he reminded Brooke. "I'm ready for another trip or a [spec] at any time."[35]

To Bob Minor Davidson put a more positive spin on the experience. "I had a splendid time in Prussia," he wrote on December 18. "They treated me like a Prince, heaping every kindness & attention upon me that could possibly be expected in time of War. The trip was not only pleasant, but very instructive for I had the opportunity of studying all their improvements in Torpedoes & subm. defences generally which may be of service to me sooner or later." Whatever hopes he entertained for another trip, Davidson resigned himself to the exigencies of his current job. He asked Minor to obtain for him copies of current Virginia laws relating to Potomac River and Pocomoke Creek fisheries. "Our last Legislature has imposed so much additional duty upon me—Fisheries—Wild Fowl &c—that I have to spend most of my time in one place fighting law questions all the time—which I know nothing about," he explained wearily.[36]

35 Davidson to Brooke, Dec. 22, 1870, BP.

36 Davidson to Minor, Dec. 18, 1870, Minor Papers. This quixotic trip to Prussia was probably the source of later newspaper stories about Davidson's relationship with the Prussian government. The

Davidson threw himself into a second two-year term commanding the Oyster Police. His political enemies assailed him as a "bully" and lampooned him and his force as nautical Keystone Kops. A Bel Air, Maryland, newspaper gleefully described a "Duck War," during which Davidson detained "what he supposed to be a suspicious *vessel*, in the shape of a *scow*," and, when challenged, asserted his authority by brandishing his pistol. "The valiant Captain was not resisted, on this evidence of power, and made his search, but found neither guns, decoys nor any other suspicious property contraband of the ducking war. Subsequently, however, Captain D. secured as trophies three sink boxes and some two hundred decoys, and proceeded to blockade the town to prevent the ingress of any ducking craft that might wish to enter.'" Davidson went about his business as political enemies continued to accuse him of inefficiency and failure to successfully prosecute supposed violators.[37]

However much he may have bristled under the criticism, Davidson characteristically proceeded with confidence in his own integrity. His keen sense of justice even crossed the color line when he pursued and arrested a man accused of drowning an African-American oysterman named John Dobson.[38]

Baltimore *Sun* in 1877 noted that "During the Franco German war he had an advisory position in Germany at large remuneration," (reprinted in *The* [Norfolk, Virginia] *Public Ledger*, Nov. 15, 1877). Davidson's son, Rev. Charles Steele Davidson, later made the fantastic claim that President Grant sent his father to Prussia "to make investigations" about torpedoes. Quoted in *The Milwaukee Leader*, Aug. 4, 1913. Those articles are the basis for this author's erroneous claim that Davidson was "already in Europe to observe the [Franco-Prussian] war for the U.S. government." (Coski, *Capital Navy*, 245).

37 "The Oyster Fleet in the Ducking Waters of Harford," *Aegis and Intelligencer* [Bel Air, MD], Nov. 18, 1870, reprinted in *Cincinnati Semi-Weekly Gazette*, Nov. 25, 1870, and other papers; *Port Tobacco Times and Charles County Advertiser*, Mar. 3, 1871; *The Sun* [Baltimore], Mar. 6, 1871; *Wilmington Daily Commercial* [DE], Apr. 27, 1871.

38 *The Sun* [Baltimore], Nov. 15, 1871. Several historians have intimated to the author that the Oyster Police was intended at least in part to restrict the freedoms of African-American oystermen. The only evidence I have found regarding the Oyster Police and race is a provision that appeared in the 1867 Oyster Law and incorporated verbatim in the 1868 law: "All owners and masters of canoes, boats or vessels licensed under this article, being white men, are hereby constituted officers of this state for the purpose of arresting and taking before any judge of any circuit court or justice of the peace, who shall have jurisdiction therein any person or persons who may be engaged in violating any of the provisions of this article and of seizing an canoe, boat or vessel engaged therein; and all such owners and masters are hereby vested with power to summon the *posse comitatus* to aid in making such arrest and seizure as fully as are constables and sheriffs of the several counties and city of Baltimore." Nothing in either law specifically or in legally ambiguous language prohibited African Americans from obtaining licenses and nothing in Davidson's reports or in newspaper coverage or in the secondary literature pertaining to late 19th-century Maryland suggested enforcement of the law against Black oystermen. Lewis Mayer, *Supplement to the Maryland Code*, 175-176 (1867 act, section 11) and 1868 act, section 12 in *Saint Mary's Beacon*, May 7, 1868. Barbara Jeanne Fields in *Slavery and Freedom on the Middle Ground: Maryland during the Nineteenth Century* (New Haven, 1985), 182-185, discusses the working conditions and the reputation of tongers (of whom one-third of were

Bad press and critical letters did not undermine Davidson's position in 1870, but, by 1872, the political winds had changed direction. At the April 11, 1872, Board of Commissioners meeting, Davidson faced a slew of challengers for the position of Oyster Police commander, including his nemesis, F. L. Griffith. Although he won the plurality of the first two ballots, Davidson lost on the third ballot to Capt. William E. Timmons, a state senator. Davidson was out of a job. He was, once again, a "hard up Confed."[39] Unemployment did not last long, however, and Davidson did not exhibit the desperation that he had felt in 1866-67. Within a year Davidson seized a new opportunity that would shape the last four decades of his life.

black, according to the 1880 census), quotes Davidson's 1872 fisheries report, and describes Davidson as a "generally sympathetic observer" of the tongers' plight.

39 MSOP Minutes, entry for Apr. 11, 1872; Annapolis *Gazette*, Jan. 30, 1872; "Oyster Police Board," *St. Mary's Beacon*, Apr. 18, 1872. Timmons consolidated his position by contrasting the effectiveness of his own administration with the inefficiency of Davidson's. *Saint Mary's Beacon*, June 26, 1873.

Chapter Eight

El ingeniero Hunter Davidson (1873–1884)

Hunter Davidson owed his new opportunity to the good offices of Capt. Thomas J. Page, late commander of the CSS *Stonewall.* The two men last had crossed paths in January 1865 off the coast of France when Davidson and the *City of Richmond* brought the supplies that helped transform the French-built ironclad into the Confederate raider. The end of the war found Page in Cuba, where he sold *Stonewall* to the Spanish. Page took a blockade runner back to England so that he could rejoin his exiled family in Italy. Hesitant about returning the United States, Page found safe haven in Argentina, where he enjoyed a high reputation and good connections thanks to his antebellum service in the U.S. Navy.[1]

In 1852, after the 20-year so-called "tyranny" of dictator Juan Manuel de Rosas, Argentina resumed its halting march toward national unity and economic development. The new leader, General Justo J. Urquiza, on August 28, 1852, issued a decree opening all the country's rivers to exploration and navigation, effective October 1. "The government of the United States was the first to avail itself of the opportunity thus offered to all maritime nations to obtain a more extended knowledge of La Plata," wrote Page in his 1859 book, *La Plata.* "An expedition charged to explore its rivers and to report upon the extent of their navigability and adaptation to commerce, was placed under my command in February 1853." Along with the paddlewheel steamer, *Water Witch,* command of the expedition was something of a consolation prize for the 44-year-old lieutenant from Virginia after

1 "Biography Outline of CAPTAIN THOMAS JEFFERSON PAGE EXPATRIATE FROM VIRGINIA" by Alfred J. Hanna and Phyllis Barbour, VMHC.

Hunter Davidson's
Argentina and Paraguay
1873-1913
0 Miles 100
Map by Edward Alexander
Asunción
Tacuru Pucu
Rio Iguazu
Pirayú
Villa Rica
Iguazu Falls
Rio Paraguay
PARAGUAY
Misiones Province
Itapiru
Corrientes
Posadas
Rio Paraná
BRAZIL
ARGENTINA
Rio Salado
Rio Uruguay
Santa Fe
Paraná
URUGUAY
Rosario
Zárata
Isla Martín García
Fulminante
Rio Luján
Tigre
Ituzaingó
Buenos Aires
Ensenada
Rio de la Plata
Montevideo
Maldonado
Atlantic Ocean

Captain Thomas J. Page, USN and CSN, was responsible for Davidson's position with the Argentine Navy. *NH&HC (NH-80507)*

he had been passed over for command of an exploration of Chinese waters the previous year. Page parlayed the opportunity into an important three-year survey that covered 3,600 miles by river and 4,400 miles by land documenting not only the rivers, but also the natural and agricultural resources of the Argentine interior. His massive and authoritative version of his final report was published 1859, by which time he had returned to Argentina for a follow-up survey that Congress had authorized. Page's son John assisted with the expedition, married an Argentine woman, and remained in the country solidifying the family's foothold there—while Lt. Page returned to New York in late 1860.[2]

Reading between the lines, modern historians detect a hidden agenda by which Page hoped to lay the groundwork for developing a prosperous slave-based agricultural economy in the region. "Indeed," insists Michael Verney, "the aggregate of Page's writings during and after the expedition reveals that he envisioned La Plata as the future scene of Southern colonialism." Page also deliberately and callously traveled beyond the line that President Carlos Antonio Lopez of Paraguay had established for the expedition, provoking a confrontation between *Water Witch* and the Paraguayan fortress at Itapiru in late 1853. Page's 1858-1859 return to La Plata was primarily a punitive expedition after diplomatic talks broke down between the aggrieved Paraguayan government and the U.S. over Page's arrogance in 1853.[3]

2 Thomas J. Page, U.S.N., *La Plata, The Argentine Confederation, and Paraguay, Being a Narrative of the Exploration of the Tributaries of the River La Plata and Adjacent Countries During the Years 1853, '54, '55, and '56, Under the Orders of the United States Government* (New York, 1859), ix-xxii, 25-6.

3 Verney, *A Great and Rising Nation*, 158-169 (quote, 163); Long, *Gold Braids and Foreign Relations*, 161-65.

In 1865 the Argentine government was only too happy to offer Page and his sons land and means of support along with a concession of land on which Page hoped to establish a colony of expatriate southerners. Only a few former Confederate naval officers took advantage of the opportunity.

Page's presence coincided with the Argentine government's determination to address the decades-long neglect of its naval forces. Argentina was then engaged in the War of the Triple Alliance, in which she, Brazil, and a faction of the Uruguayan government were fighting the aggressive Paraguayan regime of Solano López. Page recommended a naval defense system that included the construction of two ironclad vessels. After many years' delay, the government of President Domingo Sarmiento endorsed and funded Page's proposal and, in 1872, charged Page with contracting and supervising construction and arming of two battleships and two ironclads in Liverpool.[4]

In 1865, when he was Argentina's minister in Washington, D.C., Sarmiento realized the potential value of torpedo defenses for the valuable and vulnerable Rio La Plata and hoped to acquire some of the surplus weapons after the end of the American Civil War. Seven years later, President Sarmiento renewed his quest for torpedoes. At his instruction, the Argentine minister to France, Martin Diaz, wrote to Thomas Page in England on November 28, 1872, inquiring about torpedo technology. "Do you know one ex-confederate officer very well informed and practical about the matter, who must be known in Europe?" Diaz wrote. "We want some very capable man to direct this system of land defence." Page previously had queried Matthew Fontaine Maury, who was serving on the faculty at the Virginia Military Institute, about this matter and finally received a reply that Maury was ill and unable to assist him. Page then wrote to Davidson, who was in New York and had already been in contact with the Argentine consul there. Davidson wasted no time in seizing this opportunity. By the time he wrote to Page on February 9, 1873, to accept the invitation, Davidson had already signed a contract.[5]

4 Humberto F. Burzio, *Historia Naval Argentina, Series B, No. 12: Historio Del Torpedo Y Sus Buques En La Armada Argentina 1874-1900* (Buenos Aires, 1968), 9-11, 22, 36.

5 Ricardo Levene, *A History of Argentina,* translated and edited by William Spence Robertson (Chapel Hill, NC, 1937), 468-79; Eduardo C. Gerding, ""The Confederate Navy and the Argentine Hydrographic survey: Time of the Spar Torpedo," *The Buenos Aires Herald*, Sunday, Dec. 14, 2003-Focus-8 [English translation accessed via: https://civilwartalk.com/threads/the-confederate-navy-and-the-argentine-hydrographic-survey.90134/]; Burzio, *Historio Del Torpedo*, 11, 45, 36 (the quote is from a letter cited as being in the private archive of D. Franklin Page); Barbour, "Biographical Outline," 11-12; Alfred J. Hanna and Phyllis Barbour, "Captain Thomas Jefferson Page: Confederate Expatriate From Virginia," unpublished manuscript, copy in NH&HC, 480-83.

"This country is new & rich . . ."

By March 23, 1873, Davidson was in Paris meeting with Dr. Garcia and discussing details about the best torpedo system to employ. A month later, he was in Buenos Aires meeting with President Sarmiento. No doubt encouraged by the never-shy Davidson, Sarmiento recognized his new naval adviser's many areas of expertise and charged him with studying the location of a new harbor for Buenos Aires. Over the next several weeks Davidson conducted an extensive survey and reported his recommendations.[6]

Having impressed his new employer, Davidson returned home with a broad mandate and, apparently, a generous expense account. He spent the next 18 months in a whirlwind of activity, traveling among Argentina, London, New York, and home in Maryland, assembling the material and intellectual and human resources he would need in this promising new adventure.

After seven years in career limbo, Davidson finally found employment that exploited and expanded his experience, expertise, and knowledge in naval science as well as torpedo technology. It was no doubt personally and professionally gratifying to not only obtain substantial remunerative employment, but to have his knowledge and accomplishments respected and sought after. After years of scrounging for work and being indebted to friends for sinecures that brought headache and ridicule, Hunter Davidson could again feel like the talented naval scientist that he was in 1861 and the man of action he was during the Civil War. Hunter Davidson Supine was once again Hunter Davidson Rampant.

The rampant Davidson needed to burnish and broadcast his bona fides as a torpedo expert, for whom other torpedo experts would want to work. Toward this end, in May 1874, while he was in New York, Davidson wrote and published a four-page open letter entitled "The First Successful Application of Electric Torpedoes or Submarine Mines in Time of War, and as a System of Defence" (which was reprinted two years later in *Southern Historical Society Papers*). "I have but recently returned from South America, and had an opportunity of reading two works on Torpedoes, or Submarine Mines" by British officers, he began. The failure of those works to give proper credit to Confederate torpedo development generally and Davidson's own work specifically was the impetus for the open letter.

6 "Commander Hunter Davidson—USN-CSN," by Phyllis Barbour and A. J. Hanna in ZB file, NH&HC; Burzio, *Historio Del Torpedo,* 45; Davidson letter published in unidentified newspaper, Mar. 1889, enclosed in B. W. Hanna to Secretary Blaine, Apr. 6, 1889, copy in Barbour Papers. The Argentine government ultimately ignored Davidson's advice and built the harbor based on the plan of Eduardo Madero.

Davidson credited Secretary Mallory (tentatively) for originating the Confederacy's use of torpedoes and directing Matthew Fontaine Maury to undertake the work. According to Davidson, Maury began his experiments on his own initiative in the spring of 1862, which was nearly a year after Maury began his work. "He had arrived at no definite conclusion from his experiments [with electrical torpedoes], in any particular when he left the Confederacy for Europe," Davidson continued, "and I was ordered to take charge, subject to orders from the Navy Department only, and remained so until near the closing scenes of the war, when I was relieved in command by Captain J. Pembroke Jones." Davidson circled back at the end of his letter to explain that "the want of time" prevented "my ever kind and lamented friend Capt. Maury" (who had died months earlier) from achieving greater success, but most of the open letter was a shameless promotion of his own torpedo work. The thrust of this and subsequent writings was that "the *first* vessels ever *injured or destroyed in war,* by Electrical Torpedoes, were by the Torpedo department operating under my immediate command, and I may add the *only* ones, that I am aware of."

To support his claim, he quoted the letter he had solicited from Mallory in 1867 and cited others from John Brooke and William Parker. Taking a swipe at the reputation of Gabriel Rains, Davidson also belittled the importance of "contact Torpedoes" that had sunk, disabled, or destroyed vessels because they acted by "mere chance" and were "often as fatal to friend or foe." And, although others—from Horace Bushnell to Robert Fulton to the Russians in the Crimean War—had invented or experimented with torpedoes, he was the first to prove the inventions through scientific method. "Now if we are to consider *practical* success as the test of an *invention,*" he reasoned, "have I not a right to this? Am I not as much entitled to it as Morse to the Telegraph? Howe to the Sewing Machine? Colt to the Revolver?" He cited his boat lifting patent as evidence of his credentials as an inventor and of the importance of proving the efficacy of an idea. No doubt to solidify his credentials even further, Davidson conveniently elided his four-year tenure commanding the Oyster police and claimed that "I have been almost constantly on Torpedo duty ashore and afloat since our war, making the subject a study in several foreign countries and our own, and have not yet seen any material improvement or development of the original system."[7]

The elevation of his own role at Matthew Fontaine Maury's expense seems to have been deliberate and was certainly not out of character, but it was so obvious that it threatened to undermine the objective of the pamphlet. Davidson hastened

7 Davidson, "The First Successful Application of Electrical Torpedoes or Submarine Mines in Time of War, and as a System of Defence."

to conduct some damage control. "Please read this pamphlet over carefully & write me as soon as you can, if you believe that I have therein done Capt. Maury injustice in any sense, or have 'stolen any of his thunder'," Davidson appealed to Maury's protégé and former Confederate Ordnance Bureau chief John Brooke on August 2, 1874. "I have been accused by one person of having done both, and it is necessary that I should prove the accusations to be without foundation in fact—if I can." Davidson promised not to make Brooke's letter public but would "show it to friends." He further asked Brooke to solicit a similar letter from George Washington Custis Lee, who had served on President Davis's staff and in a position to know of his work. "I want the evidence of two or three strong men."[8]

Brooke obliged with a brief, but effective, letter dated August 21. "I regret to learn by your letter of the 2nd ins[t..], that the pamphlet entitled 'The first successful application of Electrical Torpedo or Submarine mines in time of war and as a system of defence,' has been construed as detracting from the well-earned fame of the lamented Maury," Brooke began. "So far as I know, the statements made in the publication referred to are true, and I believe you are entitled to the credit of having made the first successful application of Electrical Torpedoes or submarine mines in war."[9]

From New York Davidson traveled again to London (where he had been in May) to research further the type of torpedo system to employ in Argentina. He had reportedly met before with Nathaniel J. Holmes, the English engineer who had worked with Charles Wheatstone and Matthew Fontaine Maury in 1863-1864 to develop a new battery system and with whom Maury had patented electrical torpedoes in England in 1865. "My rooms are often full until the small hours of the morning," Davidson wrote Brooke. "Here are Harvey R.N. of England, [Horst?] of Prussia, Edonboro of Turkey, Kennon of Egypt and McEvoy who still pays attention to the small matters and meet with success in fuzes, circuit, closers &c." The Argentines were trying to persuade Davidson to adopt a system developed by Charles Ambrose McEvoy, a British-born Confederate naval officer who had obtained a U.S. patent for firearm improvements before the war, obtained five Confederate patents for fuses and conducted experiments on fuses and explosives under John Brooke's supervision during the war, and relocated after the war to London, where he continued his work. Frederick Harvey, who had recently resigned as captain in the Royal Navy, had, with his uncle, developed a torpedo then in vogue—the Harvey or so-called "fish" torpedo—and later joined Davidson

8 Davidson to Brooke, Aug. 2, 1874, BP.

9 Brooke to Davidson, Aug. 21, 1874, BP.

in the Argentine torpedo service. While in Great Britain, he checked on the status of a steamship that he had designed, and the Argentine navy authorized to be his floating headquarters vessel (later christened *Fulminante*). He later described it to Brooke as "a splendid ship built expressly for the purpose 182' x 30' x 15'3"[.]"[10]

The confab in London underscored the continuing reputation in naval circles of former Confederate officers, especially those who had worked with torpedoes and other emerging technologies. Beverly Kennon, U.S. Navy date of 1846, had pioneered the use of electrical torpedoes in the lower Mississippi even before Maury and Davidson laid down the torpedo barrier in the James and was among at least eight former Confederate officers recruited to work for the Khedive of Egypt in the early 1870s.[11]

Davidson was also in the process of recruiting. "I am actively engaged here organizing my department hoping to get off for S. American in January," Davidson wrote to John Brooke on August 8. Just as John Randolph Tucker had (with his employer's blessing and encouragement) recruited former Confederate comrades for his work with the Peruvian navy eight years before, Davidson turned first to veterans of the Confederate navy's Submarine Battery Service. He engaged his talented electrician/telegrapher Roy O. Crowley and the officer who succeeded him in command of the service, Lt. John Pembroke "Paul" Jones—who had also been a fellow member of the U.S. Navy Date of 1841. In subsequent years, after Jones moved back to the U.S., Davidson sent out feelers to another Date of 1841 comrade, James Henry Rochelle of Virginia, who had been an officer aboard the *Patrick Henry* during the Battle of Hampton Roads and who had been part of John Randolph Tucker's department in Peru. Davidson offered him a position as Torpedo and Hydrographic Engineer, for a salary of $3000 in gold, with rations,

10 Charles L. Lewis, *Matthew Fontaine Maury, Pathfinder of the Seas* (Annapolis, MD, 1937), 183, 204-5; Davidson to Brooke, Aug. 8, 1874, BP.; background information on McEvoy from *CV*, (July 1908), 16:352 and Knight, *Confederate Invention*, 109-110; *The Times* [London], Apr. 17, 1905; *Confederate Navy Register*, 123; Brooke, ed., *Ironclads and Big Guns* 117, 119-22, 148, 152; and Perry, *Infernal Machines*, 58. McEvoy once claimed to have been born in Virginia, but other sources suggest he was born in Ireland and immigrated with his family to America. John McKee's research (email message to Coski, July 13, 2025) suggests he was born in Glasgow, Scotland, in 1824. "CAPTAIN F. HARVEY." *The Times*, July 30, 1919; Davidson to Brooke, Aug. 31, 1875, BP.

11 William B. Hesseltine and Hazel C. Wolf, *The Blue and the Gray on the Nile* (Chicago, 1961), especially 70-75 and 253-60; Timothy S. Wolters, "Electric Torpedoes in the Confederacy: Reconciling Conflicting Histories," *The Journal of Military History*, (July 2008): 72:772-773. Wolters speculates that Kennon may have conferred with Maury about torpedoes in Richmond before departing for New Orleans.

quarters, and expenses. "Preferring the present duty and association I declined the offer," Rochelle assured Tucker.[12]

Davidson also set his sights on John Mercer Brooke. In a series of letters over the next year, the man who had so desperately begged Brooke to recommend him to the "Japs" or the Prussians begged, flattered, and cajoled Brooke to accept a position in his department—to no avail.

"I sincerely wish you could effect [*sic*] an entrance into Torpedo affairs. You are so eminently fitted for the very requirements of that service. It is such a pity that you are buried, as it were." "Nothing would give me more pleasure than to have you here in London in this the centre of Torpedo operations," Davidson wrote on September 29. Sensing perhaps Brooke's reluctance to accept a subordinate role, Davidson promised that "All my Torpedo papers, estimates, proposals for contracts &c of which I have a large quantity shall be entirely at your service if you come over." Even if Brooke were "'going for' the Brazilians or 'Jap's' instead of joining him in Argentina, Davidson would share "useful hints" from his experiences.[13]

Settled in Buenos Aires, Davidson renewed his offensive a year later. He initially offered Brooke the position of Torpedo Engineer with a salary of $3,000 per year in gold, "with fine apartments & rations allowed on board of a splendid ship built expressly for the purpose." The contract was for a year, but Davidson was confident that his department's funding was secure.

"There is much money to be made in this new country for a man of your peculiar accomplishments," he assured Brooke. Knowing that the widowed Brooke recently had remarried and started a new family, Davidson tried a different angle: "You can bring your family to this country & start a new life with a fair prospect of having something to live on when too old to labor any longer." "Now you say that $3,000 in gold per annum won't tempt you from your mountain house," Davidson wrote on December 8 after receiving Brooke's reply. "Will you come here to be Chief of Ordinance [*sic*] at a salary of $5000 per annum[?]" No doubt frustrated that Brooke was rejecting his importuning, Davidson struck an incredulous pose appealed at once to Brooke's vanity, sense of duty, glory, and self-interest: "Now—John Brooke, you have got twenty good years to live yet, & I know you want to leave a name & a fortune to your children. . . . This country is new & rich and wants everything in the way of men like you. If you will say that you will come when matters are made satisfactory to you thro' special channels, I feel pretty certain that you can dictate / write your own contract for the office

12 Rochelle to Tucker, Mar. 12, 1876, John Randolph Tucker Papers, Old Dominion University, Norfolk, VA.

13 Davidson to Brooke, Aug. 8, 1874 and Sep. 29, 1874, BP.

and pay mentioned." Before that appeal had reached Brooke, Davidson raised the ante, offering Brooke the position as Chief of Ordnance with the salary of $6,000 per year with travel and other benefits. "I have but one word to add & that is—as you love children and a great interest in the future, you have no right to 'hide your light under a bushel.'" That was apparently Davidson's final offensive. John Brooke remained on the faculty of the Virginia Military Institute until 1899 and died in Lexington in 1906.[14]

Davidson was equally unsuccessful in landing an even bigger fish: General Pierre Gustave Toutant Beauregard, a senior Confederate officer who, after initial reluctance, had embraced torpedo defenses during his command of the Department of South Carolina and Georgia in 1862-1864. Davidson tried to exploit the Creole's legendary egotism to woo him to Argentina. "I think they will willingly pay you twenty or twenty-five thousand a year, & all the travelling [*sic*] expenses,—allow you an assistant engineer & secretary—Also an office or offices, and any force you may require after your arrival in the country to assist in your duties," he wrote on June 16, 1874. "Should you go to the country you will find that there are many ways of making money there, that be in the direction of your accomplishments particularly, which you can perceive would be the case in any newly developed & prosperous country. And as there are few, if any men in the world, out there, you would at once obtain a prominence which I am sure would be gratifying to you." Much to Davidson's frustration, Beauregard was holding out for a $50,000 contract and wanted assurances of Argentina's financial stability—demands that Davidson warned "would wound the feelings of highly sensitive people. . . ." Over the ensuing year, Beauregard balked not only at the inadequate salary, but also at every report of internal or international instability in South America. By early 1875, Davidson concluded that his new employer could not afford Beauregard and told him so.[15]

After almost two years of preparations, Davidson was finally ready to leave for Argentina in January 1875. While in London he renewed his 1875 Certificate of Competency as master (the original of which, he claimed, was lost in 1869 when it was in the possession of Maryland Treasurer Robert Fowler of the Oyster

14 Davidson to Brooke, Aug. 31, 1875, Dec. 8, 1875, and Dec. 16, 1875, BP; Brooke, *John Brooke Naval Scientist*, 360-62. Brooke's business partner and his and Davidson's Date of 1841 comrade, Robert Dabney Minor, did not live to see Davidson secure the opportunity he had long coveted. Minor died of a stroke in November, 1871 at the age of 44. He had been serving as engineer of the James River Improvement Company. Coski, *Capital Navy*, 246-47.

15 Davidson to Beauregard, June 16, 1874, June 25, 1874, Aug. 11, 1874, and Jan. 18, 1875, G. T. Beauregard Papers, Special Collections, Tulane University. Beauregard's replies are in the G. T. Beauregard Papers, Library of Congress Manuscripts Division.

Police Commission). Davidson gave as his address the "S.S. *Fulminante*" at the East India Docks. As references for his certificate Davidson provided an impressive list of men and institutions that testified to the scope of his work and contacts: the London and La Plat[a] Bank, S[iemens] Brothers, London Ordnance Works, Major Moncrieff, Blake Brothers & Co., [Franco Torrome?], Esq., J. R. and J. P. Silvertown [Works], and U.S. Minister to England General Robert F. Schenck. Davidson and his vessel arrived in Buenos Aires in February 1875.[16]

Although Davidson had a contract and a secure position, there was no hint that Mary and her "little flock" planned to join him—as she had intimated about his Chilean adventure in 1865. Ten years later the "little flock" had grown to include Mary, daughter Leila (age 20) who in 1875 married to an English cousin, Bowie Campbell Gowan, and moved to England; and sons Percy (age 18), Hunter (age 13), Charles (age 10), Frank (age 6), and Maury (age 2-1/2). Hunter and Charles attended the well-regarded Episcopal School in Alexandria, Virginia. By 1882, Hunter, Jr., was a clerk living in Baltimore. Between 1873 and 1878 Percy attended Washington and Lee University in Lexington, Virginia, pursuing a degree in civil engineering He was the only child mentioned in the few known letters from this period. "Give Percy a lecture if you think he needs it," Davidson wrote John Brooke, who taught at VMI in the same town. "Please stir Percy up occasionally & tell him to study Spanish hard—and never to keep any but the best company," he wrote Brooke in December 1875. "If I remain in my present position which I expect of course to do, I shall bring him out here as Ass't Torpedo Eng. & Hydrog." Percy graduated in 1878 with a degree in civil engineering and the 1877-78 school catalogue identified him as "Percy Davidson, South America"; a Baltimore newspaper in late 1877 confirmed that Davidson's son, "a lad," was with him in Argentina. (Percy did not remain long with his father in Argentina. In early 1879 he sailed to Sydney, Australia, where he found employment as public works engineer and married an Australian woman. He later returned to the United States and worked as an engineer in Baltimore and in New York City.)[17]

16 "Application for Renewal of the Certificate of a Master, Mate, or Engineer," Jan. 21, 1875, accessed via Ancestry.com. On the application section entitled "Particulars of Service," Davidson noted *Henrietta* (a "British" vessel "sold to the Chilians thru' office of the English consul"), the *Leila*, and two other Baltimore vessels, *Nannie Merryman* and *Bessie Woolford*, which he commanded for the "Commissioner of Fisheries, Coast of United States from 1868 to 1873." Rather disingenuously, he listed his service "In U.S. Navy from 1841 to 1865."

17 Walter Worthington Bowie, *The Bowies and Their Kindred* (Polyanthos, 1971), 105; *AG*, Feb. 17, 1881; Washington & Lee 1876 catalog accessed via Ancestry.com; *Woods Baltimore City Directory, 1882*, 227 and *1883*, 255, accessed via Ancestry.com; Davidson to Brooke, Sep. 29, 1874 and Dec. 8, 1875, BP; *Catalogues of Washington and Lee University, Virginia, for the Years ending June, 1878*

By design or by coincidence, Hunter Davidson apparently was residing at home in Cambridge, Maryland, in June 1880 when the census taker came around, but such periodic visits were apparently the only time he saw his family.[18]

"We have pretty much charge of everything (except Naval Affairs)"

Available sources, including research compiled by American historians Alfred J. Hanna and Phyllis Barbour, a few U.S. government documents, and, especially, studies by Argentine scholars Eduardo C. Gerding and Humberto Burzio (the latter a retired naval officer, historian, and founder of the Argentine Naval History Division who quoted verbatim from many government document sources) provide a broad outline of the nature, scope, successes, and frustrations of Davidson's work in Argentina. "We have pretty much charge of everything (except Naval Affairs)," Davidson wrote to John Brooke shortly after settling into his new job. His responsibilities included torpedoes, hydrography, and deep sea cables, and he expected to assume control of light house buoys and "in fact all improvements of navigation in addition."[19]

Defending Argentina's rivers and harbors was Davidson's first charge. As Davidson assumed command of the new Argentine Torpedo Division, rumors of war between Argentina and Brazil gave new urgency to his work. Occupying a position as a contractor, not as an officer of the Argentine Navy, *"El ingeniero* Hunter Davidson," as he appeared in official documents, reported directly to the country's Minister of War and Navy Adolfo Alsina. Not surprisingly, this arrangement generated friction within the service. On at least one occasion, Davidson rebuffed a request from the commander of the Argentine Navy to send official communications through his office, reminding him that the Torpedo Division constituted a special service and acted under the authority of the minister.[20]

Davidson's headquarters were aboard the *Fulminante,* the iron-hulled steamship that he had designed and arranged to have built in Scotland. Completed in late 1874, her home base was on the Rio Luján, a tributary of the Rio de la Plata 45 miles upstream from Buenos Aires. By the end of 1875, the Argentine Torpedo Division had at its disposal defensive and offensive torpedoes, the torpedo

(Petersburg, Va., 1878), 14 and *Catalogues* for 1874-1879, W&L; *The* [Baltimore] *Sun* reprinted in *The* [Norfolk, Va.] *Public Ledger,* Nov. 15, 1877. Ancestry.com Davidson Family Tree.

18 1880 U.S. Census accessed via Ancestry.com.

19 Davidson to Brooke, Aug. 31, 1875, BP.

20 *WES,* Feb. 23, 1875 and *National Republican* [Washington, D.C.], Mar. 2, 1875; Burzio, *Historia Del Torpedo,* 66.

The steam torpedo vessel *Fulminante* at anchorage in the Rio Lujan, 1876. Built in Britain to Davidson's specifications, *Fulminante* was his floating headquarters until it was destroyed in an explosion in October 1877. *Historio Del Torpedo Y Sus Buques En La Armada Argentina, 1874-1900*

station ship *Fulminante,* and two other small boats used to deploy torpedoes, and a flatboat. Reminiscent of the ships Davidson used in Confederate service, the ill-fated *Teaser* and *Torpedo, Fulminante* was a floating headquarters, a laboratory, a warehouse for torpedoes, batteries, and other apparatus, and a dormitory for the officers and men of the Torpedo Division. She boasted a large boom and winch on her foremast.[21]

On September 30, 1875, Davidson submitted to Alsina a detailed report of his new department, particularly its organization, duties, and equipment.[22] He characterized *Fulminante* as a tender to be used to serve the torpedo stations established already at Martin Garcia, Ensenada, and Zárate, and others to be established. He reiterated his strong preference for electrical torpedoes—which he and Dr. Manuel Garcia, Argentine minister in Paris, had agreed would be the only type of torpedo employed—and his disdain for contact torpedoes, which he considered as dangerous to friend as to foe. He offered a technical discussion of the proper depth to place electrical torpedoes (no greater than 40 feet) and such factors as channel width and currents, and the types of anchors used depending on composition of the bottom soils.

21 Burzio, *Historia Del Torpedo,* 63, 66, 167-68.

22 Burzio, *Historia Del Torpedo,* 52-5, summarizes Davidson's Sep. 30, 1875 report, citing its source as Archive of the Department of Naval Historical Studies. File 1o / 2o Page 4 Box 47, Ministry of War and Navy 1875. The following paragraphs are from Burzio's summary.

In organizing the Torpedo Division, Davidson underscored (in his September 30 report and in subsequent documents) the importance of two positions—torpedo engineer and chief electrician—both under the command of an experienced naval officer (himself). The torpedo engineer would supervise the care, use, and placement of the torpedoes, and the chief electrician must be a teacher in electricity and chemistry, (quoting Davidson) "thus capable of gathering and applying principles, for the science of Torpedo war requires the ablest talents of the day."[23] Most of the other personnel were men to construct and care for the torpedoes, along with three engineers to serve aboard *Fulminante.* The personnel described in his report were the minimum necessary for peacetime service, Davidson observed; the Division would need more men in wartime to superintend the torpedo stations and even in peacetime the defenses would be more effective with more personnel. Davidson's 1875 department budget (possibly submitted in conjunction with the September 30 report) showed a torpedo division manager, torpedo engineer, electrical engineer, and an officer in charge of *Fulminante,* along with a boatswain, three machinists, two carpenters, a mechanic, a blacksmith, an electrical draftsman, 18 first-class and two second class seamen, four helmsmen, seven stokers, two coal bunkers, two cooks, two butlers, two waiters, secretary, and a commissioner.[24]

After a year on the job, Davidson in November 1875 submitted a 2,000-word report to Minister Alsina offering his analysis and recommendations for a system of defensive and offensive torpedoes. Davidson began his report on an encouraging note, asserting that "The Argentine Republic is the most favorably situated *of all nations* to defend itself against an enemy by the employment of offensive torpedoes in its own waters." The thrust of the report, however, was that the recently delivered ironclad warships were inadequate without a robust system of offensive torpedo boats. Happily, he asserted that six small torpedo boats, which cost far less than the ironclads, would be effective and that their use "can be taught to any intelligent young naval officer in a few days." Even with its new ironclads, Argentina could not afford a large enough navy to defend La Plata generally and Buenos Aires specifically without the use of torpedo boats—as Argentina learned during a war with Brazil 12 years before. "To complete this Division," Davidson insisted, would require two high-speed high sea torpedoes and six torpedo boats. "All the gunboats of this country should be immediately fitted with marine torpedoes in

23 Quote from Burzio, *Historia Del Torpedo,* 167-168.

24 Ibid., 165.

accordance with the system employed in the squadrons of Great Britain and the United States."[25]

Davidson advised Alsina on building a credible offensive threat against Brazil—its most likely wartime foe—underscoring Brazil's vulnerability to offensive torpedoes and specifying several ways of exploiting that weakness. He reminded Alsina of the adage that two countries knowing that the other is well-prepared for war helps preserve peace. "I have given much study and reflection to this subject," Davidson explained, "and my views, here expressed, are in conformity with those of every naval officer in England and America, among the great number with whom I have conversed on this subject." In case Alsina doubted the wisdom of Davidson's suggestions, he reminded him of his credentials: "I have also had more effective practice in warfare in commanding torpedo operations than any other has ever had, and I know perfectly well the effect produced upon an enemy fleet, and the chances of success in connection with this method of warfare."[26]

The Argentines implemented Davidson's plan, albeit using the McEvoy torpedoes that Davidson had recommended against. He had also helped lay a submarine cable across the Rio Uruguay, allowing the first telegraph communication between Martin Garcia and Buenos Aires.[27]

Davidson's command of the Argentine Torpedo Division ended abruptly on October 4, 1877, when *Fulminante* was destroyed in a catastrophic fire and explosions. The disaster occurred when Davidson and his lieutenant, Frederick Harvey, were 45 miles away from the ship's Luján River anchorage, waiting to meet with the minister of defense in Buenos Aires. The fire broke out at noon and the first explosion occurred shortly before 12:30 p.m. Immediately upon learning about it, Davidson, along with two Marine officers and other officials, rushed by train to the Luján, where they found the ship engulfed completely in fire and beyond hope of salvage. Officers on the scene tried unsuccessfully to extinguish the fire but succeeded in moving other vessels in the vicinity out of danger before *Fulminante's* magazines and other combustible material caught fire. Davidson later wrote to Minister Alsina what he had learned from others: that the first explosion occurred in the engine room, blowing off the aft deck and opening the port side and killing a dozen men. The explosion also disabled the hoses and stranded the

25 Davidson's Nov. 1875 report reproduced in Burzio, 177-181.

26 Quoted in Burzio, *Historio Del Torpedo*, 180-181.

27 Burzio, *Historio Del Torpedo*, 46, 50, 67, 175; Hanna and Barbour, "Captain Thomas Jefferson Page," 499.

ship. The fire finally reached the stores of gun cotton at 5:00 p.m., causing a massive explosion.[28]

Davidson told the minister that he could not find a reasonable cause for the fire and requested a thorough investigation to determine the cause and responsibility. "First of all," Davidson wrote, "the sentiment of humanity demands it—it is a question of the honor of the Argentine Flag—the representatives of the science of war will expect it from Your Excellency by means of Torpedoes wherever they may be in the world, and finally the cause of justice begs Your Excellency to declare guilty, or the innocence of any officer or crewman whose may have influenced this disaster." He also appended a list of dead and wounded men.[29]

Reporters' accounts published in the Buenos Aires newspaper, *El Estandarte (The Standard)* and reprinted weeks later in U.S. newspapers placed Davidson at the center of the drama. Days before the disaster a small explosion occurred as Davidson conducted an unspecified demonstration for visiting Argentine army officers, breaking windows in nearby houses and alarming residents and officials about the potential for a more serious explosion (the official report of the disaster did not mention this incident). After the fire and explosion, rumors spread that Davidson was under arrest, which proved untrue. More accurate was the reporter's account (apparently gleaned from Davidson himself) of Davidson's personal losses in the explosion. He had been living on *Fulminante,* "with the view of making her the nucleus of his department," the reporter explained. Reminiscent of the loss of *Teaser* on the James River 15 years earlier, Davidson lost everything he had with him, including papers, family documents and portraits. The reporter quoted him as saying "I care nothing for my loss, but I feel deeply for the death of 14 men; and I also regret that the Government has lost so fine a vessel."[30]

Fulminante was the sixth and last vessel on which Hunter Davidson served (after the *Missouri, Shark, Virginia, Teaser,* and *Runher*) to meet an untimely end by destruction or capture.

There was some speculation that the fire was related to the enmity that Argentine naval officers harbored for Davidson and his special command, and Davidson apparently suggested that the fire was intentional. The official inquiry that President Nicolás Avellaneda ordered on the day after the disaster did not agree. Issued at the end of December, the report by Special Prosecutor Colonel of

28 Burzio, *Historia Del Torpedo,* 70-73.

29 Davidson letter of Oct. 5, 1877 quoted in Burzio, *Historia Del Torpedo,* 73.

30 "DESTRUCTION OF THE FULMINANTE / HUNTER DAVIDSON'S TORPEDO SHIP BLOWN UP. / Thrilling News from Buenos Ayres—Davidson's Heavy Losses," reprinted from *The* [Baltimore] *Sun* in *The Norfolk Landmark*, Dec. 5, 1877.

the Navy Alvaro de Alsogaray reviewed and evaluated the testimony of *Fulminante's* officers and crew and of those of the other vessels who responded to the fire and the initial explosion. He rejected the "general opinion" that the fire owed to the mishandling of an "experiment box" (which some witnesses described simply as a torpedo) by crew member John Webb, who had a record of drunkenness and carelessness, concluding that the quantity of dried cotton powder Webb carried was insufficient to have cause a serious accident. Alsogaray acknowledged that *Fulminante's* captain, U.S. national Mason Damon, tried to save his ship, but criticized him for not trying to save two vessels anchored alongside, one of which carried explosive materials. He also noted that "the ship's crew lacked the discipline and knowledge to act in the emergency because they had not received instructions or been assigned to fire clearance." Squelching any rumors of impropriety, Alsogaray concluded explicitly that, "although Mr. Hunter Davidson believes that the fire was intentional," there was no evidence to support that assumption.[31]

Although the report rebuked Davidson's suspicions, it cleared him of any blame or responsibility, concluding that Davidson "cannot be punished for his excused absence from duty that day and for the fact that he is a private individual, placed outside the Ordinances." It commended officers of several other vessels for their courage and fast action in reducing collateral damage from the explosion and recommended short prison terms for the boatswain who failed to assemble the crew and followed others ashore and for a young midshipman who was also cited for courage, but who violated the penal code when he initially lied to investigators. Following the special prosecutor's recommendations, the Navy Department concluded that "the explosion of the '*Fulminante*' cannot be attributed to a specific event or person and according to what results from the proceedings," and that there was nothing that any officers or crew could have done differently to save *Fulminante.* It gently chided the vessel's chiefs for inadequate precautions while conducting experiments and the lack of preparedness for fires. President Avellaneda issued resolutions endorsing the inquiry's conclusions and recommended punishments, with the additional admonition "[t]hat Captain Davidson and Engineer Harvey be made aware of the irregularities that appear in this investigation, so that they may take measures to avoid their repetition in similar cases."[32]

The destruction of *Fulminante* ended Davidson's tenure as chief of the Argentine Torpedo Division. And, for a few years, the Torpedo Division ceased to exist. The

31 Gerding, "The Confederate Navy and the Argentine Hydrographic Survey"; report quoted in Burzio, *Historia Del Torpedo,* 76-77.

32 Report quoted in Burzio, *Historia Del Torpedo,* 77; decree from Navy Department, Nov. 28, 1877, and President' Avellaneda's "Resolves" both quoted in Burzio, *Historia Del Torpedo,* 77, 78.

Argentine Navy stored surviving material and retained remaining personnel, but did not attempt to reconstitute the division, reportedly for budgetary reasons. In 1881, when Davidson was still under contract with the Argentine government, the Navy created a new Torpedo Division, under the command of Marine Lt. Colonel Ceferino Ramírez. Consisting of a torpedo ram, five torpedo boats and two second class river torpedo boats, the new division also acquired self-propelled Whitehead torpedoes, making it a more modern service than the one Davidson had organized and commanded. Although Argentine naval officials praised Davidson's "valuable assistance" and "competence" in his role as chief of the Torpedo Division, the Ministry made no effort to retain him in that capacity.[33]

"Designed for Davidson's 'special skills'"

Davidson's official title as a contract employee of the Argentine government was torpedo engineer and chief hydrographer.[34] After the destruction of *Fulminante,* Davidson's focus shifted to the second of those two functions. Ultimately, it was Davidson's experience with the U.S. Coast Survey more than his expertise in electrical torpedoes that made him a valuable employee for Argentina.

Even before *Fulminante's* destruction, as part of his work in preparing and deploying torpedo defenses, Davidson had been surveying and charting river courses. Formulating his river defense plan required Davidson to survey the Rio La Plata from the Uruguay to the mouth of the Paraná, including the island of Martin Garcia. Three months before the destruction of *Fulminante,* Davidson conducted a reconnaissance expedition of the Alto Uruguay bordering the northeast province of Misiones, as instructed by Minister Alsina. Anticipating subsequent expeditions, Davidson reported extreme hardships from southern hemisphere winter storms and inadequate shelter and food. About the same time, the Minister of War and Marine informed the Argentine Congress about the recent re-discovery of a deep-water channel on the Uruguayan side of the island of Martin Garcia, attributing the discovery to Hunter Davidson. "The survey and soundings of Captain Davidson have been kept secret (so it is supposed), to prevent the use of the channel by the Brazilians in case of trouble with this government," reported the American minister in Buenos Aires to Secretary of State William Evarts in September, 1877;

33 Burzio, *Historia Del Torpedo,*68, 367-368; naval historian Luis D. Cabral quoted in Burzio, *Historia Del Torpedo,* 69.

34 Burzio, *Historia Del Torpedo,* 61.

"but as all difficulties have been, or are about to be, settled, no doubt the channel will soon be made available to commerce."[35]

Argentina's president, Nicolás Avellaneda created a Naval Hydrographic Service on January 1, 1879. Three months later, the Ministry of War and Marine appointed Davidson to command an extensive scientific exploration up the Rio Paraná—a major tributary of the Rio de la Plata—to the confluence of the Rio Paraguay. The expedition, according to military historian Humberto Burzio, was designed for Davidson's "special skills" and "taking into account" that he could no longer "provide service in the field of torpedoes." As had Thomas J. Page's expedition a quarter-century earlier, Davidson's charge included not only a careful study of the river and its tributaries, but also assessing the potential of the land for colonization.[36]

The proposed expedition went nowhere for several years, possibly owing to a renewed internal schism between Buenos Aires and the Republic of Argentina. Davidson took advantage of this interruption to make his one documented visit to his family in Maryland. And, according to an article in the Baltimore *Sun*, Davidson returned to Argentina via Glasgow, Scotland, where he checked on the progress of the warships and torpedo boats for which Thomas Page had contracted years before.[37]

Finally, in March 1882, a new president, General Julio A. Roco, and his Minister of War and Marine, Dr. Benjamin Victoria, authorized a survey of the Alto Paraná, specifically to study the possibility of laying a permanent communication channel in the river bypassing several natural obstacles. The decree created a commission under Davidson's command that consisted also of mechanical engineer Guillermo Parfitt and engineer Mario Bigi and placed at Davidson's disposal the vessels *Pilcomayo* and *Talita* and the command of Major Antonio E. Perez. Obviously eager to get underway, Davidson started out on April 19 on a preliminary partial survey.[38]

35 Letter from Davidson to Alsina, July 17, 1877 cited in Burzio, 66, also 47, 55. According to the account from *The* [Buenos Aires] *Standard* reprinted in *The Norfolk Landmark*, Dec. 5, 1877, valuable "plans and models made by Captain Davidson of the Upper Uruguay, &c.," were lost in the destruction of *Fulminante*; Thomas O. Osborn, U.S. Legation, Buenos Ayres, Argentina, to Secretary of State William Evarts, Sep. 19, 1877, *Papers Relating to the Foreign Relations of the United States, Transmitted to Congress With the Annual Message of the President, December 2, 1878* (Washington, 1878), 7.

36 Burzio, *Historio Del Torpedo*, 47.

37 Baltimore *Sun*, Nov. 15, 1880.

38 Burzio, *Historia Del Torpedo*, 67; *INFORME de una ESPEDICION AL ALTO PARANA para estudiar Las Mejoras Necesarias en el "SALTO GRANDE DE APIPE" Agosto Y Setiembre De*

Traveling aboard *Pilcomayo* with the *Talita* in tow, the expedition steamed up the Rio Paraná and reached Corrientes on April 28, then proceeded up the Alto Paraná to Ituzaingo on May 3. A new pilot guided the expedition upriver on the *Talita* to Itapúa and the rapids and falls, which were the focus of the expedition as per President Roco's decree. For the next two weeks, Davidson and his men explored the river and the rapids, mapping the channels and measuring the current. At Davidson's direction, Engineer Parfitt traveled from Posados overland to San Martin, capital of the new and relatively uncharted Federal Territory of Misiones (which Argentina had occupied only since the War of the Triple Alliance), to explore the banks and assess their potential for settlement and construction of a railroad. The careful study of the river convinced Davidson that it was erroneous to refer to the Salto Chico and Salto Grande because he did not believe they were really falls ("salto"), but merely rapids. The "Great Falls of the Apipe," Davidson informed the president, were not the great barrier that he and others thought they were, and navigation of the river not as challenging as expected. The expedition returned to Buenos Aires on June 5.[39]

The government ordered Davidson to make a second expedition to the same points in August, when the river was at low tide. Accompanied by Sub-Lt. Daniel Blanco (who had been part of the May expedition) and two Argentine Navy sailors, Davidson on August 14 took a trade steamer from Buenos Aires to Corrientes. There he learned that the small steamer that was to take the expedition up the Paraná had crashed on the rocks and was unavailable. The men had to march to Posadas to obtain another vessel.

His orders for this second expedition were to explore the lowest of the three sections of the Paraná, but Davidson found that the low water allowed him to proceed further to Tacuru Pucu above the Iguazu and collect data without compromising his orders or without additional expense to the government. Leaving Posadas on September 7, he conducted his exploration over the ensuing 12 days. As he had on his earlier expedition, Davidson returned with information purporting to revise the understanding about the river. The distances along the Paraná, he explained, had been exaggerated. Instead of being 80-95 leagues (276-328 miles) between Posadas to Pacurupucu [*sic*: Tacuru Pucu] as usually estimated,

1882 . . . Del SALTO GRANDE PRESENTADO POR HUNTER DAVIDSON Octubre 1882 [translated as *REPORT of an EXPEDITION TO THE UPPER PARANA to study the necessary improvements in the "SALTO GRANDE DE APIPE" August and September 1882 . . . From the BIG LEAP PRESENTED BY HUNTER DAVIDSON October 1882*] (Buenos Aires, 1882), 4, courtesy of Las Misiones Public Library, Buenos Aires. Translated using Google Translate.

39 Parfitt's report in Davidson, *Report of an Expedition*, 31-44; Davidson, *Report of an Expedition*, 47-49, 59-61.

Davidson believed it no more than 70 (241.6 miles). The report that Davidson submitted to the government on October 5, 1882 was voluminous and detailed, covering the Paraná and Iguazu rivers, the falls, recommendations for channel and navigation improvements, the placement of buoys, future work of the Hydrographic Commission, vessels needed for future exploration and a proposed budget—as well as thoughts on the development of railways or tramways in Misiones.[40]

The proposed future exploration occurred a year later with Davidson again in command and was the most celebrated of his expeditions. Its mission was to survey the third (upper) section of the Paraná system mandated in President Roco's March 1882 decree: the Rio Iguazu (Y-guazu in contemporary sources) beyond the river's celebrated great falls to the San Antonio barrier. Under Davidson's direct command were Argentine naval officer Lt. Manuel Domecq Garcia, Norwegian-born professor Olaf Storm, and Argentine army lieutenant Adolfo Arana with 10 other soldiers and sailors, and four native laborers. Bearing chronometers and other scientific instruments, their objective was to determine not only the river's course and navigability, but also the border between Argentina and Brazil.

For this expedition, the Argentine navy again put at Davidson's disposal the bomb vessel *Pilcomayo* under the direct command of an Argentine naval officer, for transport from Buenos Aires to Corrientes, and the Argentine flagship, *Alto Parana,* for the leg of the journey from Corrientes to Ituzaingo. The seasonal low water compelled the expedition to travel the 75 miles from Ituzaingo to Posados overland. There the expedition paused to have another barge built in Encarnacion, Paraguay. The ascent of the most treacherous stretch of the Iguazu began on September 22.[41]

The river they were to survey wound through impenetrable jungle and over a series of rapids and falls, punctuated by jagged rocks. The riverbanks were alternatively swampy and covered with thick vegetation. To ascend the river, they traveled in a raft, a shallow draft boat, a similarly shallow draft barge, and an indigenous canoe to travel through rapids. According to an account published in the Argentine English language newspaper, *The Standard,* immediately upon the expedition's return, the small boats were lashed together to increase their stability and carrying capacity when navigating through more placid sections and separated and navigated separately through the more difficult sections. "The expedition commenced at daylight, and continued from eight to nine hours of every day," the reporter wrote, "working without shelter from the sun, rain, or insects, the latter

40 Davidson, *Report of an Expedition*, 4-6, 7-29.

41 Burzio, *Historio Del Torpedo*, 47-8; "EXPLORATION OF THE Y-GUASU," *The Standard* [Buenos Aires], Jan. 1, 1884, and reprinted Jan. 6, 1884.

Two of the official photographs of Davidson's 1883 Iguazu River Expedition. In the top image, Davidson leans against the tent pole. In the bottom image, Davidson and his white beard stands out in the middle of the group. *Graphic Archive of the Department of Naval Historical Studies [of Argentina]*

being a torture which renders life almost unendurable in the vicinity of that river." Indeed, the expedition encountered no human life along the river.[42]

The party documented the river not only with measurements (revising data previously obtained by the 18th-century Spanish sailor and geographer, Andrés

42 "EXPLORATION OF THE Y-GUASU," *The Standard* [Buenos Aires].

de Oyarvide, in the 1780s) but also with 50 photographs. The *Standard* hinted that the expedition discovered information about the border issue of "the most important nature and more favorable to our side of the question than we had reason to suppose," but declined to publish it.[43]

The regional governor sent a dispatch boat to transport the party back to Posados, and it arrived back in Buenos Aires on December 29. Despite the hazards and hardships, the expedition suffered no casualties. Davidson himself nearly became one when he was taking a bath in the river, slipped, and was swept away to the edge of the falls, where his leg caught on the edge of a 21-meter falls. A comrade threw him a cable and pulled him to safety.[44]

Upon his return, Davidson filed a formal report of his expedition to the Minister of War and Marine. He also shared with his former employer, the United States Navy, his survey of the mouth of the Paraná River, which he gave to Cdr. Henry B. Seeley, of the USS *Nipsic*, who forwarded it to the navy's Bureau of Navigation.[45]

Hunter Davidson was 57 years-old when he returned to Buenos Aires at the end of 1883. The expedition had been a physical trial for him. It proved to be his last substantial assignment for the Argentine government. The Ministry of War and Marine accepted his resignation on September 10, 1885, awarding him with a commendation for his service.[46]

After a decade of sometimes satisfying, often trying employment abroad, Davidson could finally return home to his family in Maryland. That was not, however, what Davidson chose to do.

43 Ibid.

44 Burzio, *Historio Del Torpedo*, 48-9.

45 Commander H. B. Seeley, *Nipsic*, South Atlantic Station, Buenos Aires, Jan. 24, 1884, RG 37, Hydrographic Office, NARA, copy in Barbour Papers.

46 Burzio, *Historio Del Torpedo*, 50; Document from Ministerie de Guerre y Marina, Sep. 19, 1885, copy in Barbour Papers.

Chapter Nine

"A Good Rebel" (1884–1913)

"After thirteen years service with the Argentinians I left them on account of failing health and strength in 1885," Davidson explained a dozen years later to his Naval School chum, Stephen Luce, "and because they had learned enough to become jealous but not enough to be magnanimous and they were commencing to do & say nasty things." "Moreover," he continued, "I had enough laid by to be independent & came to the interior of Paraguay for health & in truth to get away from the world. I felt that I had swallowed enough to enable me to chew the cud for the rest of my life & my solitude varied by glimpses of the newspapers." He declared the experiment a success. "At nearly 71 I am a better man in health than at 59 & often ride 40 to 50 m[iles] per day & that over the worst roads in the world."[1]

"Lazy Man's Paradise"

Two letters that Davidson wrote to Luce in 1897 reveal many details of his life in Paraguay—and conceal many others. "You would laugh to see me here about the center of S. America on my Estancia raising cattle & living like a Gaucho," he wrote to Luce in January 1897. "But it is the most free & independent life in the world. Such a contrast to Naval harness! . . . I can't yet entirely realize that I am my own master and when on my Estancia 'Monarch of all I Survey.' I have a fine little boat, navigable streams on two sides of me & beautiful mountains all

1 Davidson to Luce, Apr. 19, 1897, Luce Papers.

Photograph of Davidson taken at Villa Rica, Paraguay, June 22, 1894, when he was nearly 68 years old. *Charles T. Jacobs Collection*

Admiral Stephen B. Luce and Davidson were "cheeryble brothers" in their youth and remained occasional correspondents in their old age. *NH&HC (NH2323)*

around—the water is of the purest, and there is no climate in the world more free from extremes or healthier than this of the interior of Paraguay." In his subsequent letter he described his "Estancia" (ranch) as consisting of "ten square miles beautifully situated just 4 leagues due north of Villa Rica, which is sufficient support." He noted that "The life is lonely" and reiterated how unaccustomed it felt to be out of "the naval harness."[2]

The main purpose for Davidson's out-of-the-blue communication with Luce was to consult him about the article he had written on the battle of Hampton Roads, but the correspondence also allowed the men to catch up with each other's lives and families. By 1897 Luce had retired from the U.S. Navy as rear admiral and was much revered as the founding officer of the Naval War College in Newport, Rhode Island. Luce was still active as the president of the U.S. Naval Institute, which he helped establish.

Davidson lamented that he had lost four children—"three of them by far the finest I had"—and updated Luce on the four still living: daughter Leila married an Oxford-educated English doctor, had three sons (one of whom graduated first in his class at Eton), and was living in England; son Percy was divorced from his Australian wife who "ruined him"; sons Hunter ("a trump") and Charles Steele, both of whom graduated from the Alexandria Episcopal Seminary, and were respected Presbyterian Episcopal clergymen. He conspicuously did not mention his wife Mary, who had died the year before.[3]

2 Davidson to Luce, Jan. 13, 1897, and 19 Apr. 1897, Luce Papers. Davidson's ranch may have been called "Liberty Hall." John M. McKee, "Hunter Davidson: Sailor Extraordinary," unpublished Powerpoint presentation.

3 Davidson's reference to four lost children is a mystery. His first-born son, Hyde Ray, died in infancy and his two last sons, Frank and Maury, had died a few years before. The fourth may have been a child who died in infancy.

A U.S. government document that Davidson filled out 10 years after his correspondence with Luce sheds further light on his life out of the "naval harness." According to a registration of American citizens living abroad, Davidson first arrived in Paraguay on June 24, 1884 (a year before his formal separation from Argentine service) to live "a retired and quiet life." By the time he filled out the document (September 1907), he had left his estancia at Villa Rica for the town of Pirayu 50 miles to the northwest.

Edward Norton, U.S. consul in Asuncion, Paraguay, noted in a cover letter that "Davidson's residence in Paraguay has assumed a permanent character owing to his advanced age and feeble condition." As revived as he felt at 71, another decade evidently caught up with him. Davidson, Consul Norton continued, "had, for some years, and up to a short time ago, intended to return to the United States, but it is improbable now that he will ever do so[.]"[4]

The registration form that Davidson filled out included details about his life in Paraguay that he had not shared with Luce in their surviving correspondence, details which may explain why Davidson's residence in Paraguay "assumed a permanent character." In addition to himself, Davidson's Pirayu household also included his wife, Enriqueta Silvia Davalos Davidson, and four children: Ruben (born October 25, 1892), Virginia Consuelo (born July 22, 1895), Ronaldo (born June 15, 1897), and Gordon (born March 28, 1899). Enriqueta and all their children were born in Villa Rica and now living in Pirayu, except Ruben who was in college in Buenos Aires, Argentina. Enriqueta—born on November 1, 1872—was 46 years younger than her husband. Two of their four children were born when Mary Ray Davidson was still alive in Cambridge, Maryland.

Fifty years after Davidson settled in Paraguay, a scholar characterized the country as a "matriarchate." "The country has scarcely recovered from her five years' war (1865 to 1870) against the Triple Alliance—Brazil, Uruguay, and Argentina—which halved the population and left women in an ascendancy of eleven to one," wrote Rosita Forbes in 1933. She noted that the country boasted other attractions for men of means. "In pastoral Paraguay, where everything grows without effort, anybody with two or three hundred pounds a year can live well and do no work at all." In 1904, a visiting journalist stated things more bluntly. The sex ratio was as high as 20-1 and he learned that "as recently as twenty years ago"—coincidentally the year that Davidson arrived at Villa Rica—"it was with great reluctance that any male visitor was allowed to depart. If the women could not through their

4 "Certificate of Registration of American Citizen," Form 210, Department of State and Consul Edward Norton to Assistant Secretary of State, Sep. 24, 1907, both in U.S. Consular Registration Certificates, 1907-1918, vol. 3 accessed via Ancestry.com.

hospitality induce him to stay they would forcibly detain him, so much were husbands in demand. Paraguay thus became a lazy man's paradise."[5] Certainly that was the impression that Davidson gave in his 1897 letters to Stephen Luce.

In fathering four children 20 years after he sired son Maury, the 66-year-old Davidson demonstrated his virility. He also helped his new host country address a serious demographic problem: a severe shortage of men. Davidson's second family almost certainly influenced his decision not to leave Paraguay for the United States. The question remains, however, whether the existence of his second family were causal or consequential. That is, did Hunter Davidson start a second family—and marry Enriqueta after Mary Davidson's death—incidentally or intentionally? Did he, for all intents and purposes, abandon his American family?

After settling in Paraguay, he had families on both continents, but there is no evidence that Davidson ever returned to the United States after he moved to Paraguay, even in the wake of family tragedy. For reasons unknown, he obviously was estranged from his wife Mary. She died in February 1896. Her tombstone at St. Anne's Cemetery in Annapolis, Maryland, identifies her as "MARY RAY / wife of / Hunter Davidson / Captain C.S.N. / Born / Feb. 2, 1832." Youngest sons Frank and Maury died of illness at their mother's house in Maryland in 1892 and 1894, aged 23 and 22, respectively. Davidson's younger brother Roger also died in 1894 (their oldest brother, Brevet Brigadier General John W. "Black Jack" Davidson died in Minnesota in 1881).[6] He was apparently content to monitor those and other developments from 4,500 miles away.

How Davidson's American children regarded their father and how they reacted to his apparent parental neglect is not clear. Leila named one of her sons Cecil Hunter Boyd Gowan, but that may indicate homage to a family name rather than sincere filial piety toward an absent father. Son Charles, an Episcopal minister who seems to have inherited his father's maverick streak, wrote admiringly of his father's career accomplishments and named his own son Hunter. Namesake son Hunter , also an Episcopal minister, married late and was childless. Although his attitudes about race diverged radically from his father's, he wrote in defense of Robert E. Lee as a Christian man of virtue who may have owned slaves but personally opposed slavery. In an address prepared and delivered in 1916-17, Rev. Hunter Davidson declared that he had a right to speak "because my Father risked his life for the

5 Rosita Forbes, *Eight Republics in Search of a Future: Evolution and Revolution in South America* (New York, [1933]), 101, 103; "Lazy Man's Paradise / It Is in Paraguay, Where the Demand for Husbands is Great." *NYS*, Sep.18, 1904. It's not clear how Davidson acquired his estancia, but it may have been an incentive for him to stay in the country and raise a family.

6 According to the extensive genealogical research by John M. McKee, Roger Davidson died in Texas in 1894 after living most of his latte years with his second wife in New Albany, IN.

perpetuation of those august principles which are at the heart of Virginia's charter, and which have made her a great commonwealth." He was proud to say that "my Father was one of the commanders of the Merrimac when she fought the little Monitor, and did his duty beside Captain Catesby Jones and Admiral Franklin Buchannan [*sic*] in a battle which began to revolutionize the naval warfare of the world." His pride in his father's career accomplishments did not reveal the same emotional attachment that he recorded in a poetical paean to "MY MOTHER" but neither Hunter nor Charles Davidson rejected their father.[7]

Hunter Davidson was not a "man without a country." He could have returned to the United States whenever he wanted and felt able to do so and live as he had (even without a formal pardon) from 1866-1875. Other former Confederates who refused to take the oath of allegiance—most notably former president Jefferson Davis—lived undisturbed in the reunited United States. Nearly all other former Confederates who had gone into exile at the end of the war or accepted jobs with foreign governments returned eventually. By going to South America in 1875 and never returning for more than short visits, Davidson was the outlier.

In fact, the same year he opened correspondence with Luce (and the same year that Mary Davidson died), Hunter Davidson tried unsuccessfully to obtain a U.S. passport. He was apparently distressed by reading in the October 2, 1895, Buenos Aires *Herald* that U.S. citizens who remained abroad for more than two years "without intending to return within a definite time should be denied passports or other papers for protection from our Ministers and Consuls." Davidson sent an inquiry to the U.S. legation in Montevideo, Uruguay. When informed of State Department regulations, Davidson replied with some alarm and characteristic indignation, which Minister Plenipotentiary Granville Stuart passed onto Secretary of State Richard Olney. Describing Davidson only as an American residing in Paraguay without the intention to return (without reference to his Confederate or Argentine service), Stuart quoted several questions that Davidson posed to him:

> "In the event of my death would the U.S. Consul be authorized under existing Consular Regulations, articles 352-4, to settle my estate?"
>
> "In case of any serious difficulty would I be entitled to appeal to the U.S. Minister?"

7 Sources on the family of Leila Davidson Gowan accessed via Geni.com. "Burns Vestments and Prayer Book in Repudiation," *RTD*, July 27, 1913; "Preacher Burns Vestments and Leaves Church," *The Milwaukee Leader*, Aug. 4, 1913; "Lee the Real Man; a Glimpse of a Great Soul," draft address dated Bristol, June 3, 1916, and typescript poem, "MY MOTHER," Thornton Tayloe Perry (compiler) Papers, VMHC.

Undated formal portrait of Davidson from his daughter Leila Gowan's photo album. *Private Collection*

"Which are resolved into one question—Am I or am I not, a citizen of the United States?"

"Your Excellency will at once see the vital importance of the questions, for if decided against me I must seek protection elsewhere."

"As I have not expatriated myself I am unable to find under what clause of the Constitution the State Department denies me the rights of citizenship in consequence of mere residence abroad."

"Could I have known of the ruling of the Department some years back I might have returned to the United States, to renew my citizenship, but now that I am old and suffering with heart disease I am caught in a most unpleasant position."

Even if he were enjoying the easy life on his estancia with his new family, Davidson obviously began to appreciate the practical costs of *de facto* self-exile.

Acting Secretary of State Alvey A. Adee sent a long reply emphasizing that denial of a passport did not amount to loss of citizenship. Naturalized citizens who remain outside the U.S. for two years with no intent to return and citizens who accept naturalized citizenship in other countries were subject to losing their U.S. citizenship, but those circumstances did not apply to Davidson. That said, Davidson's claim to protection was not absolute or unambiguous. Representatives of commercial firms might remain abroad for long periods but, if they intend to return someday, they might be entitled to a passport. Davidson's case did not appear to meet those conditions.[8]

A few months later, Davidson applied for a Mexican War pension. Having told Stephen Luce that he had laid aside enough to be comfortable, Davidson presumably sought the pension on principle more than out of need. On that application he cited rheumatism as the reason he was living in Paraguay instead of in the United States. He renewed his application in 1907 and in 1908 and his persistence evidently paid off. At the time of his death, he was receiving a pension of $20 per month. Similarly, Enriqueta applied for a widow's pension in 1931 and filed supporting affidavits. Upon her death in 1953, she was "the recipient of a pension from the Veterans Administration" and she and her (and Davidson's) surviving son, Ruben Osvaldo, were American citizens.[9]

8 Granville Stuart to the Secretary of State, June 24, 1896, and Alvey Adee to Granville Stuart, Aug. 21, 1896, Diplomatic instructions of the Department of State, 1801-1906 (Despatches from U.S. Ministers to Paraguay and Uruguay), RG 59, NARA (hereafter cited as Paraguay Despatches).

9 Davidson's Mexican War Veterans Records, file #2-660-379, NARA; Barbour and Hanna, "Commander Hunter Davidson," in ZB file, NH&HC; Certificate for Enriqueta Silvia Davidson

"An unreconstructed southerner"

In addition to his rheumatism and the claims of his new Paraguayan family, Davidson's reluctance to return to the U.S. owed to the political and social conditions in the United States after emancipation.

Journalist and prolific travel writer, Frank G. Carpenter, visited Paraguay in 1898 while researching a book on South America. "I found some Americans living in Villa Rica and my stay was made pleasant by them in this out-of-the-way part of the world," Carpenter wrote in a widely syndicated 1899 feature story. "One was our vice consul, Mr. William Harrison, and another Dr. Charles Chase, the druggist. A third American is Captain Hunter Davidson, an unreconstructed southerner, who left the United States at the close of the civil war [*sic*] and finally got to Paraguay." He noted that Harrison and Chase had married Paraguayan women, failing to mention—or not having been told—that Davidson had done so, too.[10]

The description of Davidson as an "unreconstructed southerner" suggests that Carpenter's conversation turned to politics. Just how strongly Davidson felt about the situation in his native country is clear from an August 1903 letter he wrote to his nephew, Reginald Barclay Leach, who had married the daughter of his younger brother Roger. Leach had corresponded with his uncle by marriage about family genealogy. After addressing Leach's inquiries, Davidson opined that he was "sorry you seem wedded to 'Old Glory' that is to say to the success of the States under Blk Republican principles—for it is going to be the greatest fiasco known in history. The Negro and Labor Questions are insolvable in a Blk Repub. form of Govt." Warming to his subject, Davidson then poured out a venomous analysis of the race question in America with proposed solutions that must have shocked his kinfolk when they read his screed:

> All negroes should be castrated at once & continued until the race was [*sic*] exterminated—& for every negro who dares to lay his hand on a white woman I'd burn his whole male family.
>
> These negro outrages are the <u>direct</u> outcome of the signing of the Emancipation Proclamation—the most Cowardly and brutal act recorded in history—;

---

dated May 5, 1953 in "U.S. Reports of Deaths of American Citizens Abroad, 1853-1974," Department of State Decimal File, 1910-1962, Box 0940 (accessed via Ancestry.com).

10 "In the Wilds of Paraguay," *Omaha Daily Bee*, Mar. 5, 1899; also in *The Saint Paul Globe* [MN], *NYS*; *Indianapolis Journal*, *WES*, *San Francisco Chronicle*, *Denver Post*, all Mar. 5, 1899.

> the Carpet bag governments in the South; the Military rule and forcing the Constitutional Amendts on the South by the Sword; the forced election of negroes to Congress & high places; the hanging of the dead body of Mrs. Surratt, and the mangled body of Capt. Wirz who had been denied med[ica]l aid.
>
> In all these brutal & cowardly acts the negro saw the deep seated hatred of the North for the South and the negro has not failed to turn it to account.
>
> Ninety nine out of every hundred negroes approve the violation of white women by Negroes & the white man whose blood is not inflamed by such acts as have been committed by the Blk Repub. Govt & are now Committed to & by the negro is not a human being.

As if to underscore how unremarkable he considered such observations, Davidson then signed off with "Love to Lou Lee & may God bless you all."[11]

Such violently blatant racist comments are abhorrent in any era, but especially in our own. Ordinarily, a biographer must be cautious about generalizing from this single private letter. But Davidson's actions over the course of his life support the conclusion that this letter expressed essential values. Born into a slaveholding society that regarded Africans and African-Americans as inferior peoples, Davidson imbibed and apparently never questioned those beliefs. Consuming written accounts of the racial violence that occurred during an era that historian Rayford Logan famously characterized as the "nadir" of American race relations and filtering those accounts through his own perceptions and values, Davidson saw Armageddon approaching. Family background alone cannot explain Hunter Davidson's beliefs or behavior. His brother, John "Black Jack" Davidson, born just a year earlier, was one of the first officers of the post-Civil War 10th U.S. Cavalry—a regiment of African-American "Buffalo Soldiers"—and reportedly treated his soldiers with respect and fairness (thus his sobriquet). About the time that Davidson wrote his racist screed, his son, Rev. Hunter Davidson, published a letter in an Ohio newspaper offering a more liberal and optimistic outlook on the so-called Race Question. "The problem is being solved, methods are improving, this country, in Church and State, is rising to her opportunity, the present is a long advance over conditions of forty years ago," he exhorted, "and while there are still many obstacles in the pathway of proper progress, the day will surely come when

11 Davidson to Reginald Leach, Aug. 25, 1903, copy in Charles T. Jacobs research collection.

the negro will recognize his duty and have his rights, the croakers and the lynchers to the contrary."[12]

Even in far-away Paraguay, Davidson confronted the reality of African-American freedom and his own reflexive hatred of Black people. In 1905-06, Davidson conspired with other Americans in Paraguay to force the removal of John N. Ruffin, an African-American educator from Tennessee whom President William McKinley appointed as consul in Asuncion in 1897. Although Davidson and the others accused Ruffin of injuring American interests in Paraguay and engaging in personal profiteering at the expense of promoting American commerce, his private correspondence made clear that racism also motivated his actions. After two 1905 letters to the State Department failed to bring any action against Ruffin, Davidson wrote to the notoriously racist Democratic Mississippi congressman John Sharp Williams in June 1906. Davidson used Williams's interest in "the Consular question" as his entering wedge but pivoted immediately to what he evidently considered his strongest arguments: "The Consul here is a vile insolent negro (Ruffin) from Tenn[essee]," he explained. He felt compelled to write Williams because he believed (erroneously) that the new American minister to Paraguay "takes the Negro's part" and that there was "a secret influence at Washington in favor of the Negro." Pandering to his audience, Davidson wrote that "I fought for the dear old South thro' all the War and for this I have reason to believe that my letters to Washington re the fooregoing [*sic*] have not rec'd due attention."

In between those appeals to their shared prejudices, Davidson insisted to Williams that Ruffin's position was unnecessary and that the State Department presence in the Rio Plata countries was redundant and wasteful of public funds. Almost casually, Davidson dropped in another nugget calculated to inflame the congressmen: "[Ruffin] lives with a white woman whom he bro't from England on board the steamer as his mistress & created a great row on board."[13]

Much to Davidson's embarrassment, Williams forwarded the letter—which he later characterized as one "written in a familiar way to a 'Confederate' friend . . . to stir things up"—to President Theodore Roosevelt. Embarrassment aside, the letter had the desired effect of stirring things up.[14]

12 Davidson, *Black Jack Davidson*, 139-40, 158-61, 174-75; Rev. Hunter Davidson, "Bishop Brown and The Negro," unidentified clipping in Scrapbook, 1886-1916, of Hunter Davidson, in Perry Papers, VMHC.

13 Davidson to Williams, June 5, 1906, RG 59, Numerical files, 1906-1910, case 915-924/119, NARA (hereafter cited as RG 59 case 915-924/119). Ruffin's file revealed that the State Department had replied to Davidson's original letters but had not acted on them.

14 Davidson to Bartleman, Nov. 22, 1906, RG 59 case 915-924/119.

Despite Davidson's suspicion that the State Department was taking "the Negro's" part over the former Confederate, it had been accumulating a file of the complaints against Ruffin. Acting Secretary of State Robert Bacon assured Williams that "The several charges made by Mr. Davidson have received the Department's careful attention and a copy of his letter will be forwarded to Mr. R. M. Bartleman, American consul General at Large, who is about to start on a tour of inspection of the consular offices in Central and South America, for his consideration in connection with his inspection of the office at Asuncion."[15]

In his December 6, 1906, report to the secretary of state, Bartleman dealt systematically with the complaints about Ruffin from the American community and the Paraguayan government. According to the department's summary of the report, Bartleman concluded that "Ruffin is doing this Government incalculable harm in remaining at Asuncion and that this is the general opinion in Asuncion." The overriding consideration in reaching this conclusion was that the Paraguayan government that had come to power in a 1904 coup had declared Ruffin *persona non grata* because it believed he surreptitiously supported the ousted regime. Acting Secretary Bacon dispatched a new consul, Edward J. Norton, to Asuncion and would accept Ruffin's resignation when he arrived there in June 1907. Ruffin rebutted the arguments of his American and Paraguayan critics, but to no avail. "I see no reason to change the Department's position in the Ruffin case," wrote a State Department official, William N. Carr, to Secretary Bacon. "The papers submitted by him do not appear to explain satisfactorily the charges against him."[16]

Davidson's letters and testimony apparently did not figure prominently in the decision to dismiss Ruffin, but they do reveal much about the old Confederate's status and mindset in the twilight of his life. As context for a letter from Davidson that he included in his report, Bartleman offered a summary of what he had learned about him: "Captain Hunter Davidson was graduated from the U.S. Naval Academy—class 1843 [*sic*]. "He was the inventor of the torpedo, and at the time of the fight between the 'Monitor' & the 'Merrimac' a 1st Lieut on the latter—I think he fired the gun which blinded Admiral Worden. Since many years he has resided in So. America. He is now about 80 years of age & in good health[.]" Despite his role in fanning the flames against Ruffin, Davidson proved frustratingly reticent in his interview and in a subsequent letter. He declined to elaborate on the charges that he had made in his initial letters as long as his allies were unavailable to corroborate

15 Bacon to Williams, Sep. 13, 1906 and Huntington Wilson to Richard M. Bartleman, Esq., RG 59 case 915-924/119.

16 Bartleman report of Dec. 6, 1906 and Department of State to Ruffin, Apr. 4, 1907 and undated memorandum, RG 59 case 915-924/119.

them. Speculating that Davidson was "somewhat piqued" at the State Department for not acting on his earlier letters, Bartleman described him as "of little assistance to the Consul General in his investigation." A note appended onto a May 1908 State Department summary report of the charges against Ruffin further minimized Davidson's influence in the case. "It is also believed that Mr. Davidson's bitter complaints against Ruffin were prompted to a great extent by personal feeling."[17]

The State Department learned much more about Davidson's role in the cabal from Ruffin himself. After arriving back in the United States, Ruffin assembled a comprehensive dossier in his own defense enclosing 38 supporting documents, including several letters from Davidson. Ruffin found the letters in the files of the recipient, Vice Consul Waldemar de Korab, who reportedly sought to replace Ruffin and who helped orchestrate the smear campaign against him. The files became Ruffin's responsibility after de Korab died in late 1905 or early 1906. They contained undeniable evidence that Ruffin had been "the unfortunate victim" of "unjust persecution" by de Korab, Minister O'Brien, Davidson, and others. Ruffin described Davidson as "a captain in the Southern Confederacy who left America to avoid taking the oath of allegiance and whom Mr. W. C. De Korab permitted to sign himself in the Consulate Registry of American citizens as a good rebel."[18]

Indeed, on June 16, 1905, Davidson replied to de Korab's letter "re the Nigger Consul" with confidence that "I think the nigger is being wound up -Vamos á ver [translated: Let's see]. He asked de Korab to tell the former vice consul, William Harrison, that they were "collecting information at the request of the U.S. Secretary of State in respect of the 'character and conduct' of the negro Consul in Paraguay." A week later he consulted de Korab again on the details of their campaign against Ruffin, to whom Davidson referred to four times simply as "the Negro." Concerned that his allies feared Ruffin's political clout, Davidson sought to assure de Korab. "The new Minister must shortly come to Asuncion in order to present his credentials & then we will have a good opportunity of ventilating the Negro question. Push the Negro all you know how & don't let him rest—His suit against you is all 'buncom[b]e'." Learning that Harrison was unwilling to assist them because Ruffin had some diplomatic dirt on him, Davidson changed tactics. "In the letter to the Secy State wh[ich] I enclosed you yesterday I propose to add the proposition ~~that~~ or suggestion to the Department that in view of the

17 Bartleman note accompanying letter from Davidson to Mr. Bartleman, Nov. 22, 1906, RG 59 case 915-924/119. The sources for Bartleman's often hyperbolic biographical details are unclear. Charges Against John N. Ruffin (Colored) of Tennessee, Formerly Consul at Asuncion, Paraguay," RG 59 case 915-924/119.

18 Ruffin to Hon. Robert Bacon, Acting Secretary of State, Apr. 27, 1908, RG 59 case 915-924/119.

accumulation of charges against the Negro that it would be best to recall him at once & thus avoid a great public scandal as an inquiry would of course get into the papers here & at home."[19] That reasoning appeared in the State Department's decision to dismiss Ruffin in 1907.

Despite Ruffin's powerful dossier, the State Department declined to reinstate him. The White House in the person of President Roosevelt's secretary, William Loeb, promised to speak to Acting Secretary Bacon about his case. That April 28, 1908, letter is the last document in Ruffin's file.

John Ruffin had been the American consul at Asuncion for almost seven years before Davidson lodged his first complaint about him to the State Department. If the presence of a Republican-appointed Black consul in his adopted country offended Davidson, why did he wait so long to act? Had he only recently learned of Ruffin's rumored living arrangement with a white English woman? It is possible that the self-righteous Davidson who had called out fellow naval officers for seemingly trivial acts learned something about the consul that genuinely offended his principles. But Davidson's scattershot laundry list of Ruffin's offenses, compared with his consistent obsession with Ruffin's race, suggest that being a (literal) Black Republican in Davidson's neighborhood was more intolerable to Davidson than any real or imagined faults in Ruffin's character or conduct. As Ruffin himself deduced, what animated Hunter Davidson was "blind prejudice."[20]

The Sage of Villa Rica

Although he remained physically in Paraguay, Davidson's thoughts and concerns often wandered northward to his old country, especially about the time of his 1897 correspondence with Stephen Luce. Even if Davidson had no intention of returning to the U.S., he sought to keep up with affairs there. Distance and isolation did not prevent him from keeping abreast of books and articles pertaining to the history of events and developments in which he had taken part. "I have never lost my interest in Naval matters but have given close attention to them, even here buried in the wilds of S. America," he explained to Stephen Luce. "We have a foreign mail twice a week and I take some twenty or more papers, periodicals, etc."[21]

19 Davidson to de Korab, June 16, 1905, June 22, 1905, and June 30, 1905, Paraguay Despatches.

20 Ruffin to Hon. Robert Bacon, Apr. 27, 1908, NARA, RG 59, NAID 19201622, frame 221.

21 Davidson to Luce, Apr. 19, 1897, Luce Papers. Similarly, in his letter of Jan. 13, 1897, Davidson told Luce that he had "never let go my interest in Naval Matters but take [several illegible words] Scientific and Naval of Europe & America & keep posted as well as I can theoretically."

Mail service worked two ways, of course, and Davidson availed himself of it frequently in 1896-97. His communication with Luce was related inextricably with his desire to set the historical record straight. He had written to Luce in October 1896 through the American minister in Montevideo to solicit Luce's comments on a pair of articles he had written (a letter that apparently went astray); he then followed up directly in January 1897.

The post-Civil War decades triggered what historian David Blight dubbed the "memory industry." Civil War veterans from common soldiers and sailors to generals and admirals wrote memoirs or contributed articles for the famous *Century* magazine series (subsequently collected as *Battles and Leaders of the Civil War*) or for the many other magazines and newspapers that tapped into the seemingly insatiable market for personal reminiscences. For some contributors, the reward was financial: otherwise unlettered men discovered that their personal memories had monetary value. For others, publication offered an opportunity to clarify their places in history and, in the process, settle scores in the ongoing inter-sectional and intra-sectional disputes over the causes and conduct of the Civil War.[22]

For Hunter Davidson, exiled by choice or by circumstance in a "wild country," publication offered an opportunity to set the record straight, vindicate his own wartime contributions, and re-introduce himself to his former fellow citizens.[23]

Davidson's opening salvo in his personal war for historical vindication was to reprint his 1881 exchange of letters with Jefferson Davis. He sent the letters to *The Sun,* a New York City newspaper which, under its editor Charles A. Dana (formerly of the *New York Tribune*), had established a reputation for publishing important articles and reviews. Its Sunday section, inaugurated in 1875, published the works of Bret Harte, Henry James, and others. On December 14, 1896, Davidson sent his Davis correspondence, and it was published in the Sunday *Sun* on February 28, 1897. The paper described the correspondence as "in its way, a contribution to the value of the literature relating to that period." Noting its original publication in the Buenos Ayres *Herald,* the editors stated that it "will of course find an incomparably greater circle of readers in this country." Perhaps not coincidentally, the editors introduced Davidson as a classmate and friend of Adm. Stephen B. Luce.[24]

22 See David Blight, *Race and Reunion: The Civil War in American Memory* (Cambridge, MA. 2001), 176-79.

23 "Wild country" quoted from Davidson, "Correspondence," *Journal of the United States Artillery*, 94.

24 "DAVIS AND DAVIDSON. / A Chapter of War History Concerning Torpedoes . . ." *NYS*, Feb. 28, 1897.

On May 9, 1897, the *Sunday Sun* published one of the two manuscripts that Davidson sent to Luce for his perusal: "MERRIMAC AND MONITOR. / The Story of the Great Naval Duel Told in a New Way." In his January 13, 1897, letter to Luce Davidson explained why he felt compelled to write the article. He had recently seen Harvard historian Edward Channing's 1896 history, *The United States of America 1765-1865,* and predictably was outraged at Channing's statement that the *Virginia* "retired from the fight and never resumed it while another combat would have been welcomed by the Monitor." Davidson complained that "the ignorance and prejudices of the author tortures beyond recognition & perpetuates the preposterous idea that the Monitor was the Victor." Reading Channing's work reminded him of two important and neglected points in the story of that epochal sea battle:

> 1st that the Merrimac entered the fight, with the Monitor as a disabled & crippled vessel—The officers & crew broken down and the vessel in complete disorder from the previous days struggle, which no time had elapsed to remedy [and] 2ndly (and the point upon which no history touches that I have seen). That the Merrimac having lost her iron beak or prow in the previous days struggle with the Minnesota [*sic*: Cumberland] was unable to sink the Monitor when she 'rammed and indented' her side, and that in consequence the Monitor owed her safety to having fought a crippled ship.—the wrenching off of the iron prow from the wooden bow of the Mer. having opened her bulkheads and caused a continuous leak—keeping men at the pumps.

Those points loom large in Davidson's narrative of the battle (cited and quoted at length in Chapter 3). Because Luce remained loyal to the Old Navy, Davidson appealed to a higher authority than Confederate partisanship in explaining why these points were important: "What we want to get at is the truth without which it is impossible to understand and appreciate the value and effect of the material used and skill displayed in using it and last perhaps not least the influence of that particular sea power upon the Civil War."[25]

25 Davidson to Luce, Jan. 13, 1897, Luce Papers. Several words struck through in the manuscript omitted from this quotation. In his Apr. 19, 1897, letter to Luce, Davidson couched his search for "truth" in "reconciliationist" terms: "The officers on both sides in the great conflict were of the same Old Stock—same education—same experiences—and there was nothing to choose between them. Had it been a foreign war they [would] have shown out alike and there [would] still have been nothing to choose between them. No 'North', no 'South'. The material used was [dead?] matter. Let us have the truth."

Davidson also thought it important to assure readers of the *Sun* that, contrary to David Dixon Porter's observation that the Confederate navy preferred *Virginia's* armored casemate to *Monitor's* turret, he and other Confederates recognized the turret to be superior. But, Davidson asked, "what means had the agricultural, pastoral South, with her ports blockaded, of building such a vessel against the Monitor? Machinery had to be especially designed for one, and I do not remember that a complete engine and boiler were built in the South during the War."[26] (By the late 19th century, large guns in armored turrets had become the standard armament in the world's warships, and Davidson no doubt wanted credit for recognizing this superiority.)

Not surprisingly, the other manuscript he asked Luce to read was about torpedoes. It, too, was published in *The Sunday Sun* on March 28, 1897 (six weeks earlier than his "Merrimack and Monitor" article). He returned to the themes and arguments that he covered in his 1874 pamphlet (reprinted in the inaugural volume of *Southern Historical Society Papers* in 1876) and would cover yet again in a final article published essentially unchanged in three different periodicals: *The Sunday Sun* (October 19, 1908), *Confederate Veteran* (September 1908 issue printed after that date), and the English *Magazine of History* (November 1908). It was only natural that Davidson authored multiple articles about torpedoes. For all intents and purposes, torpedo technology had been his profession since 1862 (although Davidson revealed no expertise in the new self-propelled torpedo technology).

Each of Davidson's articles on torpedoes was in part a response to a recent work that he believed distorted the historical record and cried out for correction. (His 1897 and 1908 articles quibbled with details in David Dixon Porter's influential 1886 *Naval History of the Civil War.*) Davidson's oversized ego and concern with his own historical reputation should not blind us from recognizing the fundamental accuracy of his arguments. Some of the histories to which he responded had indeed simplified or mangled the historical record at Davidson's expense. *The Evolution of the Submarine Boat, Mine, and Torpedo from the Sixteenth Century to the Present Time* by English naval officer Murray Fraser Sueter—the book to which Davidson's 1908 articles replied—did not ignore the incidents on which Davidson built his own reputation, but his narrative omitted the names of most primary actors and butchered the facts. In explaining the "very important step" of electrically detonated torpedoes, Sueter wrote that "This method was not

26 Hunter Davidson, "MERRIMAC AND MONITOR. The Story of the Great Naval Duel Told in a New Way . . ." *NYS*, May 9, 1897.

largely used, but had one successful issue, that was, in blowing up the 'Commodore James' a heavily armoured Federal gunboat in the Roanoke River."[27]

The main points of all of Davidson's published articles were variations on the themes he introduced in his 1874 pamphlet. Of course, the primary point was that the Submarine Battery Service (the formal name of which varied in his articles) that he organized and commanded was responsible for the first and only destruction of an enemy warship by an electrically detonated torpedo in the American Civil War. His other personal accomplishment—the *Squib's* attack that damaged the *Minnesota*—represented the only successful torpedo boat attack on an enemy vessel without loss of the attacking crew. Re-visiting the subject over a 35-year period, Davidson developed and elaborated upon a heroic narrative by which he and his associates ignored advice from friends and overcame skepticism, opposition, and interference within the Confederate navy and government, and hostility and threats of retribution from the enemy to obtain the resources, conduct the experiments, and perfect the defenses that vindicated his faith, saved Richmond from capture (temporarily), and demonstrated the value of electric torpedoes for other navies of the world. Hunter Davidson, the patented inventor, built on Matthew Fontaine Maury's foundation, to be sure, but added the tangible and intangible ingredients necessary to transform theory into reality.

The most insightful window into Davidson's mindset is his April, 1897 letter to Stephen Luce explaining his motivation for writing the torpedo article for *The Sun*. It is worth quoting at length:

> The Torpedo article I think of much importance if studied in its true bearing upon the War.
>
> The greatest men on both sides treated the question with contempt and abhorrence and were never willing to admit its efficiency much less its propriety. Ben Butler when 'bottled up' on the shores of the James styled the men of my command 'the Pirates of the Creeks' and I don't suppose it ever even occurred to him that these same 'pirates' caused him to lose the battle of Drewry's Bluff and saved Richmond for the time."
>
> Nor did the facts occur to Jeff Davis, nor to Genl [R. E.] Lee until long after the War when Lee saw this question in its true light and opened his eyes with astonishment—for he as a great Engineer should have tho't of the more than possible effect of this new Arm of War.

27 Murray Fraser Sueter, *The Evolution of the Submarine Boat, Mine, and Torpedo, from the Sixteenth Century to the Present Time* (Portsmouth, England, 1908), 271.

> He could not deny the facts of history concerning the movements of Adm. S[amuel] P. Lee & Ben Butler but he had never connected them with anything the Torpedo dept. had done.
>
> The officers of the S. Army & Navy asked to look at my arrangements with a wondering pitying expression. The only true support I had was [Navy Secretary Stephen] Mallory & at times public opinion would shake even him.
>
> Billy [Commander William H.] Parker and [Commander John Mercer] Brooke were dear good friends & kept at least quiet but didn't think this mode of warfare chivalric.
>
> Adm. S. P. Lee sent word to me by [Lt. Roswell] Lamson that I was not engaged in civilized or legitimate warfare & that he would not treat me as a prisoner of war if he caught me—but in six mos after I roared in delight when he had stuck torpedo poles on the bows of nearly every vessel in his squadron.
>
> You will see then that the feeling existing as regarded Torpedo warfare presented not only the effect from being duly appreciated & acknowledged but generally retarded its development.
>
> Had my own side encouraged me with the energy &c. that it opposed me the World would not be forgetting now what country they owe the practical use of Torpedoes in War.
>
> In writing the above, I do not pretend to ignore the Torpedo work of other men who worked with courage, ability & success, but my department was the only one working with a system in every detail—and the first to prove the efficiency of Electrical Torpedoes in War.

Obviously aware of how his written rant would strike his old friend, Davidson closed this passage with a humorous anecdote:

> Perhaps you never saw Henry Irving in his amusing play of 'The Old Waterloo Soldier', in his second childhood when he throws his arm upon the map as he almost upsets the table in his eagerness to display his knowledge of the battle. 'Why there was quatre bras & there was the sunken road—Napoleon was over there & here were we! & there you are, Mon! & what more do you want.'

I can figure you as the audience & Dave [that is, Davidson himself] as the Old Soldier."[28]

His latter-day accounts sometimes embroidered his earlier narratives. Recounting the tense May 1864 flag-of-truce encounter with Federal vessels in the James River, Davidson wrote in the *Magazine of History* that Federal officers not only met him with open contempt but opened fire at him. "One ball passed so close to my head that I could feel the wind from it." His own and other contemporary accounts did not mention those details. In his 1897 *Sun* article he invented a clever rhetorical device that both rebuked David Dixon Porter's *Naval History* for its inadequate understanding of the different torpedo systems employed during the Civil War and ridiculed Gen. Gabriel Rains's worse-than-useless contact torpedoes that Jefferson Davis considered so significant. Porter, Davidson wrote, failed to distinguish between the system of electrical torpedoes, "especially designed and perfected in every detail, and completely under the control of those operating it" and "the other a system (if it can be so called) of guerrilla torpedo warfare, which succeeded in destroying many vessels in the West, but closed all channels to friend as well as foe, and was too unreliable to be adopted as a regular service." The electric system is "now adopted by nearly every maritime nation," while "the guerrilla method is never taken into consideration as a means of warfare, although it may be again resorted to in exceptional cases."[29]

If Hunter Davidson's 1881 sniping letters to Jefferson Davis seemed blunt and impertinent, they paled before the broadside Davidson fired at him in his trio of 1908 articles (published 19 years after the former president had died). In an attack worthy of Davis's more famous sparring partners, General Joseph E. Johnston and Georgia Governor Joseph E. Brown, Davidson recounted multiple affronts in which Davis treated him with "marked discourtesy." One was the 1881 correspondence about Davis's discussion of torpedoes in his memoir. Another was a second-hand account that when Davis learned about Davidson's 1864 *Squib* attack on *Minnesota* (for which Davidson received promotion to commander), Davis "merely exclaimed, 'Humph, why didn't he blow her up?'" Davidson speculated that Davis's consistent hostility toward him might owe to a comment Davidson made to a friend in 1861 that "We will never succeed with Mr. Davis as President."

28 Davidson to Luce, Apr. 19, 1897, Luce Papers. Davidson would have roared even louder in delight about Adm. Lee's hypocrisy had he known that Lee engaged torpedo experts and advisers as early as 1862.

29 Hunter Davidson, "Mines and Torpedoes During the Rebellion," *Magazine of History* (Nov. 1908), 8:258; Davidson, "TORPEDOES."

Might this comment have gotten back to the president? In publishing a version of this article in *Confederate Veteran,* editor Sumner Cunningham added a note that "In printing the foregoing criticisms of President Davis, the VETERAN breaks its rule. The considerations are that Captain Davidson has been long absent in a far-away land. He did marvelous service for the Confederacy, and it may be the President was at fault. The VETERAN, however, stands for the President officially and personally as a great and good man. None are perfect."[30]

As he kept up with the literature on the Civil War and naval history, Davidson also felt compelled to vindicate the mode of warfare on which he staked his claim to fame. He delighted in crowing about the U.S. naval officers excoriating him for employing "uncivilized" weapons and then adopting those same weapons within months. It must have warmed his heart to read President Ulysses S. Grant's December 1875 annual message to Congress recommending increased appropriations for torpedoes. Grant predicted that in any future wars with foreign powers "torpedoes will be among, if not the most effective and cheapest auxiliary for the defense of harbors, and also in aggressive operations that we can have."[31]

Davidson observed in his propagandistic 1874 pamphlet that "every discovery of a new or improved weapon proves to be a step towards greater civilization and peace." He lived long enough to witness the evolution and destructive potential of the weapons he helped develop. Torpedoes had propelled the United States into a war with Spain (after a suspected mine sank the battleship *Maine* in Havana harbor) and played a prominent role in the 1904-05 Russo-Japanese War. He died the year before Germany—the country to which he tried to sell torpedo technology in 1870—outraged the civilized world with its "unrestricted" submarine warfare. Still, as late as 1908, he remained an unrepentant champion. "If torpedoes do nothing more than keep the enemy off our coast, what an incalculable assistance to our defence they will be," he wrote. "But the torpedo is destined to play an active part in offensive war. More than half the time the sea will be smooth enough to use torpedo boats. Battleships will be well battered and placed out of action by the gun, but will often go down with the impact of a torpedo. I have been a firm believer in torpedoes, offensive and defensive, since 1862, and they are more proportionately in evidence to-day than ever." Anticipating the evolution of torpedo warfare and extrapolating from William T. Sherman's famous adage about the humanitarian benefits of "hard war" tactics, Davidson wrote: "I believe that the more destructive the weapons employed in wars, the less apt wars are to occur,

30 Davidson, "The Electrical Submarine Mine—1861-65," *CV* (Sep. 1908), 16:459.

31 James D. Richardson, ed., *A Compilation of the Messages and Papers of the Presidents* (New York, 1902-1904), 9:4304.

and the soonest over. Long wars spread desolation and darken the earth. It would be far better to blow a whole army up in one mine and a fleet in another than that a war should last four years."[32]

Davidson's absence "in a far away land" did not prevent him from keeping up with developments and debates in his native land, but it did make it necessary for him to reintroduce himself periodically to his former comrades. When he wrote the editor of *Confederate Veteran* requesting "a sample of your esteemed journal," he also requested "the opportunity of saluting with all my heart any of my old comrades in arms of the Second American Revolution," and adding after his name "Graduate U. S. N. Academy, 1847 [conflating his 1849 graduation date with the date of warrant as passed midshipman], First Division, C. S. S. Merrimac (or Virginia), Chief of the Confederate States Torpedo Department, 1863-64." Editor Cunningham fleshed out his resume with quotations about his service gleaned apparently from the published *Official Records* and an endorsement: "This venerable Confederate may be assured that thousands will be gratified to learn that he still lives, even in far-away Paraguay, and the Southland honors him for his valuable services to the Confederacy."[33]

The *Journal of the United States Artillery* published a similar capsule biography of him in 1909, written by former U.S. and C.S. midshipman, James Morris Morgan, in conjunction with a letter that Davidson had written in response to an unspecified query. On November 26, 1908, Davidson replied to Major Thomas W. Winston of the U.S. Coast Artillery that "I regret exceedingly that I am now unequal to the task you would so kindly impose upon me, and besides I may say that my drawings and specifications, which I kept with care until a very few years past, are now nearly all lost." He then offered a few reminiscences of his childhood at Fort Monroe—Winston's current post—and closed with an old man's apology: "Excuse my digression, Major. It is a long memory from '38 thru '61-2 to 1908 and scenes events are strangely mingled in pleasure and pain."[34]

The letters in *Confederate Veteran* and *Journal of the United States Artillery* indirectly answer an obvious question about Davidson's historical reputation. Why

32 Davidson, "The First Successful Application,"3. In the conclusion of a June, 1879 letter to W. T. Walthall intended to assist Jefferson Davis in writing his *Rise and Fall*, Gabriel Rains wrote of torpedoes: "Thus Nations have been furnished with a new weapon of destruction which in augmenting the difficulties of invasion is but another step among Christian Powers to universal peace." Did Rains intentionally mimic Davidson's language? Quoted in Waters and Brown, *Gabriel Rains and the Confederate Torpedo Bureau*, 132; Davidson, "Mines and Torpedoes," 261; Davidson, "Mine and Torpedo," *NYS*, Oct. 19, 1908.

33 "Hunter Davidson, C. S. N., In Paraguay, *CV* (Sep. 1906), 14:396.

34 Davidson, "Correspondence," *Journal of the United States Artillery*, 94.

didn't a man so concerned about his place in history write his own memoir? The petty, but telling, errors in his capsule autobiography (the wrong Naval School graduation date, the wrong dates of service in a misnamed torpedo service) suggest a failing memory or unavailability of basic documentation. And, although he claimed in his 1897 *Sun* article to still possess a journal from his service on the *Virginia,* he hinted several times over several decades at the loss of valuable papers. In asking for Jefferson Davis's endorsement in 1867 Davidson explained that the "burning of Richmond caused the destruction of all my official documents, papers &, hence I am now dependent upon the expression of the good opinion of those under whom I had the honor of serving." He told his nephew in 1903 that he lost "valuable papers among them the drawing of a family tree" in 1877 "in the wreck of a vessel" (the *Fulminante*), and in 1908 told Maj. Winston that he had lost "drawings and specifications." "I have no means, in this remote, secluded region where I now live," he admitted in his 1908 articles, "of giving plans or even illustrations in order that the public in general may understand my experiments." Less convincingly, he explained why he had failed earlier to rebut the errors and slights that appeared in other books. "Like many other poor Confederate, after the war I felt too disgusted with everything and knew the folly of my writing about the war." Some of the most celebrated early memoirs and histories were penned by "poor Confederates" such as Vice President Alexander Stephens (1868) and Adm. Raphael Semmes (1869). Davidson's own self-published pamphlet about his success with electric torpedoes preceded David Dixon Porter's *History* by a dozen years.[35]

"All broken up with a hard messy uneasy life"

The recovery of the robust health of which he had boasted to Stephen Luce in 1897 proved short-lived—and Davidson may well have exaggerated it for Luce's benefit. A year earlier, in his futile 1896 effort to obtain a U.S. passport, Davidson described himself as "old and suffering with heart disease." "I have been confined to my bed for a long time and am too feeble to write you as I would wish," he confessed in a March 1900 letter to his nephew, Reginald Leach. "This month am 74, all broken up with a hard messy uneasy life." He thought often of his niece, Leach's wife, "but can't write—suffer so awfully with weakness of heart & may go off at any hour." He did not "go off" anytime soon, but his health remained

35 Rowland, ed., *Jefferson Davis Constitutionalist,* 7:109; Davidson to Dr. Leach, Aug. 25, 1903; Davidson, "Correspondence," *Journal of United States Artillery,* 94. Davidson's assertion that he lost everything in the explosion of the *Fulminante* (see chapter 7) conflicts with his 1897 article about the battle of Hampton Roads in which he claimed that he still had a "private journal" documenting that battle (see chapter 3; Davidson, "Mine and Torpedo."

tentative. Although General Consul Bartleman described Davidson in late 1906 as "in good health," a year earlier, while orchestrating the smear campaign against Consul Ruffin, Davidson complained of problems with his liver and a prolonged sickness that left him at times unable to sit up for very long or write. By 1908, Consul Norton described him as "feeble" and unable to return to the United States. No doubt his late life feebleness intensified the wistful feelings he expressed in 1908 when he described himself in 1862 as "young, energetic, strong and healthy."[36] Sometime between 1904 and 1907 he and his family moved from his estancia outside Villa Rica 50 miles northwest to the village of Pirayu.

Hunter Davidson died in nearby Paraguarí, Paraguay, on February 16, 1913, in his 87th year. He was buried there in the municipal cemetery alongside his second wife, Enriqueta, who lived until April 1953. He left behind eight surviving children and nine grandchildren on three continents. Daughter Leila's eldest son, Sir Hyde Clarendon Gowan, eventually became governor of the Central Provinces of India, and her third son, Cecil Hunter Boyd Davidson, was a lieutenant-commander in the Royal Navy at the time of his grandfather's death. At the age of 41, Davidson's son Percy also had followed Cdr. Davidson into the naval service, enlisting in the U.S. Navy Auxiliary Force during the Spanish-American War.[37]

Only a few American newspapers noted Davidson's death. Far more newspapers printed stories in 1913 about Davidson's son, Rev. Charles Steele Davidson, when he renounced the Episcopal Church and burned his raiments to protest the church's alliance with conservatism. In contrast, when Davidson's fellow Virginian, Date of 1841 USN classmate, successor to command of the Confederate Submarine Battery Service, and comrade in the Argentine torpedo service, John Pembroke "Paul" Jones, died three years earlier in Pasadena, California, newspapers throughout

36 Davidson to Leach, Mar. 9, 1900, copy in Charles T. Jacobs research collection; Davidson to de Korab, June 22 and 25, 1905, NARA, RG 59, NAID 19201622, microfilm frames 231, 232, 237; Davidson, "Mines and Torpedoes," 256.

37 According to genealogical research, the remains in the family plot were subsequently disinterred and moved to another location. Daughter Leila Gowan died in Bournemouth, England, in 1937, survived by two of her three sons. Son Hunter died in Charles Town, West Virginia, in 1939 and had no children. Son Charles Steele died in 1949 and was survived by his, sons Hunter (1906-1997) and John Carlos (1907-1990), and Charles Ray (1910-1994) and daughter Dorothy Steele Davidson Smith (1912-2003). Percy, who had divorced his Australian wife, Mary Lucy Smith, of whom his father so disapproved, remarried in 1901 to Mary (Margaret) Travers. They had one daughter, Katherine Travers Trail (1903-1923). Percy committed suicide in a New York City hotel room in 1916. Frank's son, Irving Mortimer Davidson, died in Oregon in an automobile accident in 1937. At the time of Enriqueta's death, the only one of her children still living was Ruben—who was also the only one of Davidson's South American children to have issue. He died in 1966; his daughter died in 2012. Ancestry.com Davidson Family Tree. Ruben's wife was in communication with Homer K. "Ken" Davidson, grandson and biographer of "Black Jack" Davidson, as late as 1971. Ken Davidson to Cousin Hunter Davidson, Mar. 12, 1971, copy in Charles T. Jacobs research collection.

Undated photograph of Davidson in Paraguay that appeared with his obituary in *Confederate Veteran*. *Confederate Veteran magazine, 1913*

the country published obituaries that mistakenly hailed him as the oldest living graduate of the U.S. Naval Academy.[38]

By the time of his death, Hunter Davidson had managed to rehabilitate his admittedly low-profile reputation from turncoat pariah ("HUNTER DAVIDSON, arch fiend of the torpedo corps" whose uncivilized weapons killed innocent American sailors) to sage of torpedo warfare and river navigation. He never recovered the august status he enjoyed briefly in 1860 when newspapers hailed him as the "very intelligent officer" who invented a boat-lifting device that would save lives at sea. But even representatives of the government he fought against in the 1860s found reason to overlook or forgive his transgression and praise his subsequent work in South America. The U.S. minister in Buenos Aires in 1877 called attention to a new deep-water channel "surveyed and sounded by Capt. Hunter Davidson." Seven years later, the U.S. Navy Bureau of Navigation acknowledged receipt of a valuable chart of the Paraná River received "[t]hrough courtesy of Mr. Hunter Davidson."[39] Later that year another official in Argentina wrote admiringly of Davidson's work and using a coy identification of the former "notorious" rebel:

> In my last annual report I referred to an exploring expedition, under the command of Capt. Hunter Davidson, formerly of the United States Navy, to the northern limits of the Republic. Its especial object was to verify the boundary line which separates this country from Brazil. The expedition was in every respect successful in its primary object; but the interest in Captain Davidson's report is greatly enhanced by his graphic description of the country through which he passed—rich in all the elements of national wealth, yet absolutely destitute of inhabitants. Even the Indian tribes, which are to be encountered almost everywhere else, were entirely wanting. The expedition went up the river which is navigable for light-draught steamers as far as the falls of Yguazu [Iguazu], about which heretofore so little seems to have been known, which probably had not been visited by a white man during the last hundred years. From the accounts of Captain Davidson gives of these falls, they must be one of the grandest and most wonderful sights in nature.[40]

38 "Capt. Hunter Davidson," *CV*, (June 1913), 21:307; *Army and Navy Journal* (April 22, 1913), 50:987; "Hampton's Son of Naval Fame Dead . . ." *Daily Press* [Newport News, VA], May 26, 1910.

39 Thomas O. Osborn, U.S. Legation, Buenos Ayres, Argentina, to Secretary of State William Evarts, Sep.19, 1877, *Papers Relating to the Foreign Relations of the United States, Transmitted to Congress With the Annual Message of the President, December 2, 1878* (Washington, D.C., 1878), 7; Commander H. B. Seeley, *Nipsic*, South Atlantic Station, Buenos Aires, Jan. 24, 1884, Barbour Papers.

40 *Commercial relations of the United States. Reports from the consuls of the United States on the commerce, manufactures, etc., of their consular districts. For the months of September, October, November, and December 1884.* House Misc. Doc. 34/ Serial Set Vol. No. 2319, 377.

In 1889, when he was settling into retired life on his estancia, he played the role of sage, vis-à-vis his most recent employment, weighing in on the question of the best location for the port of Buenos Aires. American Minister Bayless W. Hanna forwarded to Secretary of State James G. Blaine a newspaper with Davidson's long letter and noted its interest for U.S. naval officers. "Capt. Davidson will be remembered as an old U.S.N. Officer who, unfortunately, with so many of his accomplished but misguided colleagues, embarked in the cause of the Southern Rebellion," Hanna noted to Blaine. "He was second in command of the Merrimac in its mighty naval combat with the Monitor in Hampton Roads, March 8, 1862, and once in the Coast Survey and Harbor Improvements Service of our Navy, which fact, especially renders his opinions valuable."[41]

Even if it has relegated him to the status of footnote, History has not ignored Hunter Davidson or his primary accomplishments. Perhaps rather gratuitously, Rr. Adm. Albert Gleaves's 1925 biography of Stephen Luce introduced Luce's Naval School friend as "the famous Hunter Davidson"—an appellation few would bestow upon him. Not surprisingly, the closer a study focuses specifically on Civil War torpedo warfare or the battle of Hampton Roads, the more likely it is to mention Hunter Davidson by name—and, for that matter, to provide correct details about the subject. Surveys of Civil War history rarely mention Davidson, although the articles about Hampton Roads and torpedo warfare in the perennially popular *Battles and Leaders of the Civil War* mention him in passing and with minimal attention to the importance of the Submarine Battery Service in 1864. U.S. Naval Academy professor James Russell Soley, an early authority on Civil War naval warfare, noted that Confederate Navy Secretary Stephen Mallory relied most heavily on John Brooke (for ordnance) and Davidson (for torpedoes). Davidson's torpedo service, he concluded, "probably contributed more to the defense of the Confederacy than all the vessels of it navy." Short surveys of Civil War naval history describe the sinking of *Commodore Jones* but credit the Confederacy's torpedo warfare to Stephen Mallory and Matthew Fontaine Maury and do not mention Davidson or his Submarine Battery Service.[42]

41 Bayless W. Hanna to Blaine, Apr. 6, 1889, with enclosure, copy in Barbour Papers.

42 Gleaves, ed., *Life and Letters of Luce*, 36; Robert Underwood Johnson and Clarence Clough Buel, eds., *Battles and Leaders of the Civil War* (1884, reprint edition: New York, 1954), 1:630, 695; 4:705-707 (quote from 1:630). In contrast, the essays in Harold Holzer and Tim Mulligan, editors, *The Battle of Hampton Roads: New Perspectives on the USS Monitor and the CSS Virginia* (New York, 2006), mention Davidson twice in passing.; James McPherson, *War on the Waters: The Union and Confederate Navies, 1861-1865* (Chapel Hill, NC, 2012), 4-5, 198; Spencer C. Tucker, *A Short History of the Civil War at Sea* (Wilmington, DE, 2002), 57, 104-106; Craig L. Symonds, *The Civil War at Sea* (Santa Barbara, CA, 2009) does not give any attention to torpedoes on the James River or to Maury as a torpedo pioneer.

Studies focused on the Confederate navy typically give Davidson his due, even if they give more credit to Matthew Fontaine Maury's work than Davidson believed it deserved and, more egregiously, continued to credit the effectiveness of Gabriel Rains's contact torpedoes. Books and popular articles about Civil War torpedo warfare typically consult and credit the articles by Davidson and Crowley, insuring that students of Civil War history know his name.[43]

Davidson would be at least grudgingly pleased that studies of the development of torpedo warfare have corroborated the importance of the *Commodore Jones* incident and occasionally the *Squib's* attack, even if they did not give him the personal credit he sought so hard to win. Even those works published in Davidson's lifetime that he found deficient or erroneous in their particulars, such as those by John Barnes, U.S.N., and M. F. Sueter, R.N., acknowledged that the sinking of the *Jones* represented a landmark in the development of electrically detonated torpedoes.[44]

Perhaps most gratifying for Davidson would have been an article published in the 1940 *United States Naval Institute Proceedings* describing the sinking of the *Jones* and concluding: "Thus was accomplished what is believed to be the first destruction of a warship by submarine mine. The incident astonished the world and its immediate result was the rescue of Richmond from a second peril. General Butler, finding his army's right wing uncovered, retired to Bermuda Hundred."[45]

Military historian Timothy S. Wolters has made the most systematic effort to determine "Who among the Confederates was most responsible for developing

43 Scharf, *History of the Confederate States Navy*, 730-38; Raimondo Luraghi, *A History of the Confederate Navy* (Annapolis, MD, 1996), chapters 13 and 14; William N. Still, Jr., ed., *The Confederate Navy: The Ships, Men and Organization, 1861-65* (London, 1997), 62, 204-9; Perry, *Infernal Machines*, 110-13; Dean Snyder, "Torpedoes for the Confederacy," *Civil War Times Illustrated*, Mar. 1985, 41-4; Robert Collins Suhr, "Torpedoes, the Confederacy's dreaded 'infernal machines,' made many a Union sea captain uneasy." *America's Civil War*, (Nov. 1991), 59-62; "Confederate Submarine Service on the James River," *Blue and Gray Magazine* (Oct. 1989), 16.

44 Barnes, *Submarine Warfare*, 97-101; Sueter, *The Evolution of the Submarine Boat*, 270-71; also C. W. Sleeman, Esq., *Torpedoes and Torpedo Warfare: Containing a Complete and Concise Account of the Rise and Progress of Submarine Warfare: Also a Detailed Description of All Matters Appertaining Thereto, Including the Latest Improvements* (Portsmouth, England, 1880), 190; and William R. King, *Torpedoes, Their Invention and Use from the First Application to the Art of War to the Present Time*, (Washington, D.C., 1866; reprint, Naval Historical Center, 1992), 18.

45 Carlos C. Hanks, "Mines of Long Ago," *United States Naval Institute Proceedings*, (Nov. 1940), 66:1550. Hanks's language ("astonished the world") echoed R. O. Crowley's 1898 article quoted on page 136. In contrast, Gray, *Nineteenth-Century Torpedoes*, which focuses on the evolution of self-propelled torpedoes, does not even mention Davidson or Maury in its limited discussion of electrical torpedoes, torpedo boats, and spar torpedoes.

electric torpedoes?" He analyzed the competing claims made by and for the most prominent candidates—Stephen Mallory, Matthew Fontaine Maury, Gabriel Rains, Hunter Davidson, and Beverly Kennon—and the conclusions of other historians. He credited Maury as the "originator" of the Confederacy's work with electric torpedoes, Kennon with being the first to develop a system of electric torpedo defense at New Orleans before he was called away for other service in late 1861, and Davidson for being the first and, in fact, "the one principal to sink an enemy vessel with this new weapon of war."[46]

Hunter Davidson's ego and relentless self-promotion can obscure the rather circumscribed nature of his claim to historical fame. He did not claim to invent electrical torpedoes or to be their "originator" even in the Confederacy, or to be the first to sink an enemy vessel with a torpedo. He did not deny that contact torpedoes sunk Federal warships before May 1864; he scorned them because they were reckless weapons that were as dangerous to friend as to foe. He claimed merely that his command had been the first to sink an enemy warship in time of war using a *system* of electrically detonated torpedoes and that he and the *Squib* had been the only torpedo boat during the Civil War to "successfully attack" (defined vaguely and limply as damaging) an enemy vessel without loss to its own crew. Taken on their own terms, Davidson's claims are demonstrably true.

While trying to establish his own place in torpedo history Davidson certainly diminished Maury's role in pioneering the system that he inherited. Timothy Wolters points out that Davidson seemed to undermine his own claims when, in May 1867, he explained to Jefferson Davis that the torpedo that sunk *Commodore Jones* had been in the water for 22 months. That suggests that the torpedo was placed in about July 1862, too soon after he succeeded Maury in command of the submarine batteries to have been the product of his own work. Perhaps. In an 1866 lecture of "Torpedoes," Maury indicated that the torpedo had been in the water for only 18 months and thus credited Davidson's claim. In either case, it was Davidson's command that actually sunk the *Jones*. If the combative Davidson had an opportunity to rebut Wolters's analysis, he would declare victory after reading the second page of Wolters's article: "The shocking death of *Commodore Jones* and much of her crew temporarily halted a Union advance toward Richmond. Of greater significance, for the first time a combatant destroyed an enemy warship with an electric torpedo. The event thus marks a milestone in technological and military history."[47]

46 Wolters, "Electric Torpedoes in the Confederacy," 756, 762, 783, and 755-83 passim.

47 MFM Papers, LC; Wolters, "Electric Torpedoes in the Confederacy," 783, 756.

Beyond his importance in the history of torpedo warfare, Hunter Davidson merits attention as a representative of the generation of able young U.S. naval officers, especially those who "went South." Typical of the young officers who entered the U.S. Navy in 1841, Davidson spent two decades serving in geographically disparate squadrons and in diverse capacities. Like many of his brother officers, Davidson demonstrated intelligence and inventiveness and—despite self-inflicted wounds arising from his "unofficerlike conduct"—won plum assignments that allowed his talents to shine.

Then, in 1861, Davidson, Brooke, Minor, Catesby Jones, "Paul" Jones, and scores of others denied their knowledge and talents to the naval service that trained and nurtured them and transferred those assets to a fledgling nation determined to break up the United States. The decision to support the Confederacy against the United States in turn exacted a high cost from the men who went south. "Perhaps no biography of a class of men would be more interesting—probably sadly so—than the old Navy officers who resigned" in 1861, wrote Francis L. Galt, a naval surgeon who served on the Confederate commerce raider *Alabama,* to his old shipmate, John McIntosh Kell. After narrating his own sojourn with John Randolph Tucker in Peru and updating Kell on other mutual acquaintances, Galt mused that "many of our old families and those of resigned Army & Navy officers have had a fearful pilgrimage since the war."[48]

Few of those men expressed any regrets over their decision to fight for the Confederacy and their postwar travails, however exotic, need not elicit sympathy from us. They admitted defeat, but not that they were wrong. However "fearful" their postwar struggles to make a living and forge a new career, they managed to do so and were not compelled to renounce their actions—a phenomenon that gave birth to the "Lost Cause" interpretation of Civil War history. Hunter Davidson left no explanation of his decision to renounce the old Union and fight for the Confederacy beyond his April 1861 letter to Abraham Lincoln referring cryptically to the "principles and causes" that he and other "*freemen*" espoused. His early 20th-century racist screeds, in conjunction with his life-long contempt for African Americans, suggest that his principles included defense of white supremacy. His decision to exile himself and never return to a re-united country ruled by "Black Republicans" reinforces the impression that racism was a primary motive for Hunter Davidson.

It is tempting to make Davidson's ugly racist screed his epitaph and to hold him up as the exemplar of what many modern Americans are eager to believe true

48 Galt to Kell, Oct. 27, 1877, John McIntosh Kell Papers, David M. Rubinstein Rare Book & Manuscript Library, Duke University, Box 5.

of all Confederates. We cannot of course, generalize safely from Davidson's words to the motives of other men, and Davidson's racism alone did not define him. More challenging for the modern biographer is to comprehend how someone who considered himself a man of principle and honor—and could in fact be a man of principle and honor—was capable of such racist acts and statements.

We must also resist painting a clichéd portrait of an intelligent man of promise brought low by his own tragic flaws. As best we can know him (considering the paucity of personal letters from or about him), Davidson was, throughout his life a confident, self-righteous, plain-spoken, and self-centered man who considered his own motives and actions consistently noble. His character did not torpedo (pun intended) a promising career that might have been the subject of numerous admiring biographies over the last century. His character and his career intertwined inextricably.

The best way to understand Hunter Davidson's life is to embrace his infuriating complexity. The same principles and sense of loyalty that led him to support the Confederacy led him to serve the United States faithfully until the moment he resigned. The same man who was so concerned about being able to provide for his family abandoned his family and began a second family on another continent (although we do not know all the dynamics that lay behind that decision). The man who so obviously considered Black people his inferiors faithfully performed his duty in helping to suppress the African slave trade. The man who invented a device to save lives at sea later promoted that invention as evidence of his own intellect so that he could perfect and proliferate deadly weapons of war. His was, to use his own words, a "messy, uneasy life," made messier and more uneasy by his own beliefs, words, decisions, and actions. His service in six navies (United States, Virginia, Confederate States, Chile, Argentina, and the Maryland Oyster Police) was not the result of progress and promotion, but of necessity.[49] The variety and adventures of his life attract even as the man himself often repels. To read his biography and exclaim, "What an interesting life!" is not to say, "what a great man."

49 Davidson's Masters 1865 certificate in the British navy (renewed in 1875) could qualify as a seventh naval service.

Bibliography

Manuscript and Archives Sources

Center for Whistler Studies, Glasgow University Library, Scotland

James Whistler letters https://tinyurl.com/y6u5e7sw

Confederate Memorial Literary Society [CMLS] Collection under the management of the Virginia Historical Society, Richmond, VA

Hardin Littlepage Collection

David M. Rubinstein Rare Book & Manuscript Library, Duke University, Durham, NC

John McIntosh Kell Papers

George M. Brooke, Jr., collection

John M. Brooke Papers

Gilder Lehrman Collection, New York, NY

William McBlair Letters

Hagley Library, Wilmington, DE

Samuel Francis DuPont Papers

Charles T. Jacobs research collection

Hunter Davidson letters to Reginald Leach (copies)

Homer K. Davidson letter to Hunter Davidson [III]

Library of Congress Manuscripts Division, Washington, D.C.

Stephen Bleecker Luce Papers

Betty Herndon Maury Diary

Matthew Fontaine Maury Diary

Matthew Fontaine Maury Papers

Mariners Museum, Newport News, VA

Andrew J. Forrest letter

Maryland State Archives, Annapolis, MD

Anne Arundel County Court Docket 1849 October Term [S64-81]

Records of the Maryland Oyster Police [S302]

Minute Book, 1868-1878, of the Commissioners of the State Oyster Police [S303]

National Archives and Records Administration, Washington, DC

RG 23 Records of the U.S. Coast Survey

RG 24 Records of the Bureau of Navy Personnel

RG 24 Log of the U.S.S. *Portsmouth*

RG 45 US, Area File of the Naval Records Collection, 1775-1910

RG 45 Letters sent and received by U.S. Secretary of Navy

RG 45 Letters of U.S. squadron commanders

RG 45 Confederate States Navy area files, area 7

RG 45 Confederate States Navy subject files

RG 59 Records of the Department of State, Central files

RG 59 Despatches from U.S. Ministers to Great Britain, 1791-1906

RG 84 Records of Foreign Service Posts of the Department of State

RG 94 Turner Baker Case files

RG 94 Records of the U.S. Army Adjutant General's Office

RG 109 U.S. War Department Collection of Confederate Records

RG 109 Letters Sent by Confederate Secretary of War,

RG 109 Records Relating to Confederate Citizens or Businesses

RG 125 Records of the Judge Advocate General (Navy)

RG 405 Records of the United States Naval Academy (accessed at the Nimitz Library, U.S. Naval Academy)

Naval History & Heritage Command, Washington, DC

Annual Reports of the [U.S.] Secretary of the Navy, 1841-1843, 1845

Ship Histories

Early Record Biographies (ZB) files

Old Dominion University, Norfolk, VA

John Randolph Tucker Papers

Scott Polar Research Institute Archives, University of Cambridge, England

Henry J. Hartstene biographical note https://tinyurl.com/mppnbe4p

Southern Historical Collection, University of North Carolina Chapel Hill, NC

John Taylor Wood Papers

Tulane University Special Collections, New Orleans, LA

G. T. Beauregard Papers,

United States Naval Academy Nimitz Library

"History of the U. S. Naval Academy" by Thomas G. Ford

Records of the United States Naval Academy, RG 45, NARA (copies)

Virginia Museum of History and Culture [formerly Virginia Historical Society], Richmond, VA

Phyllis Barbour Papers
Department of Henrico Papers
Robert E. Lee Letter book
Minor Family Papers
John K. Mitchell Papers
Thornton Tayloe Perry (compiler) Papers
Washington and Lee University, Lexington, VA
1876 and 1878 catalogs

Hunter Davidson Writings

Davis and Davidson." *Southern Historical Society Papers*, 1896, 24:284-291.

Davidson, Hunter. "Correspondence" [letter to Major T. W. Winston, USMC]. *Journal of the United States Artillery*, 1909, 32:94.

Davidson, Hunter, "The Electrical Submarine Mine – 1861-65.," *Confederate Veteran*. September 1908, 16:456-9.

Davidson, Hunter, "Electrical Torpedoes as a System of Defence.," *Southern Historical Society Papers*. July 1876, 2:1-6.

Davidson, Hunter, "The First Successful Application of Electrical Torpedoes or Submarine Mines In Time of War and As a System of Defense."

Davidson, Hunter, "Mine and Torpedo," *The Sun* [NY], October 19, 1908.

Davidson, Hunter, "Mines and Torpedoes During the Rebellion," *Magazine of History*. 8:255-261.

Davidson, Hunter, "MERRIMAC AND MONITOR. The Story of the Great Naval Duel Told in a New Way . . ." *The Sun* [NY], May 9, 1897.

[Davidson, Hunter], *Report upon the Oyster Resources of Maryland to the General Assembly by Hunter Davidson, Esqu., Com. State Oyster Police Force.* Annapolis, MD: Wm. Thompson, Printer, 1870.

Davidson, Hunter, *Report on the Oyster Fisheries: Potomac River Shad and Herring Fisheries, and the Water-Fowl of Maryland to His Excellency the Governor and other Commissioners of the State O. P. Force, January, 1872,* Maryland House of Delegates, Document E, January 10, 1872.

Davidson, Hunter, "TORPEDOES IN OUR WAR . . ." *The Sun* [NY], March 28, 1897.

INFORME de una ESPEDICION AL ALTO PARANA para estudiar Las Mejoras Necesarias en el "SALTO GRANDE DE APIPE" Agosto Y Setiembre De 1882 . . . Del SALTO GRANDE PRESENTADO POR HUNTER DAVIDSON Octubre 1882 [translated as *REPORT of an EXPEDITION TO THE UPPER PARANA to study the necessary improvements in the "SALTO GRANDE DE APIPE" August and September 1882 . . . From the BIG LEAP PRESENTED BY HUNTER DAVIDSON October 1882*] Buenos Aires, Establicimiento Tipografico, 1882. Courtesy of Las Misiones Public Library, Buenos Aires. Translated using Google Translate

Official Sources

African slave trade. Message from the President of the United States, transmitting, in compliance with a resolution of the house, a report from the Secretary of State in reference to the African slave trade. December 6, 1860. House Executive Document 7. Serial Set Vol. No. 1095 (page 532).

Annual Report of the Secretary of the Navy 1847 in *Message from the President of the United States, to the two houses of Congress: at the commencement of the first session of the Thirtieth Congress, December 7, 1847.* Exec. Doc. No. 1. Washington, DC, Government Printing Office, 1847.

Annual Report of the Secretary of the Navy, communicating copies of Commodore Stockton's dispatches, relating to the military and naval operations in California, February 16, 1849. Senate Executive Document No. 31, 30th Congress, 2nd session. Washington, DC: Government Printing Office, 1849.

Commercial relations of the United States. Reports from the consuls of the United States on the commerce, manufactures, etc., of their consular districts. For the months of September, October, November, and December 1884. House Misc. Doc. 34/ Serial Set Vol. No. 2319.

"H. H. Doty." House Report No. 626, House of Representatives, 45th Congress, 2d Session, 1878.

Journal of the Congress of the Confederate States of America, 1861-1865. 5 vols. Washington, DC: Government Printing Office, 1904.

Journal of The Proceedings of the Senate of Maryland January Session, 1868. Annapolis: Wm. Thompson of R., Printer.

Journal of the Proceedings of the Senate of the United States in Executive Session, 37th Congress, 2nd session commencing December 2, 1861 (March 6, 1862).

Mayer, Lewis, *Supplement to the Maryland Code, containing the Acts of the General Assembly, passed at the sessions of 1861, 1861-62, 1864, 1865, 1866 and 1867 . . .* Baltimore: John Murphy & Co., 1868.

MEMORIA que el Ministro De Estado EN EL DEPARTAMENTO DE MARINA PRESENTA AL CONGRESO NACIONAL DE 1866 [translated as: *REPORT THAT THE MINISTER OF STATE IN THE DEPARTMENT OF THE NAVY PRESENTS TO THE NATIONAL CONGRESS OF 1866.* Santiago De Chile: Imprenta Nacional, 1866. Translated via Google Translate.

Message from the President of the United States to the Two Houses of Congress at the commencement of the second session of the Thirty-Sixth Congress. December 4, 1860. Senate Executive Document 1, part 3. Serial Set vol. No. 1080, 29.

Official Records of the Union and Confederate Navies in the War of the Rebellion, 29 volumes. Washington, DC: Government Printing Office, 1894-1921.

Pay of officers of the Navy and Marine Corps, &c . . . January 11, 1851, February 1, 1853, February 3, 1854, February 2, 1855

"Preliminary Chart of JAMES RIVER Virginia from Richmond to City Point," prepared under direction of A. D. Bache, Superintendent of the Survey of the Coast of the United States, 1855.

Register of the Commissioned and Warrant Officers of the Navy of the United States . . . Washington, D.C.: Government Printing Office, 1847-1866.

Register of the Officers of the Confederate States Navy 1861-1865. Washington, DC: Government Printing Office, 1931.

"Report of Lieut. Neil M. Howison, United States Navy, to the Commander of the Pacific Squadron...," February 1, 1847, published as House Miscellaneous Document 29, 30th Congress, 1st Session, 1848.

Report of the Commissioner of Patents for the Year 1858: Arts and Manufactures in Two Volumes. Washington, D.C.: George W. Bowman Printer, 1860, 2 vols.

Report of the Superintendent of the Coast Survey, showing the progress of the Survey during the year 1852. Washington, D.C.: Robert Armstrong, Public Printer, 1853.

U.S. Census Records, accessed via ancestry.com.

U.S. Department of State. *Papers Relating to the Foreign Relations of the United States*. Washington: Government Printing Office, 1865-1866, 1874-1906.

The War of the Rebellion: A Compilation of the Official Records of the Union and Confederate Armies, 128 vols. Washington, DC: Government Printing Office, 1880-1901.

Woods' Baltimore City Directory, 1882 and 1883. Baltimore, MD: John W. Woods. accessed via Ancestry.com.

Newspapers

Research for this book draws from hundreds of newspapers accessed via the Library of Congress' "Making of America" digital library and GenealogyBank's online archives. Although the newspaper sources are too many to include in this Bibliography, citations appear in the footnotes.

Published Primary Sources

Brooke, George M., Jr., ed., *Ironclads and Big Guns of the Confederacy: The Journal and Letters of John M. Brooke*. Columbia: University of South Carolina Press, 2002.

Brooke, John M., "The Virginia, or Merrimac: Her Real Projector," *Southern Historical Society Papers*, (1901), vol. 9, 3-34.

Bulloch, James D., *The Secret Service of the Confederate States in Europe*, 2 vols. London: Richard Bentley & Sons, 1883.

Crowley, R. O., "Making the 'Infernal Machines': A Memoir of the Confederate Torpedo Service, *Civil War Times Illustrated*, June 1973, 24-35 [reprint of "The Confederate Torpedo Service" from *Century Magazine*, (June 1898), vol. 56.

Daly, Robert W., ed., William Frederick Keeler, *Aboard the U.S.S. Monitor 1862: The Letters of Acting Paymaster William Frederick Keeler, U.S. Navy, to his wife Anna*. Annapolis, MD: U.S. Naval Institute Press, 1964

Eggleston, John R., "Captain Eggleston's Narrative of the Battle of the *Merrimac*." *Southern Historical Society Papers*, 1916, 49:166-178.

Evans, Robley D. *A Sailor's Log: Recollections from Forty Years of Naval* Life. New York: Appleton, 1901.

"EXPLORATION OF THE Y-GUASU." *The Standard* [Buenos Aires], January 1, 1884.

Foute, R. C. "Echoes from Hampton Roads," *Southern Historical Society Papers*, 1891, 19:246-248.

Gallagher, Gary, ed., *Fighting for the Confederacy: The Personal Recollections of General Edward Porter Alexander*. Chapel Hill, NC: University of North Carolina Press, 1989.

Gleaves, Rear Admiral Albert, ed., *Life and Letters of Rear Admiral Stephen B. Luce U.S. Navy*. New York: G. P. Putnam's Sons, 1925.

Himes, George, ed. "Letters by Burr Osborn, Survivor of the Howison Expedition to Oregon 1846: Reminiscences of Experiences Growing out of Wrecking of the United States Schooner Shark at Mouth of Columbia on Eastward Voyage of Expedition," *Oregon Historical Quarterly*, December 1913. No. 4. 14:355-364.

"Improved Boat-Lowering, Detaching, Attaching and Griping Apparatus." *The Scientific American*, May 19, 1860, 321-322.

Johnson, Robert Underwood and Clarence Clough Buel, eds., *Battles and Leaders of the Civil War* 4 vols. Reprint ed., New York: Thomas Yoseloff, 1954.

Jones, Catesby Ap R., "Services of the 'Virginia' (Merrimac)." *Southern Historical Society Papers*, January 1883, 2:65-75.

Kell, John McIntosh, *Recollections of a Naval Life*. Washington, DC: Neale Publishing Co., 1900.

Lamar, Howard, ed. *Cruise of the Portsmouth, 1845-1847. A Sailor's View of the Naval Conquest of California* by Joseph T. Downey. New Haven, CT: Yale University Press, 1958.

Maffitt, Emma Martin, ed. *The Life and Services of John Newland Maffitt*. New York: Neale Publishing Co., 1906.

McPherson, James M. McPherson and Patricia R. McPherson, eds., *Lamson of the* Gettysburg*: The Civil War Letters of Lieutenant Roswell H. Lamson, U.S. Navy*. New York: Oxford University Press, 1997.

Morgan, James Morris, *Recollections of a Rebel Reefer*. Boston: Houghton Mifflin, 1917.

Page, Thomas J., U.S.N., *La Plata, The Argentine Confederation, and Paraguay, Being a Narrative of the Exploration of the Tributaries of the River La Plata and Adjacent Countries During the Years 1853, '54, '55, and '56, Under the Orders of the United States Government*. New York: Harper & Brothers, Publishers, 1859.

Parker, William Harwar. *Recollections of a Naval Officer*. New York: Scribner's, 1883.

Phillips, Dinwiddie Brazier, "The Career of the Iron-Clad Virginia, (formerly the Merrimac) Confederate States Navy, March-May 1862" in *Miscellaneous Papers, 1672-1865, now first printed from the manuscript in the collections of the Virginia Historical Society*. Richmond: William Ellis Jones, Printer, 1887, 193-231.

Richardson, James D., editor, *A Compilation of the Messages and Papers of the Presidents*, 11 vols. New York: Bureau of National Literature, 1902-1904.

Robertson, James I., Jr. ed., *Proceedings of the Advisory Council of the State of Virginia, April 21–June 19, 1861*. Richmond: Virginia State Library, 1977.

Rochelle, James H. "The Confederate Steamship 'Patrick Henry.'" *Southern Historical Society Papers*, 1886, 14:127-128.

Rogers, Fred Blackburn. *Montgomery and the Portsmouth*. San Francisco, CA: John Howell Books, 1958.

Rogers, Fred Blackburn, ed. *A Navy Surgeon in California, 1846-1847: The Journal of Marius Duvalll*. San Francisco, CA: John Howell Books, 1957.

Rowland, Dunbar S., ed., editor. *Jefferson Davis Constitutionalist: His Letters, Papers, and Speeches*, 11 volumes. Jackson, MS: Mississippi Department of Archives and History, 1923.

Schneller, Robert J., ed., *Under the Blue Pennant, or Notes of a Naval Officer 1863-1865*. New York: John W. Wiley, 1999.

Smith, Charles R., ed. *The Journals of Marine Second Lieutenant Henry Bulls Watson 1845-1848*. Washington, DC: History and Museums Division, Headquarters, U.S. Marine Corps, 1990.

Stephens, Alexander H., *A Constitutional View of the Late War Between the States . . .* 2 vols. Philadelphia: National Publishing Co., 1868.

Welles, Gideon and Welles, Edgar Thaddeus. *Diary of Gideon Welles Secretary of the Navy Under Lincoln and Johnson with an introduction by John T. Morse, Jr.*, 2 vols. Boston: Houghton Mifflin, Co., 1911.

Secondary Sources

Anthis, Judith and Richard M. McMurry. "Rebels in the Sky: The Confederate Balloon Corps." *Blue and Gray Magazine,* August 1991, vol. 9, 20-24.

Barnes, Lieut.-Commander J.S, U.S.N. *Submarine Warfare, Offensive and Defensive. Including a Discussion of the Offensive Torpedo System, Its Effects Upon Iron-Clad Ship Systems, and Influence Upon Future Naval Wars.* New York: D. Van Nostrand, Publisher, 1869.

Beach, Edward L. *The United States Navy: A 200-Year History.* Paperback edition. Boston: Houghton Mifflin, Inc., 1986.

Bearss, Ed. *River of Lost Opportunities: The Civil War on the James River 1861-1862.* Lynchburg, VA: H. E. Howard, Inc., 1995.

Bearss, Edwin C. *Hardluck Ironclad: The Sinking and Salvage of the Cairo.* Baton Rouge, LA: Louisiana State University Press, 1966.

Belton, Mark Belton, Adm. "Hunter Davidson: Fighting Naturalist" Maryland Department of Natural Resources, March 30, 2018. https://tinyurl.com/yb6z9dyv.

Blight, David, W. *Race and Reunion: The Civil War in American Memory.* Cambridge: Harvard University Press, 2001.

Bowie, Walter Worthington. *The Bowies and their Kindred: A Genealogical and Biographical History.* Cottonport: POLYANTHOS, 1971.

Brooke, George M., Jr. *John Brooke: Naval Scientists and Educator.* Charlottesville, VA: University Press of Virginia, 1980.

Brugger, Robert J. *Maryland: A Middle Temperament, 1634-1980.* Baltimore, MD: Johns Hopkins University Press in Association with Maryland Historical Society, 1988.

Burzio, Humberto F. *Historia Naval Argentina, Series B, No. 12: Historio Del Torpedo Y Sus Buques En La Armada Argentina 1874-1900.* Buenos Aires, 1968.

Canney, Donald L *Africa Squadron: The U.S. Navy and the Slave Trade, 1842-1861.* Washington, DC: Potomac Books, 2006.

Casdorph, Paul D. *Prince John Magruder: His Life and Campaigns.* New York: John Wiley & Sons, Inc., 1996.

Cheevers, Jim, ed. by Sharon Kennedy, "The United States Naval Academy, 1845-2020," unpublished paper. https://www.history.navy.mil.

Cole, Allan B., ed. *Yankee Surveyors in the Shogun's Seas: Records of the United States Surveying Expedition to the North Pacific Ocean, 1853-1856.* Princeton: Princeton University Press, 1947.

Cole, Terrence. "The Strange Saga of the President's Desk." *American Heritage,* October/November 1981, 62-64.

"Confederate Submarine Service on the James River." *Blue and Gray Magazine,* October 1989, 16.

Cordell, Eugene Fauntleroy, M.D. *The Medical Annals of Maryland, 1799-1899.* Baltimore, 1903.

Coski, John M. "'A Navy Department, Hitherto Unknown to Our State Organization," in *Virginia at War 1861,* ed. William C. Davis and James I. Robertson, Jr. Frankfort: University Press of Kentucky, 2005, 65-87.

Coski, John M. "Blasting His Way into the History Books: Assessing the Role of Cmdr. Hunter Davidson," in *The Civil War on the Water: Favorite Stories and Fresh Perspectives from the Historians at Emerging Civil War,* Dwight Sturtevant Hughes and Chris Mackowski, eds. El Dorado Hills, CA: Savas Beatie, 2023, 217-224.

Coski, John M. *Capital Navy: The Men, Ships, and Operations of the James River Squadron.* Campbell, CA: Savas-Woodbury, 1996.

Cotham, Edward T. Jr. *Battle on the Bay: The Civil War Struggle for Galveston.* Austin, TX: University of Texas Press, 1998.

Crapol, Edward P. *America for Americans: Economic Nationalism and Anglophobia in the Late Nineteenth Century.* New York: Praeger, 1973.

Crapol, Edward P. *John Tyler The Accidental President.* Chapel Hill, NC: University of North Carolina Press, 2006.

Davidson, Homer K. *Black Jack Davidson: A Cavalry Commander on the Western Frontier: the life of General John W. Davidson.* Glendale, CA: Arthur H. Clarke, 1974.

Davis, William C. *Duel Between the First Ironclads.* Garden City, NY: Doubleday & Co., 1975.

Dorris, Jonathan T. *Pardon and Amnesty under Lincoln and Johnson: The Restoration of the Confederates to Their Rights and Privileges, 1861-1898.* Chapel, NC: Hill: University of North Carolina Press, 1953.

Doty, Ethan Allen. *Doty-Doten Family in America: Descendants of Edward Doty, an Emigrant by the Mayflower, 1620.* Brooklyn, NY: E. A. Doty, 1897.

DuBois, W.E. Burghardt. *The Suppression of the African Slave Trade to the United States of America, 1638-1870.* New York: Social Sciences Press, 1954.

Dudley, William S. *Going South: U.S. Navy Officer Resignations and Dismissals on the Eve of the Civil War.* Washington, DC: Naval Historical Foundation, 1981.

Dudley, William S. *Maritime Maryland:* A History. Baltimore: Johns Hopkins University Press, 2010.

Dunkerly, Robert M. *To the Bitter End: Appomattox, Bennett Place, and the Surrenders of the Confederacy.* El Dorado, CA: Savas Beatie, 2015.

Dunning, Alfred. "The Return of the Resolute." *American Heritage,* August 1959, 14-17

Fessenden Otis, "Presentation of the Arctic Ship *Resolute* by the United States to the Queen of England." *Magazine of American History.* No. 2. August, 1887, 18:97-120.

Fields, Barbara Jeanne. *Slavery and Freedom on the Middle Ground: Maryland during the Nineteenth Century.* New Haven: Yale University Press, 1985.

Forbes, Rosita. *Eight Republics in Search of a Future: Evolution and Revolution in South America.* New York: Frederick A. Stokes Company, Publishers, [1933].

Fuess, Claude Moore. *The Life of Caleb Cushing.* New York: Harcourt Brace, 1923.

Gerding, Eduardo C. "The Confederate Navy and the Argentine Hydrographic survey: Time of the Spar Torpedo." The Buenos Aires Herald, Sunday, December 14, 2003-Focus-8 [English translation accessed via: https://civilwartalk.com/threads/the-confederate-navy-and-the-argentine-hydrographic-survey.90134/]

Grady, John "Hunter Davidson and the 'Squib'." posted 6/9/2014 on "The Civil War Monitor Commentary" (URL: https://www.civilwarmonitor.com/hunter-davidson-and-the-squib/)

Grady, John. *Matthew Fontaine Maury Father of Oceanography: A Biography, 1806-1874.* Jefferson, NC: McFarland Publishing, 2015.

Gray, Edwyn. *Nineteenth-Century Torpedoes and their Inventors.* Annapolis: Naval Institute Press, 2004.

Gurney, John Thomas, III, ed. *Cemetery Inscriptions of Anne Arundel County, Maryland* (privately printed, n.d.), vol. I.

Gutman, John. "The use of ships to transport balloons during the Civil War was the first example of modern-day aircraft carriers," *America's Civil War,* June 1998, 26-28+.

Hamersley, Lewis Randolph, compiler, *The Records of Living Officers of the U.S. Navy and Marine Corps,* Fourth edition. Philadelphia: L. R. Hamersley & Co., 1890.

Hanks, Carlos C., "Mines of Long Ago," *U.S. Naval Institute Proceedings.* No. 11. November 1940, 66: 1548-1551.

Hanna, Alfred J. and Phyllis Barbour, "Captain Thomas Jefferson Page: Confederate Expatriate From Virginia," unpublished manuscript, copy in Naval History and Heritage Command, Washington, D.C.

Hesseltine, William B. and Hazel C. Wolf, *The Blue and the Gray on the Nile.* Chicago: University of Chicago Press, 1961.

Hunter, Mark C., *A Society of Gentlemen: Midshipmen at the U.S. Naval Academy, 1845-1861.* Annapolis, MD: Naval Institute Press, 2010.

Jacobs, [Charles] T. "Hunter Davidson: Unsung naval commander." *Washington Times,* February 24, 1996.

Janney, Caroline E. *Ends of War: The Unfinished Fight of Lee's Army After Appomattox.* Chapel Hill, NC: University of North Carolina Press, 2021.

Kennett, Lee. "The Strange Career of the *Stonewall.*" *United Naval Institute Proceedings,* February 1968, 80-84.

Kent, Frank Atkinson. *The Story of Maryland Politics.* Baltimore, MD: Thomas & Evans, 1911.

King, William R. *Torpedoes, Their Invention and Use from the First Application to the Art of War to the Present Time.* Reprint ed., Washington, DC: Naval Historical Center, 1992.

Kirk, Brianna and John M. Coski, "'What am I to do for a living?': Two Brothers in the Aftermath of War," *The American Civil War Museum Magazine,* summer 2017, 8-15.

Knight, H. Jackson, *Confederate Invention: The Story of the Confederate States Patent Office and Its Inventors.* Baton Rouge, LA: Louisiana State University Press, 2011.

Kowell, Brian D. "David vs. Goliath at Hampton Roads: The CSS *Squib* vs. the USS *Minnesota.*" *The Charger* [The Cleveland Civil War Roundtable]. (September/October 2021). https://www.clevelandcivilwarroundtable.com/david-vs-goliath-at-hampton-roads-the-css-squib-vs-the-uss-minnesota/

Leeman, William P., *The Long Road to Annapolis: The Founding of the Naval Academy and the Emerging American Republic.* Chapel Hill, NC: University of North Carolina Press, 2010.

Levene, Ricardo, *A History of Argentina,* translated and edited by William Spence Robertson. Chapel Hill, NC: University of North Carolina Press, 1937.

Lewis, Charles L. *Matthew Fontaine Maury, Pathfinder of the Seas.* Annapolis, MD: Naval Institute Press, 1937.

Long, David F. *Gold Braid and Foreign Relations: Diplomatic Activities of U.S. Naval Officers 1798-1883.* Annapolis, MD: Naval Institute Press, 1988.

Love, Robert W., Jr. *History of the U.S. Navy, volume One, 1775-1941.* Harrisburg, PA, 1992.

Luraghi, Raimondo. *A History of the Confederate Navy.* Annapolis: Naval Institute Press, 1996.

Mabry, W. S. compiler. *Brief Sketch of the Career of Captain Catesby Ap R. Jones.* Selma, AL, 1912.

Mahan, Alfred Thayer. *From Sail to Steam: Recollections of Naval Life.* London and New York: Harper & Brothers, 1907.

McKee, John M. "Hunter Davidson: Sailor Extraordinary." Unpublished Powerpoint presentation.

McPherson, James M. *War on the Waters: The Union and Confederate Navies, 1861-1865*. Chapel Hill, NC: University of North Carolina Press, 2012.

Morgan, William J. "Torpedoes in the James," *The Iron Worker*, Summer 1962, vol. 26, 1-11.

Mosier, Joe. "United States v. The Bark William G. Lewis: The Navy Brings a Slave Ship to Norfolk," *The Daybook* [Hampton Roads Naval Museum]. No.4 (2005), 10:6-10, 13-14.

Mosier, Joseph C. "'We Are Mere Scarecrows': A Southern Naval Officer on Anti-Slave Trade Patrol," unpublished paper presented at the annual meeting of the North American Society for Oceanic History, 2005.

Newman, Harry Wright. *Maryland and the Confederacy*. Annapolis, MD: Privately published, 1976.

Perry, Milton F. *Infernal Machines: The Story of Confederate Submarine and Mine Warfare*. Baton Rouge, LA: Louisiana State University Press, 1965.

Porter, David Dixon. *Naval History of the Civil War*. New York: Sherman Publishing Company, 1886.

Quarstein, John V. *The CSS Virginia: Sink Before Surrender*. Charleston, SC: History Press, 2012.

Quarstein, John V. and Joseph Gutierrez, "Who Won the Battle of Hampton Roads?: A Historians' Debate," in Harold Holzer and Tim Mulligan, eds. *The Battle of Hampton Roads: New Perspectives on the USS Monitor and the CSS Virginia*. New York: Fordham University Press, 2006.

Ragan, Mark K. *Union and Confederate Submarine Warfare in the Civil War*. Mason City, IA: Savas Publishing Company, 1999.

Rochelle, James. *Life of Rear Admiral John Randolph Tucker...* New York: Neale Publishing Company, 1903.

Rolle, Andrew F. *The Lost Cause: The Confederate Exodus to Mexico*. Norman: University of Oklahoma Press, 1964.

Scharf, J. Thomas, *History of Maryland from the Earliest Period to the Present Day*, 3 volumes. Baltimore: J. B. Piet, 1879.

Scharf, J. Thomas, *History of the Confederate States Navy*. New York: Rogers & Sherwood, 1887.

Schiller, Herbert M., *Confederate Torpedoes: Two Illustrated 19th Century Works with New Appendices and Photographs*. Jefferson, NC: McFarland & Company, Inc., 2011.

Shine, Gregory Paynter, "'A Gallant Little Schooner': The U.S. Schooner Shark and the Oregon Country, 1846," *Oregon Historical Quarterly*, Winter 2008, 536-565.

Shingleton, Royce Gordon, *John Taylor Wood: Sea Ghost of the Confederacy*. Athens, GA: University of Georgia Press, 1979.

Sleeman, C. W., Esq., *Torpedoes and Torpedo Warfare: Containing a Complete and Concise Account of the Rise and Progress of Submarine Warfare: Also a Detailed Description of All Matters Appertaining Thereto, Including the Latest Improvements*. Portsmouth, Eng.: Griffin & Co., 1880.

Snyder, Dean, "Torpedoes for the Confederacy," *Civil War Times Illustrated*, March 1985, 24:40-45.

Spencer, Warren F. *The Confederate Navy in Europe*. Tuscaloosa: University of Alabama Press, 1983.

Still, William N., Jr., ed., *The Confederate Navy: The Ships, Men and Organization, 1861-65*. London: Conway Maritime Press, 1997.

Sueter, Murray Fraser, *The Evolution of the Submarine Boat, Mine, and Torpedo, from the Sixteenth Century to the Present Time*. Portsmouth, Eng: J. Griffin and Co., 1908.

Suhr, Robert Collins, "Torpedoes, the Confederacy's dreaded 'infernal machines,' made many a Union sea captain uneasy." *America's Civil War*, November 1991, 8, 59-62.

Sutherland, Daniel E., "James McNeill Whistler in Chile: Portrait of the Artist as Arms Dealer," *American Nineteenth Century History*, March 2008, 9: 61-73.

Sutherland, Daniel E., *Whistler: A Life for Art's Sake.* New Haven, CT: Yale University Press, 2014.

Symonds, Craig L., *Confederate Admiral: The Life and Wars of Franklin Buchanan.* Annapolis: Naval Institute Press, 1999.

Symonds, Craig L, *The U. S. Navy: A Concise History*. New York: Oxford University Press, 2015.

Symonds, Craig L. *The Civil War at Sea.* Santa Barbara, CA: ABC-Clio, 2009.

Thurston, Arthur. *Tallahassee Skipper: The Biography of John Taylor Wood, Merrimac Guner, Soldier-at-Sea, Guardian of the Confederate Treasury, Adopted Nova Scotian.* Yarmouth, Nova Scotia: Lescarbot Press, 1981.

Todorich, Charles, *The Spirited Years: A History of the Antebellum Naval Academy.* Annapolis, MD: Naval Institute Press, 1984.

Tucker, Spencer C., *A Short History of the Civil War at Sea.* Wilmington, DE: Scholarly Resources, 2002.

Tyson, Mabry, "Believe Only Half of What You Read About the Battle of Hampton Roads," Harold Holzer and Tim Mulligan, eds. *The Battle of Hampton Roads: New Perspectives on the USS Monitor and the CSS Virginia.* New York: Fordham University Press, 2006.

U.S. Navy Department, Naval History Division, *Civil War Naval Chronology*. Washington, DC: Government Printing Office, 1971.

Verney, Michael A., *A Great and Rising Nation: Naval Exploration and Global Empire in the Early U.S. Republic.* Chicago: University of Chicago Press, 2022.

Waters, W. Davis and Joseph I. Brown, *Gabriel Rains and the Confederate Torpedo Bureau.* El Dorado Hills, CA: Savas Beatie, 2017.

Wennersten, John R., *The Oyster Wars of Chesapeake Bay.* Centreville, MD: Tidewater Publishers, [1981].

Werlich, David P., "The Allied Project to Liberate Cuba, 1866-67: Chile, Peru, and Colonel Barreda's Confederate Navy." Paper presented at the 2007 Naval History Symposium, Annapolis, MD.

Werlich, David P. *Admiral of the Amazon: John Randolph Tucker, His Confederate Colleagues, and Peru.* Charlottesville: The University Press of Virginia, 1990.

Westcott, Allan, ed. *American Sea Power Since 1775.* Chicago: University of Chicago Press, 1947.

Williams, Frances Leigh. *Matthew Fontaine Maury, Pathfinder of the Seas.* New Brunswick, NJ: Rutgers University Press, 1963.

Wilson, Walter E. and Gary L. McKay. *James D. Bulloch: Secret Agent and Mastermind of the Confederate Navy*. Jefferson, NC: McFarland Publishing, 2012.

Wise, Stephen R., *Lifeline of the Confederacy: Blockade Running During the Civil War.* Columbia SC: University of South Carolina Press, 1989.

Wiser, Edward H., "A Rough Wet Ride: The Civilian Genesis of the American Motor Torpedo Boat." Ph.D. dissertation, Florida State University, 2009.

Wolters, Timothy S., "Electric Torpedoes in the Confederacy: Reconciling Conflicting Histories," *The Journal of Military History,* July 2008, 72:755-783.

Index

Africa(n) Squadron (USN), x, 7, 44-49, 54-55
Alabama, CSS, 4, 140, 154, 248
Alarm, USS, 159
Albemarle, CSS, 128, 156
Alexander, Edward Porter, 100-102
Alsina, Adolfo, 206-210, 212
Alto Parana, 215
Annapolis, Maryland, x, 3, 20-22, 24, 55-56, 61, 63, 121, 189; Davidson's residence: 30-31, 33, 50, 52, 168, 177
Arctic, USS, 42
Argentine Torpedo Division, 206-209, 211-212, 242
Army of the James (US), 129
Army of Northern Virginia (CS), 98-100, 112, 129
Army of the Peninsula (CS), 71
Army of the Potomac (US), 98-100, 108, 112, 129
Army of Virginia (US), 112
Asuncion, Paraguay, 222, 229-232
Atlanta, USS, 130-131
Avellaneda, Nicolas, 210-211, 213

Bache, Alexander Dallas, 31, 36-38
Bacon, Robert, 230, 232
Balch, George W., 52, 66
Barron, Samuel, 67-68, 70-71, 139
Bartleman, George, 230
Beauregard, P. G. T., 123, 204
Bibb (Coast Survey vessel), 39
Birtwhistle, James, 125
Blake, George S., 50, 52, 58, 62-65
Bouncer (Coast Survey vessel), 37
Bowie, Oden, 182, 185
Brandywine, USS, 8
Bremen (commercial vessel), 45-47
Brooke, John Mercer, 59, 73-75, 94, 107-108, 119, 158, 245, 248; postwar career: 166, 168-170-171, 191, 200-206
Buchanan, Franklin, 67, 75-78, 178, 224
Buchanan, James, 58
Buckner, William P., 52-53, 61-62, 66
Buenos Aires, Argentina, x, 199, 203, 205-206, 208-209, 213-215, 217, 222, 244-245
Bulloch, James Dunwoody, 14, 16, 139-146, 154
Burnside, Ambrose E., 108
Butler, Benjamin, 129-130, 135-137, 236-237, 246
Butt, Walter Raleigh, 54, 76

Cadboro, 17
Cairo, USS, 108

Cambridge, Maryland, 39, 182, 189, 206, 222; Davidson's residence: 189, 206
Caroline E. Foote, 158
Cary, Clarence, 102
Cass, Lewis, 46
Chaffin's Bluff, 97, 107, 113, 136-137
Cheeney, William G., 96, 107
Chesapeake Bay, 4, 54, 69, 79, 81, 123, 161, 177-178, 189
City of Richmond (blockade runner), 144-149, 161, 195
City Point, Virginia, 113, 115, 119, 130
Coast Survey (US), x, 31, 33, 35-39, 43, 53, 59, 67, 72, 80, 91, 95, 100, 113, 142, 149, 212, 245
Cochrane, see *Henrietta*
Commodore Barney, USS, 115, 117-120, 123, 130
Commodore Jones, USS, 130-134, 136-138, 245-247
Commodore Morris, USS, 130
Confederate States, CSS, 70
Congo River, 45, 47
Congress, USS, 18, 76-77, 79-80
Conover, Thomas H., 46, 49, 55
Constitution, USS, 6, 8-9
Copper, Samuel, 190
Craig, William J., 76
Craney Island, 90
Craven, Thomas T., 54, 56, 58
Crawford (Coast Survey vessel), 38
Crocodile (blockade runner), 141
Crowley, Roy O., 109-111, 114, 116, 118-120, 123, 131, 136-138, 144, 171, 202, 246
Cumberland, USS, 55, 76-78, 80, 86, 88, 234
Cummings, Andrew Boyd, 45
Cunningham, J. S., 48
Cushing, Caleb, 8
Cushing, William B., 54, 128, 156

Dahlgren, John, 80, 102, 167-168
Dale, USS, 19, 43-47, 49-50, 55, 67, 186
Damon, Mason, 211
David, (CS torpedo boat), 161
Davidson, Charles (brother), xvi-xvii, 176 (illustration)
Davidson, Charles Steele (son), 122, 151, 189, 205, 221, 223-224, 242
Davidson, Elizabeth Chapman Hunter, (mother), xv-xvii, 30, 102, 223; married to William Henry Pope: xvii
Davidson, Enriqueta Silvia Davalos (wife), 222-223, 225, 242
Davidson, Franklin Buchanan (son), 190, 205, 223
Davidson, Gordon (son), 222
Davidson, Hunter, ix-xviii, 61, 175; attitudes toward African Americans: xi, xvi, 22-23, 120-121, 192, 227-232, 248-249; character and personality: ix-xi, 11, 19, 20, 21-24, 26, 31, 48-50, 64-66, 169, 186, 248-249; conflicts with other officers: 27-29, 36, 37, 47-49, 50; early naval career, 1-4, 6-20; Naval Academy: 21-25; protests U.S. Navy standing, 24-25, 33-35; passed midshipman: 26-31, 33-39; HMS *Resolute*: 41-43; African Squadron: 44-50; instructor at Naval Academy: 50, 52-55, 59; invention: 55-59; enters southern service: 63-72; duty on *Virginia*: 72-92; in command of *Teaser*: 93-95, 97, 99-105; in command of torpedo batteries: 98, 105-106; Submarine Battery Service: 107-123, 130-138; *Squib*: 123-129, 236, 238; procuring supplies in England: 139-145; command of *City of Richmond*: 145-149; end of Civil War: 149-151, 153-154; life after war: 154-156; Chilean Navy: 156-157, 160-162, 164-166; unemployed: 166-174; Maryland State Oyster Police Force: 177-197; Argentine torpedo service: 198-212; Argentine river expeditions: 212-215, 217; retirement in Paraguay: 219-227, 241-242; attempts to influence memory of Civil War: 233-242, 249; death, 242
Davidson, Hunter, Jr. (son), 72, 122, 151, 189, 205, 221, 224, 228
Davidson, Hyde (son), 35, 42
Davidson, John W. (brother), xvi-xvii, 18, 99, 176 (illustration), 223, 228

Davidson, Leila (daughter), xiii, 35, 52, 151, 181, 190, 205, 221, 242; married to Bowie Campbell Gowan: 205
Davidson, Mary Steele Ray (wife), 30, 33, 35, 42-43, 52, 72, 103, 121-122, 151, 166, 171, 177, 182, 189, 205; estrangement with husband: 221-224
Davidson, Maury (son), 190, 205, 223
Davidson, Percy (son), 43, 52, 151, 189, 205, 221, 242
Davidson, Roger J. (brother), xvi-xvii, 176 (illustration)
Davidson, Ronaldo (son), 222
Davidson, Ruben (son), 222, 225
Davidson, Virginia Consuelo (daughter), 222
Davidson, William B. (father), xv-xvii
Davis, Jefferson, ix-xi, 53, 67, 97-98, 105, 115, 148, 150, 173, 201; Davidson's disagreements: 224, 233, 236, 238-239
Deep Bottom, Virginia, 119-120, 130-131
Deer (blockade runner), 141, 144
De Korab, Waldemar, 231
Dobbin, James C., 34
Dobson, John, 192
Doty, Henry Harrison, 157-162, 164-165, 171-172
Dragon (tug), 84
Drewry's Bluff, 97, 104, 107, 113; battle of: 91-92, 236; 1864 battle: 135-136
Dupont, Samuel F., 33-35, 56

Edenborough, Henry Bolton, 161, 165
Eggleston, John R., 76, 81, 84-86, 90
Elizabeth River, 26, 69-70, 76, 79, 88
Emma Dunn (steamer), 179
Ericsson, John, 74, 76, 80
Erie, USS, 14

Falmouth, USS, 8
Farrand, Ebenezer, 67
Franklin, James S., 190
Fessenden, William Pitt, 58
Florida, CSS, 36, 140, 142, 146, 154
Flusser, Charles W., 66-67
Forrest, French, 67-69, 74, 80
Fort Caswell, 138
Fort Fisher, 138, 149
Fort Monroe, 69-70, 76, 79, 128
Foster, John G., 115, 119
Foute, Robert Chester, 54, 76, 89-90
Franklin expedition, 41-42
Freelon, Thomas W., 9-10
Fulminante (Davidson's Argentine headquarters ship), 202, 205-212, 241
Fulton, USS, 2

Galena, USS, 91
Gallatin, USS (Coast Survey vessel), 36, 38
Galt, Francis L., 248
Gansevoort, Guert, 118
Glassell, William, 161
Goldsborough, Louis M., 79
Gosport Navy Yard, 70
Gowan, Bowie Campbell (son-in-law), 205
Gowan, Cecil Hunter Boyd (grandson), 223, 242
Gowan, Sir Hyde Clarendon (grandson), 242
Graham, William A., 24, 29-30
Greene, Samuel Dana, 82, 88
Griffith, Lewis, 185-187, 189, 193
Guerriere, HMS, 6

H. L. Hunley, 123, 128
Hampton Roads, Virginia, 8, 54, 69-70, 76, 96, 115, 123, 129, 126; battle of: x, 71-73, 76-88, 93, 221, 245
Harrison's Landing, Virginia, 99-100, 105, 111
Hartstene, Henry J., 41-42, 67
Harvey, Frederick, 201, 209, 211
Hasker, Charles, 78
Henrietta (Chilean Naval ship), 156, 161-165
Henry, John C., 184
Hollins, George, 67
Home Squadron (USN), 6, 9
Housatonic, USS, 123, 128
Howison, Neil M., 14-17, 24
Huger, Benjamin, 72, 74
Hunter, John Chapman (grandfather), xiii
Hunter, Thomas T., xvii, 67, 161
Huse, Samuel, 118

Imogene (blockade runner), 149-150, 155
Ingraham, Duncan, 67

Intrepid, HMS, 41

J. B. White (dispatch boat), 90
James River Flotilla (USN), 91, 102, 128
James River Squadron (CSN), 71, 74, 88, 91, 93, 107, 135-136
Jamestown, CSS, 70, 91-92, 104
Johnston, Joseph E., 98, 105
Jones, Catesby Ap Roger, 67, 73, 76-83, 85-87, 89-90, 107, 111, 168-169, 191, 224, 248
Jones, John Pembroke, 37, 39, 67, 137-138, 200, 202, 242, 248
Jones, Thomas Ap Catesby, 11, 80

Kearny, Stephen W., 18
Keeler, William F., 90, 103
Kell, John McIntosh, 4, 248
Kennard, Joel S., 45, 47, 67
Kent (steamer), 182
Kevill, Thomas, 76
Knox, Samuel, 27, 49, 79

La Gloire (French warship), 73
La Vallette, Elie A. F., 18
Lake, Moses, 24
Lamson, Roswell H., 54, 129, 132, 134-137, 237
Leach, Reginald Barclay, 227, 241
Lee, Francis D., 123
Lee, Robert E., xvi, 68-69, 95, 98-99, 101, 105, 108, 112, 129, 168, 172, 223, 236
Lee, Samuel Phillips, 115, 127-128, 134, 136, 155, 237
Lee, Sidney Smith, 67-68
Légare (Coast Survey vessel), 31
Legg, William Henry, 178
Leila (Davidson's Maryland Oyster Police headquarters vessel), 181-183
Letcher, John, 68, 96
Lincoln, Abraham, 63, 65, 69, 79, 115, 138, 172
Littlepage, Hardin B., 54, 76
Louisa Wallace, 155
Long, James C., 76
Longstreet, James, 105

Luce, Stephen Bleecker, 25-27, 33-37, 39, 52-53, 63; correspondence with Davidson in later years: 219, 221-226, 232-236, 241, 245

Mackinaw, USS, 130
Maffitt, John Newland, 36-38, 67, 142
Magruder, John B., 74, 149-150
Mahan, Alfred Thayer, 20, 54, 155
Mallory, Stephen R., ix, 67, 73, 75, 91, 95, 97-98, 139, 142-144, 172, 200, 247; Davidson in command of Submarine Battery Service: 104, 107-109, 112, 114-116, 119, 127, 136, 138, 237, 245
Maratanza, USS, 100-104
Marmaduke, Henry H., 76, 78
Martin Garcia, Argentina, 207, 209, 212
Maryland Oyster Police, x, xiii, 177-190, 192-193
Mason, John Y., 13, 19
Massachusetts, USS, 27-29
Maupin, Socrates, 96
Maury, Matthew Fontaine, 2, 59, 68, 93-94, 105, 107, 109-110, 141, 143-144, 168, 202, 247; development of torpedoes: 95-98, 102-104, 106, 135, 137, 200, 236, 245-246; after Civil War: 154-155, 171-172, 198, 200-201
Maury, Richard, 96
Mayo, William K., 52
McBlair, William, 45-50, 55, 67
McCauley, Charles S., 28-29
McClellan, George B., 89-90, 98-99, 105, 112
Mediterranean Squadron (USN), 7
Merrimack, USS, see *Virginia*, CSS
Michigan, USS, 3
Minnesota, USS, 71, 79-80, 83-88, 234; attack by *Squib*: 124-129, 236, 238
Minor, George, 67, 69
Minor, Robert Dabney, 76, 94, 96, 159, 168-169, 171-172, 174, 189, 191, 248
Mississippi, USS, 2-3
Missouri, USS, 2, 8, 24, 210
Mitchell, John Kirkwood, 136
Monitor, USS, 73, 76, 78, 97, 100, 103-104; battle of Hampton Roads: 80-91, 224, 230, 234-235, 245
Montgomery, John B., 12-13, 18-19, 24

Morris (Coast Survey vessel), 33, 36, 149

Naval Observatory, 2, 59, 68, 94-96
Naval School, 3, 6, 76, 80, 151
Naval War College, 221
New Ironsides, USS, 123, 161
Newport News, Virginia, 76, 81, 115, 118, 127
Niagara, USS, 145
Nipsic, USS, 217
Norfolk, Virginia, before Civil War, xv, 1, 4, 8, 12, 19, 26, 30, 43, 45, 47, 54; Confederate control: 69-70, 72, 85-86, 88, 122; Navy Yard under Confederate control: 69, 74, 76; Union control: 90-91, 126
North Atlantic Blockading Squadron (USN), 79, 91, 115, 133
North Carolina (USN), 10-11
Norton, Edward J., 222, 230, 242
Numancia (Spanish Naval ship), 160

Office of Ordnance and Hydrography (CSN), 107
Olinde, CSS, see CSS *Stonewall*
Oliver, Charles B., 78
Osborne, Burr, 17
Owl (blockade runner), 142

Pacific Squadron (USN), 7, 12, 18, 26, 29
Page, John, 197
Page, Thomas J., 195, 197-198, 213
Paraguari, Paraguay, 242
Parker, Foxhall Alexander, 6, 8, 53, 121
Parker, William H., 53, 63-64, 66, 121, 200
Patrick Henry, CSS, 70-71, 91-92, 154, 161, 202
Pegram, Robert Baker, 68
Pelot, Thomas, 45-46, 67
Pennsylvania, USS, 1, 4, 30, 70
Perry, Matthew, 68, 157, 170
Philadelphia, Pennsylvania, 3-4
Pierce, Franklin, 34
Pilcomayo, 213-215
Pirayu, Paraguay, 222, 242
Plymouth, USS, 52, 54, 56, 58
Polk, James K., 11, 15
Pope, John, 112
Pope, William Henry (stepfather), xvii
Poppy (USN tug), 125-126
Port Royal, South Carolina, battle of, 35
Porter, David Dixon, 133, 235, 238, 241
Porter, John Luke, 73-75
Portsmouth, USS, 11-14, 17-19, 24, 36, 44, 54, 122
Portsmouth, Virginia, 70-73
Potomac River, xv, 2, 8, 69, 75, 112
Preble, Edward, 9
Preble, USS, 9-11, 44, 54
Preston, William B., 24-25, 27-28
Princeton, USS, 2

Rains, Gabriel, ix, 105-107, 122, 135, 137, 200, 238, 246-247
Randolph, George W., 105
Rappahannock River, 108, 112
Read, Charles W., 54
Read, Edward Gaines, 161
Read, William W., 54
Reed & Co., 143, 155
Reed, William C., 158
Release, USS, 42
Resolute, HMS, 39, 41-42, 45-46, 67
Rice, Gus, 183
Richmond, CSS, 104
Roanoke, USS, 71, 80
Robb, Robert G., 93
Rochelle, James Henry, 70, 92, 202-203
Rocketts Navy Yard, 93, 96, 98-99, 124
Roco, Julio A., 213-214
Rodgers, John, 31-33, 91, 100, 102, 134
Roosevelt, Theodore, 229, 232
Ruby (steamer), 143
Ruffin, John N., 229-232, 242
Run Her (blockade runner), 141-143, 210

St. Lawrence, USS, 80
Sampson, William T., 54
Sangamon, USS, 116, 118-119
Sarmiento, Domingo, 198-199
Savannah, USS, 13, 27, 30
Scharf, John Thomas, 92
Schley, Winfield Scott, 54
Scott, Robert W., 52, 66
Scott, Winfield, 17-19

Seddon, James, 136
Seeley, Henry B., 217
Semmes, Raphael, 67, 241
Seven Days Battles, 98-99
Seward, William H., 142
Sewell's Point, 79-80
Seymour, George, 42
Shark, USS, 14-17, 24, 140, 210
Sharksville, 17
Shaw & Co., 179, 181
Shenandoah, CSS, 140, 154
Sherman, Washington, 47-49, 186
Simes, George T., 18-19
Simms, Charles C., 76, 82-83, 85
Simpson, Edward, 58
Sloat, John, 12-13
Smith, Francis H., 68, 95
Somers, USS, 1-2
Squib, CSS, 123-129, 142, 155, 236, 246-247
Stag (blockade runner), 141
Stanton, Edwin, 115
Stellwagon, Henry S., 36
Stephens, Alexander, 69, 241
Stevens, Thomas H., 102, 104, 115
Stockton, Robert F., 18, 58
Stone, Edward E., 41
Stonewall, CSS, 144-148, 150, 154, 162, 195
Stringham, Silas H., 30, 71
Submarine Battery Service (CS), ix-x, 107-114, 116, 119, 121, 123, 130, 133-134, 136-138, 242, 245
Suffolk, Virginia, 90

Talita, 213-214
Tattnall, Josiah, 67, 89-90
Taylor, Zachary, 17, 53
Teaser, CSS, 70, 93, 97, 99-105, 109, 111, 114, 207, 210
Thomson, John Renshaw, 58
Timmons, William E., 193
Toucey, Isaac, 43, 50, 55, 58, 62
Torpedo, CSS, 109, 111, 113, 115, 207
Torpedo Bureau (CS), 107
Treaty of Washington, 44
Tredegar Iron Works, 107, 110, 179
Tucker, John R., 67, 71, 154, 166-168, 202-203, 248
Tyler, John, 8-9, 11

United States, USS, 70
United States Naval Academy, 20-25, 50, 52-55, 58-59, 61, 63-67, 75-76, 89, 161, 244
United States Navy, Date of 1841, 3-4, 6, 21, 25, 45, 52, 59, 121, 170; in CS Navy: 67, 70, 74, 76, 94, 107, 138, 159; postwar: 202, 242; Mexican War: 13-14, 17-19; Northwest Coast: 14-17; as tool of diplomacy: 8-12; Academy established: 20-21; operations against slave trade: 44-49
Upshur, Abel, 6, 8
Upshur, George P., 21-23, 34, 124
Upshur, John, 52, 66, 124, 126

Valparaiso, Chile, 12, 160-162, 164-167
Van Brunt, Gershon J., 27, 79, 84-85
Vandalia, USS, 26-27
Vanderbilt, Cornelius, 89
Vera Cruz, Mexico, 8
Villa Rica, Paraguay, 221-222, 227, 232, 242
Vincennes, USS, 48, 158
Virginia, CSS (ironclad), x, 70, 72-92, 104, 108, 122, 124, 168, 178; in memory of Davidson and others: 210, 224, 230, 234-235, 240-241, 245
Virginia II, CSS (ironclad), 161
Virginia State Navy, xv, 68-69, 80, 93, 95-96, 166

Wade, Thomas F., 130
Waldeck, Louis, 78
Walker, Leroy P., 72
Walker, Theodoric Lee, 45, 47
War of the Triple Alliance, 198, 214, 222
Warren, USS, 29-30
Warrior, HMS, 73
Washington (mail steamer), 42-43
Washington Navy Yard, 14, 68, 80, 102, 121
Water Witch, USS, 195, 197
Watson, Henry Bulls, 14, 18-19
Webb, John, 211
Welles, Gideon, 61-63, 65-66, 126, 130
Wells, Clark, 41

West Indian Squadron (USN), 6
Whisper (blockade runner), 141
Whistler, James M., 165-166, 177
Whiting, W. H. C., 138
Wilkes Expedition, 1-2, 41
Wilkinson, John, 36, 67, 153-154
William G. Lewis (slaver), 47
Williams, John Sharp, 229-230
Winder, John H., 120
Winston, Thomas W., 240-241
Wise, Charles, 45-46
Wise, Henry, 118
Wood, John Taylor, 53, 63-64, 66, 76, 85-86, 88, 90-91, 103, 143, 154
Woodhull, Maxwell, 36
Worden, John L., 83, 86, 88, 230

York River, 89, 98
Yorktown, see *Patrick Henry*, CSS
Yorktown, Virginia, 90, 98, 105

John M. Coski at Burnside Bridge. Photo by Ruth Ann Coski

About the Authors

John M. Coski spent 33 years as historian and director of research and publications at The Museum of the Confederacy (subsequently the American Civil War Museum) in Richmond, Virginia. He earned his B.A. from Mary Washington College in Fredericksburg, Virginia, and his M.A. and Ph.D. in American History from the College of William and Mary. His publications include *Capital Navy: The Men, Ships, and Operations of the James River Squadron* (Savas Beatie, 1996, 2005) and *The Confederate Battle Flag: America's Most Embattled Emblem* (Harvard, 2005). He received the Emerging Civil War Award for Service in Civil War Public History.

Charles T. Jacobs was a U.S. Army veteran, career civil servant, a founder of the Montgomery County Civil War Round Table, and author of *Civil War Guide to Montgomery County, Maryland* (1983). He began researching Hunter Davidson in 1990 and published an article about him in the *Washington Times* in 1996. He died of cancer in February 2008, shortly after entrusting his research notes to John Coski.